Educating Students with Cerebral Palsy

To Ms King,
In memory of Verna Hart,
warrior Mom and Brilliant
Artist   Adline L. Usher

Printed in the United States of America.

Designed by Megan Katsanevaskis

Illustrations pp. 10–13, pp. 20–21, p. 24, and p. 49 by C. E. McClinton

Library of Congress Control Number: 2022917398
ISBN: 978-1-951568-29-0

SMALL
BATCH
BOOKS

493 SOUTH PLEASANT STREET
AMHERST, MASSACHUSETTS 01002
413.230.3943
SMALLBATCHBOOKS.COM

Educating Students with Cerebral Palsy

A COMPREHENSIVE GUIDE FOR EDUCATORS AND PARENTS

Adine R. Usher, EdD

Foreword by Richard Ellenson

This book is dedicated to the valuable, courageous, and resilient students who find joy, meaning, and purpose in life despite the difficulties that cerebral palsy may present and who, in essence, have been my teachers for nearly six decades.

Contents

Foreword

Before leaving my advertising career to get involved in the field of disabilities; before working with the New York City Department of Education to create a better inclusive school program; before working with an amazing and brilliant team to create a breakthrough augmentative and alternative communication (AAC) device called Tango; before developing Math Paper, which enables students with significant motor challenges to finally do arithmetic; before introducing an AAC app that supplements generative communication with a much-needed focus on social engagement; before five years running a cerebral palsy (CP) foundation; before my son (who uses a power wheelchair for mobility and an AAC device to speak) wrote and starred in a one-man show that had a five-night run off-off-Broadway; before having the privilege of sitting on two advisory committees at the National Institutes of Health—before all these wonderful, magical, unexpected things, I was simply the father of a young boy who had cerebral palsy.

More precisely, I was a confused, frantic, concerned, information-starved, sleep-deprived parent of a young boy who had CP. A parent who had absolutely no idea how to discover or approach the many things I knew my son would need in order to create his own vision for a successful and fulfilling life.

That feeling of disorientation, that loneliness, that sense of not knowing where to turn—the fear that no matter how hard I tried, I'd never be able to do enough or, worse, that I would certainly do something wrong—those feelings weren't only mine. They are shared by every parent of a child with disabilities: whether it is within a family fortunate enough to be economically comfortable or within a family struggling every day to make ends meet, whether it is a single parent whose spouse has walked out or it is a parent couple whose strong bond brings a constant sense of belief, love, and resilience. Ask any parent of a child with CP: We all share these feelings.

And as we parents, and those within our large circles, struggle to adapt ourselves, to handle the unexpected, to learn new ways of thinking, we meet many people who say many things. We hear people trying to be hopeful and reassuring, trying to convince us that all will be fine. We meet people who are thoughtless: "Heavens, will you be able to be get through this?" We hear awkward platitudes, words steeped in saccharine: "You're only given what you can handle." Now and then, we meet people who can just listen, who know how to *be there* for us.

We hear so many words. But so few of them are pragmatic.

Sadly, pragmatism is too often given short shrift. It feels neither inspirational nor poetic. It doesn't look boldly into the future, doesn't promise more than it can deliver. Pragmatism can even feel just plain dull.

But at the right moment—when pragmatism is carved out of experience and insight, when it lights a murky landscape with crystalline useful knowledge, when it cuts through the torrential, shrieking concerns and worries that frighten and disorient parents of children with a disability . . . ah, in those moments, there is nothing like pragmatism.

And it was at a moment like this when I met Adine Usher.

Adine is memorable: tall and graceful, with an extraordinarily warm demeanor. Her speech is thoughtful and precise, with a lilting touch of music to it.

Her eyes smile with kindness and connection. Yet those qualities conceal a fierceness: a determination to confront challenge, inequality, and ignorance, to help the world confront and understand the wildly complex challenges of disabilities. She is determined to make change, to make things better—both for the population and also for any individual who comes her way.

I met Adine when my son was six and starting elementary school. Tom had two talented and joyful teachers. We had the ostensible support of the entire DOE. We had two world-class speech-language therapists helping train the school staff. But despite all that, Tom's school had never dealt with a child whose disabilities were as severe as my son's, and despite all the efforts to create structure and inclusion, the year had been challenging. On the day I met Adine, I shared all of my frustration with her. She listened patiently; when I finished speaking, this is what she said: "Richard, we hear that story all too often. Schools are just unable to truly understand the challenges and how much effort the children are putting out. For a student with disabilities who works so hard to accomplish basic physical things . . . well, it's as if another student were taking the class while climbing a mountain with a forty-pound backpack."

Wow! What an image. What thundering words. Suddenly I could contextualize all the effort my son had to make. Suddenly I could feel in my bones the effort that *every one of those kids* with disabilities had to make. And I sensed that as a parent, well, maybe I was wearing a backpack too.

There are so many specific skills and adaptations needed for true inclusion and progress. There must be knowledge about physical issues, psychological issues, academic issues, psychosocial issues, and emotional issues. Knowledge about how to implement technology and often how to be aware of medical needs. But there is so little tribal knowledge to fall back on. In fact, everyone feels they are on their own. Every parent feels no one will ever be able to understand their child, let alone know how to help. And, frankly, considering the way things usually progress, parents are right to feel that way.

Teachers who take justifiable pride in knowing what they're doing suddenly feel inadequate, and they are usually unwilling to share those fears and frustrations. Therapists meet with children once or twice a week yet can't share that this time is likely too short to build any real foundation. Assistive technology experts too rarely get appropriate tech firmly established in classrooms and rarely get the chance to implement supports they know can help. In school, friendships start out hopeful but grow tougher and tougher, and kids with disabilities just get left behind—in part because inclusive activities haven't been designed ahead of time and implemented proactively. Tragically, medical schools almost never teach the issues created by disabilities, despite the myriad other topics they cover. Even parents: Amid love, confusion, anxiety, and exhaustion, how can you confidently nurture a child whose challenges—despite all your efforts—you worry you may never fully understand.

No one wants to fall short, yet so few of us have had the opportunity to learn how to create more success. And so, how do you confront challenges when you can't even envision solutions and opportunities? As a result, the effervescent, striving, caring, infinitely optimistic, and determined spirits and souls living inside difficult and unruly bodies: They are far too rarely seen.

So what are we to do?

Well, this book is a good place to start. This dazzling compendium of a near infinity of things we all need to know is all laid out in a way that will enable you to take them in, get familiar with them, make them part of your world, and then share them with others.

It is only by sharing individual knowledge that we build tribal knowledge; it is only by building a communal understanding of this complex world and its challenges that we can also embrace the full range of possibilities and opportunities for someone who is born with CP *and help support the vision they will develop for themselves.* It is only by this shared effort that we will progress—as parents, educators, professionals, and as people. And, most importantly, it is how we can help individuals progress on their own.

If that seems like a Herculean task . . . well, it is. But it's certainly no more daunting than climbing that hill carrying that forty-pound backpack, no more so than the challenges faced every day by people for whom we so passionately wish joy, accomplishment, and success.

As you read this and envision all that's ahead, you may also be feeling overwhelmed. Don't worry. I felt that way once too.

I sure wish I'd had this book back then. But, instead, I got lucky; I got to meet Adine herself. And now you get to meet her too. And thirteen other remarkable professionals who have taken their lifetimes of learning and inspired thinking and contributed them to these chapters.

Learn. Enjoy. Believe.

We'll see you at the mountaintop.

—Richard Ellenson

Tom Ellenson, age twenty, at home.

Introduction

Adine R. Usher

The desire to write this book has been driven by decades of teaching, observing, and supporting students with cerebral palsy (CP) and by guiding teachers and parents in diverse educational settings. Despite hard work and noble intentions, confusion and doubt can infuse the process of educating students with CP. Some educators struggle to perceive pupils with CP as "real" students, while others find it difficult to maintain reasonably high standards for these students. These teachers need strong support to effectively educate students with CP. Joining me in this venture are highly skilled, seasoned, professional contributors who share my passionate desire to support students with CP and their families.

Scores of excellent books and research articles continue to be written about students who live with CP, the most common physical impairment diagnosed in childhood. Some of these texts are written for medical and therapeutic professionals. Some writings target the specific concerns of parents who seek support and information about caring for their children who have CP, while still other books and articles include CP in broader discussions about students with *low-incidence* physical and multiple impairments.

Many of these writings and scientific research articles have been referenced in the body of this book to bring validity and recommendation to the text. It is also hoped that citations and proposed strategies will provide classroom teachers and parents with greater access to current CP research. While I want to encourage you to seek further information on a range of CP-related topics, I hope that you find this book to be a comprehensive guide to the education of students who live and often struggle with the conditions of CP.

Although statistical estimations regarding the prevalence of CP vary worldwide, approximately seventeen million individuals live with CP. Of that number, around one million reside in the U.S. The worldwide approximations of the incidence of CP range from 1.5 to more than 4.0 per thousand live births of infants and babies who are diagnosed with this *neurodevelopmental* condition (caused by injury to brain cells).[1] CP tends to be slightly more commonly found in males and in the United States, and Black babies are born with CP at higher rates than are White babies.

The term *cerebral palsy* was first introduced in 1887 by Sir William Osler, "one of the founding fathers of modern medicine."[2] Osler's work placed strong emphasis on the neurological abnormalities and pathological features of CP and followed the work of Dr. William Little (1862), who ascribed a lack of oxygen at the time of birth to cases of spastic rigidity.[3] However, it was Dr. Sigmund Freud who suggested that *prenatal* (pre-birth) causes may account for many of CP's neurologically based motor difficulties, and Freud further suggested that CP encompassed more than just a disorder of motor dysfunction.[4]

In its purest definition, a diagnosis of CP describes a primarily permanent, *congenital* (present at birth), nonprogressive condition. Groups of motor disorders, caused by injury to or malformation of areas of the brain, play a major role in impairing body movement, posture, and muscle coordination. In some cases, a definitive diagnosis of CP is delayed until around the age of three, when motoric developmental markers have not been met and when there is uncertainty about the *etiology* (history or origin) of the child's condition.

The phrase "the conditions of cerebral palsy" is frequently used in this book because I add CP's *secondary* and *associated conditions* to the primary, motoric definition of CP. Indeed, others have referred to CP as an "umbrella" condition or that often encompasses multiple motoric, health, sensory, cognitive, communication, and social-emotional elements. These secondary and associated conditions that accompany primary motoric issues can contribute to decreased function, developmental delays, and lifelong challenges.

Secondary conditions result in muscle incoordination and compromised movement. *Associated conditions* are defined as medical, intellectual, sensory, communication, and social-emotional dysfunctions that *may* be brain-based, *may* occur simultaneously with the injury that caused the motor dysfunction, or *may* be caused by the *same* brain injury or malformation that caused the motoric dysfunction. Co-occurring associated conditions can, depending on their distribution, frequency, and severity, add to the challenge and complexity of understanding and reaching students who live with a diagnosis of CP.

Students with CP may also experience *concurrent* impairments such as attention disorders, learning disabilities and intellectual disabilities, hyperactivity, and behavioral difficulties that may be akin to behaviors on the autism spectrum. These may or may not relate to primary, secondary, and associated conditions of CP.

For some infants who were diagnosed with CP at birth, symptoms may resolve themselves before the child enters school. However, with an ever-improving survival rate for very-low-weight and premature infants, some research suggests a slight increase in the number of children born each year with CP, and other studies have not seen a decline in the incidence of CP.[5, 6, 7] Despite medical advances,[8] the incidence of CP has not changed appreciably over the last four decades.

In many cases, with therapeutic and surgical interventions, varying degrees of motoric stabilization and improved functional mobility are possible; however, as the body ages, CP may exacerbate an individual's physical decline.

For too long, our focus has been restricted to the motoric and medical effects of CP. Today there are still many who believe that CP produces only motoric and medical concerns. They fail to understand the possible correlation, association, interplay, and interaction between CP's physical, medical, cognitive, communication, and social-emotional realities. Indeed, even with mild or moderate motor challenges, associated issues may pose primary concerns. Like the primary movement disorders of CP, these concomitant secondary and associated conditions can be mild, moderate, or severe and, as they interact with one another, can vary, based on changes in a student's organic realities, environmental situations, and performance demands. The presence of multiple issues may create a highly complex, individualized set of unique challenges—challenges that affect motivation, slow the learning process, add struggle and intensity to most activities, and create lifelong disruptions to a person's daily activities and sense of self.

This book addresses educators and parents, new or experienced, who teach students with CP in both public and private educational settings: from inclusion and self-contained classrooms to dedicated special education schools. The book can serve as a reference guide to not only help educators and parents to better understand how the conditions of CP can affect learning but can also familiarize them with strategies that help to lower the barriers posed by CP. Hopefully, this book will either build on a teacher's existing skills or guide teachers to understand and embrace the educational legitimacy of a student who may learn in significantly nontypical ways.

This book aims at strengthening the teacher's ability to tap into a student's potential by deepening an understanding of how the conditions of CP can affect *all* the modalities required for learning. Armed with this deeper understanding, teachers will be in a stronger position to deliver more appropriate and effective instruction.

Internationally, with changes in public and social policies that champion inclusion, an increasing number of students who have CP are attending inclusive, local public schools, and there has been a reduction in the number of specially dedicated day or residential schools.

Students with CP who live in rural areas, where appropriate alternative special programs may not exist or are too educationally or socially restrictive, have fewer options outside of inclusive programs. In large urban centers, where a greater range of services and placement options exist, full or partial inclusion programs provide varying degrees of inclusion.

However, there remain parents of very medically fragile and cognitively complex students who believe that their child's school experience will be enriched and their preparation for adult life will be more effectively addressed in a dedicated school. These parents believe that highly specialized schools can educate their children in settings staffed by professionals who have demonstrated a high degree of expertise in understanding the learning styles and potential of students with significant CP. These parents also believe that dedicated settings build self-confidence and encourage a greater number of friendships with peers who share their child's daily experiences. This confidence is well placed if the teaching staff is certified, is highly skilled, and receives ongoing professional development that addresses the unique needs of the individual student.

Whether in full inclusion, in partial inclusion, or in a special and dedicated program, it is paramount that teachers find ways to uncover and develop the strengths and abilities that can be hidden by CP. In any school setting for students with CP, it is critical that encouraging attitudes prevail in an atmosphere where teachers forge ahead to discover what a student can do rather than retreat because of what the student can't do.

In any educational setting, the complexities that accompany CP may easily confound and overwhelm even the most dedicated and experienced teacher. My considerable experience in working with students, staff, administrators, and parents across the full spectrum of educational settings that serve students with CP leads me to conclude that each setting has its strengths and challenges, its advantages and weaknesses.

There is a tremendous range and variability in the abilities and performance of students with CP. No two students with CP are alike, and the impact of CP's conditions, even in a single individual, vary from one situation and setting to another. Some students go on to live full, successful lives despite physical and health challenges. However, many others struggle to reach their potential. Whether a student is dealing with mild, moderate, severe, or profound conditions that are related to their CP diagnosis, this book seeks to help teachers uncover and build on the student's strengths by thoughtfully and thoroughly understanding the challenges and barriers posed by CP.

Educational entities need to develop their staff's ability to understand the scope of an individual student's complex profile and unique characteristics, lest educators fall short of maximizing the student's overall performance and quality of life.

I want this book to demystify the complexity of CP and, in doing so, extend the teacher's comfort level in understanding frequently used technical, medical, and therapeutic language. The book seeks to strengthen a teacher's ability to observe, analyze, understand, and appreciate the interactions between neurological, medical, cognitive, communication, and emotional conditions that can have powerful implications for instruction, learning, and performance.

I hope that the book also awakens a deeper understanding of attitudes toward students with CP, both in school and in the wider society. Detailed information about CP can be a source of comfort and relief.[9] When discomfort, fear, and doubts about the conditions of CP can be explored, confronted, and worked through, both personally and collectively, we as educators can begin to lower those attitudinal barriers to school success and societal participation that determine, in great part, the degree to which students thrive.

The "Suitcase"

Several years ago, the parents of a thirteen-year-old client with CP asked me to make a house call. This young fellow was beginning to have doubts about his body and his overall self-worth. He lived with a diagnosis of *spastic diplegia* (primary movement difficulties involving his legs and, to a lesser extent, difficulties with his arms and hands). He used a power wheelchair, was bright and inquisitive, but experienced some visual-perception difficulties that partially explained his learning disabilities. However, he was holding his own academically in a public-school inclusion class because of the excellent support he received from teachers, related service providers, aides, and his parents.

This young teenager was expressing feelings of being isolated from his school peers and was growing uncomfortable with the secondary limitations of his CP. When I inquired about what his doctors had told him about his condition, he muttered something about his legs. (I am certain that his doctors were much more descriptive than that; however, this is what the student reported.) I suggested that we work with an imaginary suitcase that contained not only the elements related to his CP but also those personal characteristics, strengths, and strategies that helped him to circumvent and reduce the impact of some of his challenges. As he began to innumerate elements of his condition and his coping strategies, a new self-awareness seemed to emerge. He became more animated and appeared quite pleased with himself. At the completion of the little exercise, he said, "I think that I can carry this!"

This student was positioning himself to grow in understanding of the full scope of his issues and was learning to advocate for his needs as he "carried his suitcase" through life. Equally important is our ability as educators to thoroughly understand the total impact of the suitcase's contents. This book strives to reinforce the absolute necessity for an individualized approach to educating a student with CP, an approach that recognizes and accepts the unique "suitcase" carried by every student who is diagnosed with CP, a "suitcase" that is filled with a range of individual strengths and very atypical challenges. A full knowledge of this unique "suitcase" requires an introductory understanding of those neurological and medical conditions of CP.

The presence of the individualized "suitcase" demands the development of skills that oblige the teacher to adapt, modify, and at times consistently and creatively customize interventions that are integrated with therapeutic practices. By using these interventions, we guide individual students toward a more functional, enriched, contented, and productive adulthood.

Educating students who have CP requires that we, as educators, accept and embrace the idea that we are involved in a medical-educational partnership, a partnership that a teacher need not shy away from. *Medical realities inform pedagogical decisions.* They equip educators with an understanding of these relationships, promote a comfort level with medical perspectives, and introduce terminology and an investigative mindset that is certain to render more effective instruction and learning.

For school-age students, ages five through twenty-one, the book expands on and reinforces the essential and powerfully effective collaborative role of a student's school transdisciplinary team, a team composed of teachers, therapists, assistants, medical personnel, administrators, parents, and often the student. Through thoughtful, shared observations and careful data retrieved from medical, psychological, and social sources that inform educational and instructional choices, team members can collaboratively shape a student's improved quality of life in the motoric, medical, sensory, academic, communication, and social-emotional domains.

I also hope that this book will help to strengthen a teacher's awareness of the need to more fully understand and more effectively and compassionately respond to the realities and experiences of the families who love, care for, and support the health, growth, and development of these students. Here, teachers are provided with a basic, introductory understanding of the brain structure and function as it relates to the primary, secondary, and associated conditions of CP. The associated conditions that are frequently allied with a diagnosis of CP are detailed, and typically employed, standard medical and therapeutic interventions are described for each associated condition.

The following is a synopsis of the chapters in this book:

- Chapter 1 provides an overview of the brain structure and describes the medical conditions that appear to be related to brain injury that result in a diagnosis of CP.

- Chapter 2 examines CP's primary and secondary motor conditions.
- Chapter 3 describes CP's associated health conditions.
- Chapter 4 provides an overview of educating students with CP.
- Chapter 5 presents CP's sensory challenges.
- Chapter 6 defines the responsibilities of the student's transdisciplinary team.
- Chapter 7 looks at CP's impact on social-emotional growth, self-concept, behavior, and socialization.
- Chapter 8 discusses the assessment of students with CP.
- Chapter 9 explores transitioning students into adulthood.
- Parental experiences and voices are heard in chapter 10, and student voices are heard in chapter 11.
- Chapter 12 examines complementary and alternative therapies for cerebral palsy.
- Finally, chapter 13 looks at cerebral palsy research, organizational support, and publications.
- The book concludes with acknowledgments, a glossary of terms, the endnotes, contributor biographies, and an index.

This book does not offer educational cures but rather recommends strategies that are grounded in research and effective practice that have evolved out of a clearer understanding of the conditions that may appear with a diagnosis of CP. These recommended strategies target assessing and teaching to the ways in which these students learn.

The book urges us to look for and find hidden strength and surprising abilities that are blanketed by obvious barriers. It encourages us to recognize challenges that are present even in the face of mild physical impairment and guides us to use alternate paths to uncover hidden treasures of knowledge and understanding in the student by lowering or circumventing debilitating barriers. Teachers and parents will hopefully come to see that rather than mourning the gifts a student lacks, they instead come to value and develop the gifts the student *does* have.

Realizing that there are teachers who may feel unprepared to teach some students with CP, I hope the information contained within this book will give rise to feelings of satisfaction and accomplishment for professionals, parents, and students.

CHAPTER 1
The Brain and Cerebral Palsy

Adine R. Usher

This chapter is written for teachers, classroom assistants, and parents who may have limited or no exposure to fundamental information about typical and atypical brain structure, brain function, and the role of neurons. Administrators and supervisors who are responsible for educating students with neuromuscular conditions may also find value in this information. Known risk factors that may lead to a diagnosis of cerebral palsy will also be discussed at the end of the chapter.

I strongly subscribe to the concept of basic brain-based training for teachers who work with elementary, middle school, and secondary school students. Understanding the rudiments of typical brain development and function can add substantial understanding about how students learn and can be taught. Acquiring an understanding of brain structure and brain function in populations of students whose brain injury often profoundly affects school performance seems essential. These beliefs are reinforced by neurologist Dr. Judy Willis, who contends that

> teachers who are prepared with knowledge of the workings of the brain will have the optimism, incentive, and motivation to follow the ongoing research and to apply their findings to the classroom.[10]

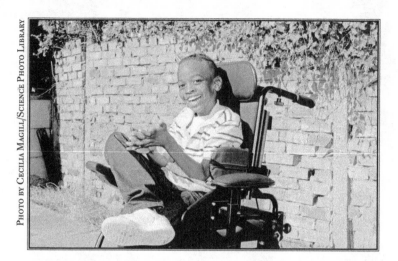

PHOTO BY CECILIA MAGILL/SCIENCE PHOTO LIBRARY

The concept of universal architectural design is becoming a part of school building codes to accomodate students in wheelchairs.

Dr. Robert Sylwester[11] acknowledges that the typical K–12 educator, who has been oriented to the social and behavioral sciences, currently lacks the biological background—specifically, the cognitive and neuroscience concepts and processes—that could strengthen an educator's grasp of brain structure and function.

I share the excitement of Patricia Wolfe, the author of *Brain Matters*, who, as an educator, not a neuroscientist, sees value in taking whatever information neuroscience can currently provide to further our understanding of why we need to teach in relationship to the ways in which a student's brain functions.

The Role of Neurons

Nearly every part of our body, externally and internally, contains nerve cells, and the nerve cells in the brain and in the spinal cord, which make up the *central nervous system (CNS)*, are called *neurons. Neurons send information to, and receive information from, other neurons in the CNS and nerve cells outside the CNS.* The neurons of the CNS carry messages from the brain, down the spinal cord, and then out to nerves in every part of the body. Sensations from our skin, organs, and joints send messages through the *peripheral nervous system (PNS)* back to the neurons in the spine and back up to the brain.

Neurons are not the only cells in the CNS. *Glial cells* and *Schwann cells* all support the work of neurons. In this book, though, we shall focus on neurons.

We are born with about 100 billion neurons in our CNS, neurons that constantly communicate with one another. Neurons interpret, control, and determine *what, how, when,* and *why* we perform an action, execute a thought, and respond to sensory input or a reflex. Injury to neurons in the brain can, to varying degrees, alter our physical, cognitive, and emotional responses.

The average developing brain at birth has more neurons than it needs, and the excess neurons purposefully die (*apoptosis*) during the first few years of life. By the time we reach middle age, the number of neurons may have declined to around 48 billion.

Neurons exist in varying sizes, shapes, and lengths, and *each neuron or group of neurons perform a distinct function.* Neurons that serve the same function tend to operate in clusters and communicate in groups (*nuclei*), thus sharing and strengthening the power of the function that the neurons are assigned to carry out. Neurons also communicate with neurons that have differing functions, thereby creating a powerful array of billions of neural pathways that connect, enable, and determine the operation of different body functions.

Problems that may occur in the developing brain (from conception to roughly age three) and injured neurons (brain lesions) are at the very heart of a CP diagnosis. Neurons in the developing brain of a fetus or infant are fragile and more easily injured. Injury to a neuron or groups of neurons in one part of a neural pathway can adversely affect the functioning of neurons along that communication pathway, creating a potentially negative impact on the quality of other brain functions.

How Neurons Communicate

A neuron receives information from the neuron that precedes it and sends information to the neuron that follows it. From the *dendrites* (which have received information from the previous neuron), information is refined in the cell body of the neuron and is then passed (by an electrical-chemical process) along the *axon* to the *presynaptic vesicle.*

From the presynaptic vesicle, the information is then passed *across* the synaptic space in the form of neurotransmitter chemicals to the dendrites of the next neuron. Physical, chemical, and electrical power contained in each of the neurons speed the communication of information (firing) from neuron to neuron. This process is repeated billions of times a minute throughout our lives.

A process called *myelination* describes the development of the fatty white protective, electrically insulating covering that protects the axons and helps to increase the speed with which information moves through one neuron and on to the next neuron. Educators and parents should be aware of the significance of injury to the myelin covering in furthering their understanding the effects of some types of CP. At birth, the neuron's axons have very little myelin protection. After birth, myelination occurs rapidly, thus allowing the infant's motor development to progress. The myelination process begins with neurons at the back of the brain and slowly, over a period of years, works its way up to the front of the brain and is completed by the early to middle twenties.

As educators, we may find references to the phrase "white matter damage" in a student's medical report. This phrase signals that damage to or loss of myelin has occurred to the axon's protective myelin sheath, and the resulting damage can negatively affect the quality of the message that the neuron or groups of neurons are trying to send. As teachers, we need to understand that "white matter damage" may partially explain the presence of altered functioning and delayed processing. White matter damage can be responsible for abnormal sensorimotor experiences and sensations or for the loss of tactile sensations.

The Relationship of Brain Structures to the Conditions of CP

Our brains are divided in half from side to side into the right and left hemispheres. Neurons communicate with other neurons *within* each hemisphere and *between* both hemispheres. The *cerebral cortex* is the outer layer of the brain's surface and covers nearly all the brain's surface. The cortex is composed of neurons that reach down to connect to other neurons in every area of the brain. These neurons *initiate, plan,* and then *execute* thoughts and actions; then they receive and respond to information that returns to the brain from peripheral nerves in other parts of the body.

Large sections of the brain are referred to as *lobes* and are equally positioned in both hemispheres. Starting at the *posterior* (back) part of the brain is the *cerebellum*. One of the many roles played by the cerebellum is to regulate and coordinate the more routine, unconscious part of movement, such as balance and equilibrium. The cerebellum also plays a role in the memory of controlled, precise, and skilled reflexes.

Just above the cerebellum are the paired *occipital lobes*, which are primarily associated with receiving, controlling, and processing visual images. Images of movement, color, depth, and shape "play a central role in human sensory processing."[12]

Above or in front of the occipital lobes lie the *parietal lobes*, which integrate much of the sensory information, including visual, tactile, and language input. The *anterior* (front) part of the parietal lobes sits directly behind the *motor cortex* in an area called the *somatosensory cortex*, which is responsible for sending and receiving movement-related messages to the body; its neurons convey sensation messages of pain, skin pressure, the position of limbs, and outside temperature.

The posterior (rear) section of the parietal lobes "continuously analyzes and integrates all this information to give you a sense of spatial awareness."[13]

The parietal lobes play a vital role in sustaining spatial attention, whether that attention is focused on a stationary object or on shifting ones. They control visual attention, touch, pain, taste, pressure, integration of different senses, orientation, and recognition.[14]

In front of the parietal lobes lies the motor cortex, which controls the precise initiation and execution of body movements. The control in this cortex is *contralateral*, meaning that the motor cortex on the left side of the brain controls movement on the right side of the body, and movement on the left side of the body is controlled by the motor cortex on the right side of the brain. The more complex and precise the body movement, as with the hands and in the face, the more space in the motor cortex is devoted to those areas of *fine* body movement. Sylwester explains that "the premotor area directly in front of the motor cortex primes the next *movements* in a motor sequence."[15] Neurons in the motor cortex activate skeletal muscles that connect to bones, joints, heart, intestines, tongue, and eye muscles.

Moving up toward the forehead are the *frontal lobes* and the prefrontal cortex. The frontal lobes control many executive functions that are necessary for goal-oriented responses such as motor activity, speech, thought, reasoning, planning, problem solving and emotional control, concept formation and abstract thinking.[16] The frontal lobes influence attention, monitor our ability to initiate or complete a task, manage stress, suppress unacceptable urges that may precipitate antisocial behaviors, help to solidify working memory, aid in our ability to monitor and shift behavior, and guide the formation of social perceptions that lead to social competence. The prefrontal cortex (part of the frontal lobe) further carries out the complex executive functioning and regulatory roles of the frontal cortex with regard to behavior, concentration, emotion, and cognition. The prefrontal cortex and frontal lobes are the last area of the brain to fully develop.[17, 18]

Functioning may be compromised due to white matter damage in the neural tracts that connect the frontal lobes both with the *basal ganglia,* in the deeper portions of the brain, and with the posterior (back) sections of the brain. A diagnosis of *periventricular leukomalacia (PVL)* may accompany this damage and is frequently referenced in a student's medical reports.[19]

In each hemisphere, above the ears, lie the *temporal lobes*. Like most areas of the brain, they serve many functions, including the storage of long-term memory, the detection of smells, and the organization of objects. The left temporal lobe is primarily associated with the perception and interpretation of sound and speech.

Deep in the center of the brain (subcortical), in both hemispheres, lie groups of neurons that comprise the basal ganglia. One of their many functions is the control and regulation of voluntary movement.

The *brain stem* sits at the base of the brain and controls the involuntary vital body functions of alertness, respiration, blood pressure, body temperature, and digestion. The brain stem is continuous with the spinal cord.

The *limbic system* (associated with emotions) is composed of the *thalamus*, the *hypothalamus*, the *amygdala*, and the *hippocampus*.

The thalamus lies in both hemispheres, above the brain stem, and regulates essential body functions through messages that are sent to the cortex. It receives input from most sensory organs—except for the *olfactory* (smell) system, whose input goes directly to the limbic system and the cortex.

These structures are involved in the formation and retrieval of long-term memory as well as the monitoring of emotions, thirst, hunger, the wake/sleep cycles, and maintenance of the body's internal balance.

The amygdala also receives sensory information from the thalamus when harm or danger is detected, and it sends warning messages by hormones, which carry them to areas of the body that can then prepare us for protective responses. The amygdala also holds the memory of emotion and fear.

The hippocampus, which lies within the temporal lobes, is also a part of the limbic system and, most importantly, helps to change information in short-term memory to storage as long-term memory in the cortex. The hippocampus also helps to control our spatial memory and aids in navigation.

Risk Factors Leading to a Diagnosis of CP

The following is a list of known risk factors for developing conditions that *may* lead to a diagnosis of CP. This listing of some known risk factors for early brain injury describes conditions that can appear in isolation or in concert with one another. The term *idiopathic* is often found in medical reports of students who have been diagnosed with CP and describes brain injury of an unknown cause.

- A low *Apgar score* (the assessment given to a newborn at designated intervals after birth that describes the newborn's general state of health, including respiration).
- Premature birth at low birth weight (before thirty-seven weeks or under 5.7 lbs. [2,500 grams]), although most babies diagnosed with CP are born near to full term.
- One of multiple births (quite frequently premature with low birth weight).
- Breech birth (when buttocks, knees, or feet emerge first from the birth canal).
- Trauma from accidents such as car accidents, near drowning, or choking.
- Trauma to the infant's head during pregnancy, labor, and delivery.
- Shaken baby syndrome.
- Pressure on the brain.
- Incomplete or abnormal development of brain structures (such as *microcephaly*, being born with a very small head).
- Physical or metabolic (life-maintaining chemical process in organisms) trauma during the birth process.
- *Hydrocephalus* (excess *cerebral spinal fluid [CSF]* on the brain, which if not drained can damage neurons).
- Infections such as meningitis and encephalitis that damage a fetus's developing nervous system.

- German measles during the early months of pregnancy.
- Fetal lead poisoning.
- Other poisoning.
- Birth defects of the brain and spinal cord (the CNS).
- *Proteinuria* (excess protein in the urine).
- Maternal fever during labor in full-term babies.
- Periventricular leukomalacia (PVL), which is frequently cited as a risk factor in CP and occurs during reduced blood flows to the tissues of the walls of the lateral ventricles (brain spaces filled with cerebral spinal fluid), resulting in the enlargement of and damage to neurons that originate in these ventricle walls. The resulting damage can affect movement and cognition.
- Poor myelination (insulation and protection) of the fatty white matter that protects a neuron's axons.
- Disruption or deprivation of the oxygen supply to the developing brain (*hypoxia*).
- Brain abnormalities present before birth and/or exacerbated during the birth process, which may contribute to oxygen deprivation or disruption.
- Rupture of fragile prenatal or postnatal blood vessels.
- *Ischemic stroke* (blood clot).
- *Intracranial bleeding* before, during, or after birth.
- Seizures during or after birth (seizures are experienced by about 50 percent of children diagnosed with CP).
- Severe jaundice in infants, which if left untreated, may be associated with brain damage that leads to CP.
- Untreated Rh incompatibility between mother and infant, resulting in jaundice in the infant.
- Fetal toxins.
- *Meconium aspiration* (in-utero feces).
- Low fetal blood sugar.

An international team of researchers now believes that based on genetic studies, inheritance or genetic mutations may play a role, because rare gene mutations contribute to the development of conditions that leave the fetal environment at risk for CP-related factors.[20]

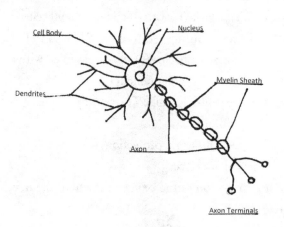

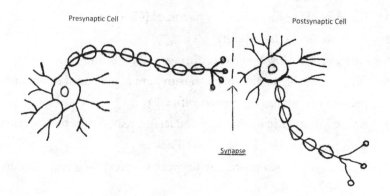

Neurons found in the brain. Top: A brain's neuron and it's parts. Bottom: Two neurons communicating at a synapse.

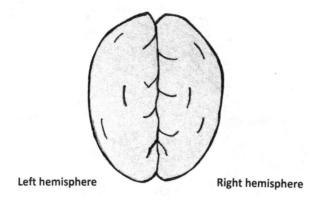

Left hemisphere   Right hemisphere

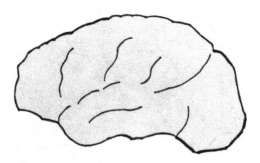

Top: The brain's left and right hemispheres.
Bottom: The brain's cortex. Neurons in the cortex reach
down to connect with other neurons in every brain area.

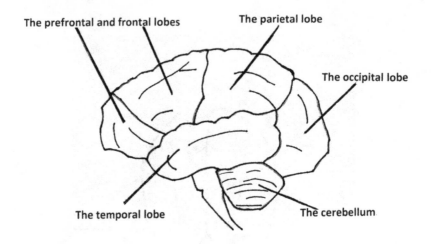

The prefrontal and frontal lobes

The parietal lobe

The occipital lobe

The temporal lobe

The cerebellum

The basal ganglia

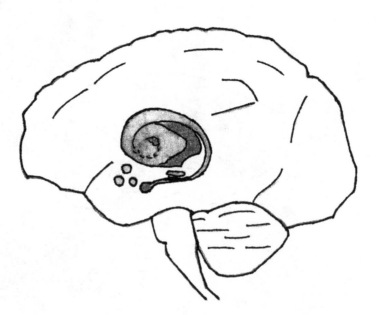

Top: Lobes are brain sections found in both hemispheres. Injury to neurons in the cerebellum is associated with ataxic CP. Bottom: Injury to neurons in the basal ganglia is associated with dyskinetic CP.

The Limbic System

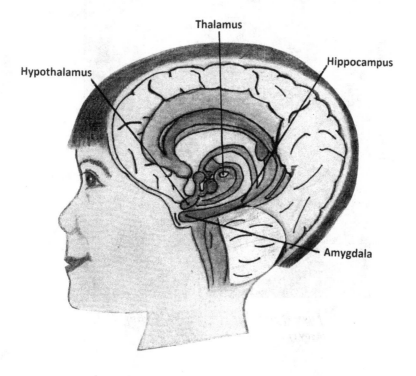

Portions of the brain that form the limbic system affect emotion.

The use of age-appropriate content and reading levels enables the joy of reading.

CHAPTER 2

The Primary and Secondary Motor Conditions of Cerebral Palsy: Surgical, Medical, and Educational Considerations

Adine R. Usher

∽

The CP "Suitcase": Mild, Moderate, or Severe Manifestations of Cerebral Palsy

Individuals *may* experience some or all of the following conditions, and there is great variability in their severity and impact.

- **Primary gross and fine motor limitation affect:** Problems with feet, legs, trunk, neck, arms, hand and finger control, speech, chewing, swallowing, and oculomotor function.

- **Chronic medical issues:** Seizures; respiratory concerns; bowel, bladder, and gastrointestinal concerns; pain; and fatigue.

- **Sensory issues:** Visual and auditory acuity issues; perception and processing difficulties; and tactile, proprioception, and vestibular issues.

- **Cognitive range:** Superior intelligence to profound intellectual limitations.

- **Communication (expressive and receptive language) issues:** Articulation challenges and language processing difficulties.

- **Social-emotional challenges (neurological and environmentally based):** Dependence, social isolation, and psychological challenges.

This chapter examines the primary and secondary motoric conditions of CP that are thought by scientists to be caused by the types of brain injuries that were discussed in chapter 1. Acquiring a basic understanding of these conditions can deepen your knowledge about how difficulties with muscle and joint movements can affect movement, comfort, feelings of well-being, attention, health, and access to all of life's activities, including learning and instruction.

Primary conditions in CP result from injured or destroyed neurons in areas of the brain that control movement, causing the brain to send faulty messages to the muscles and joints.

Primary conditions often lead to *secondary conditions*, which can be defined as pain, bone deformities, misalignment of joints, and inadequate muscle growth, resulting in *contractures* that shorten muscles and tendons.[21] Secondary conditions are consequences of primary conditions. Pain is an example of a secondary condition that results from difficult, compromised movement. Secondary conditions can significantly impact quality of life and learning in the school setting.

Compensatory conditions can grow out of secondary conditions. Stiff knees that make walking more difficult are a consequence of abnormal *muscle tone*. Swinging one's legs in a circular motion rather than maintaining legs straight when walking is another compensatory action.[22]

Gross motor involvement refers to the muscles that control large movements of limbs, the neck, and the body core (stomach and back). *Fine motor* involvement describes the control of small muscle movements in the hands, fingers, feet, and toes. Deficits in fine motor control express themselves in all the school-related tasks requiring finger and hand skills that must also be coordinated with vision.[23] Using hands individually and together requires coordination with gross muscle arm movement, vision, and *proprioception* (knowing where your body is in space). *Graphomotor skills* are fine motor skills that are required for paper and pencil activities of copying, writing, and drawing—activities that are dependent on visual acuity and visual perception. Fine motor dysfunction is also observed in weak and difficult-to-control facial, mouth, and neck muscles, which can challenge chewing and swallowing (*dysphagia*) and impair speech production (*dysarthria*).

The Consequences of Compromised Muscle Tone

As a result of faulty messages from the brain, muscles become tight, affecting *muscle tone* (muscle tension or resistance during rest in response to the need to stretch the muscle). *High tone* describes muscles that become rigid or fixed, and *low tone* describes muscles that are floppy or weak. With increased tone (tightness), contractures can develop in the joints of the wrist, arms, ankles, hips, and knees.[24] *Alternating tone* describes a fluctuation between high and low tone.

The resulting imbalance in muscle expansion and contraction is responsible for atypical performance with motor control, motor coordination, posture, and balance. This muscle imbalance also contributes to uneven muscle pull on the joints and the prolonged presence of primitive, abnormal reflexes—reflexes that should have disappeared within the early months of life.[25] Being stressed or overwhelmed can exacerbate problems with muscle tone and may add to difficulties with muscle control.

Although no two individuals who live with the conditions of CP are identical, there are movement patterns common to each type. These atypical movement patterns appear in mild, moderate, severe, or fluctuating forms and can simultaneously vary in impact in different parts of the body—e.g., low (floppy) tone in one part of the body and high (tight and ridged) tone in another area of the body.

Although CP is described as a nonprogressive condition, over a lifetime these atypical muscle movements can become more problematic for individuals as body weight increases (often from a limited access to exercise) and as the body ages.

Types of Cerebral Palsy

The three major types of motor dysfunction in CP are described as *spastic*, *dyskinetic*, and *ataxic*. A small number of children are diagnosed with *mixed cerebral palsy*, which explains the presence of a combination of two of the three types of motor dysfunctions where one form is not distinctly prominent. In reading the research on the prevalence and percentage of the different types of CP, we find that the statistics vary.

Spastic cerebral palsy (pyramidal CP) is the most common type of CP, affecting from 70 to 80 percent of individuals diagnosed with CP. It originates in injury to neurons in the brain's motor cortex. This motor impairment is characterized by fixed, ridged movements caused by muscles that are tight and inflexible[26] in their response to a rapid stretch.

The subsets of spastic CP are identified by the parts of the body that are most affected. *Spastic diplegia* describes a form of CP in which both legs are more involved than arms and hands.

Spastic hemiplegia typically affects the arm and hand on one side of the body and can also include the legs. This form of CP can produce limited awareness and sensation on the weaker side of the body; it may produce slower protective responses or dangerously rapid motions, especially when falling, and can increase a student's difficulty with two-handed coordination. Children with spastic hemiplegia generally walk later and on tiptoe because of tight heel tendons. The arm and leg on the weaker side are frequently shorter and thinner. Some children will develop an abnormal curvature of the spine (*scoliosis*). A child with spastic hemiplegia may also have seizures. Speech may be delayed, but, at best, competence and intelligence are usually within the normal range.[27]

Spastic quadriplegia can be significantly challenging, since arms, legs, trunk, and head control are all simultaneously involved. The extensive nature of spastic quadriplegia usually leaves impaired all the gross and fine muscles of the body, including those involved in speech production.

The second most common form of CP is alternately described as *dyskinetic*, or *extrapyramidal*, CP, which affects approximately 10 to 22 percent of individuals diagnosed with CP. Dyskinetic CP includes athetoid, choreoathetoid, and athetoid-dystonic types. Dystonia affects voluntary muscle movement, is marked by abnormal posture, and is found in both spastic and dyskinetic forms of CP. This form of CP is characterized by constant motion that either is rapid, random, jerky, rigid, involuntary, and unpredictable (even when the body is at rest) or is sometimes slow and writhing or marionette-type (*chorea*). Dyskinetic movement can involve the entire body, may be characterized by muscles that are weak or floppy, and may cause abnormal posture.[28] Dyskinetic CP is thought to be caused by injury both to neurons in the basal ganglia (groups of cells deep in both hemispheres of the ancient part of the brain) and to neighboring brain structures.

The least common form of CP is *ataxia*, which affects less than 5 percent of the CP population. Ataxia occurs when there is injury to neurons in the cerebellum (at the base of the brain just above the neck) and is characterized by wide-based walking, poorly coordinated steps, shaky and poorly coordinated movements, low tone when walking or changing position, and a tendency to lose one's balance when walking and/or executing a reaching movement.

According to the CDC, 77.4 percent of students with CP have spastic CP, 58.2 percent of students with CP walk independently, 11.3 percent of this population walk with hand-held mobility devices, 30.6 percent have limited or no walking ability, and 41 percent have a limited ability to crawl.[29]

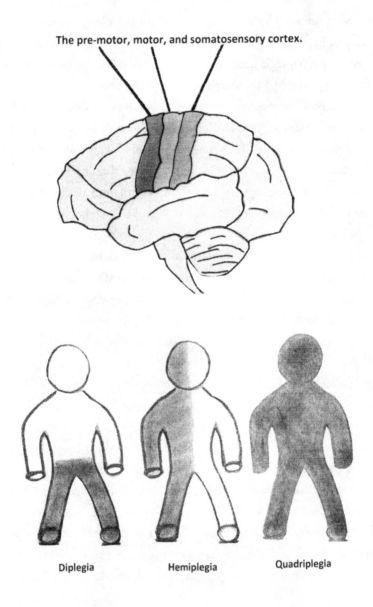

The pre-motor, motor, and somatosensory cortex.

Diplegia   Hemiplegia   Quadriplegia

Top: Injuries originating in the brain's motor cortex are associated with forms of spastic CP. Bottom: The three primary types of spastic cerebral palsy.

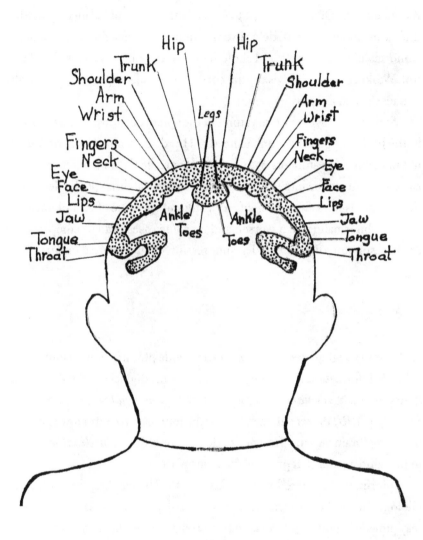

These parts of the body are controlled by neurons in the motor cortex. Damage to the neurons affect movement.

Additional Muscular and Skeletal Concerns

A student with CP may attempt to gain a better sense of balance by holding their arms in an elevated, defensive position or by engaging in toe walking. Abnormalities in the neck and shoulder muscles can compromise head control. Weakness in the body's central core not only affects posture but can also impact skeletal integrity.

Scoliosis and *kyphosis* (curvatures of the spine) occur when muscle forces in the back and pelvis are unbalanced.[30] Hip dislocations (*subluxation*) are not uncommon in students with significant spastic CP and, if left untreated, can contribute to the intensity of a student's physical disability by decreasing opportunities for safe movement. As a student ages, the effects of musculoskeletal abnormalities can worsen and, in some cases, lead to compromised cardiorespiratory function and a compression of vital internal organs.[31]

Imaging

Early brain imaging (*neuroimaging*) can provide physicians and families with valuable information about the prospective consequences and risks of brain injury. *Magnetic resonance imaging (MRI)* and *functional magnetic resonance imaging (fMRI)* detect enlargements of the four *ventricles* (hollow spaces) in the young brain and the presence of delayed or reduced *myelination* (injury to the white matter that protects the neuron's axon).

Information gathered from MRIs and fMRIs may help to explain the etiology (history) of a diagnosis of cerebral palsy.[32] Early MRI neuroimaging may provide important information concerning the specific risks of visual problems.[33] *Computed tomography (CT) scans* can also shed light on the condition of the ventricles, and *single photon emission computed tomography (SPECT)* can detect an inadequate supply of oxygen and nutrients in brain tissue.[34]

Classifications and Degree of Involvement

Developed in 1997, the *Gross Motor Function Classification System (GMFCS)* grades CP in five levels of severity or involvement, with level I being the least involved and level V the most involved and functionally and physically limiting. This system, used primarily by clinicians and therapists, was expanded and revised (GMFCS–E&R) in 2007 to include youth, ages twelve to eighteen.

Surgical Interventions for Primary and Secondary Motor Conditions

CP is a congenital condition that cannot be cured; however, surgical interventions can reduce pain and discomfort and can prevent some of the muscular and skeletal conditions of CP from worsening.

When physical therapy has not reached its desired goals, the orthopedic surgeon will seek to improve the function of bones, joints, muscles, ligaments, and tendons.[35] Surgical interventions offered to students with CP correct deformities that impact movement. These interventions improve gross and fine motor function and reduce the incidence of further *contractures* (tightening of the muscles), extend endurance, improve postural stability, extend range of motion, reduce fatigue and pain, and enhance appearance—thus allowing a student to be more functional in performing educational, personal, social, and recreational tasks.

Over the past decades, the increased benefits of bracing have decreased the number of surgeries a student with CP must undergo. When the student ceases to improve, is experiencing great discomfort, or is regressing, more surgery may be recommended. These surgeries are intended to improve function in the presence of spinal, pelvic, hip, knee, and ankle and foot deformities. Surgery is also performed to correct hand and wrist deformities. Often, surgeries are followed by *casting* or *splinting*: procedures that are designed to avoid contractures and diminish tone by immobilizing the affected body part.

A *brain shunt* (cerebral shunt) drains *cerebrospinal fluid (CSF)* that fails to circulate continually and normally from the brain, down through the spinal cord, and back up into the brain. A buildup of this improperly circulating cerebrospinal fluid is called *hydrocephalus*, which, if untreated, can cause significant brain damage and death. A student with CP may have had hydrocephalus identified soon after birth, and therefore a shunt is placed in a ventricle (hollow space) in the brain and connected, with tubing, to the abdomen. Shunts may be replaced as the student grows or if malfunctions occur.

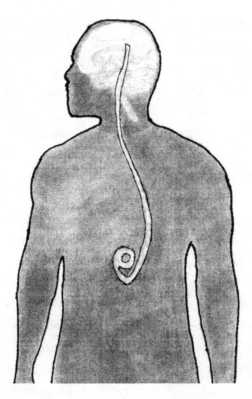

A student with a brain shunt. A brain shunt drains unwanted cerebral spinal fluid out of the brain and into the abdomen.

Tendon lengthening is the surgical lengthening of the Achilles tendon and the hamstring on the back of the knee to improve walking. This procedure reduces the incidence of toe walking and a crouching gait. Tendon transfers from one area on the bone to another can improve muscle control and are often performed on the hand and wrist.[36] Cutting tendons to relieve contractures (spastic tightness) and improve movement is referred to as *tenotomy*. A *neurectomy* permanently reduces spasticity by cutting the nerves to groups of muscles, and a *myotomy* cuts muscle to reduce contractures.

Selective dorsal rhizotomy (SDR) is a surgical procedure that clips selected nerves in the spine to disrupt the excessive flow of nerve impulses to muscles that cause stiffness (spasticity) and an overreaction to a stimulus or a change of position.[37] This procedure is primarily performed on children, and like all surgical procedures, it carries some risk.[38] Surgery may also be performed on students with CP to do the following:

- Correct limb positioning
- Manage uneven growth
- Realign hip bones with a hip osteotomy
- Reduce tremors and reduce the skeletal effects of curvatures with spinal fusion[39]
- Perform *deep brain stimulation (DBS)*, which shows promise for a CP subset of students with dystonia

Medications for Primary and Secondary Motor Conditions

Medications most frequently prescribed for students with CP are anticonvulsants, which control seizures; antispastics, which relax muscles and improve muscular control; and anti-inflammatories, which reduce the intensity of painful contractures. Medications, including stool softeners, also produce relief for a variety of CP-related gastrointestinal disorders. Antidepressants may be prescribed for depression.

Not all medications used for controlling some of the conditions of CP are appropriate for children, and many may have short- and long-term side effects. No two students with CP have the same chemistry, and tolerance to medication differs. When medications are recommended, they must be carefully and continually monitored.[40] For students with CP, medications are typically given by parents at home or by the school nurse or a designated provider. Those who have daily responsibility for the student should be aware of possible significant side effects from medication and must be observant and in constant communication with all who work with the student.

Botox is a nerve blocker and temporary muscle relaxer that quiets spastic muscles and allows weaker muscles to strengthen and function.[41]

Baclofen is another muscle relaxer that flows directly into the body's nervous system, thereby reducing spasticity throughout the entire body. Baclofen can be administered either by a pill or through a pump that is surgically implanted under the skin, over the abdomen. When baclofen is administered by mouth, the stronger dosage is likely to cause drowsiness. However, when administered by a surgically implanted pump, the steady but reduced flow of medicine is less likely to affect arousal states.[42]

Staff Knowledge of and Responses to Surgical and Medical Concerns

Teachers and classroom assistants are neither nurses nor physicians, but they must be knowledgeable and observant. Teachers should know about a student's surgical procedures and be cognizant of postsurgical recovery consequences. Teachers should also be aware of the student's medical and health conditions, the side effects of medications, and the warning signs of impending trouble that health conditions can signal. Most importantly, teachers need to know under what specific conditions the nurse and/or an ambulance must be called.

In many inclusive public schools and in special schools, routine medical procedures such as catheterization, the dispensing of medications, suctioning, and gastrointestinal tube feeding are integrated into the daily health-care plan and are usually performed by school nurses or specialized therapists. However, in those areas where nursing support is less accessible to students with CP, trained and designated school staff may have to perform some of these medical procedures.

Teachers need to know that a student has a brain shunt and understand that the shunt was surgically implanted to redirect the flow of spinal fluid, thereby reducing the buildup of fluid pressure on the brain. The teacher and classroom staff must also recognize the signs of possible shunt malfunction: fever, headaches, and nausea. These symptoms may also suggest many other less serious conditions; however, when a student has a shunt, assume the worst and know immediately how to respond and whom to contact. Have emergency plans in place if the student with a shunt appears to be experiencing signs of a shunt malfunction.

Students with baclofen pumps, which are designed to deliver medicine that relaxes spasticity, must be frequently and carefully monitored in medical facilities for signs of infections requiring evaluation, reassessment, and modification of dosages. Teachers, parents, and classroom staff can be trained to look for possible indications of pump malfunctions. Teachers should know that a student has a pump and need to learn from both parents and the school nurse the appropriate response at the first signs of pump malfunction.

Surgery

For many students with CP, multiple surgeries performed during childhood and the adolescent years are a simple fact of life. These surgeries are essential to the improvement of movement—specifically, ambulation and the establishment of muscular and skeletal stability. Surgeries are also performed to reduce spasticity-related discomfort.

Although these surgeries are often very effective in lowering CP's motoric barriers and improving the overall quality of school participation, no two students who live with CP experience the postoperative rehabilitation period identically. For some students this period is relatively uneventful, whereas others may experience a degree of physical and emotional debilitation that can include a regression of overall strength, stamina, and sustained attention.[43] For some, presurgical anxiety is not uncommon and may increase with subsequent surgeries. When this occurs, a Child Life professional on the hospital staff can provide age-appropriate information and comfort.[44]

Surgery for students and families can be difficult and stressful. Major surgery may physically debilitate a youngster for months, putting strain on families and keeping students out of school for long periods. While recovering, students may lose muscular function, may become weak, and will require postsurgical therapy. Some of this therapy is performed on an outpatient basis; other times, students recover in hospitals or in rehabilitation centers that have educational programs.

Often families and surgeons will try to schedule a student's surgery during the summer months to limit loss of school time. However, even when surgery is performed during the summer, a degree of physical, educational, and social-emotional regression may mark a student's return to school in the fall. Upon the student's return, staff members who work with them must anticipate a period of adjustment as surgical benefits emerge and the student works to regain physical, academic, and psychological strength. Discomfort, fatigue, lack of endurance, altered activity, diet limitations, health-care procedures, needs for breaks, negotiating the physical spaces of the school, and scheduling modifications all become important considerations when planning for school reentry.[45]

Medical Devices

Orthotic devices such as orthotics (braces), crutches, walkers, standers, and wheelchairs are all essential to the management of CP's primary and secondary conditions. These devices support improved mobility and overall physical functioning. However, classroom staff needs to be aware that these devices may, if not properly monitored, cause pain, discomfort, skin irritations, and skin breakdown that can add to a student's stress; therefore, close communication with a physical therapist (PT) is essential. Discomfort can be particularly challenging for students who are unable to verbalize their discomfort, and this reality may cause behavior that educators find confounding.

Structural, Architectural, and Safety Considerations

CP's primary and secondary motor conditions necessitate an internal and external school environment that ensures safety, comfort, and ease of movement and that is supportive of independence. These structural requirements enable appropriate instruction and learning.

The concept of *universal architectural design* is becoming a part of building codes worldwide for both new and old school buildings. Ramps, halls with railings, wheelchair lifts, external and internal doorways that accommodate wheelchairs, walkers, water fountains, sinks of varying heights, curb cuts, lowered accessible light switches, elevators, and accessible bathrooms are all increasingly available to expand school-wide accessibility that serves the unique physical, health, educational, and social-emotional needs of students with CP and those with other physical disabilities.

In rainy or snowy weather, floors near exits and in classrooms need to be kept dry. Snow and water from the wheels of a wheelchair can prove a hazard for students who ambulate independently but unsteadily and for those who use walkers and crutches. Appropriate nonskid rugs help to reduce this risk.

A growing number of school buildings have elevators that, depending on the age of the student with CP and the restrictions of local regulations, may be used with or without adult assistance. Since these elevators are, unfortunately, often out of service and in need of repair, school systems should have contractual agreements with repair services that quickly rectify the problem.

If legally mandated environmental and safety and accessibility standards are not in place to ensure the maximum security for the student with CP as they ambulate unaided or with crutches, walkers, or wheelchairs, a tour and examination of the school environment (with student and parents) prior to the student's arrival is highly recommended.

School safety plans and measures are essential for students with CP whose physical and health limitations may leave them at greater risk for accidents. On the other hand, once safety has been established, care should also be taken not to overprotect the student. Explore ways to balance the need for safety with the need for expanding a student's opportunities for greater independence and self-reliance.

Safety and accessibility must be considered when teachers move the students with CP outside of the boundaries of the school, and field trips will be discussed at the end of chapter 4.

Planning for Gross Motor Challenges: Posture, Mobility, and Seatwork

Since CP is primarily a condition of compromised muscle tone, gross motor dysfunction affects, to varying degrees, the ability of the body's larger muscles to control the legs, the feet, and the arms and to maintain posture in the body's core. Affected gross motor muscles in the neck may make it difficult for students with CP to maintain their head control in a steady, upright position. This inability has major implications for achieving balance using vision, for maintaining focus during instruction, and for sustaining social interactions.

If the student with CP is safe and not unduly stressed and exhausted, the use of a walker or crutches should be encouraged throughout the school day while the student participates in academic and nonacademic activities. If the student tires, a wheelchair is a perfectly acceptable alternative. An ambulating student with CP may become less steady and slower if they tire by the end of the day.

Seating

The importance of seating for students with CP cannot be overstated. Safe, comfortable, and appropriately adaptive seating increases the likelihood that concentration will be sustained and that learning can take place. Proper seating

- Prepares students for physical and cognitive demands.
- Reduces hand, postural neck, and back fatigue.
- Positions students upright, with bottoms well back in the seat of the chair.
- Maintains hips flexed at approximately ninety degrees.
- Helps to keep the student's head upright.
- Keeps the feet at a ninety-degree angle to the shins and flat on the floor or wheelchair footrest.
- May require boxes or footrests placed under the student's feet.
- Requires working with the PTs to ensure that headrests and other supports are functioning properly.
- Determines the height that allows for the comfortable resting of elbows and arms on a table.
- Permits comfortable, balanced floor sitting on mats and floor seaters, thereby avoiding W-sitting (when a child sits on their bottom with knees bent and feet positioned outside the hips), which retards hip and knee development.
- May require that chairs and wheelchairs be modified with posture cushions to ensure pelvic support.
- Can include straps, belts, and various types of side supports.
- Requires heightened awareness of the need to change a student's seating positions frequently in order to maintain attention, increase circulation, and avoid skin breakdowns.

Attention to seating and foot placement reduces discomfort, improves circulation, maintains musculoskeletal alignment, assists vision, and optimizes sustained attention and engagement. Students may use standers for part of an instructional period. Those who ambulate around the school using walkers and crutches, as well as those students with CP who ambulate unaided, may also often require adaptive seating.

Decisions regarding correct seating and foot placement are made in collaboration with students, parents, the physical and occupational therapist, and the student's orthopedist. The rationale for these seating placement choices must be thoroughly understood by the classroom staff, as they have significant implications for instruction and learning.

Equipment Needed in the School Setting

- Students with CP may depend on orthotics; they may use motorized or manual wheelchairs, walkers, crutches, or canes to stabilize movement and improve ambulation.
- Standers are used to lengthen and strengthen spastic muscles, improve balance, and increase stamina.
- A student with CP may use several large pieces of seating and mobility equipment during the school day; therefore, common areas of the class should be kept clear and free of impediments so that this equipment can be safely and effectively used to enhance the student's learning and socialization.
- Time must be allotted to move this equipment from place to place.
- Ample spaces need to be created between desks and tables to enable greater ease of independent movement for the students with CP who use bulky equipment but whose challenged movements may also be complicated by the presence of visual impairments.

Wheelchairs and Transfers as Part of the Navigational Plan

Students who use both motorized and manual wheelchairs often transfer to adaptive stationary chairs. Whenever possible, the students themselves should be trained and encouraged to assist with these transfers and to develop independent skills that will serve them well as they move toward adulthood.

Classroom staff must also be aware that a student's sensory status may influence their ability to make smooth transfers. Reduced *proprioception* (knowing where one's body is in space and in relation to different body parts) may make transferring more challenging. Difficulties with *visual perception, visual acuity,* and *visual field*, when added to movement disorders, may also increase the challenges.

Facilitating transfers in the classroom, when possible, is an important activity that has implications for both health and independence. Whether assisted or unassisted, the proximity and stability of involved seating is essential. The height of a table also becomes a safety factor when the student is moving to or from a chair. These transfers, when done easily and safely, will help to promote mobility, increase circulation, reduce pressure sores, and, hopefully, improve attention and engagement.

Wheelchair users who must remain in their wheelchairs for extended periods of time must be comfortably seated and medically stabilized. Whenever it is medically indicated, they should be able to transfer to alternative seating or standers during lessons. Having a variety of positioning choices can maximize a student's engagement, motivation, and, consequently, performance.

Wheelchairs tend to be bulky and may block the view of other students, so it's tempting to place students in wheelchairs on the periphery of a group. Awareness of—and, where feasible, avoidance of—this practice can lead to more creative, more educationally appropriate, and more socially appropriate seating arrangements, which can bring the student with CP in closer proximity to the instructor and peers. These wheelchair seating decisions, along with the knowledge of how body positions in the chair enhance attention, should also be based on an understanding of how students process what they see and hear.

Does Everyone Have to Walk?

Thinking, communicating, reasoning, and interacting with others—not the ability to walk—defines our humanity. Difficult ambulation, which is not only the result of motor dysfunction but also of proprioceptive, *vestibular*, and visual sensory disorders, often necessitates the use of wheelchairs and scooters, which spare the student with CP from expending excess energy, thus leaving more energy for learning. Students might use a wheelchair for navigating long distances in the school or on school trips and then use crutches or walkers when they arrive at their destination.

There is great and understandable pressure in society for students with CP to walk, and in many cases, this is a desirable, healthy, and medically sound goal. For others, however, the full-time or occasional use of a wheelchair or scooter is a more realistic solution. Students need to value themselves as they are and realize that wheelchairs move a person about faster, safer, and more comfortably, whereas excessive and struggling ambulation can negatively impact the well-being of other body systems and the student's overall quality of life.

Adaptive Desks and Tables to Facilitate Health and Academic Performance

Over the decades, there has been a proliferation of companies that create adaptable, customized, and medically appropriate furniture for individuals who live with a range of physical disabilities. Using metal, wood, plastic, molded foam, and cardboard, these enterprises are limited only by the reach of imagination as they work with individuals with physical disabilities, their families, and therapists to create more comfortable and effective work environments. It is not unusual for a student with CP to work on several different types of adaptive surfaces for use in different locations and for different activities that support healthy, satisfying, academic, artistic, and social endeavors.

Adaptive Desks and Tables in Conjunction with Stabilizing Educational Equipment

The desk is a hallowed and enabling place for a student with CP and must, in all ways, safely and comfortably support engagement and learning. In addition to the proper height and angle of tilt of desktops, instructional adaptations for desks or tables must be designed based on the specificity of a student's needs. There is a wide choice of commercially adaptive desks and tables for students with CP. These desks have cut-out surfaces that accommodate chairs and wheelchairs, adjustable heights, surface tilts, and adaptive writing surfaces with raised edges.

Adjustable tables and desks function in concert with adaptive seating to optimize correct posture and facilitate the use of books, computer games, writing tools, and other manual devices that support learning. Adjustable tables, desks, and seating also encourage communication and socialization, especially when these adaptations permit the student with CP to have non-isolated, closer proximity to teachers and peers.

In conjunction with adaptable desks and tables,

- Use book stands, page holders, and page turners to improved independence.
- Use a commercially made nonslip Dysem mat, which keeps educational materials from moving on the table surface.
- Work with occupational therapists (OTs) to adapt and customize typical tabletop educational materials and toys.
- Use adapted, modified scissors recommended by the OT to aid independent cutting when difficulty with fine motor tasks makes cutting stressful and ineffective.
- Determine a student's needs and acquire (in a timely manner) adaptive furniture through the committed collaboration among students, teachers, parents, PTs and OTs, physicians, administrators, and the student's funding sources.
- Do not isolate students who use adaptive desks and tables, but include this furniture within the instructional space used by other students.

Orthotic Devices

Orthotic devices are molded plastic or metal braces or splints placed on feet, ankles and legs, wrists, hands, or fingers to stabilize the affected body part. Braces may also be placed around a person's back and midsection to enhance posture and reduce spinal curvatures. These devices reduce muscle contractures, add stability to the affected body part, reduce discomfort, and improve function and performance.

In addition to knowing how these orthotic devices enhance learning, classroom teacher's assistants, therapists, and parents needs to be alert to skin irritations that may develop underneath these devices.

Smaller adaptive devices that enable writing, eating, dressing, and artistic endeavors can be found in medical supply stores and catalogs used by PTs and OTs. Some, however, are designed and customized by therapists and parents.

Alternative ways of both carrying and storing books and school equipment, if not facilitated by an aide, require book bags on walkers and wheelchairs and holders on desks and tables that are easily accessible to the student with CP.

Considerations for Special Adaptive Equipment

Equipment Storage

- Shelves for storage of clothing, personal health needs, books, and school equipment must be accessible to the student, and personal toileting needs should be discreetly stored.
- When not in use, crutches, walkers, standers, and wheelchairs should be safely stored with consideration not only for accessibility for the student with CP but also for the safe, unobstructed movement of classmates.
- Make certain that all learning devices, digital and nondigital, in the classroom's learning and play centers are accessible to the student with CP.

- Adaptive equipment that is mounted on a student's wheelchair or desk should be easily seen and reached whether or not the student is able to operate the equipment independently.

Staff Familiarity with Equipment

Students with CP use a great number of technical supports, and teachers and assistants should be familiar with the safe operation of digital and nondigital equipment. We have already covered the care of equipment that aids ambulation and seating. Classroom staff should also know *how* orthotic devices (molded forms designed to add strength and stability to legs, back, arms, and/or wrists) function, *when* they might be causing discomfort, and *how* these pieces of equipment can be maintained.

Instruction in the use and care of a student's equipment come from many sources. Parents are an excellent source for learning about the equipment's operation and care. PTs and OTs, in collaboration with parents, are the next source of expertise. Venders who sell, train, and service the equipment for either the families or the school system are an important part of the collaborative process and frequently serve the primary, informational role.

Teachers, in collaboration with therapists, should make certain that these devices are in good, safe condition, are being used safely and effectively, are not causing the student undue stress and fatigue, are not causing irritation to the student's skin, and are not exacerbating problems with posture. It is important to observe and assess when this adaptive equipment is not operating as intended or is producing discomfort.

It is not unusual for a student with CP to use several pieces of mobility equipment and adaptive seating during a school day—each piece based on the requirements of the task and the physical status of the student. This range of choices and the attention paid to the effectiveness of the choices can enhance a student's overall performance in the school environment.[46] Of particular importance is the safe use and care for power-driven wheelchairs and scooters. Some of these devices require special covers for their motors in inclement weather.

Primary and Secondary Concerns with Fine Motor Challenges

Significant learning consequences can arise when students with CP have diffi-culty executing, coordinating, integrating, and planning fine motor movements. These fine motor difficulties may coexist with the associated conditions of complex health challenges, sensory difficulties, social-emotional challenges, and/or intellectual disabilities.

Fine motor impairments that affect the efficient use of fingers and hands can significantly limit a student's access to educational, artistic, and recreational activities. Such impairments directly affect the ability of some students with CP to independently operate wheelchairs, engage in the self-care activities of daily living, and manipulate and control pencils, scissors, crayons, other art material, and books. When fine motor perfor-mance is additionally affected by distortions in tactile sensation, there can be less awareness and sensation of the intended functional movement of a particular body part. When the sense of touch fails to provide the student with appropriate information about their environment, the results can be upsetting, destabilizing, or uncomfortable.

A wide range of adaptive, educational materials, including toys, puzzles with magnets, grips, wooden knobs, and handles, allow students with CP-related fine motor challenges to engage in age-appropriate play and learning activities. These adaptive devices should be employed not only in therapy sessions but also in classrooms. In addition to being accessible to students with varying abilities to hold and explore objects, these instruments offer varying tactile sensations for students with tactile challenges. Brilliant colors and interesting sounds, when coupled with touch, strengthen the total sensory experiences and augment the learning process.

Motor Planning for Fine and Gross Motor Movement

Preparing for, understanding, and remembering the exact sequence of movements one must go through to complete a motor task is referred to as *motor planning*. For both gross and fine motor functions, motor planning is the initial, crucial element of producing the desired motoric response. The neurological injuries that characterize CP can adversely affect motor planning and are detected when a student appears to lack the motoric ability to organize and plan fine and gross movements, a challenge that can be further exacerbated by visual and proprioceptive (knowing where one's body is in space) issues.

Many students with CP do not get rapid feedback when learning or performing a motor task and require considerable repetition and practice. PTs and OTs address gross and fine motor planning issues, respectively, and teachers and classroom staff need to understand the specificity of these difficulties as they manifest themselves in specific classroom activities. Addressing this difficulty involves

- Breaking down the elements of a movement into one step at a time.
- Consistent use of verbal directionality instructions for gross and fine movements. Talk the student through the motions.

Facilitating Handwriting When It Is the Appropriate Mode of Communication

Functional handwriting (graphomotor performance) is a complex fine motor skill, which is just one of many fine motor tasks that are dependent on muscle tone, arm and hand strength and stability, posture, and hand dominance.

Fine motor skills needed for writing are also coordinated and allied with visual motor skills of eye-hand coordination and visual perception that distinguishes shapes and spaces. Fine motor skills are also dependent on coordinated eye movements, the effectiveness of the student's visual field, motor planning, memory-based organizing, and a solid knowledge of letter names, shapes, and sequencing. The student with CP may experience discomfort, fatigue, and slow and unsatisfying performance when these interrelated and coordinated tasks are difficult to perform.

Shawn Datchuk's evaluation and analyzing of writing problems faced by students with learning disabilities[47] captures exactly the challenges faced by some students with CP. His recommendations derive from practice-based and research-based solutions and point to the following writing difficulties, including those with delayed memory (*orthographic coding*); commitment of letter names, shapes, and sequencing; fine motor movement issues; visual motor coordination; and letter formation. Datchuk recommends careful observation of these students as they struggle to write, and then work to identify and remediate their breakdown points.[48]

The desire that a student with CP learn to use a pen and pencil needs to be balanced with the functionality of the task, with the legibility and satisfaction derived from the quality of the product, and with the degree of discomfort the student experiences when writing.

Effective Strategies for Students Who Experience Mild to Moderate Manual Writing Difficulty

- First establish comfortable and effective sitting posture that is correct for the task of writing after carefully observing how the student with CP uses their body. PTs and OTs can collaborate with classroom teachers to determine the most appropriate positions for writing.
- Provide sloped writing boards or slanted desks to prevent the student from leaning over into work in ways that exacerbate existing skeletal and muscular problems. These adapted surfaces can be further customized for writing, cutting, drawing, painting, and other manual tasks with the use of tape, clamps, or weights.
- For some students, improve writing posture and wrist control by stabilizing the nonwriting side of the body.

- Employ weights placed on wrists and arms to add strength and improve posture.
- Help the students to use their fingers to draw or form letters in different mediums, such as playdough, sand, or sandpaper, thereby adding tactile sensations to a motor and visual task.
- Use hand-over-hand assistance or stabilization of the students' wrists and/or elbows.
- Teach students to trace between dotted lines.

Writing Tools

A great variety of adaptive writing tools are available that make writing more comfortable and capable of producing satisfying written products by the student with CP. Pencil grips and holders can be purchased from special education catalogs or created by the OTs and teachers.

By experimenting with a variety of pencil and paintbrush sizes, shapes, and textures, you may discover the most comfortable grip for the student with fine motor challenges. Fellow students or adults in the classroom may serve as scribes when writing is slow, uncomfortable, and fatiguing. Teachers can also prepare notes and handouts that relieve the student of the physical and mental chore of writing.

Adaptive Technology When Pens and Pencils Are Simply Not a Practical Choice

As educators, we must resist the temptation to force our students with mild to moderate forms of CP into "typical" modes of writing that simply do not work effectively for them—especially when there are so many other alternatives. When the previously discussed tools are insufficient to the task of writing, modified computer keyboards or tablets and an array of adaptive technology devices are available, including speech-to-text systems that circumvent the need to deal with the physical and sensory-perceptual demands of writing.

If the student's natural voice is not comprehendible and fine and gross motor problems make writing impossible, *augmentative and alternative communication (AAC)* technology, which relies on any controllable part of a student's body (knees, head, feet, eye gaze) to control the communication system, enables students with CP to express their thoughts, both verbally and in written form. Ongoing training on these systems for students, their parents, and involved school staff is provided by adaptive technology specialists, OTs, and speech therapists. Whether the student with CP is writing, typing, or dictating thoughts through adaptive technology, it is most important that the student feels motivated to satisfactorily express their thoughts and feelings.

For students with CP, the act of writing, using any mode, should emphasize the *quality of the work* rather than the *quantity of work*. Written work by students with CP who have both fine and gross motor issues always requires *extra time for completion*. The assignment must usually be *shortened* for these students without changing the fundamental aim and content of the assignment. As with other academic endeavors, more time must be allotted for learning new skills and for making modifications that support both individual achievement and group participation.

The primary and secondary motor conditions of CP can have profound implications for learning and performance. Whether or not these motoric conditions exist in concert with intellectual challenges, primary and secondary motor conditions must be understood and constantly and effectively addressed if we are to maximize the academic and social advancement and potential of the student with CP.

Case Study

Robin, who lives with spastic CP, tries never to miss school; she uses a wheelchair even when there is snow on the ground. It can be a bit of a struggle for her parents to get her to the school bus because waiting outside in cold weather is extremely uncomfortable and potentially dangerous for an individual who is unable to move enough to generate body heat.

An additional challenge awaits the school when Robin arrives there because when snow melts from the wheels of her wheelchair onto the school's ramp and floors, new dangers wait for Robert and José, who also have CP and who use crutches and a walker, respectively.

In inclement weather special attention must be paid to drying out wet and slippery floors in hallways and classrooms, which can pose hazards to ambulatory students who also have mobility issues. This same precaution holds true for food spilled in the lunchroom, even as we are encouraging independent movement for students who have mobility concerns.

Arturo, at age nineteen, enjoys an evening out. He lives with spastic CP.

CHAPTER 3

Cerebral Palsy's Associated Health Conditions

Adine R. Usher

〜

The *associated health conditions* of seizures, pain, fatigue, sleep difficulties, oral-motor problems, gastrointestinal issues, bladder and bowel concerns, and respiratory issues often accompany CP's *primary* and *secondary* motor conditions. The associated conditions may or may not be related to the brain injury that caused the primary and secondary motor conditions. Currently in educational settings, closer attention is being paid to the effects that these associated health conditions can have on a student's overall development. The Danish Society for Cerebral Palsy believes that some of these conditions "constitute a fundamental factor for understanding the totality of the 'syndrome' of CP."[49]

This chapter aims to strengthen the teacher's understanding of the most common associated health conditions that can accompany a diagnosis of CP, conditions that can and often do greatly impact a student's health, ability to learn, and social-emotional development. With this information, the teacher is in a stronger position to understand and support strategies that reduce the impact of these associated conditions, thereby allowing the identification and promotion of a student's strengths.

Along with associated health conditions, students with CP can also live with *co-occurring* life-altering conditions such as cleft lips or palates, esophageal and intestinal malformations, skeletal anomalies, cardiac problems, asthma, autism, and *attention-deficit hyperactivity disorder (ADHD)*. Educators should be aware of the presence of these additional conditions and factor in their impact on student performance.

Epilepsy

Seizures are described as brief, temporary disturbances of electrical activity in the brain and are often experienced by students with CP. Some 15 to 30 percent of the CP population have seizure disorders, which are most frequently found in students with spastic quadriplegia or in those students whose CP also involves significant intellectual disability. Such seizures may be well controlled before the student enters school. Other students will be on medication throughout their school years to control chronic seizures.[50,51] A subset of this population has seizures that are less responsive to medication, and they may experience alterations in brain development and a deterioration of cognitive capacity.[52] The presence of seizures can also mask the atypical movements associated with CP.

The Most Common Forms of Epilepsy
Temporal lobe epilepsy produces memory impairments and poor cognition and is found in greater numbers among students with limited or no walking ability.[53,54]

Focal seizures affect only one part of the brain. If the focal seizure is *simple*, it is less likely to affect awareness or memory. If the focal seizure is *complex*, it is more likely to momentarily affect awareness or memory.

The mildest seizures, *absent seizures* (formerly described as *petit mal seizures*) are characterized by long or short periods of staring, occasionally cause short-term loss of consciousness, and are usually followed by a return to normal activity. Absent seizures are often easily missed and are difficult to capture.

Tonic-clonic seizures (once called *grand mal seizures*) are the most severe type of seizure and represent a disruption in full-brain electrical activity. Students who experience tonic-clonic seizures may cry out, stiffen, fall to the ground, shake, jerk, or bite their tongues. These seizures require skilled implementation of protocols to ensure student safety.

Seizures that respond well to a host of anticonvulsant drugs are brought under control for long periods of time or permanently. If seizures that had appeared to be controlled suddenly reappear (*breakthrough seizures*), one or several medications may be administered daily, either at home or at school or in both locations, to maintain seizure control.

In school, each type of seizure should be recorded, tracked, and reported to parents; the nurse and members of the student's transdisciplinary team should understand the physical, medical, cognitive, and social-emotional impact of a student's seizure disorder. Teachers working with a student with CP who has seizure disorders must know the protocol of proper responses to the seizure event (specific to an individual student), should have learned about seizure management from the student's parents, and, when a nurse is available, will partner with the nurse in dealing with the event.

For youngsters with difficult-to-control seizures, constant monitoring is in order. This monitoring becomes the shared responsibility of observant teachers and assistants, who may, in some cases, be assigned to the student throughout the school day because of the seizure disorder. Depending on the choice of drugs and the dosages needed to control seizures, sleepiness and lethargy are common side effects that can counter the efforts to educate the student and that necessitate the instigation of creative scheduling and instruction.

Managing more significant seizures, those that are characterized by un-controllable jerky and thrashing movements and are sometimes accompanied by unusual vocalizations, requires the adult(s) to remain calm, gently guide a seated student (who is not belted into a wheelchair) down from the chair to a horizontal position on the floor, loosen any tight clothes, and remove the student's eyeglasses. Students in wheelchairs who have seizures are usually left in their wheelchairs. Moving a student out of a wheelchair would risk injury. A student who sits, unrestrained, in a regular chair can be gently shifted onto the floor. If possible, turn the student's head to the side to allow saliva to flow out of the mouth. Move objects and furniture away from the student, place a soft towel or article of clothing under the student's head, and avoid letting the student's head hit any hard object. Do not try to restrain the student or interfere with the movements of the seizure.

Difficult-to-control seizures often contribute to cognitive problems by increasing brain injury. Learning and behavior may be negatively affected because prolonged and frequent seizures can reduce memory and, in severe cases, precipitate a permanent decline in cognitive ability.[55] At the conclusion of a tonic-clonic seizure, a student usually needs an extended period of rest and will either rest at school in a designated place or will be taken home by a parent or caregiver.

Very little appears in the literature about the need to prepare classmates in the event of a significant seizure in the classroom. Despite the legal restrictions and realities of medical confidentiality, a student's seizure activity should be explained to classmates, prior to the student's entrance to the class, by either the student, the nurse, or parents. This way, seizure activity simply becomes another inevitable reality, a different norm for the student. This approach helps the student avoid possible isolation and rejection from classmates that results from fear of the unknown.

Medications designed to manage seizure disorders can lower a student's overall arousal levels for a period of time, making it difficult for them to attend and to learn and retain information.

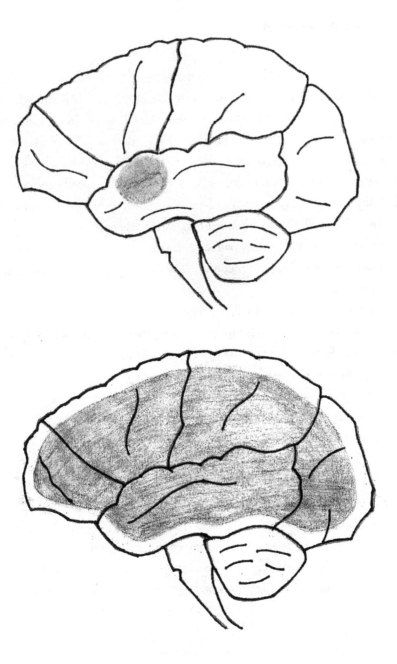

Top: A limited area of the brain affected by a localized seizure.
Bottom: Extensive areas of the brain affected by a generalized seizure.

Pain and Discomfort

Pain has been described as an "unpleasant sensory and emotional experience associated with actual or potential tissue damage,"[56] and it is thought that nearly three-quarters of students diagnosed with CP experience some degree of chronic or intermittent CP-related pain. This discomfort not only affects movement and attention but can influence the willingness to participate in the learning process. Teachers should not assume that significant physical disability automatically equates with pain, yet educators must become aware of *how* pain can affect individual students when it is present.

Of all types of CP-related pain and discomfort that some students, ages eight to eighteen years, may encounter, pain in the limbs, back, and neck is the most common.[57]

Certainly, students with CP, like their *neurotypical* (typically developing) peers, have differing thresholds for pain[58] and may experience only occasional discomfort. As with their neurotypical peers, students with CP who have chronic pain may experience degrees of depression.[59]

The following lists conditions that can precipitate varying degrees of chronic or sporadic pain, discomfort, or fatigue arising from the primary and secondary motoric conditions of CP:

- Muscle spasticity (high muscle tone and contractures) in the arms and legs (gross motor) and in the hands, fingers, and toes (fine motor)
- Low muscle tone in the trunk and neck
- Painful joints
- Muscle strain caused by muscle contractures and/or overuse
- Back, hip, and neck pain, discomfort from low muscle tone
- Fluctuating muscle tone, making it difficult to control and maintain a posture
- Hip dislocations
- Gastrointestinal pain and discomfort
- *Dysphagia* (difficulty with chewing and swallowing) discomfort
- Discomfort and/or strain and stress when communicating

- Respiratory disorders
- Seizures
- Involuntary movement and range of motion manipulation[60]
- Impaired movement affecting the sequencing of movements and necessitating the need to constantly alter sitting position

The following activities can be affected, to varying degrees, by pain and discomfort generated by primary and secondary motoric conditions of CP:

- Sustaining attention during instruction, which further complicates accompanying learning disabilities
- Completing a task
- Sitting for extended periods of time in one position
- Holding one's head up during lessons for longer than a couple of seconds
- Seeking comfortable sitting positions
- Moving around the school
- Participating in recreational activities
- Laboring with graphomotor performance when independently manipulating the implements of instruction and play, such as using books, typing, writing, drawing, painting, cutting with scissors, and holding small objects
- Dressing and bodily care
- Using eating utensils
- Dealing with pain-interrupted sleep

In some instances, when pain is intense, the student will need to miss school for a period while surgical or medical interventions are performed. Chronic pain can also raise a student's blood pressure, and this in turn may cause additional changes in the brain.[61, 62] The degree of pain and discomfort experienced by a student with CP may be difficult to determine when the student is nonverbal and/or has significant intellectual challenges.

In a desire to reduce or avoid pain, students may avoid potentially pain-producing activities by simply refusing to participate in them. This in turn can diminish the overall quality of their school experience and decrease their chances of reaching their potential in both intellectual and social-emotional domains. Students with CP

- Use fewer pain-coping strategies than neurotypical students.
- Tend to use social support to cope with pain.
- Are influenced by previous painful experiences.
- Use active coping strategies later in their teens but less in the elementary grades.
- Are influenced by the severity and discomfort of past surgeries.
- Can experience pain that ushers in emotional stress, anxiety, and overall reduced vitality.[63]

A postoperative recovery period for students with CP may be painful and debilitating and can negatively impact strength, stamina, sustained attention, and academic and emotional progress.

In the school setting, student pain has too often been overlooked. The school nurse may be called upon to assess pain; however, nurses also rely on sound observational reports from educators.[64] The following suggests ways to address and ameliorate student pain in school settings:

- Observe, record, and report student reactions to posture and movement.
- Provide appropriate, comfortable adaptations for floor seating.
- Address muscle tightness, tension, stiffness, poor circulation, and fatigue by frequently altering seating positions.
- Rearrange the placement of visual presentations and accommodate for challenging head/neck positions that exacerbate visual challenges.
- Look for information in the student's records that may indicate the presence of one or several discomfort-producing conditions.
- Use parents as a source for explaining and alerting school staff about pain and discomfort.

- Consult with related service providers.
- Make certain that paraprofessionals are aware of potential problems with a student's pain and are trained to address these problems.
- Involve the student with CP by asking the student to tell you when they are feeling pain or discomfort.
- Share information daily about the student's pain and discomfort with *all* who interact with the student.
- Be aware that a student may experience discomfort following a physical therapy session.

Physical and occupational therapists (PTs and OTs) are responsible for reducing discomfort by stretching and strengthening a student's fine and gross muscles. They often work together in joint therapy sessions to reduce discomfort, extend range of motion, improve respiratory functioning, and increase stamina.

OTs and PTs are also able to assess and recommend the need for changes in the classroom and in the school environment that can reduce the effects of pain and discomfort. They accomplish this through an assessment of posture, positioning, and ambulation; chair and desk positions; and the placement and positioning of writing. Information acquired about a student's pain is then shared with *all* who work with the student.

When students with CP have significant medical needs that require daily procedures, such as suctioning, tube feeding, and catheterization, the school nurse (and sometimes trained aides) are responsible not only for the safe execution of the procedures but also for the need to ensure that the procedures do not increase pain and discomfort.

The introduction of adaptive technology in the form of motorized wheelchairs, computers, tablets, and augmentative and alternative communication devices has significantly reduced the pain and discomfort associated with the student's being able to complete academic tasks and communicate.

Fatigue

Getting through the school day with some of the conditions of CP can be exhausting. Students with CP for whom ambulation and sometimes respiration is a challenge as they move around the school are likely to suffer from bouts of fatigue during the day that can affect their ability to attend and learn.

Students who use wheelchairs, those who struggle with vision, and those who struggle to use the tools of learning and play are all subject to fatigue. Low muscle tone that affects overall body posture and, more particularly, the ability to hold one's head up for an extended period can produce chronic fatigue.

There is often a tension between the intense desire to strengthen and develop a student's mobility and the reality that a school day filled with therapy and ambulation may leave the student too fatigued to learn. In the absence of appropriately modified and adapted equipment and instructional strategies, physical and emotional fatigue can plague a student who feels compelled to work beyond their capacity to keep up with neurotypical peers.

Although critically important to a student's health and well-being, certain medications can lower their overall arousal levels at any cognitive level, making it difficult for the student to establish and sustain engagement in both instructional and social settings.

Staff can ameliorate the condition of fatigue by

- Relying on recommendations from both the medical community and the school therapist team.
- Closely observing the student throughout the school day.
- Asking the student to self-report episodes of fatigue.
- Modifying and adapting lessons to minimize fatigue and exhaustion.
- Being aware of potential sleep problems.
- Providing periods of rest during the school day.
- Allowing ambulatory students to use wheelchairs and scooters as needed.

Sleep Difficulties

Some 23 to 46 percent of students who are already dealing with other CP-related conditions experience chronic and debilitating poor sleep, which can have profound effects[65] on the physical, emotional, and cognitive well-being of the student. Their persistent sleep problems can also significantly affect the physical and emotional health of family members and caregivers.[66] Sleep difficulties are found in populations of students with CP in greater percentages than in students without CP.[67] There is a strong correlation between sleep disorders and

- Pain from spasticity and an inability to adjust sleeping position
- Fatigue
- Gastrointestinal issues
- Obesity, which leads to respiratory disturbances
- Upper airway obstructions and narrow airways
- Pain perception
- Teeth grinding
- Excessive daytime sleeping
- Nightmares
- Drooling
- Skin ulcers
- Constipation
- Seizures[68, 69]

Sleep apnea or upper airway obstruction results from poorly operational muscles in the back of the throat. Sleep apnea in children with CP not only can seriously compromise sleep quality but is often associated with obesity in children with limited mobility and failure-to-thrive. In some cases, cardiac problems result.[70]

Sleep issues may also have strong psychosocial implications that impact performance in and out of the classroom, influencing oppositional behavior, anxiety, hyperactivity, concentration, memory, mood regulation, and consequently learning. In the school setting, the effects of lack of sleep reveal themselves in inattention, poor participation, drowsiness, lethargy, irritability, reduced memory, and sporadic concentration. In other cases, chronic head-aches and even depression can be signs of lack of regular sleep.[71]

Some students with spastic or dyskinetic CP tend to experience the greatest number of difficulties with sleep. The discomfort that is associated with spasticity and contractures, with back pain and scoliosis, and with the limited ability to control voluntary movements and make accommodations for abnormal and uncomfortable body positions—all make sleep problems almost inevitable for these subsets of students with CP.[72]

A student's sleep can be interrupted by the discomfort of gastrointestinal and reflux problems,[73] and some seizures may be precipitated by sleep dep-rivation. Researchers have found associations between sleep disorders and significant intellectual disabilities.[74, 75] The persistence of stress in a family may exacerbate sleep disturbances of a student with CP.[76]

Interventions for Sleep Disorders

The first step toward reducing the multiple effects of sleep deprivation in school involves

- Becoming aware that sleep deprivation *may* be an issue and look for daily signs of behaviors that may indicate sleep deprivation in the student with CP.
- Looking for causes of drowsiness in this population of students besides sleep deprivation.
- Knowing the additional causes for daytime drowsiness, such as medications, fatigue from gross and fine motor physical exertion, the stress of struggling with visual tasks, and the emotional fatigue from trying to perform way beyond one's capability.
- Consulting with colleagues who work with the student to ascer-tain whether they too are observing behaviors that suggest sleep deprivation.
- If possible, asking the student about the quality of their sleep, and if

sleep appears to be the issue, conferring with the student's family about their understanding of the cause of the student's sleep disturbances.

- Encouraging the family to share not only physician-identified explanations, such as reflux, sleep apnea, pain, and seizures, but also physician-recommended strategies for handling sleep issues.
- Realizing that daily exercises that extend range of motion, strengthen muscles, and improve balance and coordination may contribute to improved sleep. Exercises that involve daily stretching, slow walking, exercise bikes, and aquatic therapy may also help to improve sleep.
- Providing rest periods during the school day, thereby reducing daytime fatigue.
- Even when feeding and swallowing disorders are present, providing students healthy, sleep-supporting foods, thereby contributing to an improved quality of nighttime sleep.
- Promoting a calm bedtime routine. As with their neurotypical peers, students with CP can surely benefit from such a routine.

Oral-Motor Challenges

Compromised oral-motor dysfunction and delays describe the functions of chewing, swallowing, and speech that are compromised by impaired control over the muscles of the face, tongue, lips, and throat. This difficulty can also exist in the presence of structural anomalies of the face and mouth. Oral disabilities are caused by impaired structural disorders or by *neuromotor disorders*, where injured neurons in the brain send faulty instructional signals to the mouth, lips, tongue and throat, face, and neck areas.[77,78,79] Some oral-motor disorders may arise because of involuntary head-control problems attributable to low muscle tone. Other interrelated oral-motor difficulties may appear in the form of drooling, challenged dental health, concerns about *pulmonary aspiration* (small particles of food or drink that enter the larynx or the lungs), and the inability to smoothly pass food down into the stomach. Fine oral-motor disabilities are often classified as associated conditions of CP; however, oral-motor dysfunction can also be viewed as a primary motor condition.

Eating and Drinking

There is a range of fine, gross, and oral-motor difficulties encountered by many students with CP that affect safe chewing, swallowing, self-feeding, and speech. These serious functional concerns can all compromise independent eating and communication. Swallowing disorders (*dysphagia*) can lead to choking and pulmonary asphyxiation. Impaired lip closure contributes to drooling. All these conditions are related to the inability to smoothly pass liquids or solids down into the stomach. Also, laborious chewing and swallowing lengthens feeding time, keeping the student away from instruction and socializing.

Reduced food intake leads to malnutrition; fine oral-motor challenges are directly correlated with the difficulty of receiving sufficient nutrients, a difficulty that lowers vitality and reduces stamina. Therefore, an awareness of nutritional needs, respiratory status, and hydration is essential in teaching students with CP. Some students require highly complex feeding plans, which carefully lay out when, how, and with what consistency foods and liquids should be prepared and delivered.

Whenever possible, and with varying degrees of adult support, students with CP should eat with their peers and enjoy the social experience that mealtime provides. In a continuing effort to support independence, students with CP should be comfortably seated while eating, and their lunch, drinks, and snacks should be prepared and presented in ways that are easy for them to access and manage. It should be anticipated that many students with CP may require extra time to complete eating, and the extra time must be factored into daily planning and academic modifications.

Teachers and classroom aides should become familiar with the adaptive eating utensils used by some students with CP. Adaptive cups, bowls, cutlery, and plates, from the simplest to the most elaborate, are available through special catalogs and are usually introduced from home or by an OT. Specially designed, thicker spoons that allow for a firmer grip for those students who have trouble with fine motor control also speed the eating process and reduce spillage of food.[80] The use of such adaptive equipment further encourages feelings of accomplishment and greater student independence.

For students with CP who are completely dependent on adult assistance, avoidance of choking and aspiration is a frequent concern, and teachers and staff need to know that some students who experience swallowing difficulties may also resist therapies that use oral stimulation.[81]

However, adults who assist in feeding can also promote emotional and cognitive growth for these dependent students by explaining elements of the feeding process to them, helping them comprehend differences in the presented foods' taste, texture, color, and names and encouraging preferences. This is particularly important for students who have severe to profound intellectual disabilities. Special efforts should be employed to engage these students cognitively and socially during feeding time. By talking to students while feeding them, adults can heighten the students' awareness of the parts of their bodies that are used for chewing and swallowing, and of the presence of classmates who surround them. Teachers and therapists should reinforce these social-feeding strategies.

Gastrointestinal Disorders

Although researchers differ over the reported prevalence of gastrointestinal disorders in children and youth with CP, it seems reasonable to state that nearly half of all students with CP, many with spastic quadriplegia, must contend with varying degrees of gastrointestinal disorders that are directly related to difficulties with gross motor and oral-motor control.[82]

Gastrointestinal disorders in many children with CP result from a dysfunction of the interactions between abnormalities in the central nervous system with problems in the peripheral nervous system. These (autonomic) interactions regulate involuntary body function such as blood flow, heartbeat, body temperature, digestion, and breathing.[83] Gastrointestinal problems compound the oral-motor dysfunctions that prevent some students with CP from accepting or taking food by mouth.

Gastrointestinal disorders can make it difficult for students with CP to digest food and absorb nutrients. These disorders often cause distracting pain and discomfort. *Gastroesophageal reflux disease (GERD)* occurs when acid is regurgitated from the stomach back up to the esophagus. If untreated, GERD can exacerbate digestive problems—especially in children with CP who are unable to verbalize their pain. GERD may be characterized by belching, coughing, drooling, difficulty with swallowing, reflux, choking, vomiting, constipation, diarrhea, and abdominal pain and can necessitate prolonged feedings. Severe cases may necessitate a feeding tube.

Thorough assessments by a *gastroenterologist*, including the use of CT scans and MRIs, a determination about the scope of a student's digestive problems can be determined. A *nasogastric tube (NG tube)* is a temporary, nonsurgical approach for a student with CP who is unable to take nutrients by mouth. The NG tube is passed through the nose and down into the stomach.

A *gastrostomy tube (G-tube)* is one of several surgical options that involves surgically implanting a tube directly into the stomach or into other abdominal cavities to provide an alternate way of delivering liquid nutrients to an individual who is unable to take food by mouth. The decision to insert a feeding tube surgically into a student with CP is usually made after other, nonsurgical options have been exhausted, and as with all surgeries, infection is a risk. Some students who are tube-fed also take minimal amounts of food by mouth to provide a sensation of pleasure and to keep throat muscles from atrophying. This feeding is often done by well-trained aides who work under the supervision of nurses and parents.

Armed with information gleaned from parents, the school nurse, the student's medical records, former teachers, and directly from the student themself, the teacher is better able to work collaboratively with the school team to address gastrointestinal needs at the classroom level. Often, the speech therapist takes the lead in providing guidance for therapeutic feeding. Whether a student takes food by mouth or by feeding tube, there must be an understanding by the teacher and aides about the student's level of gastrointestinal discomfort and consequent effects on attention. Teachers should weave the need for adjusted feeding schedules into the school program and become aware of and supervise the provision of therapeutic positions for comfort and ease during feeding. As part of a collaborative effort, teachers should locate appropriate locations for feeding, in or out of the classroom, that respect a student's dignity. In partnership with parents and the school nurse, the teacher should be aware of the administration of medications that ease the feeding process and then notice and report both adverse and positive effects.

Failure-to-thrive issues occur when feeding problems impact a student's ability to receive sufficient nutrients and, like other associated health conditions, may affect stamina and alertness.[84] Physicians and dieticians will make certain that the student's dietary choices add nutrients to their diets and do not exacerbate existing gastrointestinal problems, since malnutrition is a chronic problem for many students with CP who have gastrointestinal disabilities.

Bladder and Bowel Issues

Some 30 percent of students with diplegic or quadriplegic CP have a degree of bladder dysfunction.[85] *Neurogenic bladder dysfunction* results from injury to nerves in the central nervous system or injury to peripheral nerves that control bladder function. In addition to the possibility of bladder infections, leakage, or accidents, an increased risk of dangerous skin breakdowns and infections can result in lower school attendance.

The incontinent student, because of discomfort, may have difficulty sitting still—a situation that is made more problematic if the student's motor profile includes uncontrollable movements. Unfortunately, these bladder and bowel issues may be taken less seriously, as a quality-of-life issue, if the student also contends with intellectual disability.[86] Management issues, health-related problems such as constipation, and social-emotional consequences can all arise from bladder and bowel difficulties for students with CP.

Urinary and bowel incontinence, besides exacerbating skin breakdowns and promoting infections, can cause embarrassment and precipitate distracting anxiety when these conditions take the older student with CP out of class frequently. Incontinence, especially in inclusion settings, may have powerful social implications, especially if unpleasant odors are part of the issue. The resulting isolation from classmates and the discomfort of uninformed teachers can be factors that exacerbate isolation and stigma. Unfortunate, too, is the student who has adults in his or her life who feel that the student's incontinence could be easily resolved if the student just "tried harder" to control these functions.

Chronic constipation that is experienced by some students with CP can be traced to a disrupted signal from the brain, resulting in poor coordination with muscles in the lower digestive tract. Chronic constipation can be exacerbated by restricted mobility, limited fiber intake (especially when the student is on a pureed diet because of chewing and swallowing disorders), insufficient fluid intake, and the negative by-product of necessary medication.[87]

Students with CP who have significant bladder and bowel challenges often require adult assistance. The adults who perform toileting assistance require training by school nurses and families to carry out these responsibilities in an appropriately safe, sanitary, and respectful manner. If catheters are used to drain urine from the bladder, the school nurse, aides, or the student will perform this task, often with adults monitoring the procedure to ensure that safe, sanitary methods reduce the chance of infection.

When students with CP can communicate their bathroom needs, many if not most—with medical therapy, corrective treatment, consistent management, and environmental adaptations—are able to achieve continence.[88] When continence can't be achieved, the teacher and all who support the student should be sensitive, understanding, informed, and ready to introduce and facilitate alternative strategies that do not leave the student embarrassed or feeling like a failure.

Here are further reasons for bladder and bowel difficulties with CP:

- The student may lack awareness of the messages their body is sending.

- The student may not understand the language used to explain bladder and bowel functions.
- There may be sensory sensitivity to the sounds of the bathroom.

Whether or not a student is able to achieve continence, the teacher will need a clear understanding of the student's issues and, in collaboration with school team members, must design a plan for both daily management of bladder and bowel issues and for emergencies (accidents).[89]

Even when the student's toileting needs are primarily handled in school by an aide who has been well trained by the teacher and other appropriately involved team members, the teacher themself, who may at times need to assume the aide's support role, must have full knowledge of the toileting products a student uses and see to it that the student's toileting supplies are given appropriate, private, and dignified storage. Also, students must be toileted in sanitary, private, and respectful locations. As students age, it is very important that, as much as possible, toileting support be provided by aides who match the student's gender.

While aides usually supervise the management of soiled materials, teachers should ensure that the student keep a supply of fresh clothes at school and should consider special scheduling needs surrounding school trips.

Incorporate discussions about different toileting needs into classroom discussions and help classmates understand that atypical toileting procedures are acceptable and normal. It is the school's responsibility to provide safe, appropriately sanitary accommodations for toileting routines.

Respiratory Problems

Around 27 percent of children and youth with CP are reported to experience respiratory difficulties.[90] Respiratory disorders intersect with issues of oral-motor and gastrointestinal dysfunction. In these cases, particles of food and/or saliva either enter the lungs during feeding or move up into the lungs because of aspiration. Infection in the respiratory tract may occur.

As CP is primarily a condition of abnormal muscle function, muscle dysfunction can contribute to deformities of the chest and spine. Respiratory dysfunction in CP is an associated condition resulting from musculoskeletal deformities. Poor muscle tone and weakness of the diaphragm, which controls the lungs' function, may reduce the lungs' efficiency in moving air in and out of the body, making breathing difficult.

A student with CP who was born prematurely may have begun life with immature, weakened lungs. Since these youngsters are often less able to exercise and breathe deeply,[91] they are at higher risk for lung infections and often breathe with difficulty. Problems may also arise if the student has a reduced sensitivity to coughing.[92] A student's relative immobility can also adversely impact respiratory health. Most research on the effects of poor respiration in CP focuses on mobility consequences; however, sustained classroom observations suggest that when respiratory dysfunction reduces the amount of oxygen that reaches the student's brain, fatigue, the inability to sustain attention, and reduced motivation appear as the student struggles to breathe.

For the health and safety of the student with CP, the classroom teacher needs to know the student's respiratory history and—in consultation with parents, the school nurse, OTs, PTs, and speech pathologists—needs to be aware of these struggles. The teacher and aides must look for signs of shortness of breath and asthma and be knowledgeable about those risk factors that can lead (especially during the winter months) to serious chest infections, such as pneumonia, bronchitis, and respiratory distress syndrome.[93]

Aspiration may occur if small particles of food or liquids enter the airways into the lungs, leaving the student at high risk for infection of pneumonia. A student who has these oral-motor and respiration problems may be a candidate for respiration therapy.[94]

Suctioning is the process of removing plugs of mucus and secretions that can't be swallowed or coughed up. When the brain injury of CP affects the muscles of the face, neck, and sometimes the chest, chewing, swallowing, sucking, and breathing may be compromised.

Medical and Nonmedical Interventions for Respiratory Dysfunction
- Awareness and monitoring of a student's breathing
- Oxygen therapy that involves the use of nebulizers and inhalers
- The use of high-frequency-wave vests
- The use of antibiotics to decrease infection
- Chest percussions that dislodge airwave blockages
- Maintenance of appropriate and safe nutrition
- Maintenance of body positions that enhance breathing
- Periodic draining of fluids that block airways
- Swimming, which develops lung function
- Slightly inclined seating surfaces to improve respiratory function[95]

Drooling (Sialorrhea)

Research describes the percentage of students with CP who experience drooling at between 10 to 37 percent and may be as high as 80 percent for those with spastic quadriplegia.[96,97,98] Drooling occurs when poor muscle tone in the face, mouth, and throat reduces the student's ability to maintain a closed, sealed mouth and swallow saliva. It is also thought that diminished sensation around and in the mouth may be a contributing factor. Research suggests a possible relationship in some cases between the severity of a student's motor incapacity, speech limitations, and intellectual impairment and the intensity of a student's drooling.[99] Although its impact in CP populations differs, drooling can create hygiene and management issues, requiring an extraordinary degree of adult attention that involves frequent changes of clothes and excess laundry.

There are several medical consequences of drooling. Uncontrolled drooling may contribute to aspirational pneumonia (a lung infection due to large amounts of material from the stomach or mouth that enter the lungs). Drooling is also correlated with poor dental health and can cause difficult-to-clear skin irritations around the face and mouth. For younger children, excessive drooling may complicate access to toys. As a student ages, drooling can create challenges when they use implements of instruction and can certainly negatively impact social interaction with peers, particularly in inclusion settings.

Managing Drooling

Effective responses to drooling can be placed in three categories: medical, therapeutic, and family management. Many interventions are used to reduce or eliminate drooling. These include surgery, medications including *botulinum toxin* (BoNT-A and BoNT-B), physical therapies, therapies to improve sensory function, behavioral therapies to assist the child in managing their drooling, appliances placed in the mouth, and acupuncture.[100] Current research into injecting Botox into the salivary glands to reduce salivary flow is looking quite hopeful.

Drooling may also be partially remediated by the collaborative efforts of speech and occupational therapists. Teachers should be aware of the administration of medication that eases the feeding process and hopefully can notice and report both effective and adverse effects.

Medical and therapeutic interventions should lessen the demands for both continuous school and home support. Hopefully, these interventions can limit the need for terry cloth wristbands, neck towels, and bibs and shawls that are used to continually wipe a student's mouth and chin. Effective interventions will also limit the damage drooling may cause to communication devices.

Expressive Language Challenges

Students with CP can experience varying degrees of difficulty in producing expressive language, including stuttering and *perseveration* (repetition of words or phrases). These difficulties often result from articulation and breath control challenges. The inability to produce intelligible speech (*dysarthria*) is another serious consequence of fine motor dysfunction that has significant implication for socialization and education-related communication in the population of students with CP.

Students who encounter difficulty producing comprehendible speech are severely compromised in the ability to express thoughts and feelings, articulate needs, and make choices and requests. In some instances, such students may simply retreat from communication, deciding instead to simply follow and mimic classmates.

Dysarthria appears both in the presence of and in the absence of intellectual impairment. A student with dysarthria can become isolated in school, especially if they are the only one with this condition, and may have difficulty initiating and maintaining age-appropriate communication and friendships. Oral-motor dysfunction that impairs speech articulation can result in frustration, emotional withdrawal, and a reduced willingness to express what the student knows and feels.

The active and continuous intervention of all adults who work with students with dysarthria is critical to ensuring that through conversation groups and the competent use of augmentative and alternative communication devices, students with dysarthria have a strong presence and voice in the daily life of the school.

Dental Problems

The prevalence of poor dental health is yet another consequence of fine oral-motor challenges and is highly correlated with quality-of-life and health outcomes. The Alliance for Oral Health Across Borders has determined that many students with CP are at high risk for dental disease.[101, 102] Failure to receive ongoing oral care can lead to the accumulation of disease-causing bacteria, systemic infection, and even death.

Many students who live with conditions of CP tend to have more complex dental problems than are experienced by their neurotypical peers. Some may have defects in tooth enamel and abnormal tooth formation due to developmental abnormalities.[103]

Defects in tooth enamel can be exacerbated by the difficulty the student encounters in daily brushing, thus leading to chronic tooth decay and bad breath. Untreated tooth decay and gum disease can lead to inflammation and systemic infection. Imbalance in facial muscles may lead to misalignment of teeth, and medications such as Dilantin, taken for seizures, can cause gum problems.[104]

Many students with CP face unique challenges in maintaining good dental health and hygiene and in receiving the appropriate, specialized, and adaptive dental care. Students who live in rural areas or in small communities that are distant from large medical and dental centers are at a disadvantage, lacking access to dentists who are experienced in working effectively with CP populations.

Teachers and parents should be aware not only of the presence of *malocclusions* (poor alignment between the top and bottom rows of teeth in a closed mouth) and other structural abnormalities that require specialized assessment and treatment but also of the preventative strategies that help students with CP avoid restorative or surgical care. Often, families are so overwhelmed with the tasks of managing movement and medical issues that they place less importance on dental health; therefore, there is often a lack of early and ongoing diagnosis of potential dental problems.

At the classroom level, it is important for the student's lead teacher to not only be aware of the student's medical history but also be curious about the student's dental habits and care, with an emphasis on improving and maintaining the student's overall health. In collaboration with members of the student's transdisciplinary team, teachers should be aware of the student's dietary habits, particularly his or her consumption of sugar-filled drinks. Team members should also be aware of the possible benefits of the use of fluoride in school settings.

Educators and related service professionals can enlist the help of pediatricians in identifying potential dental issues, and together they can exert pressure at the local and state level for increased funding for dental care for students with CP. Additional pressure needs to be exerted on dental colleges to expand the specialized training they offer their students, and policies need to be established that appropriately compensate dentists who need additional time, training, special equipment, and modified skills to meet the oral health needs of patients with CP.

Medical Management of Dental Issues

There is a worldwide dearth of dentists trained and dedicated to serve students with CP and to deliver appropriate but necessary dental and periodontal disease care to many students with CP. Particularly challenging is that this care must frequently be delivered under anesthesia. Research is also underway to find techniques that deliver minimally invasive restorative care.

Sensory strategies are being employed by individual dentists and clinics to lessen a student's fear and anxiety. Alternative, adaptive, and creative seating may be needed while providing dental care for students with CP. A heightened degree of privacy in clinics and dental offices may be required to meet the needs of these students, and special tools and equipment may be needed to serve this population. Medications especially designed to temporarily control dental pain can be used in anticipation of more extensive treatment.

Classroom teachers should inform themselves about the wide array of associated health conditions that can accompany a diagnosis of CP and that directly affect a student's progress in school.

Tom and his friend Desi.

CHAPTER 4

Educating Students with Cerebral Palsy: Essential Considerations

Adine R. Usher

Not all students with cerebral palsy struggle to learn, but many, many do, and as educators, our charge becomes one of turning challenges into opportunities for cognitive and social-emotional growth—and, to the greatest extent, independence and the enjoyment of life.

The Academic Model Versus the Medical Model

For years, experts in the field have discussed the relative value and relationship between the academic and medical models for students with physical disabilities. Although the academic model must be implemented in the school setting, it cannot be effectively implemented without an understanding of medical realities and considerations. The two models must establish a partnership.

For success in the classroom, teachers need to understand how the diagnosis of CP affects the student, what limitations it has caused, what strengths the student exhibits, and how and why materials and lessons must be modified and adapted.

The Educational Challenge

A pediatric neurologist once commented to me, "Ah, CP, it's all over the place." That very descriptive reflection highlights why CP's complexities are so often difficult for educators to grasp. CP's challenges encompass motor dysfunctions that may be accompanied by one or several of the secondary and associated conditions of health as well as sensory, cognitive, behavioral, and social-emotional concerns. These conditions exist in varying degrees of severity and are uniquely configured in each individual student.

Academic and social-emotional needs may be overshadowed by the sheer weight of a student's physical and medical conditions. Although a correlation exists between the severity of motor and cognitive impairments, there is no absolute correspondence; it is therefore not possible to draw conclusions about cognition from the functioning in other areas.[105] When teachers have no or limited experience in teaching students whose conditions of CP are complex and challenging, a willingness to acknowledge and confront anxieties and discomforts becomes an important strength.

Teachers, especially those in general education settings, may find daunting the addition to the class of a child who is not mobile, who may be incontinent, who may perhaps drool, who may be nonverbal or significantly dysarthric (having speech that is very difficult to understand), who may leave the class frequently for therapies or nursing support, who may miss school because of health and medical issues, who can, in addition, have difficulty interacting socially, and who may learn in decidedly atypical ways. These teachers may also not realize that the CP-related conditions that expose learning problems may exist even when the student's movement disorders are relatively minimal.

Fully informed planning is grounded in a thorough understanding of the entire scope of a student's unique physical, health, sensory, academic, and social-emotional needs. Such grounding prepares educators and therapists, if they have the good fortune to work in proximity to one another, to create environments that promote learning, that improve physical abilities, that increase meaningful participation and socialization, and that result in satisfying task completion and increasing independence.

Research- and Practice-Based Interventions

This book offers a combination of effective research- and practice-based interventions that diminish, circumvent, or overcome many CP-related barriers to physical, academic, and social-emotional achievement. However, with complex, neurologically based conditions, *evidence-based* must coexist with practice-based, commonsense interventions. The International Classification of Functioning, Disability and Health (ICF) is an evidence-based framework to describe functioning in relation to a health condition, and its standards and expectations inform the way that professionals, particularly physical therapists, respond to the conditions of CP. An important addendum to the ICF framework is the concept of the six "F-words" that need to be understood by teachers and incorporated into the overall education program: function, family, fitness, fun, friends, and future.[106]

The complexity of CP may in part account for the reduced quantity of evidence-based research that could aid the classroom teacher. Certain discrete elements of the movement—health-related conditions and socialization—have been well researched; however, the intersection of movement, health, sensory, cognitive, and social-emotional conditions with the unique, highly individual nature of these multiple conditions makes standard research techniques difficult to carry out and validate. Few studies have assessed cognitive profiles in large representative populations of children with CP.[107]

In the absence of a large body of evidence-based data, the results of effective, practice-based strategies can be quite instructive for school staff who try to limit the impact that neurological injury can exert on learning, on independence and personal agency, and on "being in the world" for many students with CP.

Cerebral palsy often erects motor, health, cognitive, communication, and social-emotional barriers that stand between the student and traditionally delivered curriculum and instruction—barriers that require educators to significantly alter not only the environments in which they work but also the materials and instructional strategies needed to reach and teach students with CP at all developmental levels. Teachers and classroom assistants will constantly need to fill in the gaps of prior knowledge and prior experience that may elude some students with CP when physical, health, cognitive, communication, and social-emotional conditions limit the student's exposure to activities that are experienced by their neurotypical peers. These limitations can decrease a student's level of interest and general state of arousal.

Students with CP vary widely in intellectual capacity. While there may be some association between the degree of motoric and health complexity and the degree of intellectual delay, there is no automatic correlation between movement and communication restrictions and intellectual capacity.

Teachers and classroom staff should also be aware of the difference between *learning difficulties* and *learning disabilities*. Both conditions may be related to neurological injury; however, *learning difficulties* describe conditions where learning capabilities would be within the average range were it not for the difficulties imposed by movement and health disabilities. On the other hand, *learning disabilities*, which are experienced by many students with CP, tend to originate from difficulties with sensory perception and processing.

Specific perception-based learning disabilities, which are found in all subtypes of CP but which are especially prevalent in students with spastic CP, are characterized by attention difficulties, motor planning difficulties that require organization and sequencing, visual and auditory acuity and perceptual difficulties, and a range of language processing difficulties. These realities can complicate learning to read, compute, write, and communicate.

No two students with CP are exactly alike, and the combination of CP-associated conditions appears in endless and different configurations. This book focuses on those students with CP whose instruction, assignments, and assessments may need to be altered, modified, and customized in ways that not only give them more satisfying access to standard curricula but also validate their own unique ways of experiencing and enjoying the world. Whether a student with CP can pursue a traditional academic program, a modified academic curriculum, a functional curriculum, or a curriculum built on purely sensory responses, the student's abilities can be maximized when teachers

- Understand the impact on learning of a student's primary, secondary, and associated conditions.
- Avoid making rapid "on the spot" assumptions about a student's challenges, performance, and potential.
- Assume that a student with CP, *at any cognitive level*, can learn and therefore demonstrate a desire to improve the student's competence.
- Dedicate themselves to discovering a student's optimal education setting and then work to create it.
- Become skilled at creating, with collaboration from others, effective modified, adapted, and customized learning paths and seek expertise when faced with confusing barriers.
- Don't allow a student's physical and medical conditions to overshadow academic and social-emotional needs.
- Go that "extra mile" by attempting atypical approaches.
- Believe that the most appropriate intervention is the most effective one.
- Carefully study, question, and research student responses and their possible relationship to specific conditions of CP.
- Rely on observation, assessments, and prior educational and medical reports to better understand a student's barriers.
- Realize that the reality of dealing with multiple challenges may limit the amount of persistence and stamina a student brings to a task.
- Understand that many students with CP, because of physical limitations and health and cognitive complexities, may lack the physical and sensory access to daily experiences of childhood that add comprehension and meaning to tasks.

- Understand that students with CP may additionally lack enriched social and emotional contacts with those outside of their immediate families.

- Understand that students with CP at all cognitive levels have functional as well as academic needs that may differ from those of their neurotypical peers. Therefore, the teachers should leave themselves open to thinking and teaching outside of their repertoire of traditional techniques and goals.

- Set realistic goals for students and allow them to work toward their own, individual "personal best." It is not important that the student always keep up with others, since they may find alternative ways to achieve desired goals.

- Present instruction in multiple modalities.

- Set goals that have the student working within the framework of required academic standards (to the greatest extent possible) while simultaneously strengthening those functional goals that are equally meaningful for the student's future endeavors and are needed to help the student satisfactorily negotiate their involvement in the wider community as a person with a disability.

- Realize that students with CP may have to process multiple physical, sensory, and expressive elements within the context of delayed processing.

- Try to gauge the student's ability to learn, realizing that elements of CP may appear to block or significantly complicate learning pathways.

- Know that students with CP may respond to complexity or information overload with frustration, withdrawal, or total shutdown.

Capturing the Contents of Each Student's Uniqueness

The scope of cognitive impairments varies between and within the spastic, dyskinetic, and ataxic subtypes.[108] Realizing that no two students with CP are identical, the following three performance categories loosely lay out a structure that may help teachers, assistants, and parents to better understand the educational implications of CP's many complex presentations:

Category 1

Movement and health disorders challenge physical access to standard educational tools and curriculum. *Even with the presence of mild sensory dysfunction, these students, with adaptations and modifications, have average or superior cognitive abilities and have the potential to demonstrate average or superior educational performance.* Students in this category may live with dysarthric speech, may be nonverbal, and may also experience social-emotional and psychological challenges related to neurology, limited social experiences, overprotection, frustration, or hostile environments.

Category 2

Movement, communication, and health-related issues not only impact access to standard educational tools and curricula, but *these students also have moderate to severe neurological and sensory-based learning disabilities that impact academic performance.* Students in this category may frequently face social-emotional challenges.

Category 3

Movement, health, and communication challenges coexist *with profound brain injury–based or brain structure–based sensory, communication, and cognitive disabilities.* Many of these students are nonverbal, and it is not uncommon to find significant behavioral and social-emotional challenges in this population due to their cognitive and communicative inability to express frustration, thoughts, feelings, and desires. These students are more than just bodies to be managed; they are valuable human beings who deserve satisfying experiences in all dimensions of their lives.

The Educator's Attitudes and Actions

A teacher's positive attitude can make the teaching and learning experiences more productive and effective for both the teacher and the student with CP. Teachers and classroom staff may work hard and strive to be effective; however, having a student with CP may reveal attitudinal barriers that can retard a student's progress. These attitudinal barriers may blunt a teacher's ability to look for and see strengths and possibilities in student performance and can impede the teacher's ability to accept the inherent worth and value in the student with CP.

Although a student's understanding, skills, and knowledge may not be immediately apparent, assume that with a willingness to be innovative, to attempt the untried, to be comfortable with trial and error, and to employ out-of-the-box teaching strategies, students will start to learn despite the complexities of CP. Try to assume that if a student does not comprehend an activity, we may not be using the appropriate intervention or we may not have identified the nature of the problem. The student with CP often requires that our responses widen and deepen.

The teacher-as-researcher approach requires genuine curiosity and a degree of flexibility that transcends the traditional view of what appropriate assessment, curriculum, and instruction look like. Certainly, educational institutions are defined by rules, regulations, and parameters of practice; however, the effective execution of modified, adapted, and even customized educational solutions demanded by the presence of CP often requires a widening and stretching of these parameters if one hopes to reach in and extract a student's potential.

The Intellectually Curious Educator

The intellectually curious educator asks questions before making assumptions and continually seeks a deeper understanding of the challenges that CP can present. In the small world of the school, this teacher can be a researcher and child-study specialist by following the emergence of observed, unexpected, or confusing behaviors, by first asking "why," and then by determining to seek answers.

Rather than assume that the unexpected response or behavior is a result of the student's failure to attend or comprehend, we need to ask ourselves if our instruction is failing the student; if we have failed to understand a student's thoughts, feelings, or confusion; and if we have failed to consider the consequences of disability-related factors and how they impact the way the student responds to our instruction.

Owing to preconceptions about members of this *low-incidence* student population, it is far too easy for educators, experienced or not in teaching these complex students, to undervalue a student's cognitive and communicative potential. This undervaluing of students with CP is often the result of educators not having received ongoing support in the form of detailed, concrete information about the physical, cognitive, communication, and social-emotional ramifications of CP conditions and in not being trained in the *art* of using both formal and informal observation.

Given this scenario, the blame for lack of progress frequently falls on the child when the problem really lies elsewhere. Where there is limited staff preparation and limited understanding of a student's complexities, where there are barriers within the educational environment, and where curriculum, instructional tools, and strategies are insufficiently customized and tailored to a student's unique physical, health, communication, cognitive, and social-emotional profile, we fail the students.

It is also difficult for some educators, and indeed for some school systems, to admit that they are initially at a loss about how to approach these challenges. Educators need to give themselves permission to observe, study, and engage in trial-and-error approaches that lead to the crafting of the most appropriate approaches. This honest, realistic approach is much preferred and is more effective than simply going through the motions of educating the student with CP.

An inquisitive state of mind is essential to the delivery of effective instruction to students with CP because new and interrelated issues and challenges are certain to arise. The educator who is willing to take the time to review the contents of rich, descriptive reports and who seeks out those who understand more about the student's condition is the educator who is most likely to maximize the student's potential. The teacher who, when confronted with unwanted or unexpected student responses or behaviors, responds with "This is very interesting; I need to find out what this means" is the teacher who moves in the direction of uncovering rational explanations and deciding on effective interventions. Through acquisition of knowledge, observation, reflection, collaborative discussion, and action, *you become a student* of your student's growth and development.

Doubts and Questions That an Educator May Express

It is perfectly understandable that a teacher with limited or no experience with CP may feel apprehensive. We don't have to pretend to know everything; however, we hopefully are willing to learn and grow. This book aims to answer some of your questions. Even an educator with considerable experience with CP may find value in reviewing the following list:

- Why do I feel uncomfortable around this student?
- How do the conditions of CP (in this student) affect learning and instruction?
- Why do I need to know about the student's physical and medical challenges and understand medical terminology?
- Am I able and willing to use the student's family as a valuable resource for understanding this student?
- What can this student learn?
- How does this student learn?
- What does this student *need* to learn?
- Am I having difficulty seeing this child as a "real" student?
- In what settings and with what classroom configurations does this student learn most effectively—whole-group, small-group, one on

one, or a combination of all three?

- Does the student have to perform exactly like their neurotypical peers?
- What must I adapt, modify, or customize to support effective learning?
- How do I create a learning environment that does not make the student's physical and neurological difficulties even more challenging?
- How can I meet this student's highly unique needs and not ignore the needs of others in the class?
- Where do I find the time to plan for this student?
- How do I support the family during times of stress and struggle?
- How do I learn to work collaboratively and effectively with the aide who is assigned to the class or directly to the student?
- How do I learn to work collaboratively with other staff and related service providers assigned to the student?
- Do I have a responsibility to become proficient at using and programming the student's assistive technology devices?
- Can I look for, listen to, and value the student's unique input and perspectives?
- What responsibility do I have in ensuring that the student has healthy social-emotional school experiences?
- Can I—do I—want to change the way I teach?
- How do I become intellectually and emotionally comfortable with a youngster who appears appreciably different from the neurotypical student?
- How do I effectively assess a student's potential?
- When and how do I adapt, modify, and customize the general curriculum and instructional strategies for students who present with the complexities of CP?
- Am I aware that the student is becoming socially and emotionally isolated from their neurotypical peers?
- How do I address this problem and help the student with CP to become a well-adjusted and valuable member of the class?

Vygotsky's Zones

The Russian psychologist Lev Vygotsky (1896–1934) described a learning paradigm in which struggling students move through three phases, called *zones*. In the first zone, the struggling student is unable to understand or perform a task independently. In the second zone, the *zone of proximal development*, the student begins to understand or perform a task with intense adult support or *scaffolding*. Scaffolding requires initial intense adult support, which is gradually removed as the student begins to master a task. By the third zone, the zone of achieved development, the student understands and performs the task with varying degrees of independence.

Many students with CP begin the instructional process in the first zone. Depending on the activity, their movement into the second zone may require adaptations that may need to remain in place for a considerable period before the student moves successfully and more independently into or closer to an interpretation of the third zone.[109]

Greenspan's Floortime

For the "difficult-to-reach student," a category that includes many students with CP, familiarize yourself with the groundbreaking research of the late Dr. Stanley Greenspan (1941–2010), who, in collaboration with Serena Wieder, PhD, and numerous other professionals, formulated the concept of "Floortime." The Floortime Approach® is suggested for many students who are on the autism spectrum; however, it works equally effectively for students who have CP that leaves them nonverbal, profoundly introverted, and significantly intellectually challenged. Students who benefit from the Floortime Approach are often so consumed by the realities of their own physical, medical, and intellectual challenges that they have limited awareness of the world outside of their own bodies. Using the strategies of Floortime, teachers seek to literally pull students out of their disability-imposed shells.

Floortime directs the adult to initially engage the difficult-to-reach student by entering the student's world and following the student's lead. Once the student allows the adult access and engagement into their world, the student begins to take notice of the adult's presence and allows the adult to participate in actions that interest the student. Once a trusting relationship has been developed between adult and student, the adult can gradually move the student out of their narrow world and into the activities and expectations of the wider classroom community.[110]

Differentiated Instruction

Following as much as possible the curricular guideline and standards for both academic and functional programs, differentiated instruction acknowledges that students learn differently. This may be particularly true for students who have CP; therefore, every conceivable strategy (different pathways) must be attempted to make instruction and curriculum accessible and meaningful for students who simultaneously may deal with movement, medical, learning, communication, and social-emotional challenges.

Degrees of Adaptation, Modification, and Customization

If a student with CP is unable to access a lesson because of motoric, communication, or health realities, their learning environment must be adapted, modified, or customized. The same holds true if accessibility is compromised by sensory and cognitive abilities. A classroom environment that presents neither physical nor instructional barriers to any student is using *universal instruction design*—for example, words posted in the classroom that, because of their size and clarity, are accessible to all students, including those with a range of visual challenges.

Case Study

Six-year-old Andy was diagnosed at eighteen months of age with CP spastic diplegia. He uses both a walker and a wheelchair (for distance and fatigue), has fine motor limitations in both hands, has slightly dysarthric speech (is difficult to understand by an unfamiliar listener) but attempts to communicate, and is friendly and loves to watch and play adaptive baseball. Daily medications control his seizures, and an aide accompanies him as he moves around the school to help him navigate classroom activities. Andy has been in school since he was an infant—starting in early intervention and then moving on to preschool and kindergarten.

Andy's mother told the school that, despite his physical limitations, he was very smart. When he was four, his orthopedist told the family that Andy should not have any difficulty in school, and so consequently, the family was alarmed when his first-grade teacher reported that Andy appeared to have learning difficulties.

This is a familiar scenario. In the early years of Andy's schooling, under-standably, great emphasis was placed on his health, strength, communication, and mobility issues. With ongoing support from parents, physical therapist, occupational therapist, and speech therapist, Andy had shown improvement in physical independence, communication, and social development; however, he was just beginning to face the academic challenges of learning to read, write, work with numbers, attend to the lessons, and consolidate short-term memory into long-term storage.

Andy is currently beginning to face the academic challenges brought on by sensory-based learning disabilities. His issues are not unlike those encountered by able-bodied youngsters who are diagnosed with a learning disability; however, his learning problems are exacerbated by additional com-plexities. A neuropsychological assessment administered by an experienced neuropsychologist revealed that Andy was dealing with significant challenges to both visual acuity and perception. Hearing acuity and hearing processing presented no apparent problems in this instance, and his conversation, thought difficult to understand, was age-appropriate. However, Andy was frequently distracted, had a very short attention span, and seemed unable to retain much of the very concrete academic material he was being taught. Additionally, Andy was not sleeping well at night and appeared frequently fatigued by the physical demands of daily activities.

The Power of Information

Like other students, a student with CP has strengths and challenges, likes and dislikes, and hopes and fears. Often, however, because the student moves, speaks, and may learn in atypical ways, it may be too easy to underestimate the student's potential and value and far too easy to miss the need to deliver instruction using atypical strategies.

Whether you have had extensive experience in working with students who live with the conditions of CP or have had relatively limited or no experience with this population of students, you need information. You need *general* information about the range of primary, secondary, and associated conditions that may exist with a diagnosis of CP. Since no two students with CP are identical, it is critical that you have detailed information *specific* to the individual student.

In addition to the internet, there are numerous books, journals, and articles that can add to your general fund of knowledge about CP. References and websites that provide a broad overview of the *etiology* (medical history) and the medical and therapeutic and educational management of CP are listed in chapter 13.

Physicians and therapists who generate reports can provide valuable support to educators and parents by remembering to define medical and technical terms when speaking and writing about a student. Teachers and parents should *never* hesitate to ask for further explanations and definitions.

If the student has been in school for a while, reading records from the previous years and speaking with faculty members who have worked with a student in the past also provides critical information and insight. When they are available, the student's medical, intellectual, psychological, social, and therapeutic records yield vital information and give meaning to the impact of CP. Lack of familiarity and discomfort with medical terminology can also be overcome by using numerous online medical reference dictionaries.

Unfortunately, because of multiple demands on their time, there is a tendency for educators to spend too little time reading these documents, and, indeed, some have never read them. Others may feel uncomfortable with medical issues, fail to understand the correlation between cognitive processes and medical realities, and don't delve into a student's medical and therapeutic history. This is a mistake, since once understood, the information gleaned from these documents often provides substantial guidance in understanding the student's challenges and in informing effective instructional choices.

Privacy laws vary throughout the world, and within the structure of local, state, and national regulations, the rights of children must be protected against abuse or prejudice. However, in an educational setting, understanding medical references provides greater instructional information to those who work most closely with children with CP. Teachers and therapists should share information with assistants who need to know as much as possible about how CP can affect performance. Local educational entities must find acceptable and legal ways to deliver this information by balancing confidentiality with the need to know and understand. Armed with a clearer picture of how the conditions of CP may affect all aspects of a student's life, we begin to demystify CP.

The Family as a Valuable Source of Information

A student's parents or guardians are a powerful resource for medical, health, safety, functional, intellectual, and social-emotional information. They can draw a profile of the student's past and current strengths, challenges, moods, likes, and dislikes. They can describe conditions that promote maximum states of alertness, and they can explain reactions to medications and causes of pain and discomfort. Parents and guardians can share general management strategies for the full range of daily living activities. And, most importantly, they can, with their passionate support and love, raise an educator's expectations of the student's potential.

Schools

Educational opportunities for students with complex diagnoses of CP vary greatly around the globe and have undergone significant changes in the last fifty years as attitudes toward these multifaceted challenges have evolved and improved. Unfortunately, there remain countries where little or no governmental support is provided for the education of students with complex CP-related needs. In these circumstances, there is a dearth of affordable schooling for children who are nonambulatory, nonverbal, and not toilet-trained. Also, stigma and cultural practices, combined with poverty, can leave parents unable to work, feeling isolated and depressed. Even in more industrialized countries, the primary emphasis on expected productivity may limit societal desire to maximize the potential of students with significant and complex CP.

However, with growing parental activism, pressure on governments, and self-advocacy, the urge to change national mindsets is slowly evolving. The moral leadership of the United Nations Convention on the Rights of Persons with Disabilities, which was signed in 2007 by 164 countries, will hopefully begin to play a significant role in this evolution. Subsequent to the convention, medical and therapeutic programs for students with CP are being allied with educational programs, thus leading to improved function, greater independence, and a more meaningful quality of life for these students.[111] The ICF framework, referred to earlier in the chapter, illuminates a broader construct than previous biomedical and impairment-based approaches to chronic health conditions and adds environmental and personal factors as contributing to greater participation and well-being for individuals with CP.[112]

School and Class Placement Options

Placement options for students with special needs are varied.[113] Options for students with CP are often determined by the intensity of services needed and range from placements in

- Hospital schools to residential schools (which may also serve day students)
- Special day schools that are dedicated to students with a range of neurologically based physical disabilities
- Self-contained classes within general education programs with both academic and functional programs
- Full- or part-time participation in general education programs (often with the daily added support of aides and special education teachers in *resource rooms*)

Another model for service delivery for students with CP in general education classes is team teaching, which requires the presence of two fully certified teachers—one who is certified in general education and the second certified in special education. Dual certification in both general and special education strengthens a teacher's ability to handle the developmental diversity that is represented in the entire school population.

Inclusion Programs

Increasingly, students with CP are being educated in *inclusive,* local neighborhood schools. This placement decision is being made and supported by families, by research, by school systems, and by federal and state laws in the strong belief that education in general settings provides many students with CP the best opportunity to acquire academic and social-emotional skills that will lead to independence and meaningful lives in the wider society.

Students with CP who attend inclusion programs require appropriate environmental and instructional adaptations and modifications if they are to function within or near the standard academic range. As part of the process, these students must have their medical, physical, communication, and mild to moderate sensory-based learning disabilities addressed.

In inclusive settings teachers and therapists are often supported either by one-on-one aides or by one aide assigned to several special-needs students; these aides operate under the guidance and directives of the teacher and therapists.

Students with CP in inclusive settings who have complex movement, learning, and communication disabilities will undoubtedly benefit from the academic pullout program typically referred to as the *resource room*, which offers learning in small-group settings under the tutelage of a special educator who breaks down the general education curriculum into smaller steps, adapts and modifies the curriculum as needed, provides greater individual attention, and offers greater time on task. This smaller setting offers a quieter, less cluttered environment and a greater teacher-student ratio, which improves student engagement and fosters motivation.

Social isolation and loneliness in the inclusive setting may be encountered by some students who live with the complex and multiple conditions of CP. For far too many of these youngsters, their primary conversation partners and friends are the adult aides who support their needs.

Especially in inclusive settings, the need for customization, whether minor or extensive, may initially challenge the educator's perception of their traditional role. The consequences of the interaction among discrete elements of motoric, health, communication, learning, and social-emotional challenges require constant intense, objective, and nonjudgmental observation of the student. Ongoing observation provides essential insight into how the student is experiencing their physical, cognitive, and social-emotional environments from moment to moment.

Some students "fall through the school placement cracks." Although significantly challenged medically and physically, these students may be deemed too high-functioning for schools dedicated to the significantly multiply disabled, and therefore, an educationally effective place must be created for them in an inclusive setting.

In some geographical areas, there are simply no alternatives to inclusive general education programs, and even students with a profound combination of motoric, medical, and intellectual challenges will be accommodated in inclusive settings. In the United States, under the federal guidelines of the Individuals with Disabilities Education Act (IDEA), inclusion is not mandated but rather strongly suggested.[114]

Special, Dedicated Schools

Most specialized schools are housed in day programs; however, a few have residential components. Parents and educators who support the education of students with CP in special, dedicated schools believe that the total learning and social environments of these settings are designed to accommodate and address the unique challenges that are encompassed in a diagnosis of CP. They also believe that students there are surrounded by a skilled and knowledgeable staff that knows how to unlock a student's hidden potential.

In these special, dedicated settings, teachers and related service providers usually have had extensive experience working with students with CP, and although students have less access to neurotypical peers, the educators have woven into their modified, adapted, and customized instruction the practical tools of living successfully in the wider society.

Students with CP who are educated in special, dedicated settings may experience a greater degree of social acceptance and have interactions through in-school friendships to a greater degree than students with CP may experience in inclusive school settings. However, some students may miss the typical behavioral role models that can be found in inclusion settings.

In both inclusive and special, dedicated settings, the students with CP vary greatly in ability, motivation, and drive for independence. In both settings, the students need a school placement that welcomes their presence and pursues the use of established and experimental strategies that enable students to experience satisfaction, achievement, competency, and greater control over their environments.

Cognition and Cerebral Palsy

Sibylle Gonzalez-Monge and colleagues suggest that one factor that may affect intellectual ability in populations of children with CP is the age of onset of (preterm) brain lesions, the size of the lesion, the presence of seizures, and the degree of motor impairment.[115] Although IQ tests are often imperfect instruments for students with CP, extensive research and reports from skilled classroom observations highlight the fact that many students with spastic quadriplegia have IQs of less than 70. Around 50 to 60 percent of students with dyskinetic CP fall below the 70 IQ marker, 22 to 33 percent of students with spastic diplegia CP fall below the 70 IQ marker, and 11 to 19 percent of students with spastic hemiplegia fall below the 70 IQ mark.[116] Many of these students contend with the academic consequences of varying degrees of learning disabilities, which in some cases are correlated with the extent of motoric challenges. Executive functioning with particular focus on attention, reasoning, and problem solving are challenging for many of these students.

With dyskinetic (*athetoid*) CP and, to some extent, ataxic CP, the learning profile may be different from that of many students with spastic CP. When cognitive delays appear in students with dyskinetic CP, these delays tend to exist because of the physical difficulty of accessing the typical tools of learning. In these instances, significant physical involvement (including difficult-to-produce intelligible speech) is less likely to be accompanied by sensory-based learning disabilities. It is unfortunately too easy for an educator to underestimate and fail to recognize the cognitive strengths of a student with dyskinetic CP.

Students who are diagnosed with ataxic CP generally have slower motor output and have lower scores on timed tests; however, despite some indicators of minor learning disabilities, their overall intelligence is usually not affected.

Not only can damage in the primary motor cortex and the presence of a thin *corpus callosum* (which integrates and transfers motor, sensory, and cognitive information between the brain's hemispheres) affect lower and upper limb functioning, head and trunk control, and the ability to produce intelligible speech, that situation can also impair attention, produce calculation problems, and compromise short- and long-term memory (which allows for the consolidation of learning and enables abstract thinking).[117] Research findings in the *Journal of the International Neuropsychological Society*[118] looked at executive control of learning and memory in children with bilateral spastic CP and found some delays in learning, memory processing, and *inhibition* because of disruptions in the *prefrontal lobe* (the site of executive functioning).

CP in the Presence of Average and Superior Cognition

A diagnosis of CP does not *automatically* mean that a student will have cognitive challenges that present either as mild to moderate learning disabilities or as profound intellectual impairments. Many students with CP have strong cognitive abilities. For some, these strengths can be challenging to identify and develop because the cognitive strengths coexist with complex, significant movement, communication, and health impairments. Unfortunately, many of these related associated conditions and their interactions with one another may not be well understood by general educators.

With the consistent use of appropriate environmental and instructional adaptations, these students can function within the average or above-average intellectual ranges. Environmental and instructional adaptations provide physical, visual, auditory, and tactile access to acquiring knowledge and demonstrating what has been learned and retained.

These cognitively strong students can become "disabled" and frustrated when educational systems, and society in general, too often allow the mere presence of obvious physical differences to predetermine attitudes and assumptions about a student's intellectual strengths and capabilities. In these situations, low expectations may dampen the willingness of educators and families to recognize and explore ways in which movement, health, and communication impairments can mask intellectual strengths and impede and delay learning. It is critically important for educators to understand this fact and allow students with CP sufficient time to perform at a speed that works for them rather than insisting that they achieve the "fluency" of the neurotypical student.

Learning Disabilities

While it is impossible to generalize about the effect that a diagnosis of CP has on cognitive functioning, we know from research and practice that cognitive challenges span a spectrum from mild to profound among and within subtypes of CP. Like learning disabilities that are experienced by students who don't have neurologically based physical and health disabilities, CP-based learning disabilities frequently appear to result from complex brain injuries or malformations of the brain structures that are involved in sensory processing.

These sensory-based learning disabilities coexist with the gross and fine motor and health impairments that define the diagnosis of CP and often yield an uneven cognitive profile that slows and confounds the learning and teaching processes. Many students with CP experience difficulties at the readiness level, struggling with basic skills and content.[119] From the beginning of their formal education, these students will require varied and less typical methods of instruction. The most salient facts of a lesson must be identified and then creatively presented in order to bring the student closer to understanding. Keep in mind that if a student is a struggling reader or never becomes a proficient, functional reader, there is a good chance that the student can gain and retain information by using their auditory strengths.

Significant Intellectual Disability

When early diagnosis of CP reveals profound intellectual disability, the student's medical records may report *global developmental delays.* These profound intellectual challenges are often accompanied by significant movement, health, communication, and sensory disorders. Students who fall into this category typically require school programs that are more sensory-based and functionally oriented in order to awaken them to the world around them and to prepare them, when possible, for the acquisition of basic life skills. This functional curriculum improves independence and provides as much involvement in the community as the students are capable of.

Although students in this category vary greatly in their ability to comprehend, attend, remember, and respond, most if not all can do and understand much more than is typically expected of them. Despite limitations, each student, through the use of intense individual sensory stimulation, can improve their performance. It is incumbent upon teachers and assistants to dig deeper, to look further, to demonstrate a willingness at a moment's notice to change strategies to one that yields greater promise, and *to use a student's intentional responses to build on and connect to new learning.*

The goals of the complex and profoundly intellectually disabled student with CP may not align with the goals of the neurotypical students, and decisions need to be made to determine which strategies and goals appropriately produce meaningful engagement for the student. If these students find themselves in inclusive programs, the following questions should always be asked: In what ways is this student truly benefiting from learning strategies intended for students who function at a considerably higher level? Is this student simply a class of one? Are the student's unique educational and functional needs being consistently met? Would the student benefit from being a part of a critical mass of those who share the student's common experiences and goals and who learn in similar ways, or is the student absorbing important lessons simply from proximity to neurotypical students?

If a profoundly intellectually disabled CP student spends considerable time in a general education setting, he or she, even though not on an academic track, may be able to absorb some elements from the general curriculum while also being offered a highly individualized, functional program on an individualized basis or in small-group settings.

When there are alternatives to inclusive placements, low-functioning students with CP tend to be educated in self-contained, public-school classes or in special or residential schools. The students receive instruction commensurate with their cognitive level while being provided with limited yet meaningful access to neurotypical students either in school or out in the community. Interaction between the students in special programs with students in general education often comes in the form of nonacademic activities and programs.

General Attention and Distractibility

Many students with CP are easily distracted (have short attention spans) and find it difficult to concentrate when experiencing frustration in the face of complex, fast-moving instruction in inclusive settings. This distractibility may have roots in various forms of physical discomfort and a limited exposure to the topics. Poor memory or delays in both physical and cognitive processing tied to wide-ranging sensory dysfunctions also add to the problem. Some youngsters with CP find it difficult to focus on a lesson unless the instruction is being directly and individually addressed to them.

Inhibition of Return (IOR)

Inhibition of return (IOR) is a term used to describe the reduction of attention to an item that had previously been attended to. In populations of students with forms of spastic CP, this condition has been traced to the development of perinatal (during the birth process) injury in the anterior (front) parts of the brain, areas that play a role in visual attention.[120]

Addressing Issues of Attention, Distractibility, and Disengagement

Instructional responses to attention and distractibility in CP require an understanding and awareness of the student's entire sensory and physical status because all or many of the previously mentioned primary, secondary, and associated conditions that may accompany a diagnosis of CP can contribute to attentional and distractibility deficits. Students with CP who struggle with attention will come closer to reaching individual goals when the quality of their work leaves them feeling satisfied, acknowledged, and appreciated. The following are recommended instructional strategies that can lower the attentional barriers:

- Provide visual presentations that the student can see and comprehend.
- Make certain that the student is comfortable and free of pain or physical stress.

- Create calm, orderly, yet stimulating, learning environments.
- Refocus the student by reshaping the immediate learning environment.
- Create an office or use a carrel in a corner of the classroom that blocks distracting objects and people (a space that other students can use at different times) and that may reduce visual and auditory distractibility.
- Move the student into a separate, isolated space that minimizes visual and auditory distraction, especially when working with new concepts or materials.
- Make certain that the room temperature is appropriate for the student's medical condition.
- Be alert to any tactile-defensive responses that may appear with the introduction of instructional materials. Don't just automatically assume that you are dealing with a behavioral issue.
- Make certain that students can hear presentations.
- Avoid attention loss caused by slow auditory processing by reducing the pace of instruction and by using repetition.
- In consultation with the OT, use weighted clothing to help calm and focus the student.
- Teach the student individually or in small groups where intense proximity to the instructor can improve attention.
- Deliver instruction in small doses, which allow for review, repetition, feedback, and increased student engagement.
- When introducing independent work, make certain that assignments are modified so that the student can be physically and intellectually engaged in the activity.
- Give the student ample time to respond.

Understanding Memory

Memory, both short- and long-term, is an invisible, very complex brain process that requires neural communication among many parts of the brain. Short-term memories, if they last long enough, are thought to be distributed throughout all areas of the brain through neural connections and can be retrieved when needed. When reconstructing memory (remembering), we retrieve *parts* of a memory to form a complete memory.

Repetition strengthens memory retrieval and retention when there is a strong emotional association attached to the memory.[121] If we are focused, can sustain our attention, and are not distracted, memories form when groups of neurons repeatedly fire together.[122] When we look at working memory, temporary storage and manipulation of information is necessary for such complex cognitive tasks as language comprehension, learning, and reasoning. Working memory requires the simultaneous storage (long-term memory) and processing of information and is dependent on effective hearing, vision, and executive control to monitor and regulate attention.[123] To be effective, working memory not only must be supported by *visual sequential memory* and *phonological memory* from spoken information but also is dependent on sensory input from other sensory sources. When deficits exist in these sensory sources, memory retrieval and information consolidation are weakened.

Learning difficulties can be found, in varying degrees, in all types of cerebral palsy. Around 50 percent of students with CP experience learning difficulties that are related to memorizing, consolidating, and applying presented knowledge.[124] This also applies to students who have weak short-term memory, which slows learning even when the students are functioning within the normal IQ range.

Difficulty with short- and long-term memory, attention, sustained concentration, organizing, and processing information affects the student with CP's ability to master academic subjects at a basic skills level. These types of learning challenges characterize the learning difficulties experienced by many students with CP.

Students with poor working (short-term) memories tire easily, which may affect their ability to discriminate between relevant and irrelevant facts when reading and attempting to solve math problems. Memory problems with CP can induce slower processing, thereby rendering self-instruction more difficult.

Whole-Group Versus Small-Group Instruction

Although the use of whole-group instruction appears to be favored by many teachers, its exclusive use, a strategy employed in both inclusive and special-school settings, may be less than effective for students with moderate to significant levels of CP-related learning disabilities—disabilities that are compounded by the presence of complex motor, health, and sensory issues.

There will be students with CP who, in an inclusion classroom, may not quickly or easily comprehend and/or respond to what is being taught in the context of whole-group instruction. Although these students may have average or above intelligence and are coping with or without sensory-based learning disabilities, health and motor challenges may slow their educational processes. For such students, instruction in a small group of students or instruction delivered on a one-on-one basis may be more productive and yield greatly improved student comprehension. These small groups can function very effectively within the general classroom setting, in resource rooms, or in special education classrooms.

Benefits of Direct Instruction in Small Groups

Direct, systematic instruction that uses repetition and frequent prompts, delivers information in smaller, shorter segments that later can be extended, and offers positive feedback with less attention to errors made during instruction can often be more effective and less upsetting than whole-group instruction for many students with CP.

Using the small-group model, teachers can investigate creative ways to present the material, can use dramatic voices to emphasize important words and concepts, and can give the student with CP ample time to accept, make choices, demonstrate preferences, and register thoughts and feelings. Student response modes can be made either independently, with the use of digital assistive technology, or with adult assistance.

Successful direct instruction, coupled with observation for students with

CP who appear unable to self-instruct, should also be accompanied with ongoing informal assessment and monitoring, making it more likely that the teacher will reach the most difficult-to-reach student. Modified small-group instructional strategies, along with environmental modifications designed for students with CP, may also prove beneficial and effective for some students who are otherwise designated as neurotypical learners.

Effective Instructional Strategies in *All* School Settings

Although teachers and assistants in special-school and special-class settings have had considerable experience with modifying instruction and curriculum, both special and general settings require constant observation, and sufficient time must be taken to explore and identify areas of difficulty and strength. The following are some direct instructional strategies:

- Ensure that the student understands the goal of a task.
- Present instructional materials in less complex yet interesting ways.
- Help the student with CP develop sustained curiosity by frequently asking comparison questions.
- Many students with CP will simply need more time to learn and master new skills. Provide shorter periods of instruction interspersed with short periods of "downtime" to help deepen each student's understanding of the subject matter. Hopefully, the student will in time feel better prepared to engage in greater class participation.
- Understand that the slow pace of a student's work production may not only be caused by movement irregularities but can also be interrelated with slower cognitive processing.
- If needed, provide demonstrations that may include physical, verbal, visual, and auditory prompts.
- Use any acceptable manner of communication and resist the temptation to always deliver teacher-directed instruction.
- Dramatically identify a starting point and verbalize each step in a sequence. When appropriate, write steps down.

- Whenever possible, use the student's own ideas, feelings, and preferences, undampened by adult judgment. Neuronal connections strengthen and grow (plasticity) when strong, positive emotions are involved.

- Use the multiple, sensory modalities of vision, hearing, speech, touch, and proprioception (position of the body in space and the relation of body parts to one another), which give the student with CP the greatest possible opportunity to comprehend a concept and demonstrate understanding.

- Reduce the complexity of instruction, but keep the lesson sufficiently challenging.

- Suspend your initial discomfort with slow responses and extend times for intentional student replies.

- Use age-appropriate content and reading levels, even when major curricular modifications become necessary.

- Use curriculum and instructional materials guided by a student's cognitive abilities, sensory status, and functional and future needs.

- Consistently apply curricular and instructional modifications and adaptations.

- Motivating a student with CP who has spent most of their life sitting in a wheelchair, and perhaps observing and not participating, may not be easy. Work hard to ascertain that which leads the student to happiness, curiosity, creativity, strength, and pleasure. Then build academic tasks around these strengths and emotions.

- Help the student with CP to stop and think before executing a plan.

- Always check on the student with CP to determine if your instruction is exceeding the pace of the student's natural, slower processing speed.

- For students with CP who function most effectively in a less traditional academic setting, look for more practical, functional components that can be derived from and woven into a general-education academic curriculum.

- Use a student's interests to encourage cooperation with a lesson.
- Do everything possible to promote student engagement.
- If the entire curriculum content cannot be used or comprehended, choose the key and most salient points to present and review with a slower, more deliberate presentation.
- Purposely give activity-specific feedback and appropriate praise for minimum effort or success.
- When the student with CP meets a roadblock, don't stop instruction with the assumption that nothing more can be learned or taught.
- Apply the strategies of *task analysis* to identify the causes of the learning breakdown and look for missing skills that are required to complete the desired task. Teach these skills or replace them with other skills; then work to complete the task.
- Monitor learning and constantly assess and adjust instruction.
- Commit yourself to using adaptive and augmentative technology to reach the student.
- Leave open space for independent, student-directed activities and responses.
- When possible, gradually withdraw assistance.
- Counter student tendencies to "give up" by stressing the importance of persistence, seeking help, learning from mistakes, and giving oneself time to look for hidden clues and strategies.
- Provide considerable sensory stimulation for the student with CP.
- Examine the academic and social benefits of instructional stations.

Here are some general instructional considerations:
- Keep class routines consistent.
- Encourage *all* adults in the classroom to work with the student with CP.
- In the face of multiple physical and health needs, make certain that the academic and functional learning needs of the student with CP are not shortchanged.

- Don't assume that commercially manufactured materials will be appropriate for a student with CP. Carefully balance the use of commercially prepared materials with the need to customize materials based on the student's sensory, intellectual, and movement issues.
- Consider peer tutors to assist the student with CP.
- In team-teaching settings, observe ways in which a student with CP benefits or struggles with the instructional style of the general educator.

CP in the Presence of Profound Learning, Medical, and Movement Disabilities

The most significantly multiply disabled students with CP often have complex movement, medical, communication, social-emotional, and intellectual profiles that place them in Life Skills programs. In some school systems, these students spend some time in general education settings, although their instructional goals may be greatly altered. Usually, these students receive their education in special education settings. The recommended instructional strategies for students with fewer intellectual challenges may be modified for students with more significant and profound intellectual limitations. Addressing the unique challenges is much more important than pushing the student to keep up with others. Here again, instructional processes and goals need to be individualized. These programs tend to use strategies that focus on

- Increasing the use of visual, auditory, olfactory, and tactile stimulation to elicit responses that can be allied with a functional life-skill goal.
- Developing a functional understanding of and relationships with objects and people in the student's school and community environments.
- Developing verbal and nonverbal communication that allows the expression of wishes, thoughts, and feelings.
- Learning strategies of self-protection and self-advocacy.
- Engaging in training programs that allow for participation (with or without supervision) in the wider community.
- Observing students to ascertain reasons for challenging behaviors, and then crafting remediations.

It is extremely important that the curriculum for students with profound intellectual difficulties be age-appropriate. Although it may be difficult for educators to find high-interest, low-academic-level materials, it is unacceptable for the middle school student with CP who lives with significant intellectual challenges to be offered educational materials found in preschool programs. A class of profoundly disabled fourteen-year-old students with CP should not be singing "The Wheels on the Bus."

Depending on the student's degree of awareness and sensory connections to persons and objects outside of their bodies, curriculum and instructional strategies are centered around attempts to use vision, hearing, touch, taste, smell, and proprioceptive positioning to increase the student's awareness of their body and the presence of others in their environment.

- These strategies seek to elicit curiosity and exploration that can hopefully lead to further learning and discovery.

- Sounds, music, clay paints, liquids, and toys of different textures are all used to literally bring a student out of the isolation of their own body and into greater emotional, sensory, and gross motor participation and awareness of the world around them.

- Close attention, through intense observation, must be paid not to overload a youngster's sensory faculties. The loud singing and drum beating that excites one student with CP may deeply upset and drive another deeper into themselves and further away from the aim of the lesson.

Care and honest appraisal must be employed if these significantly involved youngsters are placed in inclusive settings, and we must be certain that the student is not simply "auditing" the class with the hope that something will "stick," when in essence, the student could be working on projects that are more likely to benefit the life they will live as an adult. The following instructional tips for the severe and profound CP populations should yield some improvement in performance:

- Begin at a student's level of performance, not at the level we'd like them to be at.
- Use task analysis to reach back and find the student's breakdown areas.
- Provide instruction that addresses the issues revealed in the breakdown points.
- Look for episodes of anxiety and rejection that may block learning.
- Read to the student in a dramatic and emotional manner. Read slowly, emphasizing key concepts, and recognize that commercially prepared stories and songs often move too rapidly for a student whose auditory processing may be considerably slower than that of the neurotypical student.
- For this population with severe or profound intellectual disability, learning the days, months, and year; learning the alphabet; counting; working with shapes and colors; learning through music and rhyme (in an age-appropriate format); and caring for plants and animals are all solid learning activities.
- Art projects that involve not only colors but also satisfying textured sensory experiences (which will differ from student to student), all with a great deal of varied repetition and with as much individualization as the program can provide, will benefit this population.
- For students whose CP is accompanied by severe intellectual disability, social enterprising projects such as baking, selling cookies, running classroom stores, and making and delivering handmade soaps all enhance functional skills and develop a greater awareness of their environments. Such activities help students to express wishes in an environment that strengthens social connections.
- As much as their intellectual capacities permit, students with CP in the severe and profound intellectual groups need access to education that prepares them to develop skills needed for adult living, for functional financial skills, for food shopping, for vocational opportunities in the wider community, and for access to social relationships and self-determination.[125]

- Even when the student is younger, educators along with parents need to ask themselves the following: What skills will this student need when he or she is thirty? What skills will propel them toward a satisfying quality of life?

- Understand and accept that because of cognitive limitations and/or impaired receptive visual and auditory function, success with phonics-based reading programs may be unattainable.

Instructional Group Size for Profoundly Intellectually Challenged Students with CP

Decisions about group size for this population of students with physical, health, communication, and cognitive challenges are of critical importance. For these students, the large, whole-group experience, unless conducted by an exceptionally skilled teacher accompanied by equally skilled and involved aides, is unlikely to maximize student potential.

Often in classrooms for profoundly disabled students with CP, the go-around-the-circle method of instruction is used. Although aides may be assigned to sit behind and support one or several students with CP, the pace of instruction is determined by the lead teacher, who directs the lesson with a one-size-fits-all model. A close observation of this method yields several flaws. On the average, each student receives only three seconds of contact with a manipulative or a spoken interaction with the instructor during an entire class go-around. When students are not able to respond in a reasonable period, they have a response provided for them or are simply passed over in favor of the next student.

When these students can work with adults in small groups of two or three, their overall engagement is greatly increased; they have more time to respond and to explore and perform an activity. The adult who is leading the activity has greater opportunity to observe student responses and readjust instructional interventions. After prior planning with classroom aides, the lead teacher introduces the activity to several small groups of students—each group led by an adult. The teacher then allows the assistants to conduct the activity in their own small groups. At the completion of the activity, the lead teacher brings the activity to a close.

Although this instructional strategy is unfamiliar to many educators who are wedded to the whole-group, teacher-led approach, for those who are willing to try another strategy, the results can be amazingly successful. Teacher-student interaction is increased, and instruction moves along slowly enough to permit in-depth exploration. Students experience much longer time on task, which in turn increases retention and extends memory. Students are more likely to interact with and learn from one another, and this strategy allows teachers and aides to observe student responses. Instruction delivered in these small-group settings, using a high adult-student ratio, encourages students to develop their own strengths, creativity, and problem-solving skills. In this manner, elements of a more traditional curriculum can be absorbed in this more functional setting.

The Phenomenological Approach

The term *phenomenological* describes planned, intense, skilled, informal, nonstandardized, and often recorded observation over a long period. The phenomenological approach is essential when teaching students with CP. The observations guide the observers (teachers, aides, related service providers, and parents) in learning as much as possible about the student with CP in a variety of settings. In the classroom, these long-term phenomenological observations usually commence after a battery of formal assessments have initially chronicled the overall status of a student's motoric, communication, sensory, health, cognitive, and social-emotional situation.

The operation of a classroom is a highly organized, choreographed, labor-intensive endeavor, with teachers and assistants constantly playing defined roles (although many teachers would say that there is scant time for the intense observation of a single student). Hopefully, observation of the student with CP's responses or lack thereof can become a natural part of the instructional day and can be performed by all the adults who work regularly in the classroom as they see with "different eyes."

Ongoing informed observation is the most essential and powerful tool available for gathering information about students with CP, whose presentations can often be exceptionally complex. Observation helps steer educators in effective directions, allows them to use task analysis to target discrete challenges, helps to determine the exact level of each challenge, leads to a determination of methodology, and helps them pinpoint a student's strengths and weaknesses.

The classroom teacher who primarily uses a whole-class instruction model often lacks the luxury of time for the kind of intense one-on-one observations that are afforded to related service providers. For students who struggle with the multiple complexities of CP, much more may be required. Ideally, when teachers or assistants can arrange to sit on the sidelines for a designated period and remove themselves from direct interaction in order to intensely observe a student, the rewards of discovery can be immensely revealing.

Phenomenological observations chronicle how a student's strengths, behaviors, coping mechanisms, and CP-related challenges shape the student's responses to activities at different times during the school day and reveal valuable information about how the student interacts with adults and fellow students. Information extracted from skilled observations in one setting needs to be compared with reactions in other settings and should be shared with all of those who interact with the student. And if the teacher is afforded the opportunity to observe a student with CP during an out-of-the-classroom therapy session, excellent insights might be gained that can lead to new ways of delivering instruction to this youngster in the classroom.

Unfortunately, in some educational environments, when dealing with a student who is severely disabled with CP and who has compounding health, communication, and intellectual challenges, teachers who have not been trained to work with this population may perceive the student as being too difficult to assess, reach, or teach. Not only is the student's potential underestimated, but there is often an unspoken attitude that these students are hardly worth the considerable expenditure of time and effort needed to reach and teach them. These students may not receive the kind of intense, effective instruction that could develop their intellectual and social-emotional potential.

Observation of a student's every response is a strategy that helps us to demystify CP, gives us insight into the student's capabilities, and forces us to replace "Let's pretend that we are reaching this student" with "Let's find out exactly how we can promote learning in this student."

Combining What Is Observed with What Is Known

In many countries, an *Individualized Educational Plan (IEP)* is generated for special-needs students, based on results from batteries of formal assessments and from objective and subjective assessments of those who have worked with the students. Teachers and related service providers should ponder and look for solutions to how the roots of observed, puzzling responses are informed by facets of educational, psychological, and medical reports.

The results of planned observations, once communicated to support team members during scheduled team meetings and through informal collaborative contacts, help all who work with the student to gain a deeper, clearer understanding of the evolving nature, extent, and complexity of the student's strengths, challenges, and progress.

An Informational and Observational Profile

The following are lists of observational points that are directly related to many of the primary, secondary, and associated conditions of CP. As the teacher begins to work with a student, he or she should seek answers to these questions.

Status of Physical Ability and Comfort

- What is the full extent of the student's gross motor strengths and limitations?
- What is the full extent of the student's fine motor strengths and limitations?
- How effectively does the student carry out tasks that require gross and fine motor planning?
- Does the student's medical history suggest the presence of episodes of pain or discomfort?
- Under what situations have you noticed that the student may be experiencing pain or discomfort?
- Do the student's mobility and positioning limitations add to the discomfort of pain or fatigue?
- Have pain and discomfort impacted distractibility and/or the ability to attend to learning?
- If the student is medicated, what effect does medication have on the student's mood, attention, and participation?
- Do the student's seizures negatively impact the student's safety or their academic and/or social performance?

Visual Status: Acuity and Perception

- Does the student have any visual challenges?
- Has the student had a recent vision assessment that is available to the school?
- Under what specific conditions does the student's vision appear to be less than effective?
- Does the student currently appear to be experiencing problems with visual acuity?
- Does the student have difficulty coordinating visual and manual tasks?
- Does the student appear to be experiencing problems with visual tracking?

- Under what condition and to what extent is visual distractibility a problem?
- Can you be certain that the student's visual perception (interpretation or representation) of what they see is similar to that of a neurotypical student?

Hearing Status: Acuity and Perception

- Does the student have a history of hearing difficulties?
- Has the student had a recent hearing assessment that the school has access to?
- Do the student's responses to sound appear to vary with pitch and volume?
- Have you observed the student misinterpreting spoken or environmental (ambient) sounds?
- Has the student demonstrated any discomfort with sound?
- Does the student exhibit auditory preferences?
- Does the student require sound amplification during instruction?
- Does the student require spoken instruction to be delivered at a slower pace?
- Can the student comprehend and follow spoken instructions?
- Does the student pay attention during whole-group instruction, or do they rely solely on direct, individual attention? (This is very typical in a population of students with complex CP.)

Touch Status: Acuity and Perception

- Have previous school records recorded difficulties with or sensitivity to touch?
- Have you observed any instances of behavior that might signal issues with touch sensitivity or tactile aversion?
- Does the student use tactile sensations to explore their immediate environment or to learn about or communicate with others?

- What tactile experiences appear to engage the student?
- To what extent does the student integrate their sensory functions?

Cognitive Indicators

- What information about the student's past and current cognitive status has been provided by school records, including educational, psychological, or neuropsychological assessments?
- What is the status of the student's attention span in a variety of activities?
- How would you describe the student's working memory (short-term memory)?
- How would you describe the student's long-term memory?
- Can the student demonstrate the ability to understand and perform concrete tasks?
- Can the student demonstrate the ability to comprehend and perform in abstract domains?
- At what grade level is the student able to demonstrate problem-solving ability?
- Does the student learn new material more effectively in large-group, small-group, or individual settings?
- How much repetition and review does the student require to imprint a new concept? (Is this need activity-specific?)
- Can the student generalize existing cognitive skills to new tasks?

Communication: Expressive and Receptive

- Does the student have difficulty with articulation?
- Is the student able to express thoughts and feelings using age-appropriate language?
- Can a typical communication partner comprehend what the student is trying to express?
- If the student is nonverbal, do they have a repertoire of nonverbal

strategies—for example, signing, body language, or sounds that allow them to communicate thoughts, feelings, and needs?

- If the student is nonverbal, are they able to use any type of assistive technology to foster communication for both academic and social purposes?
- Is this communication-enhancing technology affordable for the family and school system?
- Is ongoing training available for these assistive technology systems (since too many systems, once ordered, are never effectively utilized)?
- Can these technology systems be maintained and upgraded?
- If the student is verbal, can they receive the language instruction needed to communicate thoughts, feelings, and needs?

Emotional Status

- What appears to bring the student happiness and contentment?
- Under what conditions is the student unhappy, agitated, disengaged, or upset?
- How does the student handle frustration and discomfort?
- Is the student aware of and concerned about the rights and needs of others?
- Are there instances in which the student appears to be unnecessarily self-focused?
- Is the student able to establish and sustain effective relationships with peers?
- Is the student able to establish and sustain effective relationships with adults?
- For how long and under what circumstances does the student explore or play independently?
- Does the student appear to be isolated or lonely in the class or school community?
- Does the student appear to be overly dependent on adults?

- How does the student make, maintain, and extend social interactions?
- Under what circumstances does the student demonstrate initiative and independence?

Ideally, every adult who works with students with CP is continually gathering information that sheds light on these and other questions through intense, recorded observation and is sharing this information with colleagues and parents. Phenomenological observations help to promote a deeper understanding of CP's impact on a student. These observations should also be accompanied by a continual questioning of the meaning and causes of a student's observed responses or the lack thereof.

Approaching Core Curricula with Needed Adaptations and Modifications

Initially, the teacher may want to use curriculum and instructional strategies that are research-based and that have proved effective for other disabling categories. However, we must not expect a perfect fit or assume or pretend that the student with CP is learning when, in essence, they are not. We must always look for ways to tailor and customize curriculum and/or employ unorthodox strategies for a student with complex CP when the student's reactions or performance alert us to the inefficacy of an intervention and keep the student from reaching a desired goal. Frustration may arise and valuable instructional time may be squandered if the student is expected to comply with interventions and strategies that are unproductive for them.

Educators are constantly reminded that instruction must be implemented with fidelity to standardized goals if lessons are to be considered valid.[126] However, for many students with CP, adjustments and sometimes significant modifications and adaptations *must* be part of the instructional process if some or all of a lesson's core-related goals are to be achieved.

An in-depth knowledge of the student's strengths and challenges, a clear identification of barriers that elements of CP can present to instruction and learning, rigorous documentation of adaptations and modifications used, and a transparent rationale of why, how, and when modifications are needed lay the foundation for the decisions to employ modifications and adaptations. Educators in both inclusive and special settings should collaborate with transdisciplinary team members and avail themselves of professional development in order to strengthen their ability to modify and adapt lessons in ways that maximize the academic accomplishments of students with CP.

Daily Transportation Responsibilities

Many or most students with CP require some degree of special transportation to participate in school. In many cities around the world, special transportation for this population is legally mandated. This service engages the use of large and small buses with hydraulic lifts that safely transport students who use wheelchairs as well as those who ambulate with difficulty. Ambulettes and private vans with ramps also transport students with CP. For older students, when it is available, accessible public transportation may fill the need.

Oversight for the school transportation process usually falls to an administrator or designated teacher; however, members of the school-based support team, particularly PTs and nurses, may have a valuable role to play. Safety is the primary concern when transporting students with CP to and from school, and the teacher needs to know that a student can safely enter the bus and is safely secured once on the bus.

A student's medical and physical profile can dictate where and how the student is positioned on the bus, and it is not uncommon for some students with CP to require the attendance of a nurse or transportation aide in cases of medical emergencies.

The teacher also needs to be aware when the student's morning wait for the bus is unacceptably long, especially in cold weather, since wheelchair users are more sedentary and have more difficulty keeping their bodies warm and may need extra outdoor covering.

Drivers and bus matrons must be aware of potential medical or health complications during transit and should be in phone or radio communication with both home and school. Buses have accidents and break down, and particularly on return trips, teachers may have to extend their workday by waiting with students for replacement buses.

Preparing for Field Trips

Patrice Kuntzler

Field trips are essential educational activities that must be well thought out when they involve students who have the complex medical and motoric conditions of CP. These field trips, day or extended, require preplanning after the educator has considered all the CP-related barriers that have the potential to limit the student's enjoyment, safety, and well-being. The following are lists of recommendations that will make out-of-school adventures safe, comfortable, enjoyable, and educationally relevant for many students with CP:

- Consult the student's IEP for trip planning guidance.
- Be aware of and plan for weather and environmental conditions that can produce difficulties for the student.
- Learn from the student, school team, and parents about needs and roadblocks the student faces when leaving the home or school environments.
- Consult and collaborate with OTs and PTs about trip planning.
- Select sufficient staff and designate the appropriate staff to meet all of the student's needs.

- Do not depart from medical schedules.
- Contact the field-trip site to determine the facility's readiness to accept students with specific physical and medical challenges.
- Determine the site's degree of accessibility.
- Look for potential gaps in accessibility guides related to travel in a particular area or site.
- Consider routes, traffic conditions, station closures, and construction delays that can be problematic for the student with CP.
- Before the trip, visit the site and
    - Examine the terrain from the school bus or car to the trip location.
    - Check the availability and condition of bathroom facilities.
    - Find areas of privacy to attend to medical and bathroom needs.
    - List extra supplies that may be needed, such as water bottles, straws, garbage bags, and any articles that the student with CP may need.
    - Prepare to transport special equipment and find temporary storage.
    - Factor in fatigue and discomfort.
    - Identify opportunities for seating, rest, and downtime.
    - Identify accessibility to exhibits and events.
    - Locate sites for administering medications, being fed, and eating meals.

Planning for Emergencies
- Be able to contact local emergency personnel quickly if needed. Emergency contact information should be readily available. For example, if you are taking a boat trip, it might become necessary to contact a harbormaster if there is a medical emergency for the student or other personnel on the field trip.
- Include staff who are equipped to respond to medical emergencies.

- Identify in detail situations in which the student's vulnerabilities pose a threat to their safety and well-being.
- Review or create school policies around medical emergencies, fires, natural disasters, evacuations, or other potential threats to the well-being of the student.
- Write, in collaboration with parents and school team members, and duplicate safety plans for the student that are immediately available to classroom teachers, nurses, and school administrators.

Overnight and Extended Trips

- Be fully aware of accessibility and accommodations for sleeping, personal care, and being fed and eating at the arrival site.
- Take both trained daytime and nighttime staff.
- Allow a student who can't travel with the class to make the trip with a parent or caregiver.

There are several benefits of an extended school trip: It allows the student with CP the experience of first-time travel away from home. It promotes and tests the student's independence. And it expands the student's experiential fund.

CHAPTER 5

The Educational Impact of Cerebral Palsy's Sensory Challenges

Adine R. Usher

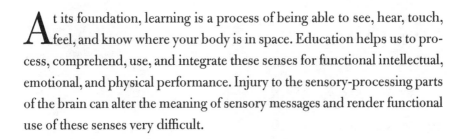

At its foundation, learning is a process of being able to see, hear, touch, feel, and know where your body is in space. Education helps us to process, comprehend, use, and integrate these senses for functional intellectual, emotional, and physical performance. Injury to the sensory-processing parts of the brain can alter the meaning of sensory messages and render functional use of these senses very difficult.

Overview of the Sensory Brain

The exchange of information through electrical/chemical processes and between neurons in different areas of the brain is continuous. These informational exchanges are sent through neural pathways in the brain, down the spinal cord, and then out to the *peripheral nerves*, which are found throughout the body. When these message signals from the brain reach the peripheral nerves, those nerves act upon the sensation and then inform the brain of specific responses.

Whenever possible, students with CP should eat with their peers and enjoy the social experiences that mealtime provides.

When educators refer to receptive and expressive sensory performance, they are speaking primarily of the consequences of reciprocal, neurological, and informational exchanges that affect vision, hearing, touch (*tactile*), taste, smell, *vestibular* (balance) and *proprioception* (sensing where the parts of your body are in space).

Contributors to Sensory-Based Learning Disabilities in CP

Students diagnosed with CP may experience challenges in some or all of the sensory domains that are required for processing and learning. These challenges can distort and affect the student's ability to interpret and integrate the performance of these senses. It is worth repeating that there are found, in varying degrees, learning disabilities in nearly 70 percent of students with spastic CP; learning disabilities are less frequently found in students diagnosed with dyskinetic (including *athetoid*) CP.[127]

Sensory processing is allied with sensory integration (the ability to integrate several senses), allowing students to link tasks and to expand and construct meaning from their physical and social environments. Since we know that neurons in one part of the brain, even injured neurons that can distort a message, are in continual communication with neurons in other areas of the brain, it is therefore not surprising that many students who have CP experience sensory problems that can coexist with, affect, and exacerbate movement difficulties.

In chapter 1, we learned that neurons in the brain's *parietal lobes* assume a pivotal role in organizing much of the brain's sensory functions.[128] Neurons in the *motor cortex*, which control movement, lie directly in front of the *somatosensory cortex*, which itself sits in the front part of the parietal lobes. The somatosensory cortex is a strip of neurons going across the top of the cerebral cortex that receives information from other areas of the body about touch, temperature, pain, pressure, and the position of our limbs. The proximity and communication between the motor cortex and the areas of the parietal lobes can influence the presence of learning disabilities in students with spastic CP. To be effective, the use of research-based sensory strategies, prior reporting, observation, commonsense approaches, and an awareness of *all* of a student's sensory responses are needed to teach students with CP.

CP-Related Visual Challenges

The student with CP in your class is exhibiting one or several of the following behaviors: She appears to have poor visual concentration, is consistently inattentive, and is struggling to read or seems unable to read or remember what she has read despite intense, specialized instruction. She can't seem to comprehend and perform the most elementary of math activities, rarely looks directly at the person speaking to her, cannot do puzzles, seems not to comprehend the purpose of toys, and does not visually track objects or people.

Damage to neurons in the visual centers of the brain can contribute to mild to significant reading difficulties; can impair the student's ability to fixate, gaze, and track in a smooth fashion; can limit the size of the student's visual field; and can severely affect the ability to attend and focus attention.[129]

Vision is a neurological function. The eye receives an image, sends the image along the neurovisual pathways to the visual cortex in the *occipital lobes*. There, in collaboration with the work of *associative vision areas* in neighboring parts of the brain, the visual image is understood and interpreted, then sent back to the eyes as vision.[130] Vision is a function influenced by many brain areas, and over 50 percent of the brain's cortex is devoted to visual function.[131] Certain types of damage that cause visual dysfunction may be related to the infant's gestational age.[132]

Although several areas of the brain play a vital role in vision, the parietal lobes, which lie directly in front of the occipital lobes, play a significant role in visual perception.[133] Vision guides movement, shifting and maintaining attention, making sense of confusing surroundings, recognizing emotional situations, and making sense of moving or stationary objects or people. Effective vision allows us to move our head and eyes in concert with one another, thus allowing us to track and scan. The constantly fluctuating nature of visual abilities vary and are dependent on several factors: the motoric requirements of a task, the effectiveness of a student's positioning, the status of often conflicting sensory demands, and the effects of medication. Fatigue and stress in the student's immediate environments also affect the quality of vision.

There seems to be a correlation between the location of neurological injury, the extent of brain injury, and the severity of visual abnormalities,[134] and both research and careful classroom observation lead us to conclude that students with varying forms of spastic CP are at greater risk of experiencing visual problems. Impaired *visual acuity* is more prominent in students with dyskinetic CP, whereas *spatial problems* and complex difficulties with visual perception are more commonly found in students with a diagnosis of spastic CP.[135] "The spectrum of visual problems in children with CP is extremely broad"[136] and may emerge only in response to the demands of academic and social performance. Although well researched, the overall picture of CP's effect on vision is still blurred.[137] Nearly 50 percent of students who are diagnosed with the conditions of CP experience some form of visual impairment, and visual-perception problems occur in concert with motor dysfunction.[138]

One cannot overstress the role that *visual perception*, *visual acuity*, and *oculomotor* (muscle-dependent eye movement) challenges can play in the learning process for students with CP because these students may experience great difficulty with reading and math.

Visual-perception difficulties are found less frequently in students with *extrapyramidal* (athetoid) CP, although some have *cortical visual impairments (CVIs)*.[139] The percentage those whose ability to read, write, and comprehend mathematical concepts is affected by a wide spectrum of visual dysfunctions, spanning all the subtypes of CP. Visual deficits in this population often interact with and exacerbate the consequences of motoric dysfunction. Some of the research on CP refers to vision challenges as associated disorders. Other studies view vision difficulties not as an associated condition but rather as a function of central nervous system (CNS) dysfunction, which describes the coordinated work of the brain and the spinal cord.

CP and CVIs are described as sharing a common origin in damage to developing neurons caused by oxygen deprivation.[140] Other researchers find a relationship between injured neural pathways in the primary motoric regions of the cortex and damaged or malformed visual neural pathways that emerge from the brain's visual cortex in the occipital lobes.

Unfortunately, because parents and professionals may understandably be strongly focused on the movement and health-related priorities of CP, significant visual issues are too often misunderstood, undiagnosed, and unattended to. Parents and educators may lack access to the research on vision problems in CP and are often unaware of the frequency with which problems with visual acuity, oculomotor function, visual perception, CVI, and a compromised visual field can occur and further complicate the learning process.

As this chapter progresses, you will come to realize that visual symptoms and problems may have several causes. It is therefore absolutely critical that families and teachers be observant and informed about the visual status of the student with CP, insisting that the student receive a thorough vision assessment performed by vision specialists who understand the potential link between CP's complex conditions and visual dysfunction.

Visual Acuity

When asked about a student's vision, it is not uncommon for parents of the student with CP to report that they have checked their child's vision and reported that no problems were noted. These parents are usually thinking about problems with *visual acuity* that results from *refractive errors*, which describe the degree of clarity and precision of one's vison. *Hyperopia* describes farsightedness, while *myopia* describes nearsightedness, and both terms refer to the degree of clarity and precision with which an object can be seen. A student with CP may also have difficulty changing eye focus to maintain a sharp image of objects at various distances. Some students with CP must contend with the blurred and distorted images of *astigmatism.* Teachers should be aware that "vision [affects] children with CP differently depending on their movement disorder. Children with spastic CP [perform] worse with eyes closed while those with dyskinetic CP [have] improved head stability with eyes closed. Our results demonstrate that children with mild to moderate CP have deficits in head stability even during quiet sitting."[141]

Problems with visual acuity can be corrected (to varying degrees) by the student's wearing corrective lenses; however, parents and educators need to understand that improving visual acuity does not preclude the presence of other, significant visual challenges.

Oculomotor Dysfunction

Oculomotor dysfunction, which is secondary to fine motor problems, describes the lack of coordinated motion of both eyes as they sweep the visual field to gather information. In these instances, eye muscles are not properly controlling smooth, coordinated eye movement, including in vertical and horizontal planes (*visual convergence*). Many students with CP live with varying degrees of oculomotor dysfunctions, which can significantly affect learning when

- Both eyes turn in or out and can't work together (*strabismus*).
- One or both eyes turn in (*esotropia*).
- One or both eyes turn out (*exotropia*).
- One or both eyes turn upward (*hypertropia*).
- Visual acuity is reduced when one eye moves from side to side (*amblyopia*, or "lazy eye").
- Involuntary, rhythmic eye movements reduce visual acuity and impair binocular vision (*nystagmus*).
- Eye muscles misalign during rapid eye movement (*motility*).

Oculomotor difficulties are made more challenging when coupled with visual acuity, with visual perception, and with the limited size and strength of a student's visual field. Some observable consequences of oculomotor dysfunction appear when a student has difficulty

- With smooth and steady visual tracking that is needed for reading from left to right, which may also be exasperated by visual-perception difficulties.
- In tracking coordinated eye-hand movement on a linear plane.
- When coordinating the sense of touch with eyes and hands.
- When both eyes have difficulty shifting focus rapidly (*saccadic movement*) as they move (scan) from one object to another.
- Sustaining focus on a stationary object (*fixation*).
- Shifting focus from one important activity to another.
- Visually following an auditory cue.
- Moving back and forth between a screen or blackboard to a keyboard or paper-and-pencil tasks on a desk.[142]

Visual Field Restrictions

Visual field restrictions refer to visual limitations in the entire area of vision that ideally can be taken in without shifting one's gaze. Visual field problems may reflect significant vision loss in either the peripheral areas or in the central areas of vision; the problems may also be pronounced when students are diagnosed with *cortical visual impairment (CVI)*, a condition resulting from injury to the optic nerves, which run from the eyes to the brain's occipital lobes. The condition is found in populations of students diagnosed with CP. As a result of this injury, the brain is unable to process and correctly interpret visual information.[143] CVI may exist in combination with other brain-based challenges that occur with a diagnosis of CP. Certainly, reliable assessments and learning can be challenged by the presence of CVI, but in its milder forms, there does not appear to be an association between cognitive function and CVI.

Visual field difficulties are less well understood by educators and may be falsely interpreted as total blindness. Indeed, the formerly used term *cortical blindness* misleads some teachers to believe that students had no sight. Fortunately, the current terminology of CVI, an impairment that includes visual field restrictions, implies an imperfect but not totally absent visual field.

In the most severe cases, the visual field is significantly limited, images are blurred, and sections of the visual field appear to be missing or are altered by the presence of numerous blind spots. Students with CP who have a diagnosis of significant visual field restrictions may be considered legally blind but are not totally blind.

Visual field restrictions not only impact learning but, when paired with motoric deficits, can negatively affect safe movement through the school. Socialization can be a challenge because the student may experience delays in fixing on and tracking the faces of those with whom he or she is communicating. Visual field restrictions can be present when a student with CP

- Looks without appearing to register understanding.
- Appears to have distinct color preferences.
- Fails to see objects or people in their field of vision.

- Is exceptionally partial to familiar objects and toys.
- May have difficulty viewing objects at a distance.
- Is observed often gazing at sources of light.
- Exhibits weak visual attention.
- Appears to avoid attending to objects that are visually complex.
- Engages in excessive blinking or eye rubbing.
- Has difficulty attending to moving objects.
- Has trouble remembering inanimate and personal associations that have previously been seen.
- Focuses exclusively on the familiar and appears to avoid the novel in activities of daily living.
- Favors the upper areas of a limited visual area, missing objects in the lower visual areas, thereby increasing the risk of tripping or falling.[144]

Visual Perception and Integration

Visual perception describes the process of visually interpreting and making sense of what is seen. Deficits in this area play a prominent role in explaining the significant barriers to learning and socialization that may be experienced by students with CP. Visual perception is integrated with the movements of our bodies and the movement of objects in our environment. It permits us to plan, anticipate, and predict our own responses and correctly interpret the responses of others based on visual clues. Visual-perception problems may affect both motoric and cognitive tasks and often precipitate functional difficulties in several domains.[145]

Students born with CP who have congenital lesions in the brain's visual areas may have elementary *visuospatial* perception difficulties that render them unable to reorganize and process complex visuospatial and *visuo-constructive* functions.[146] Educators should be aware of the rate at which specific changes in visuospatial functions may occur (based on a variety of visual demands) so that they can plan and adapt their educational strategies.[147]

Cognitive visual dysfunctions (CVDs) also describe the inability to process visual information. Elisa Fazzi and her colleagues found that children with CP displayed an uneven cognitive profile, with deficits in visual object recognition, visual imagery, visuospatial skill and visual sequential memory, visual associative abilities, nonverbal intelligence, and face and letter recognition.[148] These findings were explained by the widespread resulting involvement of higher visual processing systems because of not only tissue destruction from brain injury in the newborn infant but also impaired and subsequent brain development.[149]

Difficulties visualizing the concrete makes it exponentially more challenging to envision objects in the abstract; therefore, many students with CP struggle with visual sequential memory. This difficulty becomes apparent in learning to read an analog clock or to work with geometric concepts. Visual-perception impairments and visual integration problems may be present when students with CP have difficulty

- Perceiving and comprehending spatial distances and relationships.
- Visually perceiving or reproducing the complete outline of the shape of an object.
- Consistently identifying, isolating, and distinguishing individual numbers, letters, and words from one another on a page, board, or classroom wall display.
- Sustaining visual attention.
- Establishing *visual sequential memory*.
- Consistently recognizing and distinguishing letters, shapes, numbers, and objects.
- Comprehending and establishing spatial order when working with letters, numbers, and shapes.
- Establishing a one-on-one correspondence in counting numbers or objects.
- Associating numbers with their quantitative equivalents.
- Perceiving important details that distinguish one object from another.

- Reversing letters and numbers well past the primary grade years.
- Discriminating the foreground from the background.
- Recognizing the sequence of patterns of objects.
- Recognizing and interpreting facial expressions.
- Recognizing variations in spatial arrangements.
- Reproducing the complete outline or shape of an object.
- Visually constructing (visuospatial) and reconstructing objects in the learning environment.
- Recognizing the relation of objects to one another (particularly prevalent in students who were diagnosed with periventricular leukomalacia [PVL]).
- Discriminating the whole from its parts.
- Recognizing missing parts of an image (*visual closure*).
- Creating visual closure of pictures, objects, letters, and numbers.
- Visually comprehending directionality (*laterality*)—that is, left-right, up-down, next to, above-below, first-middle-last, and in between.
- Differentiating between horizontal and vertical motions.
- Visualizing images in two and three dimensions.
- Recognizing space as a separate entity from an object.
- Avoiding walking into objects or people who would be seen and avoided by most persons.
- Differentiating and interpreting facial expressions that denote moods.
- Processing an overload of visual information.
- Comprehending visual information that is presented too rapidly.

Visual Motor Integration and Hand-Eye Coordination

During our waking hours, we are integrating visual information with information provided from all our other senses, including sensations from gross and fine movement. Visual motor integration difficulties can significantly impact all aspects of the school experience for students with CP when

- The eyes are unable to guide the fine motor tasks required for the manipulation of the typical implements of academic performance and recreation, such as writing, coloring, painting, cutting with scissors, or manipulating toys and puzzles.

- The student has difficulty spacing letters and numbers while writing.
- The student has difficulty staying on the line while writing.
- Graphomotor impairments compromise the ability to write and copy numbers, letters, pictures, and patterns.
- The eyes are unable to guide and aid in the coordination of self-care activities.
- The eyes poorly guide independent walking or navigating with a wheelchair or walker in the school and neighborhood environments.
- The student is unable to visually comprehend and integrate information that does not come equally from both eyes (*bilateral integration*).
- The student has difficulty copying shapes, numbers, or letters.

Handwriting

Handwriting is another skill that very much depends on fine motor function and visual-perception skills. Even if they can functionally use a pencil, some students with CP have trouble writing on a line when one is clearly present, and they cannot internally visualize or perceive the presence of an invisible line.

Parents are often insistent that the student with CP learn to use a pen and pencil. Where developing this skill does not cause great discomfort, stress, or fatigue, it can be pursued. However, it is not important that the student perform as others do. It is only important that the student perform in a manner that produces a satisfying product that leaves them with a feeling of accomplishment. This is more important than producing a volume of written work.

Writing considerations and remediations include the following:

- In inclusion settings, accept shortened assignments from a student with fine motor and/or visual-perception difficulties.
- With the guidance of the OT, introduce a regular or appropriately adaptive keyboard as soon as its need becomes apparent.

- Before the student uses a pencil, have the student trace letter shapes, and stress directionality.
- As the student writes, ask them to visualize whether the letter is standing on the line, sitting on the line, or sitting on the line with its legs dangling below the line.
- If manual writing is not an option, explore computer access with head sticks (pointers attached to headbands), voice-to-text computer technology, eye gaze (using eye fixation and movement to track words and numbers), or any part of the student's body that allows for a functionally consistent degree of control.

Visual-Proprioceptive Functions

Student performance can be challenging when coordinated eye function does not respond to the body's position and movement in space. Here, students with CP may be

- Visually unaware of their bodies in space as they move toward objects.
- Unable to perceive far and near objects during movement.
- Unable to easily integrate balance (vestibular difficulty), vision, and movement.
- Likely to miss a chair when attempting to sit.
- Likely to encounter difficulty when attempting to simultaneously see, move toward, and interact with peers.

Visual Functions at the Executive Level

The term *executive* describes visual activities that are partially regulated in the *frontal cortex*, the primary seat of executive functioning, including self-regulation and decision making. In some students with CP, the observation of the concrete does not lead to the ability to make visual abstractions—that is, to imagine the movement and manipulation of letters, numbers, and objects. This requires higher-level thinking skills. Problems ensue if this visual function is poorly regulated, and students may have difficulty

- With visuospatial processing.

- Planning, anticipating, and predicting responses based on visual cues.
- Recognizing parts within the whole and creating a whole from several parts.
- Envisioning objects in the abstract, a difficulty that weakens visual memory and is apparent when the student is trying to read an analog clock or comprehend geometric concepts.
- Combining vision with mental processes.
- Mentally manipulating visual images (a task that is particularly essential when learning math).
- Visually recognizing sequences of objects or patterns.
- Internally visualizing or perceiving the presence of the invisible line on a page.
- Differentiating between horizontal, diagonal, and vertical lines.
- Maintaining attention, maintaining motivation, and directing the monitoring that is needed for visual exploration.
- Sustaining visual stamina that is not necessarily tied to inattention or lack of interest.
- Visually comprehending that a task has been completed.
- Paying nondistracted attention to visual detail.
- Comprehending and interpreting the meaning of printed material.
- Understanding and interpreting the relationship between larger categories and the individual characters and/or objects that are found within those larger categories.

Vision-Dependent Communication

For the sighted, the ability to maintain social connectedness is dependent on our reaction to what we see and interpret as we interact with others. When this brain-based visual function is poorly regulated, a student with CP may fail to

- Consistently recognize familiar faces.
- Use vision to understand the posture, facial expressions, movements, and gestures of others.

- Understand the movements and gestures of others.
- Coordinate vision with speech (visual-verbal integration).

Social Consequences of Visual-Perceptual Challenges

It is not uncommon for a student with CP to have trouble differentiating and interpreting facial expressions that denote moods. There is some research to support the concept that damaged mirror neurons, which enable us to mimic one another's facial expressions, may also be a contributing element, although the current body of research on mirror neurons and CP centers around movement difficulties. Visual challenges, which affect navigation, may also impact behavior and socialization.[150] Learning requires visual and nonverbal responses. Deficits in this area can compromise both academic and social interactions.

Visual Memory

Visual memory requires that we remember and make sense of what we have seen in sharp detail. Often paired with attention deficits, visual memory problems can pose major academic challenges for students with CP, consequently negatively impacting academic progress that depends on

- Remembering the letter arrangements that make up the word.
- Remembering words, numbers, and patterns.
- Remembering what was read, even when the student can see and sound out a word.
- Remembering and describing visual images (visual abstracting).
- Having sufficient repetition and practice with visual images in learning environments.

Case Study

AR is a student with ataxic CP. As she was learning to walk, she would fixate on something in space in front of her and then would move. As the PT explained, this student used that strategy to help stabilize herself. The teacher digested this information and then realized that AR used this response when she was asked a question. The teacher learned to repeat a question and give AR time to "fixate" and then respond. Her rate of success increased in lessons that required responses.

Medical and Therapeutic Interventions

For students with CP, eye surgery is performed when less invasive treatments (glasses or vision training) have failed to correct the problems of cataracts or of misaligned eyes (*strabismus*) due to *oculomotor dysfunction*. Surgery is performed to realign the eyes by restoring their muscle balance. With surgery, the eyes will begin to work and move together—improving vision and reducing visual strain.

Problems with *visual acuity* (the clarity with which one sees) and oculomotor function (synchronous movement of the muscles that control eye movement) can be detected in routine eye exams; however, visual perception and processing, visual integration, and sensory processing, as well as visual field performance, require much more specialized attention.

With effective vision therapy, heightened and informed teacher awareness, and consistent instructional adaptations, the impact of CVI and visual field impairments may be reduced, though not eliminated. If treated early with surgical, medical, and therapeutic interventions, many of these oculomotor conditions can be improved or reversed.[151]

Teacher and teacher-assistant awareness of vision-dependent behavioral characteristics in populations of students with CP through direct observation in both special- and general-education settings is essential. A diagnosis of CP *should* signal the need for a visual system evaluation as early as possible, with obligatory follow-up examinations.[152] Then, with a clear diagnosis of vision challenges, it is imperative that all who work with the student learn to lower environmental and instructional barriers while providing necessary vision services.

Any visual information gleaned from reading the student's records, from speaking with former teachers, and from talking with parents should immediately inform not only the way the classroom is arranged but also the way instruction is delivered. Based on the results of the assessment, adaptations to the classroom environment should begin to lower the barriers of visual impairment and stimulate the student visually at a functional level. Not only will many generalized visual modifications in the class help the youngster with CP who has demonstrated a need, but these modifications will in no way harm those students whose visual functioning is within the normal range; in addition, the modifications may reap unexpected benefits for other students whose visual issues are yet unidentified.

Visually Appropriate Environmental and Instructional Strategies

- Provide adequate classroom lighting that is appropriate for specific individual needs.
- Resist the temptation to crowd pictures, letters, and words on walls and display boards.
- Allow spaces between words and between the lines of text on the board and on walls to increase visual accessibility.
- Make certain that pictures, lettering, and numbers are large, bold, clear, well-spaced, and visually accessible.
- Have the student write on dark, bold lines.
- Bring objects, letters, words, and numbers close to the student.
- Use a moving cutout window to help a student with oculomotor problems to maintain left-right eye tracking when reading.
- For youngsters with figure-ground issues, use paper or cardboard cutout windows to isolate words, groups of words, columns of numbers,

or objects that you wish the student to exclusively focus on.

- Avoid the random use of colored letters in a word (for decorative purposes) unless you are highlighting a specific instructional aim—for example, the first letter in the beginning word of a sentence, compound words, or phonetic sounds.
- Place heavy black letters on a light or white background.
- Use heavy, bold contrasting colors to highlight instructional points, such as the appropriate use of a capital letters, commas, periods, question marks, and exclamation marks.
- Reduce visual distractibility and increase visual attention by covering up educational material not immediately needed in cubbies and shelves that line the walls of the classroom.
- Place no more than between one and four objects, numbers, or letters on a page, outlining separate boxes for each. This increases visual focus and decreases visual overstimulation. This is a successful strategy that can be employed at any age or grade level.
- Paste individual objects from standard workbook pages into these boxes, thereby eliminating the clutter of the standard worksheet that produces such visual confusion for many students with CP.
- Use a contrasting color to highlight part(s) of a word that represent specific instructional goals.
- Bold characters, enlarge them, and provide spaces between words and lines, even when using the whiteboard (e.g., SMART® board).
- Outline or underline, to aid tracking, with a heavy, usually black, marker anything that you need the student to focus on.
- To assist in making directionality more understandable, make use of boldly written arrows.
- Realize that sometimes, when writing, the student with CP can't visualize the size of a space that exists between letters, words, and numbers.
- To force spacing, initially have students write words in rectangular boxes that are separated by sizable spaces.

- When visual perception causes letters, words, or numbers to run into or overlap one another, use vertical lines or symbols of any shape to *force* spacing between words, letters, numbers, and objects—for example, "1***2***3***," "a***b***c***," and "The----house----is----red----."

- You can create spacing by placing one or two fingers at the end of a word before beginning the next word. A pencil eraser placed between words also serves this purpose.

- Use computer and other digital presentations that are large and colorful but not too busy or overwhelming.

- Use spoken descriptions (by both student and teacher), and touch what the student is both seeing and doing. This adds the sensory input of speech, touch, and hearing.

- Based on what you are learning about the student's visual status, change their location and seating position in the class to provide the most advantageous visual accessibility.

- The student with visual field deficits may have trouble when sitting on the floor and expected to sustain an upward gaze at the teacher. The same student may not experience visual stress when sitting at their desk and seeing the teacher at eye level.

- For the student who has difficulty visually transitioning from board to desk, make duplicate copies of work written on the board for use at their desk.

- Avoid the use of the commercial workbook when the print is too small for the student and when the cluttered printed background (figure-ground) causes confusion and may decrease motivation.

- Significantly limit the number of words, sentences, or numbers to a page if the student is visually confused and distracted by the clutter on a standard printed workbook page.

- Use commercially produced light boxes with commercially produced overlays or handmade images painted on acetate sheets to evoke the student's interest and curiosity that aligns with instructional objectives.

Employing this strategy in a dark room may be particularly beneficial for students with CP whose profile includes a diagnosis of significant CVI. Use of tablets and computers may also provide a similar effect.

- Help the student with CP to distinguish the foreground from the background by placing activities on a plain-colored place mat with reduced background clutter.
- Create space between words and lines of text on the board and on wall displays.
- Boldly underline passages or words in the student's writing to increase focus.
- Eliminate background visual distractions.
- Rely on a whole word rather than a phonetic approach when the latter is unsuccessful and stressful.
- To improve visual attention and extend visual sequential memory, present small, isolated groups of letters, words, or numbers of concepts one at a time. Then gradually add and introduce new materials against a neutral background.
- Vary the types and presentations of reading materials and, through observation, determine which types of presentations appear to be most effective.
- Use age-appropriate, multisensory reading programs in both print and digital forms that take full advantage of auditory, visual, and kinesthetic domains and that are specifically designed for students with learning disabilities.
- Use reading programs that are flexible, diagnostic, and prescriptive. Multisensory reading programs use explicit instruction, are sequential in structure, are language-based, and emphasize sound-symbol correspondence strategies of decoding.

Guided reading strategies, providing teacher-led instruction in small groups, are beneficial to students with CP who struggle with vision-based reading challenges. Guided reading allows students to learn to read using text that is accessible to them: easy and interesting enough for them to read and comprehend but challenging enough that, with adult facilitation and the introduction of various learning strategies, students can clearly demonstrate growth and proficiency.

Some students with CP who have average intelligence will simply *never* learn to read despite the use of adaptive reading programs that have proved successful for other students with sensory- and language-based learning disabilities. In these instances, vocabulary, object identification, and concept formation may have to be taught primarily through a student's auditory and non-letter-based visual strengths:

- Allow the student's hands, fingers, or toes to trace over the heavy, bold markings in sand, on sandpaper, or on any other materials that encourage visual, motor, and tactile sensations to work simultaneously. This strategy is also successful when students with CP continue to reverse letters and numbers well past the primary years.

- Tracing shapes on the student's hand increases their kinesthetic awareness of visual shapes.

- Copying block patterns and sequences, sorting and matching, dot-to-dot games, puzzles, and spot-the-difference games all contribute to improved hand-eye function.

- Support the student's understanding of how letter shapes are formed by talking about the direction of lines and circles during the writing process (using the support of auditory input) and use small arrows to point in the direction of letters that are frequently mistakenly interchanged—for example, *d* with *b* and *g* with *q*.

Visual Difficulties That Can Challenge an Understanding of Numbers, Quantities, and Mathematical Functions

Comprehending numeration and mathematical concepts can be particularly challenging for students with CP, and oculomotor, visual field, and visual-perception difficulties appear to lie at the root of these challenges. For some of these students, difficulty establishing one-on-one correspondence continues well into the elementary years. Even with the extended use of manipulatives to aid counting and grouping of numbers, some students with CP have considerable difficulty moving from the concrete level of understanding to an abstract understanding of numerical groupings and operations. Visual-perception challenges can be exacerbated by poor working memory, which adds to the difficulty of perceiving and discriminating relevant from irrelevant facts.

Frequently, math strategies used for neurotypical students are less successful for the student with CP because of the complexity of their sensory and learning challenges. These challenges necessitate a careful analysis of the student's unique difficulties and a crafting of interventions that address these specific challenges. The following are some instructional responses to math difficulties caused by visual challenges:

- Use tangible, hands-on manipulatives for as long as they are needed to increase the student's ability to move from the concrete to the abstract. Manipulatives add tactile reinforcement to existing visual and auditory stimulation, and they reinforce long-term memory.

- Employ creativity and innovation to bring numeration, counting, and problem-solving concepts to students whose physical and sensory limitations have curtailed their exploration of numbers.

- Separate objects to be counted by drawing heavy lines or similar barriers between numbers or around objects to be counted.

- Place objects to be counted in separate, well-spaced containers.

- Use hand-over-hand guidance and strong verbal support to gradually help the student to internalize the concept of separate yet connected numerical progression.

- Visual-perception challenges make reading an analog clock difficult for many students with CP. Try representing time intervals with pie-shaped cutouts to help students internalize the shape of a time interval. If this instruction fails, allow the student to find satisfaction with a digital clock.

- After adult modeling, have the student place number symbols in small containers that hold objects representing quantitative equivalents.
- Understand that visual-perception problems may limit the transferability of "play" money to real currency. Try to use real money.
- Basic geometric concepts can prove exceptionally challenging for some students with CP. Finger tracing of shapes with verbal supports and geometric puzzle manipulation may improve perception of geometric shapes and properties.
- Use bold, contrasting colors in drawing and distinguishing geometric shapes and use print, digital, and three-dimensional figures for demonstration formats.
- Place no more than one to four math problems per page in order to reduce the confusion caused by clutter and figure-ground difficulties.
- Choose digital math programs that can be paced to the student's functional rhythm and that take into account the realities and range of the student's visual challenges.

Assistive and Adaptive Technology

While the terms *assistive technology* and *adaptive technology* are often used interchangeably, they are different. *Assistive technology* refers to "any item, piece of equipment, or product system, whether acquired commercially, modified, or customized, that is used to increase, maintain, or improve functional capabilities of individuals with disabilities," while *adaptive technology* covers items that are *specifically designed* for persons with disabilities and would seldom be used by nondisabled persons.[153]

Certainly, the presence of computers and tablets has reduced the CP-related barriers posed by the interaction of visual dysfunction and fine motor challenges. Adaptive devices can now be activated by different parts of the body, including eye gaze. A wide array of modified computer keyboards can be equipped with keyguards that reduce the physical strain of pencil-and-paper tasks, especially when the task is confounded by visual-perception dysfunction and eye-hand incoordination. Assistive technology can lower the barriers of

CP-related vision challenges by

- Using read-along digital stories with uncluttered backgrounds and adjustable font sizes.
- Using digital word-recognition programs that feature large print and color coding for visual distinction.
- Adapting a kinesthetic approach (which improves mental visualization and retention) by tracing letters and words in the air.
- Saving read-aloud stories that the student with CP has made up and dictated.
- Making certain that the student has full and ongoing access to digital devices and programs that allow for a variety of customized print presentations (font size, clarity, spacing, highlighting, and bolding).
- Helping the student with CP physically activate and control these programs with the collaborative efforts of the PT, the OT, and the assistive technology specialist.
- Employing the skills of a vision specialist to facilitate the digital presentation of written material.
- Conferring, when necessary, with schools or programs that serve legally blind students with sensory-based vision disabilities.

CP-Related Auditory Challenges

Hearing (auditory) disorders are associated disorders that may or may not be directly related to the primary motoric disorders of CP. Auditory dysfunction, like visual dysfunction, may be the result of either anatomical defects or neurologic injury to the auditory nerves or a combination of both.[154]

Students with CP appear to be more prone than their neurotypical peers to have hearing problems.[155] Auditory defects often may go unrecognized in cases of mild, moderate, or significant CP. Students with CP whose profile also includes intellectual disability are at higher risk of hearing problems due to prenatal and perinatal *neurodevelopmental* damage, including fetal-maternal infection, neonatal sepsis, and other severe illnesses found in newborns.[156]

Deficits in *auditory acuity* (how much and how clearly one can hear) and *auditory perception* (how one processes and interprets what one hears) are experienced by some students with CP. These hearing defects can significantly impact a student's ability to acquire, retain, and use auditory information.[157] "Estimates of hearing loss in children with cerebral palsy range from 3 percent to 10 percent (Evans et al., 1985 as cited in Pellegrino and Dormans, 1998)."[158] However, because of the difficulty of identifying hearing disorders in this population, the true frequency may be much higher. This dysfunction is characterized by difficulties with auditory acuity and/or auditory perception and often accompanies premature birth.

Although infants are screened for hearing loss within the first few weeks of life, often hearing deficits are not of primary concern when they exist in concert with so many more overt physical and medical issues that command the immediate attention of parents and medical providers. However, methods for testing for hearing loss in preterm infants may be improving.[159]

There are two primary types of hearing loss found in CP populations: *sensorineural* and *conductive*. Sensorineural (permanent) hearing loss occurs where there is injury to the neural receptors in the inner ear, injury to the auditory nerve cells in the *neural pathways* in the brain, injury to the sensitive hair cells that are found in the cochlea, and injury in the parts of the brain that receive auditory stimuli.[160]

Neural hearing difficulties tend to occur more frequently in students with athetoid (dyskinetic) CP, as well as in those with intellectual disabilities. The hearing status of students who fall into these categories should be carefully observed and monitored.

Problems with auditory acuity are described as *conductive* hearing losses and occur when sound is disrupted and poorly conducted from the outer ear canal, through the middle ear, and then past the small bones of the inner ear before it reaches the nerve receptors of the inner ear.[161] For some students with CP, *otitis media with effusion* results from the accumulation of fluid in the inner ear and the presence of inflammation.[162]

Auditory discrimination describes the ability to perceive and distinguish discrete sounds. *Auditory perception* describes the student's ability to comprehend and give meaning to sounds. Both skills may be compromised with CP and can result in a range of language-based problems.

Educational Consequences of Auditory Dysfunction

Students with CP may have average or above-average visual skills while dealing with below-average auditory-visual skills. Conversely, strong auditory skills may help to lower the barriers posed by problematic visual difficulties. Concerns with short-term auditory memory and auditory retrieval, whether they are allied with issues of auditory acuity and auditory perception, are not unfamiliar to some students with CP and can significantly affect academic comprehension and recall. The following is a list of some of the educational barriers that may result from auditory dysfunction when a student with CP

- Is required to repeat numbers and letters in sequence.
- Must remember important parts of narratives and organize orally delivered materials in a timely manner.
- Experiences inattention and distractibility when their brain has difficulty filtering out ambient sounds.
- Experiences a reduction in the ability to hear sounds within a normal hearing range.
- Has difficulty hearing discrete decibel levels.
- Struggles to distinguish between phonetic sounds.
- Is unable to rapidly distinguish auditory stimuli.
- Has difficulty with articulation.
- Is unable to fully participate in the academic program.
- Exhibits a loss of interest in classroom and school activities.
- Has overall diminished academic performance.

- Is challenged by spelling and reading comprehension.
- Has delayed acquisition of speech.
- Has difficulty retelling a story.
- Experiences frustration and behavioral problems that may be related to hearing loss.
- Experiences constraints on social participation.[163]

If the student is *dysarthric* or nonverbal, hearing difficulties can exacerbate efforts to make sense of principles of basic phonics and the blending of letters—all prerequisites to reading. Since our sensory functions are integrated with and mutually dependent on our motoric functions, auditory deficits in both acuity and processing can pose a challenge to motoric performance by failing to provide cues that guide our movements in the environment.

Surgical and Medical Interventions

Myringotomy is an intervention for some students with CP that drains fluid buildup in the inner ear (which causes otitis media with effusion) after hearing problems and speech delays have been diagnosed through a comprehensive assessment. A small incision is made in the tympanic membrane, which allows the drainage of fluids in the middle ear that had become infected. When these infections become chronic, corrective surgery may be used to alleviate this problem with the brief insertion of ear tubes into the eardrums to equalize the pressure there.[164] These tubes are associated with improved rates of survival; however, they can themselves cause additional health problems (chronic drainage, scarring of the eardrum, thickening of the eardrum) and gastrointestinal issues.[165]

Hearing aids and *cochlear implants* are often helpful to students with CP. Hearing aids need no explanation, but cochlear implants bypass the normal hearing process and provide, after extensive training, a modified sound experience.

Environmental and Instructional Responses to Auditory Acuity and Processing Issues

- If a youngster with CP, no matter the severity and complexity of their motoric conditions, is struggling in the early grades and appears to be falling behind neurotypical peers, screening for hearing loss, like screening for visual problems, is critical to the student's cognitive, speech-language, and psychosocial development.[166]

- Teacher, school team, and parental awareness, observation, and collaboration are essential in providing an understanding of the exact nature of auditory issues.

- Identify problems with auditory discrimination especially when there seems to be a discrepancy in the student's ability to distinguish between sounds that are heard and sounds that the student attempts to produce.

- Look for signs of inattention, poor concentration, and withdrawn or inappropriate behaviors that may signal hearing challenges.

- Use *FM systems* that mike and raise the decibel level of the teacher's voice and amplify sounds in the classroom.

- Be aware of the volume, the clarity, and the pacing of instructional speech.

- Use musical tones, sung or played on instruments, to heighten the student's awareness of sounds.

- Use soothing music to help settle and center the student.

- In the presence of hearing loss or auditory processing challenges, provide instruction in quiet areas.

- Encourage small-group instruction, which not only enhances the clarity of instructional voices but also allows for socialization in a more controlled auditory environment.

- When subvocalization (internal, silent speech) is poor, strong auditory presentation will help.

- If auditory dysfunction is established, communicate, collaborate, and learn strategies from centers or organizations that serve the deaf and hard of hearing.

- For auditory perception deficits, play "I hear" games, which involve listening to instructions and clapping to rhymes.
- Be aware that the student's auditory deficits can negatively affect behavior.
- Strategically position the student with hearing deficits in such a way that, during periods of direct instruction, their ability to hear and respond is optimized.
- Develop a sensitivity to and an awareness of the student's response to specific decibel levels that may cause discomfort or pain.
- Explore the use of lipreading and sign language training for student and staff.
- When you speak, face the student.
- When the student is facing the person who is speaking, focus them on visual and auditory stimuli.
- Keep spoken instructions clear and concise, deliver instruction at a moderate pace, and use relatively short phrases.
- Employ repetition for students whose problem involves auditory perception (interpretation of what is being said) and auditory memory issues.
- As a classroom teacher, maintain ongoing collaborative communication with the speech and language pathologist (SLP) who is assigned to the student.
- Some of the SLP sessions with the student with CP should be held in the class so that the specialist can assess the challenges of instruction in a group setting.
- Make certain that the SLP's thoughts and observations are shared with all who work with the student.
- Assure that other staff members who interact with the student throughout the school day are aware of and understand the student's specific

auditory challenges. Ascertain that they are employing, daily, the agreed-upon interventions that address these challenges.

- Be alert to the presence of *auditory cognition* challenges (problems in identifying a sound) in students who have been diagnosed with athetoid CP and some forms of spastic CP, subtypes that are associated with dysarthria (difficulty producing intelligible speech).

- Auditory-verbal dysfunction may compromise speech. Hearing ourselves speak enhances the quality of our speech production. Dysarthria diminishes the quality of the auditory-verbal relationship.

- Be aware that in addition to being easily distracted by environmental sounds, some students with CP may be extremely sensitive to the frequency and volume of sound. A student who appears to tune out may be responding to an auditory hostile environment.

- Know that the student may have several hearing challenges.

- Realize that poorly articulated speech (non-dysarthric) and delayed language development can also signal problems with hearing acuity and processing.

- Suspect the potential influences on hearing of frequent upper respiratory tract infection and nasal obstructions, and recommend that the family seeks medical advice.[167]

CP-Related Tactile Challenges

Touch is central to our humanity. Brain-based disruptions in the student's ability to tolerate the sensations of touch and pressure can prove extremely unsettling and uncomfortable for some students with CP as they deal with the implements of daily care, play, and learning. Since feelings and emotions are so strongly tied to touch, appropriate touch plays an important role in soothing the more significantly involved CP students, who can't easily express feelings or levels of comfort and discomfort.

Tactile challenges arise when the sense of touch, controlled by neural pathways coming from the brain's parietal lobes to the skin, provides the student with inaccurate information about their immediate environment. It is thought that both tactile and proprioceptive function are primarily determined by the status of neuronal activity and neurologic pathways that originate in the somatosensory cortex of the brain (part of the parietal lobe), just behind the motor cortex.

The conditions of hypersensitivity (being oversensitive) and/or hyposensitivity (being undersensitive) are two of the most common sensory distortions that may appear in some students with CP. The student exhibits an exaggerated, excessive, and unmodulated reluctance to touch or taste certain objects or textures. Their responses of discomfort are observable in signs of agitation and distractibility. A student who seems unable to settle themself comfortably in a seated position may also be experiencing tactile dysfunction. The student with a diagnosis of CP hemiplegia may experience more sensation difficulties with the more involved side of the body.

CP-Related Challenges to Smell, Taste, and Texture

Although there has been research on difficulties with taste and smell in populations of adults who suffer from neurological disorders, little is known about reactions to taste and smell in populations of children with CP. Teachers and therapists must therefore rely on their intense and repeated observations to identify those situations in which a student with CP appears to repeatedly avoid certain smells, tastes, and textures of food. These adverse reactions may reflect personal preference or demonstrate varying degrees of sensory dysregulation. An awareness of an aversion to taste and food textures is important for the speech pathologist who works in collaboration with physical therapists and parents in executing feeding programs for students with CP who require assistance with and training for chewing and swallowing.

If sensitivity to smell is suspected, try to eliminate strong odors in the classroom, chemical odors during art or science activities, and strong odors from cleaning products. When introduced by therapists, essential oils may provide comfort to students.

Students with CP who exhibit aversions to taste and smell may be showing either oversensitivity or undersensitivity. These extremes may be exacerbated by challenging reactions to normal internal body functions.

CP-Related Proprioceptive Challenges

Proprioception refers to perceiving where your body parts are in relationship to one another, in relation to the immediate environment, and in relation to the space around you. Messages between the brain and receptors in the joints, muscles, ligaments, tendons, skin, and connective tissues inform the central nervous system (CNS) about the quality and location of movement.[168]

Brain injury can distort information sent out to nerve receptors in the joints, thereby making it difficult for the student to know where their body is in space. The problematic effects of proprioceptive dysfunction can further complicate gross motor incoordination.

Proprioception is critical to the ability to move independently around one's immediate and distant environments. Brain-based body and joint orientation dysfunction is often common in students with CP, especially when paired with problems of visual perception.

Instructional Responses to Tactile and Proprioceptive Issues

From reading a student's records and speaking with OTs, PTs, and parents, learn to recognize signs that may signal tactile, proprioceptive, and sensory integration dysfunction. The following is a short list of remediations for tactile and proprioceptive issues:

- Gross motor activities such as climbing frames, obstacle courses, and tunnels provide for body awareness activities.
- Swings and rockers are particularly calming for students with CP.
- Know that tactile or proprioceptive dysfunction may become more problematic when integrated with dysfunctional visual perception, visual processing, and/or visual discrimination.
- When teaching youngsters with CP, help to increase their awareness of what their bodies are doing and where body parts are placed by talking them through activities.
- Whether seated in chairs or in wheelchairs, students with CP may benefit from extra work space that allows for freer movement and greater opportunity to grow their awareness of their bodies in space.
- Be aware that the feel of clothing, room temperature, and vibrations can be disquieting and unsettling.

Vestibular Processing Concerns

Vestibular processing is dependent upon the work of sensors in the inner ear that control balance, the eyes that guide and confirm direction, and the muscles of the legs. Signals for all these systems must be integrated in the brain to help establish and maintain a sense of movement and of balance.[169]

Vestibular sense, in responding to gravity's pull, establishes information about the head's relationship to the ground and, in doing so, uses information from our other senses to coordinate movement.[170] Vestibular proprioception describes the coordinated movement of head and body, an ability that can be severely taxed in some students with CP. Vestibular challenges can be of concern for students with CP who are hypotonic (with floppy, low muscle tone) and who have accompanying oculomotor difficulties. Students with vestibular issues may experience dizziness when lying down or moving their heads. Their injured vestibular systems fail to provide gravitational security. This lack of gravitational security can lead to systemic discomfort and a lack of social-emotional connectivity.[171, 172]

Instructional Responses to Vestibular Issues

- The physician may prescribe vestibular rehabilitation.
- Use swings and sensory integration techniques prior to instruction, which can possibly improve attention, reduce stress, improve sitting and standing posture, improve movement in space, encourage emotional well-being, and extend social and academic participation.
- Provide a balanced sitting position on a mat or chair before a lesson.
- Give verbal prompts for the positioning needed or for position changes.

Dyspraxia and Motor Planning in CP

A term that educators may find in reports and hear about from therapists is *dyspraxia*, or *developmental dyspraxia*. The term refers to a condition in which coordinated motor planning and organization is adversely affected by neurological damage. Dyspraxia is thought to result from poor discrimination of proprioceptive messages from the brain to the rest of the body.[173]

With dyspraxia, the student with CP (often with diplegia) may have difficulty constructing a plan, action, or motor task and may know what they want to do but can't plan or execute a plan. Rushing, disorganization, unhelpful expenditures of energy, and performance anxiety can all be consequences of dyspraxia. Other functional consequences of dyspraxia parallel many of the challenges described in this chapter on interrelated sensory functioning.[174]

Once a student with CP has been satisfactorily positioned in the school setting for motoric comfort and stability, accounting for and addressing sensory issues becomes the determining factor for delivering, receiving, and using academic information.

CHAPTER 6
The School-Based Support Team
Adine R. Usher and Contributors

T he members of a school-based support team address a student with CP's unique needs. Under optimum circumstances, the team works collaboratively through observations, evaluations, and shared planning in order to implement mutually agreed-upon goals,[175] to elevate the student's skill level, to help the student grow in independence and develop self-confidence, and to move the student closer to leading a fulfilling life.

A full team's membership includes the participation of parents, students, administrators, teachers, physical therapists, occupational therapists, speech therapists, resource room teachers, vision and hearing therapists, assistive technology specialists, school psychologists, social workers, counselors, and nurses. When they are available and play an active role in the student's education, art and music specialists may be included.

The intervention of each member of the team begins with a thorough assessment of a student's status and needs, based on observation and formal inventories. Once a clearer picture of the student emerges, goals are developed and strategies are executed.

In school, the primary educational focus of developing academic skills coexist with the need to develop effective communication and social-emotional

153

*A transdisciplinary team works collaboratively to
determine a student's educational plan.*

competency. For the students with CP to navigate their lives outside the classroom, they also need effective life skills. With therapeutic intervention, students
learn to navigate buildings, use bathrooms, manage meals, use transportation,
and understand their own medical needs; they also learn how their equipment
works and can instruct others in how to assist them with specific tasks.

In response to a student's unique health and medical needs, and with
parental consent, medical personnel and outside specialists can engage in
phone consultations with staff members, or they may be brought in to discuss
specific issues that are not usually covered in regularly scheduled meetings.
This occurs when it is of critical importance that the team get a perspective

from a specialist who is working with the student outside the school setting.

Some members of the team who provide direct, specialized service to the student with CP are referred to as *related service providers (RSPs)*. Their role is critical to the safety, physical development, academic progress, and social-emotional success of a student with CP. Paraprofessionals and aides will also be included in this chapter's discussion, for they, too, intensely interact with students and collaborate with teachers and RSPs.

The "Pull-Out" Versus "Push-In" Conundrum: Where Are Services Provided?

For many years, most therapies were performed in individual or small-group sessions in therapy rooms outside of the classroom. This is the "pull-out" model. The "push-in" model dictates that the therapist provides related services within the classroom setting. The effectiveness of both models has been widely discussed, but for many students with CP, the use of *both* delivery models serves students best if skills are to be acquired and retained.

Managing a push-in approach requires careful planning, as therapists may initially question the validity of working in a classroom setting, and the classroom teacher, particularly in inclusion settings, may not initially realize the value of sharing their space and/or merging their goals with others. However, once the push-in model is well organized and effectively executed, the student with CP can benefit tremendously when classroom teachers and therapists work in a collaborative space to combine their professional skills.

First, a student may need to learn a new skill in isolation, where task analysis is done. By breaking the task into smaller components, the student can master the fundamental components of the skill in a pull-out setting. This is where the therapists initially determine which adaptations must be incorporated into the intervention. Once mastered, the skill is transferred, "pushed in," to functional use in the classroom. Here, the therapist, with the support of the teacher and the teaching assistants, helps the student with CP to incorporate newly achieved skills into their everyday activities. When it is determined that the student no longer exclusively needs pull-out assistance, the skill becomes fully incorporated into the student's daily routine.

Based on the student's needs and skill level, the directives of the educational plan, the nature of the lessons being taught, and the need for highly specialized therapeutic equipment, the therapist and other members of the transdisciplinary team will determine the optimum location for service delivery.

SECTION I

The Physical Therapist (PT)

Amanda Buonora Jung

Traditionally, people think of the physical therapist (PT) as helping a person recover from a sports injury or a stroke; however, in the school setting, with students who have CP, the PT's role is considerably broadened. The PT is at the cornerstone of habilitative and rehabilitative responses to CP's gross motor challenges and directly addresses those gross motor impairments and environmental barriers that impede safe access to the tools of learning.

In early development, infants learn by exploring their environments through moving. They start with their eyes and random movements of the arms and legs. The body further develops in a head-to-feet direction. Infants start to explore, and through cause and effect, they learn how things work. Through trial and error, they learn to solve problems. Motor development in conjunction with perceptual development provides the foundation for cognitive processes. Many children with CP often miss most if not all the early motor experiences. This lack of typical development and movement can cause gaps in a student's learning.

Students with CP, whose bodies have withstood orthopedically driven musculoskeletal disabilities, require proper management, care, treatment, and therapy to retard the worsening of the conditions, such as skeletal deformities and the body's premature aging.

PTs are movement specialists who enhance the student with CP's learning experiences by maximizing gross and fine motor functioning and ambulation.[176] They help the student negotiate and function safely in all areas of the school environment, and they aid the student's ability to explore and understand how their body works.

A major feature of the PT's therapeutic responsibilities in the school setting is to improve the student's access to the school building and curriculum. Exercising and functional activities support daily stretching, which keeps muscles loose and reduces the pain of spasticity and contractures. These exercises and therapies also improve range of motion, strengthen muscles, and increase function for participation in educational activities. Additionally, PTs monitor the correct use of adaptive equipment, teach the correct methods of lifting and transferring, and supervise the correct application of orthotic devices.[177]

Since the official rationale for offering these related services in a school setting is to enhance, to the greatest possible extent, the educational program of the student with CP, PTs try to align their therapeutic goals with the educational goals articulated in the student's educational plan. In communication and collaboration with the student's family, the student, and the student's medical professionals (who prescribe, guide, or shape the nature of some therapeutic interventions), the PT determines the best mode of movement for the student. The options are many, ranging from walking independently to using an assistive walking device, such as a cane, crutch, walker, motorized or manual wheelchair, or any combination of those options—options that may change and must be continually assessed.

It's not just about stretching and getting stronger but also about using the student's skills in the most efficient way to obtain success in the educational setting. As part of the educational team, the PT's primary goal is to help the student develop motoric skills in ways that bring them closer to reaching educational goals.

PTs serve as consultants to classroom teachers, aiming for open dialogue about modifying and improving access to educational environments by making them as barrier-free as possible. They help decide where desks are positioned and how much space is needed for aisles. PTs recommend educational furniture and constantly create opportunities for students with CP to use their newly acquired skills. Here are some classroom and school-wide considerations:

- Does an ambulatory student with CP need an assistive device?
- Where will this device be safely stored and easily accessible and yet not pose a danger to other students?
- If a wheelchair is needed, should it be standard or will it require adaptive features such as headrests, armrests, and special back and side supports?
- If the student does not have the stamina to keep up with classmates, can his or her schedules be altered? Can the student be given extra time to move from class to class? Are there locations for rest, or can a student who usually ambulates use a wheelchair or a scooter when tired?
- How will potential fatigue be accommodated on long distances or school trips?
- Can the manual or motorized wheelchair user negotiate the school building independently?
- Are all areas of the class (tables, rows, centers) accessible to the student?
- Does the student require a height-adjustable desk?
- Does the student need assistance in moving from a sitting to a standing position?
- Is the student able to readjust their own sitting position?
- If a book bag can't be carried by the student, can it be placed on the back of a wheelchair and set up during class so they can access its contents?
- Can the student have "double books"—meaning a set at home and a set in the classroom(s) so that they don't have to be carried throughout the day?
- How much of a student's necessary academic information can be digitized and placed on easier-to-use digital devices?

Before or when a student with CP arrives at a school, the PT will assess the appropriateness and safety of areas, including the cafeteria (to ascertain if the student with CP can carry a tray or set up their lunch), bathrooms, special class areas, the playground, the auditorium, and the area for boarding and leaving the school bus.

Whatever the student's school setting or class size, we know that a multisensory instructional approach is most effective for students with CP. Realizing that all students have different learning styles—and that especially pertains to many students with CP—the multisensory approach appears to be more effective for these students than the lecture format delivered to primarily stationary pupils. The PT can enhance lessons by allowing the student to see, hear, and physically interact with an activity in a variety of ways, including the provision of alternate positioning and the use of transdisciplinary, team-developed lessons.

After having conducted extensive observations of the student in both classroom and out-of-classroom settings, the PT consults with the teaching staff to answer questions and make recommendations for seating, positioning, adaptive equipment, and opportunities for movement that enhance social and academic engagement throughout the school day.

How and Where Does the Student with CP Sit?

How and *where* students with CP sit is an important but, unfortunately, frequently overlooked topic that can have major effects on their ability to learn. Many such students have poor trunk control, making it difficult for them to sit upright and/or maintain their heads in a central, midline position. Sometimes, the students lean to the side or sit flexed forward. This creates difficulty for them to see what's being presented and can also hinder the efficiency of their breathing. Decreased oxygen leads to decreased attention and, consequently, decreased learning.

How does the student sit? Can the student sit on their own, and what are they sitting in or on? With stability comes mobility, and with a stable base, movement can happen, so if the core (trunk) is stable, the hands, arms, and head are freer to move.

The PT works on improving the strength and endurance that assists the student in maintaining an optimal sitting position. PTs can also recommend the type of chair(s) the student requires to complete classroom tasks. A standard classroom chair may be appropriate for a student whose physical disability is minimal. However, a student with moderate to significant physical involvement may need an adaptive chair or customized seating within a wheelchair that allows the student to sit upright. Some students may need straps to support and stabilize the body so that they can use other parts of the body to enhance academic functioning.

Bench sitting is another therapeutic strategy that can be practiced both at school and at home. If a student with CP has a weak core, sitting on a bench, for a short period of time while performing ordinary activities, causes the student to use more and different muscles, thereby strengthening core muscles over a period.

Where does the student with CP sit? Where should we place the student within the classroom? Optimal placement is often forward, facing toward the area where the teacher presents the lesson. Placement on the side of the classroom can be problematic if the student has difficulty turning their head or holding it up to see from an angle. There is also the possibility that added to the physical problems described here are visual perception, oculomotor, and visual field concerns that add to the student's inability to benefit from the lesson. The PT's consultation with classroom staff on room setup and student placement will help to reduce these barriers.

The PT will assess whether there is enough room for a student's wheelchair to pass around desks and access all areas of the room to ensure inclusion in classroom activities. The PT will also assist teachers in deciding where to place walkers during lessons so that the student with CP is able to reach the walker without interfering with the safety of classmates.

There may be a need for alternate positioning of the student with CP during the school day. People move and shift their bodies all day long without even realizing it. We do it to avoid feeling stiff, tired, and groggy. A student with CP may not be able to shift body position by themself. This inability may account for the student's "zoning out" and having difficulty paying attention during lessons. Improved positioning is accomplished by adjusting wheelchair positions, bracing body parts with orthotics, inserting pillows in chairs and wheelchairs, and exploring safe and effective handling and management techniques.

The PT can introduce strategies specific to that student, to help improve attention and interaction with lessons. Sometimes, something as easy as allowing the student to stand up for a few minutes during a lesson can do wonders. Another option may be to have the student tilt their motorized wheelchair to relieve pressure on buttocks. Placing a student with CP in a stander for part of a lesson or, if possible and with appropriate support, joining the entire class in sitting on the floor are activities that can stimulate brain function.

Although PT sessions in school settings may often be reduced as the student with CP moves into the teenage years and appears to have reached a plateau, sometimes the benefits of such sessions are continued and accelerated through athletic endeavors. Indeed, there are those in the therapeutic and medical communities who believe that, given the early decline of function and strength often seen with CP, there needs to be a plan for lifelong access to physical therapy.

SECTION II
The Occupational Therapist (OT)

Kate McGrath

Whereas the PT is primarily responsible for gross motor development, the occupational therapist (OT) is primarily responsible for fine motor development. Both disciplines blend perfectly and, with other therapeutic and educational professionals, work collaboratively to support the student with CP.

In this section OT Kate McGrath describes the work of improving fine motor and visual motor functioning for educational and self-care activities such as writing and keyboarding skills, dressing, feeding, and the manipulation of learning materials. They ensure the effective placement of learning materials and secure adaptive materials that support a student's academic program.[178] School-based OTs are responsible for identifying and remediating underlying CP-related motor, sensory, cognitive, and/or psychosocial barriers.

In addition to remediating skill deficits, OTs often teach students modified ways to perform daily school activities (dressing, eating, toileting) with or without adaptations and assistive technology. The OT aims to ensure that, to the greatest extent possible, students with CP can actively and independently participate in school-related tasks with a sense of satisfaction and accomplishment.

In elementary school, middle school, and high school, students are expected to attend to teachers' instructions, follow directions and rules, locate and manipulate instructional materials and tools, make sense of visual materials, manage personal belongings, take care of personal needs, and relay information in a variety of forms—all while remaining engaged and ready to learn! These seemingly basic classroom routines often become difficult, complex, multifaceted tasks for students with CP. CP-related brain injury causes breakdowns in many performance areas, and students with CP require ongoing practice of skills throughout their life span if they are to achieve and maintain a degree of function and independence. The OT targets these challenges.

Ongoing observations of student performance in varied locations in the school environment (classroom, locker area, cafeteria, and schoolyard), in addition to communication with transdisciplinary team members, yield valuable information about student strengths and challenges. Together, these team members can help the OT facilitate a plan of action for the student that produces individualized and meaningful goals.

Students may be required to produce written texts many times during the school day, either on paper or on the computer. This can pose challenges for some students with CP, whose gross motor, fine motor, visual motor, and visual-perception issues create substantial barriers to producing written work. Some students with CP may have legible handwriting, but because of fatigue, muscle weakness, muscle stiffness, abnormal posture, bilateral incoordination, and uncontrolled or extraneous movement, they find writing challenging. OTs use graded therapeutic activities to remediate upper-extremity motor control (affecting reach, grasp, manipulation, release, and bilateral coordination). OTs work collaboratively with PTs, exploring and teaching the students alternate ways to position their bodies.

Optimal positioning of writing materials is also a focus of the OT. Low-tech adaptations such as slanted writing easels are often utilized to give the student with CP a surface on which to position the forearms and lean into if there is decreased postural control.

Pencil grips may be used to relax grip and relieve tension in the hand musculature, and a soft lead pencil may eliminate the need for excessive downward pressure on the paper. A weighted wrist cuff or forearm cuff may dampen extraneous movement for students experiencing tremors or ataxia. Smart pens, such as the Livescribe, can record and play back everything a student has written or heard presented in class. By tapping on an unfinished passage, the pen plays back the teacher's completed message. The Livescribe can later be loaded up and stored on the student's computer or smartphone.

Many students with CP have difficulty making sense of letter forms, the visual-perception component of writing. These students may have trouble discriminating between forms that are either the same or different, and this difficulty consequently interferes with the physical act of writing, which involves the integration of both the visual and the motor systems.

OTs frequently adopt a sensorimotor approach when teaching writing and will often use manipulatives that promote tactile feeling and movement to enhance an awareness of shape, size, and spatial orientation. Therapeutic handwriting programs use a variety of materials and sensory strategies (large and small wooden lines and curves) that reinforce correct formation and spatial orientation of letters.

Students with CP who deal with visual-perception and organizational difficulties may find assistance in the use of stationery whose lines provide distinct tactile feedback and, for beginning writers, drawn boxes placed in different positions to guide and prompt the consistency of letter sizing. A visual cue that highlights the starting and ending points on a line may help the student to internalize left-to-right writing directions. Exploration of font style and size and visual contrast (i.e., yellow letters on a black background) may help the student with CP to visualize letter forms and decipher details. Positioning writing materials at the optimal height or angle can also facilitate hand-eye coordination.

For many students with CP, physical handwriting may not be a realistic or desirable goal; therefore, assistive technologies are often explored as an alternative to manual writing. OTs work closely with assistive technology specialists who are hired by school systems to assess student needs, determine which systems meet a student's needs, and train students, parents, and classroom staff in the use of these systems.

Adaptive keyboards, such as mini-size keyboards, may improve motor accuracy and conserve energy for one-hand users or students with limited reach span. A mini keyboard may also improve speed and accuracy, as well as improve visually scanning and locating letter keys. High-contrast Zoom text stickers placed on keyboard keys may also ease letter location by facilitating visual discrimination. For other students with CP, a macro keyboard may be more forgiving when overreach is a problem or when the student requires greater spacing between letters. Frequently, a keyboard with a keyguard can improve motor accuracy for students with spasticity, tremors, or ataxia.

On-screen keyboards (accessed via mouse or switches) prove useful for students who have difficulty physically pressing keys on a standard keyboard. An adapted mouse such as a roller ball or glide pad may decrease the degree of physical movement required to move the cursor onto letter keys.

Parameters can be set that allow minimal finger movement to move the cursor long distances. Cursor size, shape, color, and speed can also be explored to ease visual and motor accuracy while directing the cursor to a target. A more robust joystick may help those who have difficulty grading motor control or effectively using mouse click functions. For students who cannot directly access the on-screen keyboard with a mouse, a scanning system can be created that allows the student to select letters using a switch.

On-screen keyboards may also ease visual access, since the keyboard and word processing programs appear in the same visual field (at the same distance). The appearance of the on-screen keyboard can be modified to ease visual access—for example, by using color contrast. Adaptive software, such as word-prediction or abbreviation-expansion software, can eliminate the number of keystrokes required to complete a word and often improve spelling accuracy. Auditory-feedback software can facilitate accuracy and attention for students with CP.

Tablets such as iPads are commonly used by students with CP to produce text. A variety of on-screen keyboards with different visual arrays, with or without auditory feedback, are available. Apps such as Notability and SnapType allow students to photograph and complete worksheets using a finger to draw lines or letters on the touch screen. Direct and indirect access techniques using a keyboard, switch, voice, or vision are all possible on tablets.

Beyond enhancing the physical ability to write, OTs also assist students with CP to develop the cognitive aspects of writing by addressing organization, planning, and sequencing of thoughts prior to writing.

The motor impairments of some students with CP may be severe enough to necessitate an exploration of body parts other than the hand to facilitate writing. Alternate methods may include the use of pointers and switches affixed to the forehead, chin, mouth, knee, or feet to help written expression. Complex technologies such as eye-gaze computer systems, voice-to-text systems, or switch interface (with scanning software) may warrant investigation. Students in motorized (power) wheelchairs often have sufficiently sophisticated electronics to interface with computer systems and provide an alternate means of accessing the academic curriculum. A school-based OT, in collaboration with team members, has a responsibility to stay current about the new advances and ever-changing technologies as they become available in order to ensure that technology continues to match the changing needs of the student with CP.

OTs are dedicated to ensuring that students with CP have motor, sensory, and/or cognitive opportunities to physically interact with classroom materials. Interacting with and controlling the physical environment, with or without adaptations and assistive technologies, adds meaning to activities, enhances learning, and maximizes satisfaction.

Simple modifications that are easy to set up and be used in multiple settings of the school environment are important for students with CP. Stabilizing a classroom object on a stationary surface eases access, as the object "stays put" when the student swipes toward it. The materials and tools themselves can be adapted with straps and hooks to facilitate grasp. Object size, shape, texture, and weight may also be modified—for example, knob-shaped paintbrushes or pull strings attached to locker doors. Electronic or battery-operated equipment may be adapted to allow for single-switch access.

In the school setting, the OT plays a crucial role in teaching staff and students alternate ways of performing everyday school tasks. Simple adaptations and sophisticated assistive technology provide the student with CP the opportunity for skill practice and generalization of skills. Teaching students how to accurately communicate their needs, receive the necessary level of assistance, and maximize participation and independence (for even a portion of an activity) helps to strengthen skills and add student satisfaction. Even the most physically disabled student desires to be actively involved in some aspect of their daily classroom activity, even when this participation must be facilitated by others. These students, more than any others, need to move their arms and hands in a variety of ways to preserve flexibility, deepen sensation, and give greater meaning to their time spent in the classroom.

The following are low-to-moderate modifications frequently used by OTs who serve students with CP:

- Standard and nonstandard computer keyboards, modified by shape, size, color, and texture, that enable typing when fine motor and/or visual challenges make typing difficult
- Modified pens and pencils with or without grips that ease manual writing
- Whenever possible, encouraging the student to work bimanually (using both hands) when holding a book, supporting a paper while writing, and manipulating a toy or game

When Does a Student with CP Need Assistive Technology?

- A student's gross motoric positioning and fine motor limitations preclude the use of typical educational tools and strategies.
- A student's handwriting is consistently labored, uncomfortable, and barely legible, and it fails to produce a satisfying and effective output for both the writer and the reader.
- The student struggles to develop organizational skills.
- The student's comprehension and functional use of letters and numbers is challenged by motoric and/or sensory difficulties.
- Students with CP may experience attention and concentration difficulties when using instructional materials that are designed for neurotypical learners.

SECTION III

The Speech Therapist

Adine R. Usher

Effective communication, whether through speech, body language, art, or music, lies at the heart of the human experience and is essential to lifelong independence, feelings of personal satisfaction, academic achievement, and social and emotional competence.

Although a truly complex ability, speech can be simply categorized as symbolic or nonsymbolic. Symbolic speech refers to spoken words, symbols that represent words, and sign language. Nonsymbolic speech is found in utterances, facial expressions, gestures, and body language.

Verbal communication challenges in CP vary in type and intensity; however, students need to be provided with the tools that enable them to express their needs, feelings, preferences, thoughts, and knowledge. Doing so enhances self-worth, confidence, and the hope of becoming meaningful members of the wider society.

With guidance from families and collaboration between the speech therapist (often referred to as speech pathologist) and other team members, the classroom teacher can learn to identify and deal effectively with CP-related challenges of producing spoken, *expressive* language. Other students with CP encounter difficulty with language development involving the complex processes of perceiving, comprehending, and interpreting language; this is referred to as *receptive language*. Both expressive and receptive language challenges can exist concurrently with other sensory-perceptual challenges. These difficulties are thought to arise because of damage to neurons in the motor cortex and in other intersecting neural pathways that include the frontal and left temporal lobes. It is thought that nearly 50 percent of students with CP exhibit some degree and form of speech challenges.[179]

Mild to Moderate Expressive Communication Challenges

Students with mild to moderate CP-related communication challenges who use natural speech may still encounter difficult articulation and expressive and receptive language processes. These students need teachers who understand the exact nature and scope of the student's communication strengths and challenges and who are willing to identify and lower environmental communication barriers and alter accustomed teaching practices to better accommodate the student's communication needs.

Mild to moderate speech challenges that are apparent during academic lessons can impact learning, performance, and self-confidence. Classroom teachers should be alert to the ways in which CP-related communication challenges can hinder peer relationships and, consequently, healthy emotional growth. It is in these classroom settings that the keen observation and intervention of the speech therapist is of critical value.

In addition to individual speech therapy, these students may need therapist-facilitated, small conversation groups comprising peers who either share the student's expressive challenges or are neurotypical. In either situation, the peers must be encouraged to exhibit patience as the student with CP learns to communicate effectively. If the student is observed to be having trouble negotiating peer-to peer communication, it is well not to simply assume that they can correct the situation without skilled adult intervention.

Conversation strategies employed in one-on-one speech therapy sessions can be replicated in classrooms, in lunchrooms, and on the playground. Extracurricular activities such as drama, sports, and choral music provide additional means for expanded interaction, for building confidence, and for applying consistent communication opportunities.

Students with mild to moderate CP-related verbal communication difficulties may, in their early elementary years, need low to moderate technical communicative support to supplement their natural speech. These low-tech systems must be available to the student throughout the school day, and their operation should be well understood by all who work with the student. Rather than serving as a crutch that hinders the development of articulate speech (as is feared by some parents), these simple communication systems may relieve some of the stress and tension associated with communication difficulties and can reduce the kind of frustration that may lead to nonproductive behaviors. Low-tech solutions can motivate the youngster with CP to attempt greater social interaction and verbal communication with peers and adults.

Significant Communication Challenges in Students with Average Cognitive Ability

Approximately 20 percent of students who are diagnosed with CP have difficulty producing comprehendible speech (dysarthria).[180] Complex verbal communication issues exert a significant impact on the academic and personal lives of these students. The inability to produce articulate, intelligible speech comes from weak fine muscle control in the face, tongue, throat, and neck. Weakness in the chest muscles that control breathing exacerbates the situation. Sensory and cognitive status may also influence the quality of articulate communication.[181]

Students with dysarthric speech, who have difficulty producing smooth, uninterrupted, fluent speech, or those who are nonverbal learn to use varied and alternative ways of communicating with those who are closest to them, usually family members.

There appears to be an association between the ability to produce speech and levels of gross motor functioning in CP subtypes. Although a high proportion of nonverbal students have concomitant intellectual disabilities, it is very important for educators to understand that there is *no* automatic correlation between dysarthria, nonverbal status, and reduced cognition. Nonverbal status does not mean that a student is incapable of learning.

Communication with those outside of the family can be exceptionally challenging for nonverbal students, and paths that support communication with nonfamily members depend on the needs of the environment, the willingness of others to communicate, and the availability of and training on devices that support alternative communication.

Regardless of the complexity and extent of a student's communication challenges, it is unacceptable to leave them with no or limited means of communication. We need to appreciate the difficulty of "interpreting" what a nonverbal student is trying to say, as eye gaze and body movements are hard to interpret. Besides the skilled intervention of a speech therapist, other therapists, parents, and classroom staff should always look for indicators of communicative intent. Therefore, it remains the school's responsibility to see that every conceivable avenue of alternative communication be explored and encouraged, including both low- and high-technology solutions, gestures, facial expressions, and utterances.

Teachers and peers who have neurotypical speech may find it difficult and unsettling to communicate with a student with dysarthria, or they may simply *pretend* to understand what the student is attempting to say and then proceed to speak *for* the student. The inability to smoothly communicate with teachers can reduce the quality of a student's learning and significantly limit opportunities.

Students with dysarthria can expend considerable energy attempting to communicate and subsequently can become exhausted and frustrated when unable to make themselves understood. In some instances, this fatigue and frustration leads to unacceptable behaviors or to the conscious decision to limit communication attempts. Dysarthria requires speech therapists to work on improving the following conditions: use of rhythm, low pitch (prosody), phonation, nasal resonance, intonation, harsh-sounding vocalization with limited pitch variation, shallow and irregular breathing, jaw movement, and reduced pockets of residual air that make it difficult to rapidly produce, articulate, and extend whole utterances during one short breath.[182]

Stuttering, when combined with dysarthric speech, only makes it more difficult for a student to communicate, and when both conditions are severe, the student may simply retreat from attempts at verbal communication. Therapy for stuttering for a student with dysarthria may not be easily found; however, if one is needed, every effort should be exerted to find a specialist who can address this challenge.

Perseveration (neurologically based, repetitive speech patterns) can slow and complicate the communication process.

Communication Challenges with Intellectual Disability

Some students with CP have significant intellectual disabilities in addition to movement and medical challenges, a condition that impedes their ability to articulate feelings, thoughts, and needs. For this population, switch-activated toys and low-tech communication interventions are effective. Their use is predicated on careful observation and ongoing analysis of *how, when,* and *what* the student is capable of understanding and responding to in various settings.

Observation of communication patterns helps speech therapists, classroom teachers, assistants, OTs, PTs, and parents to closely examine the verbal and nonverbal choices a student uses daily. Recorded observations then provide a solid basis for crafting interventions. When successful, these interventions can be carried forward and generalized into novel situations and settings.

Many students with intellectual disabilities and CP are very or totally dependent on others for their physical care and management. This care is too often performed in silence, thereby denying the student the full awareness of another's presence. Speak to these students continually and in an age-appropriate manner in the following situations:

- When they are being fed, explain what you and they are doing.
- As you dress them, talk to them about their clothes.
- Speak with them as their toileting needs are being met.
- Describe the characteristics of toy and instructional tools as they are presented and explored.
- Use language to make these students more aware of their social and physical surroundings.
- Encourage families and caretakers to talk to these students.
- Use spoken and sung language to elicit interest, curiosity, and the joy of human contact.
- Acknowledge and respond to all the student's attempts to communicate.
- Accept that with this population, most communication will be nonverbal.

Receptive Language Disorders

Some students with CP encounter difficulty understanding the meaning of spoken language. They have difficulty making sense of and replicating the (pragmatic) speech they hear from others. While some receptive language disorders are directly related to losses in hearing acuity, others are perceptual in origin and can significantly affect comprehension, memory, and social interaction. Some receptive language challenges experienced by students with CP are

- Finding words needed for self-expression.
- Initiating and maintaining conversations.
- Naming objects.
- Requesting or making choices.
- Comprehending and describing abstract concepts.
- Comprehending what is read.

These challenges may go unnoticed if the student with CP becomes adept at watching and following peers.

Language delays in CP, even in the absence of articulation problems, have many causes. Some delays may be attributed to a student's general limited attention to language in both the school and home environments. Other delays may be attributed to a student's difficulty sustaining conversation from lack of practice and limited social and experiential exposure. It is not uncommon for concentration on a student's physical and medical management to reduce cognitive attention, resulting in limited emotional and conversational interaction with the student.

Speech is inextricably tied to memory; therefore, problems with short-term memory and rote recall can negatively impact language development.

The varied associated conditions of CP, while not always clearly understood, often appear to be interrelated. Kathryn Straub and John Obrzut cite research that suggests that, in some cases, there might be a correlation between hand impairment and deficits in phonological and visuospatial skills.

Oral-motor problems also may appear suggestive of phonological deficits. Altered visual perception can distort the effective collaboration between vision and hearing, thereby reducing the comprehension of language.[183]

For students with all subtypes of CP, speech therapy aims to improve low pitch, poor breath control, and imprecise articulation.[184] The speech therapist, working one-on-one, in small groups, or in classroom settings, meets these challenges with a wide variety of exercises that are tailored to the exact nature of a student's needs and designed to improve verbal communication over a period of years.

Classroom Supports for Expressive and Receptive Language Challenges

Use simple language and break down instructions into smaller steps.

- Slow the pacing of your speech.
- Speak in shorter phrases.
- Speak dramatically.
- Exploit the use of meaningful facial expressions and as well as body language itself.
- Realize that the student may need to have the response time extended.
- Encourage alternative methods of response, such as switch scanning, pointing, eye gaze, body signaling, and vocal utterances.
- Repeat instructions; provide additional cues, such as gestures, pictures, and written words; or demonstrate what you are doing.
- To ensure understanding, ask the student to repeat the instruction or respond in *any* effective manner.
- Encourage the student to ask for help if instructions have not been understood, using all modes of response.
- Encourage all attempts at communication and provide opportunities for students to demonstrate understanding in their own, perhaps atypical, way.

- Use expressive language strategies that help the student to find the right word or thought.
- Learn and use sign language.

Low-technology systems are used by many students with CP-related verbal communication challenges. These systems enable the student with articulation challenges (which may be accompanied by breathing and swallowing disorders) and writing difficulties caused by both gross and fine motor challenges to leave the isolation of their own bodies and initiate social connections, make choices, register disapproval, learn early language rules, and become grounded in the fundamentals of learning to read, spell, compute, write, tell stories, and recount events.[185] Here are some examples of low-tech communication devices and strategies used for verbal communication:

- Nonelectronic or minimally electronic devices such as communication boards, chat books, schedule boards, conversation books, talking toys and games—as well as pictures, symbols, photos, words, and/or concrete objects and toys that can be placed on laptop trays, tables, and magnetic boards
- Digitally based graphic organizers for writing
- Toys and switches with voice output and handheld systems that have preprogrammed messages
- Sign language
- Uniquely individual strategies of nonverbal communication, including hand pointing, head or mouth pointers, light pointers, and distinctly understood body motions that indicate yes or no

Multilevel Systems of Assistive Technology (AT) and Augmentative and Alternative Communication (AAC)

With the certainty that students with CP have more strengths than we can initially see, we need to be willing to reach past the more obvious aspects of communication disabilities to release what may be a hidden core of student thoughts and feelings. This requires the constant employment of every conceivable form of low, medium, and high technology that encourages and supports student communication. These devices, both aided and unaided, bolster a student's self-esteem, enable more independent performance, reduce the impact of CP-related communication barriers, and place students with CP in closer proximity to social and recreational interactions of classroom life.

The fields of electronic and digital communication systems are constantly growing and changing. New devices address a wide range of individual needs, are becoming easier to acquire, and are more affordable. Often, after extensive assessment, when they are deemed essential to the educational process, these devices are included in a student's IEP and paid for either by the school district or by insurance. This assessment process will often go through a period of trial and error before the most effective and efficient communication device is found. It is common for a student to use several types of systems for communication.

The student with CP who has had early intervention and preschool instruction hopefully arrives in first grade with a well-laid-out educational plan. This plan spurs the creation of a profile that includes the rationale for providing adaptations and modification, and it must closely track the student's ability to effectively use low- and high-tech adaptive devices.

In many locations, the task of assessing a student's need for *assistive technology (AT)* and *augmentative and alternative communication (AAC)* systems falls to regional technology centers that assess the student's performance on various systems, make recommendations to local schools and families, help the school to acquire the systems, and commit themselves to the extensive training of staff, family, and student.

Although provisions for funding may vary, when the need for AT is established, it is written into the student's educational plan and supplied by the local school system. Special schools that serve students with CP usually have their own technology specialists on staff.

Students with moderate to significant CP will use a combination of low-tech and high-tech digital systems that serve their changing needs to read, speak, and write throughout their school years.

In the broadest sense, AT includes any device external to the student's body that aids their participation in *all* areas of school activities and helps the student to access the curriculum through physical, sensory, intellectual, and social modalities. In a global sense, AT refers to a product that is commercially bought or made in the school or home setting and that enables the student with CP to increase and improve functioning. In this section, AT refers to those devices that enable the student with CP to read, write, and speak more effectively, since reading and writing, in addition to speaking, are themselves tools of communication.

Although larger appliances, such as wheelchairs, walkers, crutches, standers, adaptive furniture, and orthotics that assist students with gross motor challenges, all fall under the category of assistive technology, they have been more specifically discussed in chapter 2.

There exists a continuum of support from simple teacher-made or commercially prepared, modified teaching materials, games, and toys to simple low-tech instructional and communication devices and, finally, to the most advanced digital hardware and software that supports every aspect of the academic and social curricula. Sophisticated digital hardware and software enables students who can neither speak nor write to communicate with degrees of satisfying effectiveness at an age-appropriate level.

The effectiveness of the technology requires continual assessment, alteration, and adaptation as physical, medical, academic, and social needs arise and change. The fear that these supports might become a crutch that would impede a student's ability or desire to function more traditionally is generally unfounded and may reflect parental difficulty in accepting the reality of the student's condition. However, technology should not supplant the development of skills that, in time, can be learned. Once the need for AT is determined, first try the simplest-to-use device that supports an academic goal.

When hand and finger access is not possible, AT devices permit alternative physical access to activating digital communication systems. These systems use head-control, eye-gaze, knee-control, foot-control, and breath-control systems on switches that control visual and auditory output on computers of any size. The systems not only enhance the user's ability to choose and share letters, words, numbers, and pictures but also control the movement of a wheelchair and other devices of daily living in the environment. These systems reduce stress and fatigue and, most importantly, endow a student with CP a stronger presence in the world. Students gain the opportunity to learn from and interact with their environments with greater safety, comfort, efficiency, and independence. Using the innovative interventions of biomedical and engineering research, one can only imagine the development of future creative strategies that will make life easier for individuals with CP.

Augmentative and alternative communication (AAC) encompasses every type of communication except oral speech, and it gives the student with CP an alternative to speech when speech is not an effective tool. From a simple picture to the most sophisticated computer that allows for the storage and retrieval of messages and contains many pages, AAC systems allow users to communicate with the world. (Dedicated AAC systems are designed specifically for communication, and nondedicated systems are computers that serve multiple purposes.)

Speech therapists are conversant with the multiple and ever-changing improvements in types of high-tech AAC systems and carefully match them to the student's needs. Speech therapists use these devices to improve student access to basic academic skills, strengthen functional daily-living skills, and expand limited socialization opportunities to prevent the isolation of students from the nuances of social communication with peers in both special and inclusive settings.

Determining the most comfortable and effective mode of student access to AAC systems is of paramount importance, and even under the guidance of the speech therapist, the systems may take years to master. However, as the systems are mastered, with appropriate professional training for all who interact with the student, their use promises independence and access to work opportunities as students with CP reach adulthood.

Typically, students who rely on AAC systems do not use them in family settings. More recently, speech therapists are encouraging greater use of AAC systems outside of the school, thereby strengthening the proficiency of communication along with the continued use of vocalizations, body language, and sign language.

Medium and high AT and AAC devices may be programmed to accommodate and circumvent the verbal communication, visual, auditory, tactile, and gross and fine motor challenges that students with CP often encounter, and their successful use is predicated on the quality of training, individual skills, and student motivation. Besides speaking and writing for the students, these devices offer them access to vast subject-related vocabularies. Students can actively engage in the normal question-and-response flow of instruction and can strengthen their development of math skills, language arts, and writing by using

- Body parts, switches, and joysticks to allow access and indicate responses
- Alternative computer mice and modified or adaptive keyboards
- Computers that respond to changes in eye gaze
- Devices that record instructional material for later use
- Language boards
- Tactile symbols for students whose CP includes visual challenges
- Watches used for transition training and reinforcement when needed
- Voice-to-text computer systems that don't tax a student's voice
- Print-to-speech software
- Software packages that present appropriately enlarged, highlighted, and uncluttered visual presentation of pictures, words, numbers, music notes, and picture symbols (icons)
- Touch screens

- Multiple methods that control the ability to scan a screen
- Wheelchair mounts for communication devices that are safe and functional, both inside and outside
- Switch control of cell phones
- Modifiable digital textbooks in subject areas
- Wireless page-turning devices

Here is how to use technology to lower the barriers created by dysarthric speech:

- Starting at an early age, provide intense speech therapy coupled with access to and the continuous use of low-, medium-, and high-tech communication systems.
- Program into the communication devices the answers to instructional questions.
- Coordinate and create an interface between all the student's digital equipment.
- Prepare the student to give oral reports to the class using digital devices.
- Call on students that are dysarthric, give them a choice of simple responses, and then wait for that response.
- Program into AAC systems, in game format, questions that the student with CP can ask their classmates.
- Program age-appropriate conversations into communication devices and then make sure that they are used daily.
- Give students jobs and assignments around the school that require communication with less familiar individuals.
- Provide scripts that are programmed into communication devices that promote engagement in the class, the school, and the community.

The school's responsibilities include the following:

- Make certain that every member of the classroom staff is knowledgeable about and comfortable with the operation of the student's AT and AAC systems.

- Acknowledge that time and consistency are needed to gain student and staff efficacy in the operation of many devices.
- As much as possible, encourage and enable students to always keep their communication systems with them.
- Make certain that all homework that needs to be digitized is consistently prepared in a digital format.
- School systems that serve students with CP should engage a speech therapist and an OT who are knowledgeable and up to date in the use of AT and AAC communication.
- These specialists need to establish connections with local technology centers who can aid in the performance of AAC assessments and help in the acquisition of appropriate devices.
- Speech teachers and technology specialists should implement effective, ongoing training for students, teacher, assistants, and parents.
- It is essential that several individuals on the student's team be able to program high-tech devices and make certain that they are consistently synchronized with the contents of a student's academic program.
- High-tech devices can be expected to break down; therefore, a support system needs to be in place, not only for timely repairs but also for the acquisition of loaner devices that ensure a continuity of instruction and learning for the student.
- Enlist all members of the transdisciplinary team to devise ways of collaborating on the student's communication needs.
- Write functional communication goals for AAC systems into the IEP that address social and learning interactions throughout the school day.
- Regularly analyze and monitor the effectiveness of communication device interventions.
- Train a team composed of the speech therapist, the classroom teacher, and the OT to appropriately program the software on AAC devices,

thus ensuring access to all academic and nonacademic domains.

- Begin AT and AAC training when children begin to speak, since it takes years to develop the skills to use assistive tech effectively and independently outside of the school setting.

The functional use of AT and AAC devices should be equally weighted between academic and functional social communication. Many students with CP will be, to various degrees, dependent on aides for support during the school day, and it is the responsibility of these assistants and the classroom teacher to guide neurotypical peers in respecting, understanding, and engaging in conversations with students who communicate in atypical ways.

There are too many students with CP who communicate only with adults at school. The attempt to foster communication between neurotypical students and students with significant communication difficulties becomes more challenging as students advance in the grades, since older students mediate their own social connections. However, it is of paramount importance that technical and nontechnical interventions be crafted and that communication partners be found and trained so that the student with CP is not isolated but becomes an integral part of the class and school.

Students with CP who have significant communication difficulties in special education settings will also benefit from structured social group communication activities where many of the students rely on AT and AAC devices. These structured groups provide social motivation and functional practice and reduce isolation and dependence on others while giving the student some power and control in both home and school environments.

When both external environmental conditions and the internal realities of CP make it difficult for students to move, sit, stand, speak, write, hear, and see, ways must be found not only to enable these students to approach these skills as independently as possible but also to help them to diminish the effects of their disability by exerting some degree of power and control over their environments, both comfortably and effectively. AAC systems provide this power.

Here are some general thoughts on AT and AAC usage:

- Using AT does not prevent a student from eventually developing more typical speaking, reading, and writing skills if that eventuality is possible.

- AT and AAC systems are effective aids that enable the students with CP to reach outside of themselves and begin to connect to people and objects in their environments.

- AT programs that use speech-to-text or word-prediction software that prompts the writing process further enable reading, organizing, and writing.

- Many students with CP use AAC technology only in formal, instructional settings but unfortunately not in social settings.

- AT and AAC systems can be consistently used along with natural speech and sign language.

- From the earliest age, provide consistent use of appropriate low- and high-tech AT and AAC devices.

- Technical communication solutions should be effective, interesting, interactive, and integrated into academic lessons, play experiences, and social opportunities.

- Allow for sufficient setup, instructional, and transitional time for AT and AAC devices.

- When home-based communication strategies are effective and considered rational, effort should be made to implement them in school.

- Speech therapists who serve students with CP will want to be aware of and use evidence-based practices that revolve around AT and AAC.

The Speech and Hearing Connection

There is a correlation between speech production, language development and processing, and the status of a student's hearing. Some 15 to 20 percent of students with CP experience some degree of either *conductive* or *sensorineural* hearing impairments,[186] which can affect a student's speech, communication skills, academic performance, and socialization. A student with CP can also have mixed hearing loss involving both conductive and sensorineural impairments.

The difficulty of producing intelligible sounds may also influence the quality of the sounds the student hears (phonology) and attempts to produce. Even if the student's hearing acuity is intact, distorted speech production, as in dysarthria, can distort a student's perception of their own speech and suggests the need for skilled, modified reading and speech instruction.[187] Spelling also requires a degree of auditory decoding that some in this CP population, because of articulation problems, may find quite challenging.

The speech therapist, with or without the active support of a hearing therapist, needs a thorough understanding of the student's hearing status. This understanding will be strengthened by the results of an auditory evaluation that

- Measures the student's response to sound through speakers.
- Tests the flexibility of eardrums.
- Tests the workings of the tiny hairs in the inner ear.
- Examines the functioning of hearing nerves.
- Looks for processing disorders where the ears and the brain fail to coordinate the meaning of sounds.

Speech therapists and other team members often recommend the use of FM systems in classrooms when students with CP need amplification of voices, as ambient noises can affect hearing and understanding. Many students with CP use hearing aids, and some acquire cochlear implants that may vastly improve hearing and consequently improve speech. Classroom seating for hard-of-hearing students with CP should position each student near teachers and other support personnel, who in turn should constantly be aware of this need for proximity whenever adults are delivering important information. For these students, developing lipreading skills may also be introduced into a student's program.

Teachers, in collaboration with speech therapists and other members of the transdisciplinary team, must exert every possible effort, through a thorough understanding of the mechanisms of speech and hearing and AAC systems, to enable students with CP, regardless of age, severity, and nature of the communication challenges, to build independence in their ability to communicate thoughts, knowledge, needs, and feelings in both academic and social modalities.

The Speech Therapist and Feeding

Much of the musculature that controls speech also controls chewing and swallowing. When chewing and swallowing are impaired, speech therapists share their awareness of the concomitant health and safety problems of delayed growth, insufficient nutrition, poor hydration, fear of choking, and the danger of aspirating food. Therefore, these specialists work closely with caregivers and other team members, including aides and paraprofessionals, to improve the student's ability to chew and swallow and to make certain that the student is properly hydrated.

SECTION IV

The Vision Therapist

Adine R. Usher

An acute awareness of the prevalence of visual impairments in populations of students with CP necessitates the need for visual assessments, corrective or therapeutic treatments, the establishment of a learning environment that considers a student's unique visual profile, and the use of instructional strategies and curricular materials that lower the barriers of vision difficulties for students with CP.

The medical and surgical responses to difficulties with visual acuity and oculomotor functions (eye movement), following an assessment, are provided by medical professionals called *ophthalmologists*. Following their medical interventions and often recommendations for glasses, they ideally share their findings and recommendations with transdisciplinary team members who daily strive to improve the potentially complex visual functioning of the student with CP. In-depth discussion of visual impairments in populations of students with CP is further developed in chapter 5.

Although there continues to be strong disagreement between ophthalmologists and *optometrists* over the value and efficacy of vision therapy,[188,] [189] many parents reach outside of the school setting (if vision therapy is not provided by a school) to secure private vision therapy sessions provided by a *developmental optometrist* who is trained to target the effects of oculomotor visual processing and integration and visual-perception difficulties in students with CP.

If a school system has access to a vision specialist, that person may work regularly with students with CP whose visual profile includes one or several of the following visual issues: convergence of both eyes, difficulties with eye tracking, focusing, and visual processing. Laterality, visual discrimination, directionality, visual sequential memory, spatial relationships, and visual motor integration are all skills that are essential for learning and movement.[190]

With or without the services of a vision specialist and using guidance from formal assessments, informal assessments, and observations, OTs and classroom teachers are responsible for creating a visually supportive educational environment for the student with CP. This environment reflects a thorough understanding of the student's visual issues by limiting or eliminating visual barriers that are usually not a problem for the neurotypical student. Classroom teachers, with the support of the OT, PT, and other team members, will employ vision strategies recommended by team members, especially by the OT, as part of their instructional interventions to enhance the student's academic, pragmatic, and visual motor efficiency.

The student with CP who has minor or complex visual challenges is optimally served when a school can provide access to vision-enhancing assistive technology. The choice of low, intermediate, or high technology that enlarges, simplifies, reduces background distractions, and highlights letters, numbers, and pictures is determined by the scope and severity of a student's individual visual needs. Background color may have to be coordinated with a student's visual status.

Educators who seek appropriate vision aids for students with CP in both specialized and inclusive settings should also seek additional guidance from teachers of the visually impaired.

Types of Visual Aids That Can Help Students with CP

Some of the following visual aids can offer improved academic products: computers, tablets, modified keyboards, magnifiers, tactile and auditory devices, audiobooks, adaptive and modified computer software, head pointers and stick pointers for tracking, touch screens, Morse code switches, word-prediction software, augmentative and alternative communication (AAC) systems, and voice-recognition software.

Because these visual aids and devices offer a wide variety of font sizes, appropriately contrasting colors, shapes, spacing, and icons and picture presentations, students with CP are given an opportunity to master, to the best of their ability, educational, self-care, independence, and social tasks.

SECTION V

The School Nurse

Judy Portelli

The primary and secondary conditions of cerebral palsy require medical monitoring and interventions if students are to be safe and comfortably benefit from an educational experience. The school nurse, when available, becomes critical in managing these medical needs. In addition to being an ongoing source of information for school personnel who need to fully understand how a student's CP affects his or her schooling, the school nurse provides direct services to the student with CP and frequently acts as an intermediary between home and school in matters of physical well-being, health, and safety.

Nursing responsibilities fall under the following general categories:

- Administering medications.
- Assessing student health status.
- Responding to medical alerts.
- Monitoring feeding procedures.
- Monitoring challenges with elimination.
- Taking on additional educational roles:
    - Providing medical management support that promotes student independence.
    - Optimizing health by placing students in effective learning positions.
    - Offering professional development.
    - Working with families.

The delivery of these school-based nursing services to students with CP varies throughout the world and is greatly dependent on national and local policies, on financial allocations, and on the availability of qualified nursing professionals.

Administering Medications

Up to 50 percent of students with CP have seizures. These seizures can vary in severity, and many students need anticonvulsant medication from school nurses because failure to consistently control these seizures can increase cognitive decline and be life-threatening. Side effects from anticonvulsant medicines that may interfere with learning can include behavior alterations and may decrease levels of attention and precipitate mood swings.

Many students with CP were born prematurely and therefore have chronic lung disease because of lung injury secondary to treatment. In these instances, and for the many students with CP who have asthma, the nurse may have to administer nebulizer treatments.

Pain is unfortunately common for students with CP, and the school nurse may administer over-the-counter or prescription medications that reduce the pain of spasticity, contractures, pressure ulcers, or frequent surgeries as well as reduce the discomfort of the stiffness that results from sitting in a wheelchair for long periods. The nurse may also, in consultation with the PT, recommend tilting wheelchairs (to redistribute weight) and removing students from wheelchairs prior to medicating.

Assessing Student Health Status

Students with CP exhibit a variety of visual and hearing deficits—50 percent and 25 percent, respectively. The school nurse, in collaboration with other specialists, may be called upon to assist with screenings and assessments. Ongoing observation and assessments for scoliosis, which affects up to 25 percent of the population, and hip subluxation (dislocation), found in up to 60 percent of students with spastic CP, are also the responsibility of the school nurse in collaboration with the PT.

Responding to Medical Alerts

Seizures:

The school nurse plays a critical role in helping the classroom teacher, and concurrently other students, in responding to seizures that occur in school. In collaboration with parents and physicians, the nurse (who is usually called at the onset of a seizure) has previously made certain that the teacher understands the underlying neurological causes of seizures, knows the student's seizure history, and is physically and emotionally prepared to safely support the student with CP during a seizure episode. The nurse will also have prepared the other students to anticipate what may happen if a seizure occurs and even encourage students to notice and report their observation of staring, which may precede a student's seizure. This preparation has the effect of reducing student fears and enlisting peer aid in moving aside potentially dangerous furniture.

The nurse determines that a safe environment has been created, optimally with the student placed on their side, away from objects that could cause injury. While the seizure is occurring, the other students should be removed from the room. The nurse times the seizure and documents the student's movements and breathing. (The staff member who witnesses the seizure should begin the timing at its onset.) In cases where seizures are prolonged, abortive medication (if the student has it on hand) may be administered by the nurse to shorten a seizure.

Throughout this entire process, the nurse will speak calmingly and reassuringly to the student, then provide a quiet, private area where the student can recover from the seizure. With more difficult-to-control seizures, the nurse may work with the neurologist to share recorded observations in an effort to identify seizure type and, if necessary, alter medications.

Choking:

A school nurse, in consultation with a speech and language specialist and the assistant who feeds the student with CP, must discuss all precautions to avoid the risk of choking in students who have difficulty with oral-motor control that includes swallowing saliva.

Intrathecal baclofen pump malfunction:

Malfunction of the intrathecal baclofen pump can occur in those students with more severe spastic CP whose families have opted to have the pump surgically implanted. The pump is placed in the abdominal cavity and the tubing in the *intrathecal space* in the spine. Running by itself, the pump reduces spasticity by delivering a continuous flow of baclofen to the student's system. A malfunctioning pump can deliver too much baclofen, or if the tubing gets kinked or if the reservoir empties, the student abruptly stops getting baclofen, thus causing baclofen withdrawal. Minor responses to this situation are drowsiness, nausea, headache, muscle weakness, a return of spasticity, or light-headedness. More severe reactions to baclofen withdrawal include *hyperthermia*, seizures, *disseminated intravascular coagulation,* multisystem organ failure, cardiac arrest, coma, and death.

With guidance from the school nurse, the classroom teacher and staff are made aware of these signs of trouble and can alert the nurse, who then intervenes either by administering oral baclofen (which should always be on hand) or by getting the student to the doctor or hospital.

Shunt malfunction:

Some students with CP have concurrent or resultant *hydrocephalus* (a buildup of cerebral spinal fluid [CSF] that is not circulating, unobstructed, through the brain and around the spinal cord). These students require the implantation of *brain shunts* (brain drains), which direct CSF from the brain to organs in the body's core for fluid elimination. Typically, they are *ventriculoperitoneal shunts.* It is essential that teachers and classroom staff be alerted to the signs of shunt malfunction. Failure to do so could result in the student's death. Training teachers to recognize the following warning signs is the role of the school nurse:

- Subtle changes in behavior, with a student simply "not looking right," which may indicate the beginning of a shunt problem
- Headaches
- Fever
- Vomiting
- Altered states of consciousness or disorientation
- An altered appearance of eye pupils in the later stages of shunt malfunction

Respiratory difficulty:

The school nurse will make certain that the student with CP, their parents, and school staff are well informed about the need for pulmonary care and the potential for pneumonia and aspiration. Students with CP may occasionally need to receive oxygen or be suctioned during the day to clear their airways. The school nurse will perform and/or monitor the administration of these treatments.

Monitoring Feeding Procedures

Some students with CP receive *gastrostomy tube (G-tube)* feeding because of their inability to safely take food by mouth. These feedings of formula, or blended, food use either a formula-filled syringe to administer a bolus (dose) from a can of food or a continuous-feed pump that sends formula through feeding tubes into the stomach or intestines. Part of these feedings may occur in the classroom, but the teacher and assistants must be alert for vomiting and (providing they are trained) should immediately turn off the pump if this occurs. If staff members are not comfortable touching medical equipment, they should either bring the student to the nurse or call the nurse to start the process.

The school nurse will monitor these feedings, making certain that the staff responsible for feeding the student is doing so properly. The nurse will determine that the student is kept in an upright sitting position during the feeding and for thirty minutes after the feeding. In collaboration with team members, the nurse will ensure that physical therapy is not scheduled directly after feedings.

Monitoring Challenges with Elimination

Urinary and bowel incontinence are quite common in populations of students with CP, and the nurse—in consultation with parents, teachers, aides, and therapists—will contribute to toileting management solutions. In order to build toileting independence, and through using repetitious attempts, toilet training needs to begin as soon as feasible. Creating bathroom schedules at two- to three-hour intervals is one strategy. The nurse will also encourage some parents of students with CP to consult with a neurologist, since toileting challenges result from brain-based *neuromuscular* dysfunction. Constipation and potential bowel obstructions can also become issues of concern, and bowel movements may have to be documented by the staff member who provides toileting assistance.

School nurses will also monitor fluid intake for students with CP (and encourage staff to be aware of this issue), since incontinence and immobility leave them at increased risk for urinary tract infections (UTIs). This concern may be magnified if the student has oral-motor difficulties, has difficulty swallowing (dysphagia), or may not be sufficiently hydrated.

Students with CP who have little or no control of urinary function because the messages from the nerves in the brain and the spine fail to signal the bladder to tighten or release have *neurogenic bladder dysfunction.* The school nurse, in collaboration with the OT, will explain this condition to the student and carry out catheterization, which drains urine from the bladder, or when the student's fine motor coordination allows, teach the student how to perform self-catheterization. If a school nurse is not present, parents or other designated caretakers will perform this responsibility.

The staff member responsible for providing toileting assistance needs to be alert to signs of skin redness, pressure areas, rashes, possible infections, and/or signs of potential abuse. All this information is reported to the nurse.

Taking On Additional Educational Roles

When a new student with CP starts school, the school nurse reviews the medical information on the student for all concerns and conditions related to the diagnosis that impact the student's well-being and their ability to benefit from the educational program. Ensuring that the teachers know all they must about the student, the nurse creates alert cards and lists and enters detailed up-to-date descriptions in the student's educational plan to document important health and safety considerations.

The school nurse also joins other members of the transdisciplinary team in supporting parents who experience difficulties managing the student's CP. The nurse discourages parents from sending a sick student to school, because return transportation during the school day may be difficult or impossible to accomplish.

In the absence of a school nurse and depending upon local and state regulations, in-school responsibilities that are usually carried out by licensed nurses may have to be performed by parents, assistants, or members of the teaching faculty. Indeed, in many areas of the world where the needs of students with CP are not easily accommodated, mothers are unable to work outside of the home, because they bear full responsibility for school health-care tasks.

SECTION VI

Psychosocial Support: Psychologists, Counselors, and Social Workers

Ronald Friedman and Elizabeth Viducich

School Psychologists and Counselors

In a perfect world, students with disabilities and their families would have access to as-needed, lifelong, supportive services of psychologists, counselors, and social workers. These services are of particular importance for students with CP and their families, considering the impact that CP-related conditions can exert on cognition, movement, health, communication, and social-emotional health and overall development. Additionally, psychologists, counselors, and social workers help teachers to understand a student's pressures, realities, and hidden potential more fully. Counseling provided by psychologists and school counselors addresses student anger and frustration and offers coping skills to manage these feelings.

In the school setting, the psychologist may assume one or both of two primary roles: that of a diagnostician, who administers and interprets educational and/or neuropsychological assessments, and that of a clinician, who provides individual or small-group counseling to a student with developmental disabilities, including CP. The school counselor is a certified or licensed educator who performs short-term counseling and works with the transdisciplinary team to advance the student's unique educational and social-emotional needs as they move through the school program.

The following describes the role of one school psychologist:

> In his diagnostic role, Dr. Ronald Friedman, an experienced child psychologist at a special school for students with physical disabilities describes how an assessment of a student with athetoid CP in an inclusion program confounded a psychologist who was less experienced with this population. The student, while intelligible, had speech and language deficits. She had fine motor issues but could write, eat finger food, and walk short distances before she needed her wheelchair.
>
> At age six, she tested within the normal range. By age nine, her overall scores on educational testing instruments were beginning to drop, particularly in areas that required abstract reasoning, vocabulary usage, spatial relationships, and nonverbal reasoning. This student was lagging developmentally and could not make the jump from concrete thinking to more sophisticated abstract thinking. She was experiencing increased isolation from her classmates and was observed in the lunchroom and the schoolyard alone with her aide. In the classroom she was hesitant to volunteer information and required considerable prompting to get her engaged in classroom discussions. This scenario represents some of the issues that many, but not all, students with CP confront.

A psychologist must consider a broad range and depth of physical, cognitive, health, communication, and social-emotional issues before undertaking an assessment:

- Is the student verbal or nonverbal and are their utterances intelligible?

- If the student is nonverbal, can they produce reliable nods, grimaces, or eyeblinks that correspond to yes or no responses?
- Can sign language be used as a practical tool?
- If the student is verbal, do they express complete thoughts or fragmented utterances?
- Does the student have an augmentative and alternative communication (AAC) device that serves as an intelligibility backup and that permits responses?
- How independent or dependent is the student's ability to navigate fine motor manual skills?
- Can the students use eye gaze or other physical methods to indicate responses?

Broadly speaking, the school psychologist assesses and addresses challenges and competence in the domains of cognition and emotional health, including self-concept, socialization, and a move toward independence.

Cognitive considerations:

The intellectual range of students with CP can cover the gamut from very gifted to having profound intellectual delays. Many students with CP present with scattered, uneven intellectual profiles characterized by highs and lows among different cognitive domains. For them, cognitive assessments require skill, flexibility, and the experience to choose subtests that accurately reflect the student's strengths and weaknesses.

When testing a student with CP whose physical limitations affect task performance, a psychologist will make the material as accessible as possible to accommodate the student's physical abilities and limitations, remembering that the purpose of testing the student is to find out what they know and where the breakdown points exist.

Reasonable accommodations can and should made if they are described and fully acknowledged. When alternative tests are used, the modified testing process needs to be understood, and its results and reliability should be verified and compared in relation to other assessments. Cognitive assessments of students with CP should hopefully be both descriptive and prescriptive.

It may be difficult to find assessments that are normed for complex CP populations, and the psychologist will have look for subtests that are used with the general populations and then factor in some of the following adaptations when administering the subtests:

- Extend testing time limits.
- Generate multiple- but limited-choice answers in the presence of severe intelligibility issues or in answers that require lengthy verbal responses.
- Enlarge pictures or diagrams.
- Use masks or markers to filter out or reduce distractibility, and—for those with visual limitations, such as *cortical visual impairment (CVI)*—limit the visual field.
- Look for assessments that are not biased by the physical disability but rather measure the intellect.
- Factor in fatigue and break up testing sessions into shorter periods.

Students with CP who have intact verbal skills have repeatedly been observed to experience perceptual visual and motor challenges. Vocabulary usage and the ability to identify similarities may be average; however, matrices and visual puzzles may prove quite challenging. These students may require extended periods to succeed with manipulative tasks.

Counseling and communication:

Counseling and communication with students and parents is the psychologist's hallmark responsibility, one that is shared collaboratively with counselors and social workers. Social capability, adjustment, and self-acceptance issues define the psychologist's responsibilities to both students and their families.

Counseling a significantly dysarthric CP student can be very challenging, although augmentative and alternative communication (AAC) systems—in addition to language boards, sign language, and pictorial representations of emotions and feelings—improve the process.

Areas of counseling for students with CP usually center around the topics of independence, socialization, acceptance, and isolation—areas that can be a source of frustration for some youngsters with CP. The following is a list of considerations when counseling students with CP:

- Understand the importance of context, listen carefully, and recognize shifts in topics.
- Use eye contact and facial expressions as important ways of establishing a rapport with the student.
- Do not "fake" comprehension or try to complete a student's thoughts, because doing so risks losing the student's trust.
- Realize that the quality of an interaction is more important than its quantity.
- Know that a student may be "stuck" between home and school when the home is encouraging the student to "pretend" that the disabling conditions are "not there."

Socialization:

Psychologists and counselors directly address the isolation and lack of appropriate peer interaction that is a common occurrence for many students with CP, especially nonverbal students with significant movement limitations who attend inclusive programs. Social-emotional concerns requiring professional attention also arise among students with CP who are being educated in special-school settings by virtue of a student's dependent status.

Psychologists and counselors relieve the stress emanating from anger, fear of rejection, and frustration. They teach, strengthen coping strategies, and provide a safety net for students with CP who

- Have limited opportunities to play, communicate with, and be challenged by students with average cognitive and social abilities in inclusive settings.

- Face increased isolation as they move into middle and high school.
- Can benefit from the introduction of interactive activities and social media platforms that can minimize some degree of isolation but that do not substitute for face-to-face interactions.
- Are often not invited to out-of-school activities with neurotypical peers.
- Need opportunities to practice social skills in an unembarrassing, safe and comfortable space.
- Appear more likely to have a fuller, more accepting social life in and out of school if they attend specially dedicated programs that offer a full range of sports and artistic activities.
- Face significant challenges in establishing social networks.

Another challenging question is whether a student with CP has strong connections with others with similar physical, health, communication, and learning needs or whether and how they can and do interact with the non-disabled world. The answer to this question depends on attitude, personality factors, upbringing, and the availability of educational and recreational activities in the community. Usually, people connect with common interests. The more one is involved with photography, sports, art, or politics, the greater the likelihood of finding similar-minded individuals. When students can present themselves as self-confident, interesting, and as having skills and passions, their disability may become a less important part of the package they present.

Developing self-care and independence within the context of a realistic need for lifelong, intense personal care and dependence can create a challenge and a dilemma for students with CP and their families. Early in a student's life, there is a need to understand the fine line between unhealthy dependency on others and the reliance on others to facilitate the completion of a task—that is, to see others as auxiliary assistants rather than enablers.

As students with CP age, the school psychologist plays a major role in patiently helping the students to honestly assess the range and scope of their needs and strengths, to ask for help when it is obviously needed, to advocate for themselves, and to cope with periods of physical and emotional regression that can affect students and parents alike.

The psychologist, in collaboration with other team members, works to encourage students with CP to take charge of their own bodies and enlist the help of parents in encouraging independence whenever possible. This requires ongoing psychological support in preplanning and structuring the student's ability to appropriately respond to their own unique needs in a variety of settings throughout the school day. Students with CP need to grow toward becoming their own experts by knowing what works or doesn't work for them and by knowing how others can *assist with*, but not *do* for them, skills they can modify and develop for themselves. The psychological supports needed to reach these goals of greater control and independence involve mapping and planning for a self-navigation that works around limitations, making certain that all equipment and accommodations that ease the student's life are provided, customized when necessary, and used.

Psychologists face an important challenge in helping nonverbal students with CP express their needs, wishes, and independence, using both technical and nontechnical solutions. By inculcating in dysarthric students the expectation that they should take as much control of their lives as possible, psychologists are supporting and developing a lifelong sense of control and self-worth.

Students with CP should begin to learn at an early age how to efficiently and respectfully direct caregivers, and the psychologist or counselor can be extremely effective in this tutelage, since dependent students can too often demonstrate behaviors of entitlement and self-involvement. Caretakers should, whenever possible, defer to the student's preferences and feelings, and through discussion and role-playing, the psychologist or counselor can guide the student with CP to interact with caregivers in thoughtful and considerate ways while still demanding respectful care.

Peer sensitivity training and disability awareness programs benefit both students with CP and their neurotypical peers. These programs are frequently facilitated by the psychologist or counselors, often with the guidance of parents and, when possible, with the major participation of the student with CP.

Disability transparency is essential if a student with a disability is to be understood, valued, and respected by neurotypical peers and regarded as just another student. This is particularly important in inclusive settings, where fears and misunderstandings about disability can further a student's isolation. Parents, nurses, doctors, counselors, or psychologists, particularly in inclusion settings, can explain and attempt to demystify CP for classmates, but when students with CP speak for themselves and answer their classmates' questions, they project a sense of ownership and control that leads to greater understanding and respect. Students gain in strength and self-confidence when they explain their disability and disability-related experiences to classmates, and they can describe the adaptive tools, devices, and equipment (a discussion that can be fun, new, and interesting) that enable them to master the academic program and participate in school life. This confidence reduces the chance that neurotypical peers will shy away from the student who needs special tools.

These students with CP are the *real* experts who may be able to portray themselves as resilient people who happen to have a disability. Peer sensitivity discussions often include psychologists or counselors and lead to conversations centered not only around the differences all students experience but also to the way in which students share experiences and can assist and support one another. During these discussions, which can become group problem-solving sessions, all students can weigh in on how activities can be modified to include the participation of students with physical limitations.

If the student with CP is unable or unwilling to engage in sensitivity activities, then nurses, parents, psychologists, and/or teachers, after careful preplanning, can shoulder the responsibility of demystifying disability. Private organizations may also be engaged to provide disability awareness programs that reach student populations at different age levels.

Paraprofessionals, with guidance from classroom teachers and psychologists and counselors, are in a unique position to build disability awareness and respect while also fostering social interaction in less formal ways that are embedded into informal daily contact. The schoolyard, the lunchroom, and other nonacademic venues offer ample opportunities for the neurotypical peer to witness and appreciate the challenges and strengths of the classmate with CP.

Social skills group training may be extremely beneficial for students with CP, who, because of physical limitations, brain-based social perceptual challenges, isolation, and overdependence on adults, have not been afforded the opportunity to informally learn and practice accepted socialization responses.

Psychologists or counselors who conduct these groups allow the student with CP to practice social interaction skills in small, safe, structured groups that enable confidence building in larger, more diverse social situations. New social skills can be learned and modeled for similarly challenged peers in the safety of the smaller group, and students with CP can be reminded of their options for problem solving when they get "stuck." In supported social skills training, students with CP can practice conversation skills that enable them to join activities, venture to take social risks, and request social interaction.

In both inclusive and special-school settings, in grades one through twelve, using the voluntary buddy system, under the guidance of a psychologist or counselor in both academic and nonacademic settings, can create models and pathways to improved socialization skills for the student with CP. In counseling sessions run by psychologists or school counselors, the professionals can learn how students with CP perceive their challenges and abilities in academic, recreational, leisure, and social interactions. The psychologist or counselor can brainstorm ideas with the student to encourage the creation and articulation of modifying strategies that enable participation in a range of activities.

Finally, psychologists and counselors play crucial roles in supporting parents of students with CP by learning about the parents' expectations, fears, stresses, and hopes for their child. These professionals, in their interaction with caretakers, not only focus on a student's strengths that guide the development of realistic goals but may also need to guide important conversations that attempt to steer parents away from unrealistic, unattainable goals that negatively affect the student's self-esteem. It is difficult for parents to see other children advance while their own special-needs child sometimes stagnates or physically and/or emotionally regresses.

Psychologists and counselors encourage and support parents who may be in mourning for years and who may withdraw emotionally because of the loss of the child they "expected" to have. Parental guilt and sadness are just as real as the determined stance to maximize a student's potential and not let the disability define the student. Psychologists, counselors, and social workers deal with all these complexities. These difficult conversations, facilitated by psychologists or counselors in collaboration with other transdisciplinary team members, can occur over a period of years and may need, over time, to have their focus readjusted. Counseling for parents of students with CP, although not generally provided by school systems, can be invaluable for parents as they manage the journey with their child or young adult.

Social Workers

Hadassah Rubin and Adine R. Usher

School social workers, in collaboration with members of the student's transdisciplinary team—especially psychologists and counselors—support not only students who live with the conditions of cerebral palsy but also their families and caregivers. CP forces students and families to deal with a plethora of concerns that center around social-emotional coping, and social workers can provide referrals to a range of services outside of the school, including the location of appropriate housing.

No two students or families are identical, and family and student responses to the challenges of CP vary greatly. For many families, the diagnosis of CP is devastating and disorienting—particularly in the early years, when developmental milestones remain unmet or are severely delayed. For example, extraordinary parental effort can be expended toward getting the student to walk. If these efforts are disappointingly unsuccessful, social workers, along with counselors and psychologists, attempt to help parents through repetitive periods of grieving and support students through feelings of failure by highlighting strengths and rephrasing ideas of "normal."

Helping students with CP to feel good about themselves and to focus on their strengths, capabilities, and growing independence while simultaneously and realistically supporting them to successfully cope with the constraints placed on them by physical health, communication, and sometimes intellectual limitations—these are some of the primary responsibilities of the social worker.

Some students with CP, particularly starting in the middle school years, deal with increasing pain and discomfort from spasticity. When school time is lost because of surgical intervention, periods of convalescence can also bring depression and emotional regression. Social workers support students with CP through these emotionally challenging periods, helping them to see these episodes as either temporary setbacks or necessary opportunities for improvement. A social worker may also provide emotional support for the student whose twin is more physically able.

Social workers operate in the trenches with parents as they provide essential life service referrals, including transitions from high school to college, from high school to community participation, or from high school to work. Transitions from high school can bring anxiety to both student and parent, as there may be a limited understanding of the scope of barriers in a college or work setting faced by the student with movement, sensory, medical, and perhaps cognitive concerns. The social worker helps the student and their family to realistically view disability not as a sickness but as an opportunity to strengthen skills and increase independence.

The challenge is significant for the social worker in inclusion settings, where because of motoric, communication, or perhaps intellectual reasons, socializing with peers and overall diminished participation, including exclusion from parties and social events, may prove emotionally difficult for the student with CP. In the mainstream, a social worker may suggest ways to decrease a student's dependence on a personal aide that fosters further isolation from peers.

Social workers who serve students with CP are credentialed to handle many of the following concerns:

- Addressing immediate physical, emotional, and behavioral concerns that affect the student at both home and school.
- Looking for the roots of sudden shifts in student performance and behavior.
- Helping to establish behavior management plans.
- Seeking the availability of appropriate housing.
- Recognizing the presence of physical and sexual abuse.
- Locating and coordinating mental health services in the student's home community.
- Mediating cultural conflicts between home, school, and community.
- Providing coping skills for family members.
- Knowing about family adjustments to and attitudes about disability.
- Addressing family economic struggles, including medical expenses and the acquisition of necessary medical equipment.
- Implementing crisis intervention strategies.
- Elevating levels of student and parental self-acceptance.
- Presenting CP-specific training to staff and parents.
- Coordinating community resources, including social services.
- Joining transdisciplinary team members to develop alternative programs and investigate solutions.
- Providing case management services that teach the student with CP to find and use multiple life-improving resources.

Summary

Living with CP can be challenging. Lifelong struggles with movement, health, cognition, learning, communication, independence, socialization, and self-perception issues are real, and psychologists, counselors, and social workers play a critical role in the educational success of a student with CP.

CP-related emotional and pragmatic challenges, if left unattended, can leave students with CP and their families feeling overwhelmed and powerless. The constant presence of psychologists, counselors, and social workers offers support that inculcates resilience, perseverance, and problem-solving abilities.

Section VII
Adaptive Physical Education (APE)

Dan Cuddy

Access to appropriate, satisfying athletic and recreational participation can be challenging for many students who live with the primary, secondary, and associated conditions of cerebral palsy. This section explores the benefits of adaptive physical education (APE) programs that lower or eliminate challenging barriers to athletic activity while promoting active, enjoyable participation that, in some instances, leads to para-athletic competitive sports.

Adaptive physical education (APE) is a modified physical education program that promotes individual gross motor skill development, organized group activities, modified individual and team sports participation, and in-door/outdoor therapeutic recreational activities. An effective APE program is designed to meet the specific gross motor, fine motor, tactile, communication, visual, auditory, social-emotional, and intellectual needs of students with disabilities. Through careful planning and, when needed, the use of adaptive athletic equipment, programs and activities are designed to maximize the growth potential for students, especially those with CP, who may not safely or successfully engage in more traditional physical education, sports, or recreational programs. Athletics should be an important part of a student's program both in and outside of school.

In the United States, APE is a federally mandated component of special education services in the Individuals with Disabilities Education Act of 1975 (IDEA); therefore, APE becomes a part of the student's Individualized Educational Plan (IEP), and the APE teacher is a direct service provider who is trained in assessing and working with special-needs students and who can modify and adapt activities to meet the specific needs of those students. The plan must include assessment information about each student's strengths and challenges, the amount of APE the student is to receive, and the amount of time the student spends in receiving one-on-one services, participating in small-group classes, or, for some, participating in carefully chosen general physical education activities. Goals with measurable objectives are set for each student.

The APE teacher first learns, in detail, about the strengths and needs, the likes and dislikes, of the student with CP from records, from consultations with members of the student's transdisciplinary team, from their general education counterparts, and from direct observation. The APE specialist then creates a program designed to reduce the barriers to athletic and recreational participation. These barriers are related to the level of the severity of voluntary and involuntary gross and fine motor movement disorders, communication and sensory-based learning disabilities, social-emotional issues, and chronic health challenges.

Many students with CP who need APE services use wheelchairs, walkers, and crutches. Others, with milder physical disabilities, may still have visual, hearing, tactile, and processing issues that complicate athletic and recreational participation. Additionally, pain, discomfort, fatigue, and often being overweight can exacerbate the sedentary lifestyle of far too many students with CP. This inactivity can leave the student at further risk for secondary health complications.[191]

Many students with CP have decreased muscle tone, limited strength, coordination challenges, and limited flexibility. These physical aspects of CP may also contribute to low levels of self-confidence and self-esteem and to limited social skills. These secondary complications appear in the form of lowered fitness, poorer and declining health, musculoskeletal fragility, and—as the students move into adulthood—a loss of ambulatory skills, obesity, cancer, cardiometabolic diseases, and early mortality.[192]

Research studies that have investigated CP's limitations on physical activity find that students with CP tend to participate in fewer activities than their nondisabled peers, have a more sedentary lifestyle, participate in activities closer to home (primarily with family members), and are less likely to participate in spontaneous peer-involved social activities.[193]

After examining twenty-nine articles on activity limitation for children with CP, an Australian study[194] suggests that a range of measures is required to evaluate physical activity, and that assessment should include examining the difficulty of executing an action. Activities need be tailored to the individual needs of children with CP, particularly as they relate to participation in real-life situations.[195]

Far too many students with CP return from school to watch TV or to stare out the window, watching the world go by; they are isolated, with few, if any, friends. These students need a sense of belonging that athletic and recreational participation can provide. Minus the availability and accessibility of effective, appropriate school or community athletic and recreational programs run by skilled and knowledgeable practitioners, students with CP lose valuable health benefits, social and emotional satisfaction, opportunities for leadership, independence, and the sense of enjoyment that accrues from athletic, recreational, and sports-related social participation.

Environmental factors may also influence the type and degree of athletic participation for students with CP. Family preference for physical activity, family fears for the students' safety, parental understanding, appreciation of the value of athletic and recreational participation, family socioeconomic status, neighborhood locations, transportation, scheduling, and the availability of adaptive equipment are all to be considered. In the United States, federal mandates require that the physical education needs of special populations necessitate the kind of reasonable modifications and accommodations that parallel, as much as possible, those athletic programs that are designed for nondisabled students.

In many areas of the world, there is still a scarcity of adaptive equipment and a lack of available athletic expertise in addressing the unique needs of students with CP. Too many students with CP are left on the sidelines as spectators, feeling excluded. However, there is a growing awareness of the social-emotional and physical benefits of participation in athletic endeavors, and we daily see greater and more creative athletic participation for students with CP, although still more must be done.

The following are the APE teacher's general goals:

- Provide participation in an adaptive physical education program that meets the specific needs of the student with CP.
- Encourage camaraderie, fun, and self-worth.
- Build up the student's muscular strengths, skills, and interests.
- Improve eye-hand coordination, cardiovascular endurance, and balance.
- Encourage the motivation to be competitive.
- Promote choice, decision making, and self-advocacy.
- Set up the conditions for memorable and enjoyable athletic and recreational participation.
- Expand socializations by helping students with CP to become less self-focused.
- Help students with CP to interact with others in groups or on teams.
- Strengthen age-appropriate social skills that are derived from belonging to a group.
- Improve student moods and diminish episodes of depression.
- Help the student to plan for a better future by endowing the student with the belief that they are entitled to the joy of athletic participation.

The benefits of participation in an adaptive physical education program are numerous, and research studies, including one by Connie Johnson,[196] have found that participation in physical activity and sports leads to elevated levels of well-being and physical health.

The APE instructor

- Simplifies and modifies the language of athletic rules and instructions, thus enabling the student with CP to feel successful and engaged.
- Provides one-on-one instruction and guidance, uses visual aids, and demonstrates correct techniques.
- Adapts physical education equipment to meet specific student's needs:
  - Students in power wheelchairs can play soccer with either homemade or commercially designed foot guards that attach to the chair and allow the student to independently manipulate a soccer ball that is larger than standard size.
  - When playing baseball or kickball, a student using a wheelchair can independently play at a base and, when handed a ball, can "make an out" for their team.
- Improves and manipulates available physical playing space by changing the size of playing areas through the use of cones and floor tape.
- Seeks the updating of accessible outdoor turf fields, playgrounds, and fitness centers for students, many with CP, who need more outside time in fresh air.
- Understands that physical exercises greatly benefit brain function by dilating blood vessels, thereby sending more oxygen to the entire body.

Appropriate activities stabilize posture, engage large muscle groups, and improve balance and gross motor function. Speed walking can improve endurance, and work on a stationary bike strengthens leg muscles. Regular, appropriately modified exercise for students with CP that is found in athletic and recreational activities can reduce obesity, improve physical conditioning, improve respiration through strenuous movement, increase muscular strength, stretch muscles and tendons, act as an antidote to pain and fatigue, and improve overall health and well-being.[197]

The APE teacher needs to have detailed knowledge about the physical, health, cognitive, and social-emotional barriers that can impact the student. With this information, the APE teacher can use the following strategies to circumvent and compensate for these barriers:

- Plan intentionally in collaboration with OTs and PTs.
- Provide or create a greater diversity of activities that reflect an understanding of the complexity of the student's needs.
- Develop athletic and recreational activities that are emotionally satisfying and welcoming.
- Help students with CP to become knowledgeable about and interested in spectator sports that they may never participate in.
- Encourage the kind of teamwork in students that may lead to the acquisition of leadership skills.
- Involve the student with CP in deciding how an activity can and should be modified.
- Use consistent verbal prompts when necessary.
- Discourage frustration by explaining that sometimes just extra practice and extra instruction on specific game-related skills are needed by everyone.
- Offer recreational activities that encourage movement, excitement, competition, and socialization.
- Reduce or modify the skills needed for a specific activity when the student with CP lives with significant motoric disability.
- Encourage direct support from experienced peer-participants in the activity.
- Understand issues of safety, pain, fatigue, and lack of prior experience.
- Consider transportation, scheduling, accessibility, and activity location.
- Help develop in students with CP a sense of accomplishment and pride when participating in athletic activities.

- Observe students with CP as they take part in free play in natural settings in order to gain information about their ability to generalize their skills to new recreational activities.

The benefits of a well-executed APE program carry over into classroom settings for students with CP. The hands-on nature of APE programs leads to cognitive improvements in

- Following directions.
- Sustaining emotional self-regulation.
- Accepting healthy competition.
- Learning to challenge oneself.
- Engaging in decision making.
- Participating in teamwork.
- Focusing on specific goals.
- Expanding verbal communication.

Community-based special athletic and recreational programs are separate athletic programs that parallel as much as possible programs designed for nondisabled students. The international Special Olympics and the Little League Challenger baseball program, which to date have over thirty thousand special-needs athletes in ten countries worldwide, are only two of many programs that provide after-school athletic and recreational activities for students with a range of developmental disabilities, including CP.

Here are some types of adaptive athletic and recreational activities and strategies:

- Hippotherapy normalizes pelvic movement, stabilizes posture, and improves gross motor function.
- Speed walking improves endurance.
- An adapted sailing program gives students with CP widened access to sports.
- Adapted skiing and snowboarding build muscle strength and improve balance.

- Low-impact or nonimpact physical activities, such as swimming, the use of adaptive tricycles, stationary cycles, and other forms of cycling that strengthen muscles, may be appropriate and enjoyable for some students with CP.[198]
- It is speculated that various gross motor functions of posture and movement, in addition to improved respiration in CP, may improve in warm-water pools by stimulating sensorimotor systems.
- Warm-up, strengthening, and stretching exercises show improvement for stiff muscles, reduce the chance of fainting, and are recommended as sports therapy for CP populations. All warm-up exercises aid rolling, walking, and climbing.[199]

Here are some modifications that enable greater athletic and recreational participation:

- Typical sports equipment can be modified and, when necessary, stabilized.
- Balls can be suspended from ropes, and extra grips can be added to equipment.
- When modifying and individualizing equipment for students with CP, in addition to establishing safety with authorized persons, consider the size, weight, texture, and firmness of the athletic or recreational objects.
- Choose the most appropriate equipment for athletic and recreational participation for the student with CP, then modify further when needed.
- Whether a student with CP is in a self-contained setting or an inclusion program, movements, positions, and rules for athletic and recreational activities may require modifications. This is especially important in inclusion settings, for without these modifications, it is likely that the student with CP will simply be left as an observer.
- Space parameter and/or distances can be modified to accommodate

physical limitations and fatigue.

- The number of participants in an activity can be modified.
- Scoring system can be changed, especially when students are competing with themselves.
- When the student with CP is facing participation challenges, pair them with an able-bodied student.
- In inclusion athletic and recreational programs, some activities may involve allowing the neurotypical student to have a turn at being in a physically disadvantaged position.
- Make limited use of asking students with CP to be referees or scorers. They should have more active roles.

The Parents' Role in Athletic and Recreational Activities

Parents who fear for the safety of the child with CP should have their concerns addressed but will hopefully be encouraged to see the health and social values of athletic and recreational participation that is safely and appropriately designed for their child. Just as parents should be involved in their child's rehabilitation and educational programs, so they need to be involved in athletic and recreational choices.

Parents are the experts in their child's abilities and needs.[200] Parents have ways of meeting challenges and supporting needs. The APE teacher should be prepared to explain APE programs, goals, and benefits to parents and to supply them with a list of community-based athletic and recreational activities that can serve the needs of students with CP.

As more students with CP are being included in mainstream school programs, the expectation that they will contribute meaningfully to athletic school life must be accompanied by an awareness of what CP is, what adaptations are needed, and how, at the individual level, unique needs are to be met by skilled, encouraging athletic professionals who allow for enjoyable participation in a diversity of activities.[201]

Nonacademic subjects and activities have long been considered essential to the total educational experience of students in all types of educational settings. The physical, health, aesthetic, and social-emotional value of physical education and recreation are without question.

SECTION VIII

The Creative Arts: Music, Dance, Drama, and the Visual Arts

Adine R. Usher

Students with CP derive a high degree of pleasure and pride through participating in the universal language of artistic endeavors. Participation in the creative arts opens a world of pleasant, exciting, emotionally valuable, and personally enriching experiences. New interests are explored, new methods of communication are created, meaningful ways of socializing with both disabled and able-bodied peers are forged, and expanded ways of participating in family life are developed. For most students with CP, creative-arts activities are enjoyable, avocational experiences, and for some, these artistic endeavors can lead to professional paths in the postsecondary years.

Participation in the creative arts affords students with all levels of CP opportunities to become inventive, imaginative, and engaged in empowering activities that leave them in control, often for the first time. Skills learned through artistic participation can be integrated into academic work. Artistic endeavors aid students with CP in working through challenges where there is often no right or wrong, there is just doing!

All the creative arts can improve both the verbal and nonverbal communication skills of students with CP, and artistic accomplishments, no matter how simple, enable these students to share their gifts and receive positive feedback.

Whereas this book focuses on creative-arts programs in a school setting, teachers should be aware that community-based, public, private, nonprofit, therapeutic, and professional music, dance, drama, and visual-arts programs can be recommended for students with CP and with other developmentally disabling conditions. Very Special Arts (VSA) is an international organization of arts, education, and disability that is headquartered in Washington, D.C., and is currently known as the Department of VSA and Accessibility at the John F. Kennedy Center for the Performing Arts. This organization provides opportunities for disabled people of all ages to learn, participate in, and enjoy the arts.[202]

Music

Exposure to music holds particularly powerful rewards for many students with CP. The multiple and well-researched value of music programs for students who live with all the subtypes of CP encompasses improved movement, palliative influences on mood regulation and behavioral control, and greater opportunities for enjoyable socialization and musical participation.

Musical services can be delivered to students with CP in a variety of settings. These services are found in general and special educational music programs and in private, individually delivered music therapy sessions directed by a specially trained music therapist. Occasionally, the music therapist will be engaged by public or private schools where they may co-treat with physical and occupational therapists.

Music is provided for students with CP either on an individual basis or through group participation, as students listen to music, make music on instruments that have been modified (when necessary) for each student's use, and, when they are able, join their voices (to the best of their ability) with their peers in song. Students with CP whose articulation problems include stuttering cease to stutter when they sing because the act of singing improves breath control.

Music therapy for students with CP uses music with the distinct instructional goals of

- Relaxing movement
- Eliciting language
- Improving literacy
- Increasing focusing
- Deepening listening
- Improving socialization and elevating self-esteem
- Reducing heart rate and blood pressure
- Lowering general levels of stress
- Heightening enjoyment

The goals of a music therapy session are most often met in one-on-one sessions with music used to strengthen the bond of trust and musical exploration between student and therapist as they move toward an articulated goal of heightening alertness, strengthening concentration, following directions, copying physical and auditory cues, and enhancing a feeling of shared participation and accomplishment.

As with other members of a student's transdisciplinary team, the music teacher or therapist must have an in-depth understanding of the student's physical, health, intellectual, sensory, and social-emotional strengths and challenges. The music specialist can draw on the student's engagement with music to reduce the barriers posed by CP-related physical, health, intellectual, sensory, and social-emotional conditions.

There is often an overlap between the goals of the music therapist and those of the school-based music teacher. Both educators seek to use music to improve gross and fine muscle functioning, extend movement, instill music appreciation, extend verbal and nonverbal communication, offer opportunities for social-emotional growth and joyful participation, and, as a physiological benefit, stimulate plasticity in the brain's motor cortex.[203]

Therapy sessions also attempt to use rhythmic sounds to activate and coordinate muscles in the auditory-motor pathways.[204] For example, lively, fast-paced passages seem to improve the spatial tasks of walking, dancing, and upper-body movement in a wheelchair user with CP.[205] Behavioral challenges, motivation, and cooperation may also improve with music therapy, since

- Vocalizations become reciprocal.
- Eye contact is established.
- Relaxation occurs.
- The student with CP begins to make musical connections between familiar sounds and melodies.
- Fine motor skills improve as fingers strike and scratch instruments.
- With music and rhythm, more child-directed movements appear.

The following are some health benefits of music for students with CP:

- Listening to or making music can reduce the perception of pain.[206]
- Singing often improves the control of respiration, improves posture, allows for better control of vocal cords, and allows phrases to be paired, which makes lyrics easier and clearer to produce.[207]
- Movement to music, in or out of a wheelchair, may extend stamina and lower heart rates.[208]

Music and rhythm have demonstrated the ability to

- Connect the cognitive, motor, and emotional functions of the brain.[209, 210]
- Improve and strengthen fine and gross motor skills and sensorimotor skills.[211]
- Stimulate movement and particularly improve walking speed and distances.[212]
- Improve kneeling, standing, and crawling.
- Stimulate, guide, and challenge the repetitive movement of upper-body muscles.[213, 214]
- Improve motor function in the arms, hands, and head movement.
- Connect motor and cognitive skills.

- Provide some restorative benefits for the reduction of muscle tension found in spasticity.[215]
- Respond to instructions and conversations that are sung.

Playing keyboards improves fine motor and eye-hand coordination, strengthens fingers, provides discipline and focus, and assures that the student both receives and gives pleasure.

Music produces cognitive and emotional benefits:

- Music-induced interest and pleasure produces a surge of dopamine in the brain.[216]
- Deep resonances, harmonious tones, and gentle rhythms may comfort psychological distress.[217]
- Memory is improved by the recall of humorous lyrics.[218,219]
- Music modifies cerebral processes by capturing the student's attention.[220]
- More avenues for expression of feelings, opportunities for control and choice, and strengthened self-confidence are experienced by students.[221]
- Opportunities are expanded for decision making, emotional release, mental stimulation, and personal satisfaction.
- Handling instruments, singing, and listening to music improves a student's emotional state.[222]
- Students are taught to take turns, make eye contact, and respond with appropriate facial expressions.[223]
- Researchers suggest that music may play a powerful role in strengthening working and verbal memory in a damaged brain.[224]
- For some with CP, music reduces the anxiety, frustration, and self-consciousness that can foster muscle tension and thereby dramatically set back physical progress.
- Reducing or speeding up the rhythm improves a student's performance or mood.[225]

- Focus and attention are improved in response to musical sounds.
- Music provides a student with CP a much-needed experience of freedom.
- If a student with CP is exposed to engaging music that is in touch with the student's feelings and that encourages object recognition with name repetition, they can name objects with the help of repetitive songs, can express curiosity at new sounds, and can make musical associations.

Adapting Musical Instruments for Students with CP

It is not important that the student with CP play an instrument in the same manner as the neurotypical student. It is only important that they participate in any manner possible that expands emotional and sensorimotor experiences.

In any school setting—inclusion, special-class, or special-school—the student's fine and gross motor issues and communication challenges may necessitate the adaptation and modification of instrumental music instruction. These modifications will ensure that for these students, music making will be a successful social and joyful enterprise. Music and classroom teachers can enlist the adaptive expertise of OTs and PTs to make musical activities accessible to students with CP in the following ways:

- Accessible head wands, mouth sticks, pointers, and finger extensions that function on computer keyboards can also be used on electronic and nonelectronic musical keyboards and xylophones.
- Musical notations can be enlarged, simplified, and modified for students with CP who also deal with visual-perception challenges.
- Switch-activated, prerecorded musical instruments can enable participation in instrumental and vocal activities.
- Instruments can be played with finger scratching and striking motions.
- Classroom instruments (including small keyboards) can be taped down on the student's desk or table, and if motor processing is slow, a student need play only one or several notes in a measure.

- Placing the words to songs, written large and well-spaced on large sheets, will help the child with CP (and those with other developmental disabilities) not only to learn the words to a song but also to increase reading skills.
- Bells, mallets, and drumsticks can all be rendered functional with the use of tape and Velcro that aid in grasping.
- Arms, knees, feet, and wands held between the teeth can all be adapted to give a student with CP accessibility to musical participation.

The music instructor needs to be aware that some students with CP have auditory sensitivities that appear when music is either too loud or too fast. Keen observation and information in the student's records may alert the instructor to the presence of these sensitivities or signs of tactile defensiveness and tactile rejection.

Music teachers and therapists should acquire information about local music programs that include students with varying degrees of CP and be prepared to share this information with parents. Once the student with CP is comfortably positioned and has access to musical participation, an observant teacher can look for improvements in hand-eye coordination, attention, concentration and focus, and attempts to extend range of motion while hitting switches, striking drums, or touching keys.

Dance

Dancing, for students with CP who are ambulatory or for wheelchair or scooter users, is a magnificent combination of body motion connected to the endless power and strength of music. Whatever the mode of dance, the following benefits accrue:

- Dancing expands the student's range of motion.
- Wheelchair dancing maximizes upper-body strength and improves

fluidity of motion in response to the emotional power of music.

- Dancing can improve upper- and lower-body muscle tone and balance.
- Dancing may lead to acrobatics skills.
- Dancing inspires self-confidence, pride, and joy.

For students with CP, dancing presents the "different body" as beautiful and accepts movements that are natural and normal for the student's body and spirit.

Somatic therapy is a form of dance therapy that enables music to help the student with CP focus on their body's internal sensations. This is done to create a mind-body connection.

Drama

Drama programs in all school settings open excellent and exciting ways for students with CP to express themselves. And particularly in inclusion settings, meaningful roles must be found or crafted for them, independent of the severity of their CP. The creativity and self-expression inherent in dramatic performances benefits mental and physical health, improves memory and communication skills, strengthens cognition, and reduces the anxieties the student with CP may initially have about being in the spotlight. Indeed, many students with CP find acting freeing and cathartic.

There are increasing dramatic opportunities in schools and communities for students with CP to perform, either in groups or in one-person shows, and students can practice their creativity aided by modification to their mobility and communication equipment.

The Visual Arts

A student with CP should never be denied the enjoyment of visual-arts experiences because of perceived or faulty assumptions about their complex CP-based conditions. CP, with all its complications, can profoundly and negatively affect a student's intrinsic sense of self-worth, but, just as with music, the visual arts open avenues for the student who communicates with difficulty. Art expands imagination and permits healthy ways for the expression of positive and negative emotions to reach a wider audience. Like music, dance, and drama, the visual arts permit students with CP to appreciate what their bodies can do to build self-esteem, pleasure, and pride through artistic engagement.

Art teachers and therapists, whether in special, inclusive school, or community settings, work to invent ways to make the visual arts accessible and emotionally meaningful for students who live with the movement, health, cognitive, sensory, and social-emotional realities of CP.

Although the gross and fine motor difficulties encountered by many students with CP appear initially to be exceptionally challenging, a provider's creative inventiveness can modify and adapt art activities that, when augmented by a student's determination and effort, can transcend the student's motoric and communication limitations. This, in turn, sets the path for feelings of joy, self-confidence, competence, and accomplishment to emerge from a visual-arts activity. Taking part in, completing, and sharing well-crafted art activities permits a student with CP to receive positive feedback, appreciation, and the admiration of others—a gift that frequently eludes this population of students.

While the fundamental principles of art, which emphasize color, shape, texture, and form, are offered to all students, it is not important that the student with CP engage in art activities in ways like that of his neurotypical peers. Art by its very nature is highly individual, with no right nor wrong; it simply is!

It is of critical importance that art teachers or therapists become aware of how the student's emotional presentation, interests, neurologically based tactile sensitivities, visual status, and levels of stamina influence artistic exploration.

Art teachers will often use easy-to-modify, atypical approaches that give meaning to concrete and abstract concepts. Art can also be produced by students with CP on digital devices. When permitted and with support from an OT, an effective light restraint on a student's less-difficult-to-control upper arm may enable more effective and satisfying use of hands and fingers. Modifications for students with CP who need them range from easels that can be attached to wheelchairs and spillproof containers on tables.

Rather than despairing about what a student with CP can't do, an inventive, creative art instructor will search for what the student *can do*, no matter how limited the student's physical abilities or how atypical the instructional response. Here is the experience of Eiko Fan, art teacher at the HMS School for Cerebral Palsy in Philadelphia:

> Some kids cannot move their bodies in conventional ways. I invent many different ways to create art. Some kids paint with their feet. Some kids cannot hold paintbrushes the regular ways, so I invent ways for them to hold the brushes. The paintbrush can follow the student's natural movement from side to side. Sometimes I pair my students off with students from other schools who don't have CP.
>
> We want people to understand that our kids have abilities. Each child with CP has different abilities, and I try to invent different ways to make sculptures to show who each student is. Every kid gets to experience different things, such as using a long stick to reach the painting. Parents get to know that each kid can do things, not just sit in a wheelchair. The student with CP may paint with a brush fastened to fingers, arms, feet, or head; indeed, any stable part of the body can be used.
>
> The students express choices even if they can't say them. Choice comes by watching their eye movements. One student

paints with his middle finger that he moves up and down, but that does not keep him from creating something. I enhance finger movement by inventing a device that allows the student to make larger movements. When the student bounces on the device, he gets better painting movement, and he understands what I am getting him to do. A lot of passion comes from this one movement, and adding music enhances his movements. It takes a lot of patience to have CP, but the student's reaction is often "Look at me! I can do this!"

We (both teacher and the students with CP) make art for people to see in public spaces. They paint on big shirts for their parents to wear. When a dad wears the shirt, people stop him to ask, "Where did you get this?" and the father explains the whole story. Experience is innovative and creative. We decorate canes for others to use in performances.

I focus on the reality that each student with CP can participate, no matter the severity of the disability, and I invent specific ways for each student to fully participate. In a student's mind, pieces of art can come together. As the student uses touch, art becomes alive as the fingertips talk to the brain.

Students can also see by using their imaginations. I believe touching makes people smart. Touching awakens an important sense and connects with other senses in the brain. For our kids, artwork is a kind of language: Even for a child who doesn't have a clear way of expressing yes and no. When a child selects one color and moves that paint to go this way and that way ... that is a way of communication. The child is showing curiosity, a desire to participate, and an ability to make decisions.

We purposely use more permanent art materials, such as canvas, which parents will not easily want to toss away. It gives

the child with CP respect—a can-do presence—and parents can
brag and appreciate the student's gifts.

Art therapy, like music therapy, is delivered by skilled professionals who
assist students with CP or other disabling conditions, in order to resolve deeply
embedded personal conflicts and challenging behaviors in a calm, relaxed,
and creative environment. These art therapy sessions may occur in school,
in the community, or in medical settings. Using guided art activities—such as
brush painting, finger painting, drawing, coloring, clay sculpting, and working
with mediums of cloth, metal, and stone as therapeutic tools—students with
CP can move toward new, more effective behaviors and feelings. Some art
therapists believe that successes with art therapy can merge into improved
academic performance.

SECTION IX

Teachers in Both Inclusive and Special Settings

Adine R. Usher

The transdisciplinary process is an ideal platform for collaboration among
classrooms. Each member has strengths and needs, and through shared observations and experiences, teachers in both inclusive and special settings feel
supported as new strategies and solutions are tried, discarded, or retooled.

The classroom teacher, whether experienced with CP or not, has a tremendous responsibility to meet the varied, unique, and often complex needs
of students in their classroom setting. Students with CP who appear on the
full spectrum of associated conditions learn, like their neurotypical peers, from
everything and everyone in their environments. It is their ability to comprehend
and respond that *may* differ from that of the neurotypical student.

Teachers in both inclusive and special settings have hopefully received
a thorough grounding in typical child development. This foundational

knowledge must be augmented by an understanding of the scope of nonsequential learning and developmental delays, including significant intellectual challenges, that may be present in a student with CP. These delays may be compounded by a lack of experiential events in a student's life that impact motivation and learning.

Although the training that special educators have received has usually given them a broad pedagogical grounding in a range of disabling conditions and learning challenges, one cannot automatically assume that all special educators are familiar with the range of possible complexities found in students with CP, since these students represent a low-incidence population whose multiple needs may not have been covered in a teacher's training. Also, the consistent use of whole-group instruction, even with a group of twelve, is not the most effective for students who require intense student-adult proximity and interaction.

Teachers in inclusion settings, depending on the extent of their exposure to special-needs populations, may be unfamiliar with the movement, medical, and associated conditions of CP and therefore will, in addition to staff development and personal research, benefit greatly from frequent formal and informal exchanges of information delivered within the transdisciplinary model.

Without training and transdisciplinary exposure, teachers in inclusion settings may unwittingly underestimate the potential of the student with CP. Teachers should also be aware of how knowledge about a student informs day-to-day expectations and interactions, not solely with traditional pedagogical interactions but also in the casual comments and responses that convey equally important information about a student's understanding.

Many of the instructional strategies used for less medically complex, nonphysically disabled but learning-disabled students may work effectively for students with CP, but teachers in both inclusive and special environments should be aware that more creative and innovative modifications are frequently needed.

The Resource Room Teacher

Resource room teachers are special educators who work in their own class-rooms and teach through small-group instruction. They meet several times a week with special-needs students from inclusion classes who bring unique and complex learning profiles, requiring more individual attention and more rep-etition at a reduced pace of instruction. The resource room teachers generally reinforce the curriculum being presented in the general-education inclusion class and are free to use a wide array of modified and adapted instructional strategies, which include the use of digital and assistive technology. Students with CP who are assigned to inclusion programs often receive resource room services several times a week. Collaboration between resource room teachers and other members of the student's transdisciplinary team is essential, as this specialist has observational skills in the small-group setting that makes them sensitive to the discrete ways in which the conditions of CP can affect processing, learning, and instruction.

Co-Teaching

Co-teaching is a form of instructional collaboration that is often found in inclusion programs when special and general educators share teaching re-sponsibilities throughout the school day. In some models, the neurotypical students receive the focus of the general educator while the special-needs students, including the students with CP, receive major attention from the special educator. However, as previously discussed, the student with CP benefits when both general and special educators jointly devise curricular and instructional modifications and adaptations that bring comprehension to the student. This teaching model enhances the skills of both teachers. When co-teaching works smoothly, teacher role reversals are likely to occur.

Section X
Classroom Assistants, Paraprofessionals, and Aides

Adine R. Usher

Sometimes, the terms *assistant*, *paraprofessional*, and *aide* are used inter-changeably. Other times, these titles strictly define designated roles of support for students with CP. Depending on the scope of a student's needs and the availability of personnel in a school, assistants will need to be well trained in safety measures, feeding, toileting, ambulation support, positioning, and academic assistance. Under the best of circumstances, the teacher will have sufficient information about a student's strengths and challenges, has shared this information effectively with assistants, and then can competently direct and monitor the assistant as he or she works to support the student with CP.

The most effective instructional strategies that are employed by both the teachers and the classroom assistants are those which have been collaboratively modified and adapted in consultation with the appropriate related service providers (RSPs). Teachers will make certain that they and their assistants are fully conversant with any technology that the student is dependent on and will ensure the delivery and monitoring of ongoing assistive technology training for class assistants.

There will always be a need for individual support for some students with CP. In inclusive settings, there are more individually assigned support personnel for students whose CP is significant and complex. In special education, unless there are critical health imperatives, these assistants tend to serve several students and monitor their needs.

Depending on their titles and concomitant responsibilities, these assistants play a crucial role in safely bringing the student's physical, health, academic, and social-emotional performance close to the student's "personal best." How these support personnel are trained and function can determine the success of a student's school experience. That said, the overuse of support personnel can significantly impede a student's self-determination and independence of thought and action, and in those cases, a psychologist may want to intervene when it appears that the student's overdependence on an assistant is being encouraged.

Although there are some students with CP who unquestionably require the presence of an individual, one-on-one aide, within the past decade, there has been considerable discussion and research on the topic that questions the advisability of assigning individual assistants, paraprofessionals, and aides whenever parents or school districts request them. Those who propose a reevaluation of the widespread use of individual, one-on-one assistants point to the following observations:

- The constant presence of an adult aide may isolate the student from peers.
- The assigned assistant may be the student's only "friend" in school.
- Some students with CP become very dependent on the assistant and exhibit little need to initiate or express independent thoughts, initiate actions, exhibit self-determination, or explore beyond the limited parameters of their lives.[226]
- The constant attention of an assistant ("the helicopter aide") might limit motivation and self-determination and might reduce the desire for modest risk taking.
- With constant adult attention, a student with CP may become self-involved and exhibit feelings of entitlement.
- A red flag should go up if the assistant is teaching the student with CP with minimum input from the classroom teacher, who has left the bulk of the teaching to the assistant.
- An assumption that the aide "owns" the student can lower levels of teacher involvement.
- The assistant may be insufficiently trained to independently assume most of the teaching to a neurologically complex student.
- Excessive assistant attention may slow a student's ability to mature.

- The assistant's constant presence may embarrass the student with CP.
- The assistant's close relationship with the student's family may place a strain on school-family relationships.

Training for Assistants, Paraprofessionals, and Aides

Ongoing staff development and training for assistants, paraprofessionals, and aides is extremely important, even though this critical training, in many schools, is often minimal and of limited effectiveness. There is a need to constantly evaluate the appropriateness and effectiveness of individually assigned assistants. School systems that serve students with CP and other neuromuscular disabilities should

- Make certain the teacher's pre-instruction planning decisions are shared with the assistants.
- Expand and deepen the assistants' understanding of the underlying medical and health causes for the complexity of the student's condition.
- Expand the assistants' understanding of the combined influences that CP's movement, health, cognitive, sensory, and social-emotional conditions can have on learning and instruction.
- Encourage patient, studied observation of the most subtle, nuanced changes exhibited by the student that coexist with environmental factors.
- Find ways to share with classroom assistants research-based information about CP that comes from the disciplines of medicine, education, and psychology.
- Periodically provide disability-specific presentations delivered from internal staff and external resources.
- Challenge, when they exist, preconceived attitudes about the limitations of a student's potential.

Assistants need to

- Build up the student's ability to function independently, safely, and effectively in physical, academic, and social-emotional and self-care areas.

- Provide individual or small-group academic, physical, and sensory support and instruction under the guidance of the classroom teacher(s) and RSPs.
- Use all adaptive and modified instructional procedures that have been determined necessary by the transdisciplinary team.
- Continually work to improve the assistants' powers of observation so that they can add to and share valuable information about the student's strengths and challenges.
- Assist students in safely moving around the school environment.
- Safely aid in activities of daily living (ADLs), such as feeding, dressing, and toileting.
- Serve as a scribe for the students with limited fine motor skills (when a fellow student cannot perform this task).
- Provide assistance if the student is not able to physically manipulate or perceive the process of manipulating books, papers, pencils, or computer keyboards.
- Use all the low-tech modifications designed for desk and table work that are recommended by therapists and parents.
- Receive training on all the adaptive technology devices that the student needs to maximize academic and communication performance or guide the student toward knowledgeable proficiency. Then assist the student with knowledgeable proficiency.
- Adhere to accepted protocols, and with guidance from the family, the physician, and the school nurse, be prepared to respond appropriately and effectively when the student has a seizure or other medical emergency.
- Respond, monitor, and appropriately guide, with support from transdisciplinary team members and behavior specialists, when the student with CP experiences behaviors that are unstable and cause problems

for themselves and their peers.

- Facilitate socialization with peers and encourage independence rather than allowing students with CP to spend the school day solely dependent on the company of adults.
- Provide academic support, using modified and adaptive strategies, in middle and high school settings, where the work can be especially challenging (particularly in inclusive settings) due to the increased pace of instruction, the use of the lecture format, the presence of difficult-to-achieve and unrealistic academic expectations, and—unfortunately—the unwillingness of some teachers to "go the extra mile" for the student.
- Realize that socializing for some students with CP in inclusive middle and high school settings may be exceptionally challenging. Participation in socializing activities may also require sensitive adult assistance at a time when teenage socializing is not generally monitored by adults.
- Encourage and help neurotypical peers to appreciate the student's strengths.[227]

Optimizing the Use of Assistants, Paraprofessionals, and Aides

- Use peers to provide sporadic support when student safety is not put at risk.
- Assign one or two assistants who can provide shared support to several students, including the student with CP.
- Engage parents in determining the levels and varieties of support that assistants, teachers, and peers can provide to the student with CP.
- Employ the greater use of alternative strategies and specialized equipment that allow for increased student independence and personal agency.
- Train assistants to recognize when they need to step in to engage the student and when it is time to step back and allow independent action.
- Whenever possible, independent of a student's cognitive level, involve

students with CP in appropriate problem-solving activities.

- Recognize the benefits of helping students to embrace new opportunities to practice and acquire improved social and communication skills.

Michael Giangreco suggests that decreased reliance on assistants, paraprofessionals, and aides can increase in students with CP feelings of belonging in the wider school community.[228]

Activities of Daily Living (ADLs)

The term *activities of daily living (ADLs)* refers to those self-care activities and tasks that are essential to daily existence. For the temporarily able-bodied, dressing and undressing, eating independently, attending to one's toileting needs, moving unaided, and caring for one's personal effects are rarely a challenge. However, for many students with CP, one or more of these tasks can present significant challenges that often require assistance. Meeting these needs is part of an assistant's responsibilities; it is their responsibility to help create a bridge to the student's independence and self-confidence. The efficacy of staff members who help in these areas may vary greatly, depending on the availability and quality of staff training.

Toileting:

One of the most personal of ADL tasks is toileting. Toileting issues may be compromised by incontinence, by the physical inability to attend to one's toileting needs, or by the inability to physically negotiate bathroom facilities. If regular or adaptive toilet facilities cannot be used, then changing tables may be needed.[229]

When needed, toileting functions are carried out by specially assigned aides or by the student's individually assigned assistant. As students with CP age, every effort should be exerted to provide a toileting assistant who matches the student's gender. Situations may arise that require a classroom teacher or available trained adults, regardless of their official title, to assume this role and assist a student.[230]

As some students with CP get older and heavier, mechanical modes of lifting these students onto a changing table are used that may require the assistance of more than one adult.

Even when the student with CP remains dependent on others for their toileting needs, every effort should be exerted to provide aid in a respectful manner that maintains the student's dignity and builds confidence as they learn to assist themselves to the fullest extent possible.

With the move toward greater architectural accessibility, students who require minimal assistance benefit when schools are modified with one or several safe, accessible bathroom stalls complete with elevated toilet seats, grab bars, and lower sinks. PTs and OTs work with aides, paraprofessionals, and parents to ensure that the student with CP who needs toileting assistance can receive that help in an environment where their needs are appropriately met.

Dressing and undressing:

The consequences of CP's fine and gross motor limitations can make dressing and undressing challenging. OTs, parents, and frequently aides play major roles in helping students with CP to become more independent with dressing and undressing. As teachers observe aides and therapists assisting students, they too can become adept at assisting students when needed.

Certainly, if there are medical proscriptions in regard to moving and manipulating a student's body, those proscriptions must be thoroughly understood by all members of the classroom staff. However, teachers need to know that most students with CP are not exceedingly fragile, and staff should therefore not fear assisting these youngsters.

Parents are encouraged to dress students in roomy clothing that is easier to don and remove. Over the past decade, more attractive clothing and footwear is being designed and sold for individuals who spend time in wheelchairs and who encounter difficulty with buttons, snaps, shoelaces, and zippers. Looser-fitting clothes secured with Velcro closings, shoes that close with Velcro straps, and elastic waistbands for pull-on pants and skirts are becoming more in vogue.

Here again, facilitating independence is the goal, with a reminder that "it is easier to dress the weaker side of the body first and undress the weaker side last."[231] Teachers should also make certain that spaces and hooks for hanging coats and book bags are within easy reach of the student with fine motor, gross motor, and sensory limitations.

Although eating and drinking are also activities of daily living, they are discussed in chapter 3 under the heading "Oral-Motor Challenges."

SECTION XI

Parents as Team Members

Adine R. Usher

Caregivers, whether parents, grandparents, relatives, or nonrelated guardians, should always play a prominent and guiding role in the transdisciplinary process. It is they who offer unwavering affection and discharge ongoing responsibility for the physical, medical, educational, and social-emotional well-being of the student with CP, usually well into the student's adult years and often to the end of the caregiver's life.

Chapter 10 will delve more deeply into the reported experiences of parenting a student with CP; however, team members should never diminish the passion, deep love, anxiety, struggle, and commitment that parents bring to the team. Although not "specialists" in the formal sense, they indeed are the "experts" who know the student best, and as such, they may at times disagree with school policies, thereby finding themselves in an adversarial stance with transdisciplinary team members.

School professionals are bound by legal and administrative restrictions, and even in special school or class settings, where they have extensive experience in working with students with a range of CP conditions, limits may exist in their ability to comprehend and respond effectively to parental passions and demands.

Parents of students with CP can be understandably fiercely determined that their child receive every opportunity to succeed. At different periods in a student's schooling, caregivers and professionals may have differing priorities for the student. Federal legislation also grants parents legal redress when differences with school authorities cannot be easily resolved.

Often parents see strengths that we as educators have yet to discover. Sometimes, however, parents see strengths that simply are not there. Compassion, empathy, and sincere respect must be offered to parents who struggle with the often-immense challenges of CP. Schools are most effective when they can offer family-centered care that provides interventions that focus on multiple areas of family need. Parental suggestions and recommendations, whenever possible, should be adopted, and every effort should be made to ensure that parents leave the table feeling listened to, respected, and hopeful.

The world COVID-19 pandemic, which has forced so many students with CP to learn virtually, has strengthened the parents' role of coach, when parents are trained by and collaborate with service providers.

SECTION XII
Students as Team Members

Adine R. Usher

In the United States, federal and state directives may determine the age at which students can take part in their transdisciplinary team meetings. It is of great importance that the student with CP be assisted in developing skills of self-advocacy and independence, and participation in team meetings is an excellent way to work toward that goal. A growing movement, often from state and federal directives, is encouraging students with disabilities to not only take part in their team and IEP meetings but, when possible, take the lead in running these meetings. Student-directed IEPs can amazingly inspire higher academic achievement, improve communication, spur motivation, and develop wider self-advocacy skills.[232] Colleen Thoma and Paul Wehman clearly outline how to prepare students for IEP participation.[233] As part of this preparation, students with CP should do the following:

- Understand the concept of advocacy, and become aware of their range of options.
- Deepen their understanding of their strengths and challenges.
- Become familiar with the IEP process.
- Use strategies to calm nerves, build leadership capacity, and incorporate parent involvement.
- Learn to articulate their perceptions of their school experiences, express their goals and aspirations, and offer suggestions and solutions.

All forms of communication augmentation, including assisted speech, should be employed to enhance the student's participation in these meetings.

SECTION XIII
School Leadership

Diane Gallagher and Beverly Ellman

Superintendents, school directors, principals, or special education supervisors who monitor and guide the delivery of services to schools in an educational district all play pivotal, critical, interrelated, and interdependent roles in providing program-wide leadership. One important role is communicating with and guiding transdisciplinary team members who are responsible for delivering direct services to students with CP.

School leaders, as active members of the transdisciplinary team, model the collaborative nature of the team process and convey their belief in the value of team members. Mistakes will happen, but with team support, everyone learns.

Leaders, in their various capacities, help families, educators, and RSPs to fully understand the legal parameters and requirements of local, state, and federal dictates that drive the delivery of services for students with CP. Administrators also enable the acquisition of, dissemination of, and training on the use of needed equipment and the enhancement of essential programs.

The building principal, school director, or education supervisor often assumes the role of mediator in resolving differences of opinion between parents and staff members and, when successful, helps the faculty to deal more empathetically with overwhelmed parents. Administrators and supervisors are called upon to listen to, respect, empathize, commiserate with, and help parents to deal with the realities of their child's disabilities while navigating the minefield that can be a school system. When administrators realize that they can never walk in the parents' shoes, they will be sensitive to the parents' challenges and can articulate the strengths and limitations of an individual school program while ensuring that the student with CP is fully supported by educational law and effective practice.

It is incumbent upon school leadership to become conversant with those aspects of a CP student's motoric, health, cognitive, and social-emotional issues and to provide all staff members with the necessary ongoing professional development and adequate consultation time that strengthens and further informs staff efficacy and collaboration. A leader's pedagogical knowledge, intellectual curiosity, managerial style, and interpersonal skills can advance an educator's efforts to effectively meet the complex needs of students with CP.

Leadership Responsibilities
- Demonstrate a solid understanding of child development for both neurotypical students and students with neuromuscular challenges.

- Make certain that all direct service providers have the equipment needed to support students with CP.
- Determine a teacher's knowledge and skills and be available to discuss challenges and brainstorm possible solutions.
- Supervise and guide teachers in engineering class environments that meet the unique and individual needs of students with CP.
- Stay abreast of new strategies and perspectives, and be willing to try new methodologies that address challenges as they arise.
- Understand that the directives on confidentiality must be balanced with the staff's need to understand a student's challenges if they are to respond intelligently and effectively.
- Devise ways of assessing teacher effectiveness.
- Realize that the teaching staff is dependent on concerned, supportive, and informed leadership.
- Supervise with an understanding that each discipline's priorities are balanced and blended into workable solutions that offer learning opportunities for each student with CP.
- Facilitate collaboration, consultations, and regularly scheduled team meetings.
- Set up timelines for transition programs, and assign appropriate faculty to these tasks.

Staff Training Responsibilities

- While capitalizing on student abilities, consider limitations and inconsistencies.
- Supervise the process of helping teachers to acquire new skills and breaking out of more traditional silos.
- Equip yourselves to understand the full scope, ramifications, and complexity of low-incidence disabilities, or align yourselves with those who do.

- Help classroom staff to see life through the eyes of the student with CP.
- Help staff to realize that students with CP learn from everything and everyone in their environments.
- Appreciate and allay staff fears and apprehensions, and convey to the staff that trial and error, experimentation, boldness, and innovation are necessary steps on the path to student progress.
- Encourage staff to adopt a Child Study approach that relies on observation and recording.
- Ensure that teachers understand that as models of effective communication, they can demonstrate to students acceptance, encouragement, and resourcefulness.
- Help members of the direct related service teams to broaden both the scope of their interventions and their expectations about students with CP.
- Make certain that teachers understand that well-coordinated, adapted, and modified activities "that allow students to successfully handle academic challenges on their own" require extended time, extra space, and trained, specialized personnel.[234]
- Provide teachers, assistants, and related service staff with a firm grounding in the federal Individuals with Disabilities Education Act (IDEA), state special education directives, and local school district requirements.

Staff Collaboration

- Meet the challenge of getting teachers and RSPs to work together, compromise, and support one another in framing realistic interventions that move beyond specific discipline frames.
- Appreciate the perspectives and points of view of the direct RSPs.
- Explore and support teaching models that enhance collaboration.

Environmental and Student Health and Safety Considerations

- Ensure that every issue of accessibility and safety, both in the physical layout of the school and in access to instruction, has been considered, planned, and executed.
- Understand that within the structures of safety and accessibility lies the need to bolster student independence.
- Determine that every member of the school staff is completely versed in the health and safety needs of each student with CP.

Advocacy, Resources, and Research

- Make certain that school leaders communicate effectively at the state and federal levels about the exact nature of the complex and unique needs of students with CP.
- Collaborate with organizations that provide CP-specific information, and then transmit this information to special and general education classroom staff.
- Provide perspective-widening staff training, which can be generated not only from parents and internal school expertise but also from expertise in the medical and academic communities.
- Provide general and special education teaching and support staff with research-based information on CP, including access to journal articles specific to the conditions of CP.
- Be involved in legislative efforts that support the needs of low-incidence populations at the local, state, and federal levels.
- Join special education professional organizations to remain up to date with trends, legislative activities, and changes to policies.

Home-School Communication

- Listen to and value parental wisdom and experiences.
- Apprise parents of students with CP about the disability services they are entitled to.

- Interact with and provide guidance for parents and caregivers of students with CP by lowering the significant degree of tension, stressors, and friction that may be encountered in home-school relationships.
- Understand, at a personal level, that personal, financial, health-care options, daily management, and social stigma concerns may consume a family of a student with CP.
- Provide information to parents of students with CP about school policies and training that can augment their child's school programs.
- Establish close ties with parent groups of special-needs students, and encourage them to share resources, networks, and blogs.
- Encourage teachers to share a student's personal accomplishments with parents, since in many cases, the student with CP cannot effectively communicate those successes.
- Inform parents about the assistance from and access to entitled educational, social, and financial services, such as Social Security Disability Insurance (SSDI), which provides a range of services, from monthly allotments to home improvement grants.
- Facilitate the opportunity for parents to publicly make their voices and concerns heard by providing accessibility to policy makers.
- Lead the school in becoming an agent of needed change for students with CP and their families.

SECTION XIV

Optimizing the Effectiveness of the School-Based Support Team

Adine R. Usher

The school-based support team convenes on a regularly scheduled basis to collaboratively support and advance the physical, health, educational, and social-emotional development as well as the independence of the student with CP. The frequency of meetings may be flexible and changeable. Weekly, monthly, quarterly, and/or triannual meetings are convened in some settings. Partial team meetings may also be called by any team member at a moment's notice to discuss a particularly pressing issue. A well-functioning school team's membership may vary in response to the discrete needs of a student with CP, with members constantly involved in sharing and exchanging information about the student that is gathered from observation and practice.

Hopefully, team members listen to and respect one another, and they serve as powerful resources for educators, both experienced and inexperienced, who strive to comprehend the intricacies and educational impact of a CP diagnosis as they provide effective instruction. Team members bring different perspectives and skills as they work to further their understanding of the medical, educational, and functional intersections of a student's conditions.

Members of an effective team become skilled at communicating and approaching each student as a uniquely individual package of challenges and strengths, and when exchanges are going well and team members allow themselves to learn from one another, role reversals and role exchanges frequently occur. An effective team is the perfect setting for ongoing training and growth for all its members.

Depending on the administrative structure of a school or school system, classroom assistants—variously referred to as aides, teaching assistants, or paraprofessionals—who provide direct support to students with CP either individually or in small-group settings, may be official or ex officio members of the team, as they often have much to offer.

Ideally, team members should have, in addition to team meetings, frequent interpersonal contact with one another, thus expanding the time that members can discuss the student with CP. In school systems where a rich array of support is not available, extra effort must be exerted through outside resources to find, understand, and share valuable information about a student.

In addition to formal and informal contacts, team members can communicate their thoughts about, and work with, the student with CP through reports, emails, phone contacts, and daily journals, which all strengthen communication both within the school setting and between home and school.

Unlike therapies that are delivered in hospital and clinic settings that provide postsurgical care, school-based related services are primarily designed to strengthen and support all elements of a student's academic and social-emotional performance. Those related service goals are written into a student's Individualized Educational Plan, which meshes therapy goals with learning goals. In the United States and in other parts of the world, this legal plan is referred to as an IEP.

Effective collaboration in any setting is a skill that must be constantly honed. The team that is assembled to meet the needs of the student with CP has the profound responsibility to do all it can to minimize the effects of the multiple barriers that can arise from this complex condition. Creating an effective school-based support team for the student with CP encompasses utilizing some of the following skills and practices:

- Demonstrate a respect and appreciation for the expertise and perspectives of other team members.
- Develop empathy and understanding for varying perspectives, and adopt the ability to develop new positions and perspectives.
- Learn to compromise.
- Develop the flexibility to listen to innovative approaches that have a basis in developmental experiences.
- Become equally effective as a communicator and a listener.
- Develop a mindset that allows you to work as a team member, not simply as a solo provider.
- Focus on the immediacy of the issue being discussed, but see the interrelationship of concerns and challenges.
- Share effective strategies with team members.
- Learn from others by adopting and modifying some of their interventions for your own practice.
- Distribute formal written reports for scheduled meetings *many days*

prior to a meeting so that all team members will have the opportunity to read and digest the contents of the reports.

- Present both written and spoken reports in an explanatory format that can be easily understood by meeting participants; carefully define acronyms and technical, medical, and pedagogical terminology.
- When the terminology of other disciplines is foreign to you, don't hesitate to ask for clarifications during the meeting. This will advance your own knowledge.
- Do all within your power to build up a strong, respectful, and empathetic working relationship with families,[235, 236] realizing that the student with CP is with you for a relatively short time, whereas the family's responsibilities to his or her welfare last a lifetime.

An example of supportive seating.

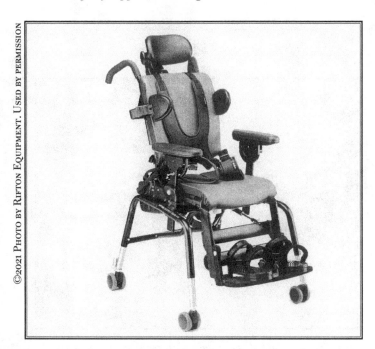

The Activity Chair provides supportive seating for a wide range of school-related activities.

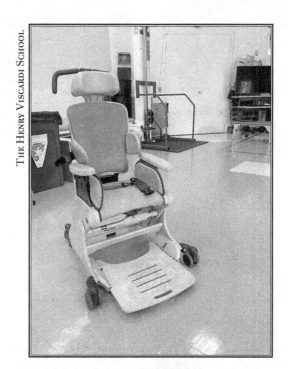

An activity chair in a different style.

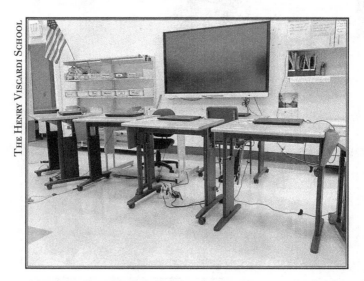

Adaptive, adjustable desks accommodate seating at varying heights.

A custom-made, adjustable-height table.

Low- or no-cost custom furniture made from accessible cardboard building techniques.

A custom-made booster seat using cardboard building techniques.

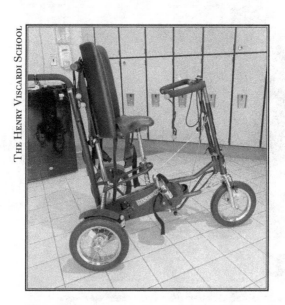

The activity tricycle promotes greater freedom of movement and socialization; improves lower body strength, balance, and posture; and aids visual planning.

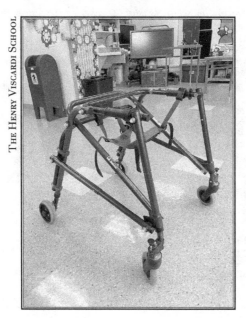

A gait trainer targets and improves those movements and sensory skills essential to walking.

A posterior, posture-control walker enables safe ambulation.

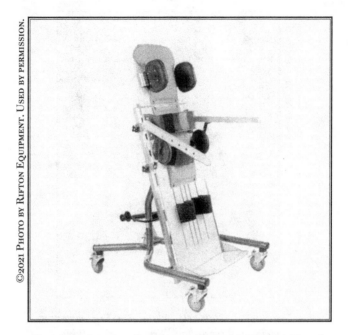

The Supine Stander offers the multiple health and social benefits of standing for students who use wheelchairs, including freer use of their arms.

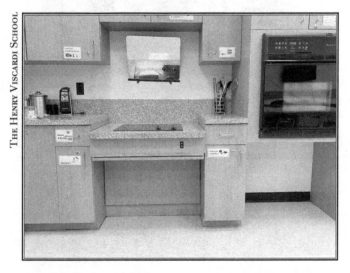

A modified, adaptive kitchen.

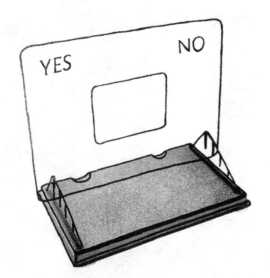

The low-tech, eye-tracking Eye Talk Communicator.

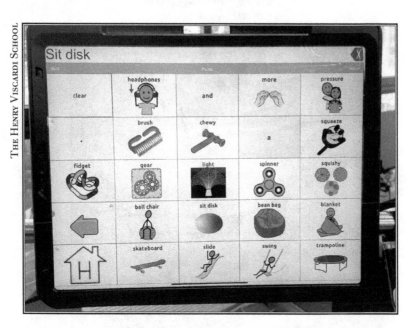

An augmentative and alternative communication system that can be accessed touching the screen with your hand or touching body parts on a switch, laser pointer, or head-tracking device to access a tablet or smartphone.

A custom-made, cardboard vocabulary stand.

*A switch can be a stand-alone communication device
or used to activate toys, computers, and mobile devices.*

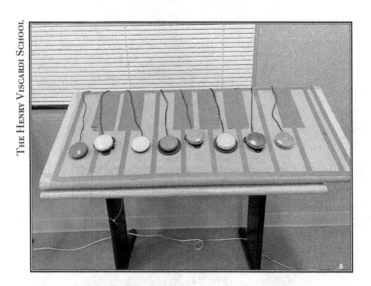

A switch-activated musical keyboard.

Adaptive playground equipment.

A wheelchair swing.

An augmentative and alternative communication system that gener-
ates speech through eye-gaze control of a computer. (Reproduced with
permission from Tobii Dynavox, LLC ©2021 Tobii Dynavox.
All rights reserved.)

Tom hanging out with his buddy Sam.

CHAPTER 7
Social-Emotional Development:
Self-Concept, Behavior, and Socialization

Adine R. Usher

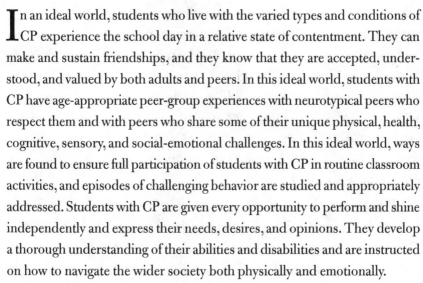

In an ideal world, students who live with the varied types and conditions of CP experience the school day in a relative state of contentment. They can make and sustain friendships, and they know that they are accepted, understood, and valued by both adults and peers. In this ideal world, students with CP have age-appropriate peer-group experiences with neurotypical peers who respect them and with peers who share some of their unique physical, health, cognitive, sensory, and social-emotional challenges. In this ideal world, ways are found to ensure full participation of students with CP in routine classroom activities, and episodes of challenging behavior are studied and appropriately addressed. Students with CP are given every opportunity to perform and shine independently and express their needs, desires, and opinions. They develop a thorough understanding of their abilities and disabilities and are instructed on how to navigate the wider society both physically and emotionally.

In this ideal scenario, students with CP have developed a strong sense of self-worth and, propelled by their own persistence, drive, and determination, learn to deal with and anticipate life's challenging physical, medical, educational, and social situations. At the completion of their formal schooling, students with CP have developed, to the best of their abilities, pride in their own strengths and accomplishments. In this accepting and supportive environment, students with CP are provided with the tools that maximize their capabilities. The results of their best efforts represent an acceptable norm, seen through the lens of "personal best." They are surrounded by family, friends, therapists, administrators, and teachers who hold high, yet realistic, expectations for them, who encourage and support their independence, and who accept their physical, medical, and learning differences. These adults help the students to accept and truly value their own unique gifts while gently and firmly propelling them toward further achievement and the greatest possible independence. These students will never be overlooked or discounted.

Unfortunately, we don't live in an ideal world!

When students with CP whose physical, medical, communication, educational, and social-emotional challenges are appropriately recognized and accommodated, and when these students acquire the cognitive and social-emotional skills needed to interact successfully with peers, both with and without disabilities, the barriers posed by CP need not be insurmountable. This chapter addresses the reality that not all students who live with the conditions of CP inhabit this ideal world. As no two students with CP are identical, it is therefore not surprising that a review of the research on the social and behavioral adjustments of students with CP is mixed in its findings.

We cannot make a definitive association between emotional and behavioral problems and CP,[237] and it is incorrect to assume that *all* students with CP exhibit characteristics of low self-concept.[238] However, as students with CP become more aware of their limitations, they can become overwhelmed as they deal with the discrepancies between their strong cognitive strengths and their physical, learning, and perhaps communication challenges. When this occurs, they may be less cooperative and may exhibit frustration.

For students with CP whose profile also comprises significant associated conditions that include intellectual challenges, frustrated responses may appear in the form of challenging behaviors. Céline Vignes and her colleagues found that negative peer attitudes are commonly considered to be a major barrier to full social inclusion.[239]

This reality can render the school environment emotionally frustrating and overwhelming. Therefore, it is not unusual for students who live with the moderate to severe conditions of CP and who also have average intellect to experience periods of sadness, leading them to prefer the more accommodating and understanding company of adults to that of their nondisabled peers.

Internal and External Influences on Social-Emotional Development

A student's innate personality and sense of self-worth in the presence of significant movement, medical, communication, and learning differences play a major role in determining the student's emotional responses not only to the unique configurations of their own CP-related conditions but also to the ways in which their culture views them.

Social-emotional adjustment, self-concept, and behavioral control in most students with CP are also related to and dependent on a variety of factors external to the student. Beyond the limits placed on physical accessibility in the student's physical environments is the quality of their social involvement in school, within the family, and in the wider community. Acceptance and involvement, whether positive or negative, welcoming or nonwelcoming, can have a profound effect on the mental health and social-emotional development of the student with CP.

Self-Concept

Self-concept is a complex construct that describes the interactions of many variables, both internal and external, and that speaks to the ways in which students perceive themselves. The ways in which students with CP perceive and value themselves is contingent upon the scope of their own emotional strength, abilities, and limitations and upon the perceptions of peers, family, and members of the larger community. Students with CP who value their strengths even in the presence of physical, academic, communication, recreational, and social limitations may indeed be living with a positive, realistic self-concept. Unfortunately, this is not universally true for many students.

Motivation: Passivity and Compromised Initiative

Passivity and the subsequent lack of (or inability to) initiate can characterize the responses of some youngsters with CP. However, even in the presence of strong intellectual capacity, the presence of dysarthric speech may enforce a degree of passivity and resignation as students work to communicate wants, needs, thoughts, and feelings.

The presence or lack of motivation and persistence to engage in the social, academic, and recreational activities of student life are very much dependent on personality, physical, health, communication, and cognitive variables that influence the lives of students with CP. For those with limited access to social engagement, motivation may be dampened. Research suggests that in some instances, parental attitudes toward their child's disability may influence the child's desire to participate as a student. However, other students, who have access to empowering environments and supportive adults, develop a strong inner drive. These students can be highly motivated to stretch their abilities.

Limited mobility, pain, fatigue, the effects of medication, social isolation, overprotective caregivers, low adult expectation, and reduced opportunities to act with independent self-agency can all contribute to lower levels of motivation and can increase student vulnerability. Reduced motivation may impact the effectiveness of therapeutic interventions, increase passivity, limit the curious desire to explore environments, and exacerbate emotional responses to failures when the student is unwilling to attempt challenging tasks.[240]

Limited Experiential Background

When motoric, health, and social access to the world limits the experiences of a typical childhood, a child's experiential background and fund of general information may be restricted. Additionally, unnecessary dependence on others and low levels of socialization can further delay potential growth and development.

Neurological Roots of Social-Emotional Challenges

While some behaviors and social-emotional challenges for a student with CP have their roots in the student's innate personality and in their social environment, other social challenges may be associated with neurological injury, and as is often the case, the youngster will have to contend with the interactions of all these variables.

Lability is a neurologically based condition that describes the disrupted ability to control and modulate emotional responses in the face of frustration or disappointment. Difficulties with lability are occasionally found in elementary and middle school boys who have spastic quadriplegia.[241, 242] There is a possibility that brain injury disrupts neural pathways or networks, thereby making the brain less adaptive to emotional and behavioral challenges. Subtle subsequent learning challenges may make it more difficult for students to cope with situations and monitor their own behavior.[243]

Richard Lavoie described the inability of children with learning disabilities to understand and utilize nonverbal language or paralinguistics, and he tied this difficulty as a powerful contributor to rejection and social isolation.[244] This neurologically based condition makes it difficult for some students with CP to perceive and react to the body and facial language of others in ways that are considered socially appropriate. When *mirror neurons,* found in the brain's frontal cortex, fail to fire properly, it may be difficult for the student to understand the behavior and responses they see in others. Under these circumstances, it can be challenging to establish social connections or to develop empathy for others. Behavioral difficulties experienced by some students with CP may also have their roots in psychiatric disorders. In my decades of observation, I have witnessed many incidents of paralinguistic challenges in students with CP.

Society's Potential Impact on Social-Emotional Development

We live in a world that worships and rewards perceived physical perfection, and those who appear to lack this perfection often pay the heavy social-emotional price of stigma and exclusion. Negative attitudes that perceive disability as an undeniable tragedy, sometimes with religious and cultural overtones, may lead to avoidance and devaluation of the student with the disability and result in a lingering reluctance to fully meet the special individual needs of the student with CP. This further restricts the student's access to fuller physical and social inclusion. According to disability advocate Trisha Lynn Sprayberry, "The real issue of those with disabilities needs to be better addressed. We need to shift this sad and pitied, shallow, discriminating, and oppressive perspective and change the way we see and deal with disabilities as a whole."[245]

In many countries, conditions for individuals who live with CP have been steadily improving, however, research has well established that many individuals with moderate to severe CP often still struggle for acceptance and parity with able-bodied citizens. Students with CP may live isolated lives if governments don't provide accessible transportation, public accommodations, and safe sidewalks.

The Home Environment's Potential Impact on Social-Emotional Development

A student's behavioral and emotional compass can be swayed by the multi-layered dynamics of family structure. Like neurotypical peers, students with CP are, in part, affected by

- The coping skills, the degree of acceptance, and the emotional health of adult family members
- The family's ability to deal with fluctuating levels of frustration and competency
- The realities of caregiver stress and the availability of caregiver support
- Siblings' levels of understanding and comfort with the student's disability
- Expectations that, as much as possible, the child with CP adhere to family rules, routines, and values
- The ability of the family to provide and afford appropriate medical and educational services
- The family's willingness and ability to promote independence and avoid overprotection, even when a high degree of dependence is unavoidable
- The stress that parenting a child with CP can place on a marriage

A literature review by Audrey Guyard and colleagues confirms that parents of CP children have greater risk of experiencing a sense of burden than parents of typically normally developing children.[246] A family's coping mechanisms can be sorely strained by the challenges of raising a youngster with CP. Family members may even have difficulty controlling their own behaviors, emotions, and reactions in the face of stress, and they may be reluctant to set behavioral boundaries for the student with CP, thus assuring further instability for both student and parents.

The School Environment's Potential Impact on Social-Emotional Development

Experience and observation have shown me that many teachers who rarely have had the opportunity to work with students with CP too often exhibit attitudes of discomfort around significantly physically disabled students while concomitantly expressing great pity for them. Given these attitudes, teachers may fail to understand the roots, complexities, and nature of the student's CP-related behavioral and social-emotional issues and are therefore unable to respond in effective ways.

Students with CP may regress emotionally if adults don't take the time, or lack the skills needed, to explore the reasons for behaviors and emotions. For too many students with CP, these challenges go unrecognized, unexamined, misinterpreted, and poorly responded to.

Solveig Sigurdardottir and her colleagues found that 40 to 50 percent of preschool children with CP in early intervention programs have exhibited significant behavioral and emotional difficulties.[247] We might reasonably expect that these challenges will follow some students into their school-age years. School-age students with CP appear to be more at risk for behavioral and emotional difficulties than are their neurotypical peers. Regardless of their origin, even if less serious, these behaviors can be disruptive, stressful, and upsetting for both student and staff.

Research exists that indicates that many students with CP struggle at times with issues of poor self-concept. Adolescent girls with CP may be at greater risk of lower self-concept than are their male counterparts. These girls generally are perceived differently, have fewer reciprocated friendships, exhibited fewer sociable and leaderships behaviors, and are more isolated and victimized.[248]

When present, difficulties with self-concept may suggest a correlation between frustration and behavioral responses to the range of limitations imposed by CP's primary, secondary and associated conditions.

The Role of Program Placement in Social-Emotional Development

Across the globe, increasing numbers of students with mild, moderate, and severe CP are being included, with varying degrees of success, in local general education classes. Growing numbers of educators, families, and students vigorously applaud this trend toward inclusion, firmly believing that a student's academic and social-emotional growth can best be enhanced in inclusive environments. Despite the universal push for research-supported, inclusive education for students with CP, however, some studies suggest that the social isolation experienced by many students with significant, complex CP in inclusive school settings impedes the development of positive self-esteem.[249]

Other educators, parents, and students themselves believe that some students with significant CP will thrive educationally, socially, and emotionally, especially during their formative years, in a highly specialized educational setting in which the student's exceptionality is the norm. For these students, it is believed that special schools facilitate improved self-awareness and self-concept. In schools dedicated to the unique medical, physical, educational, and social-emotional needs of students with significant CP, feelings of social isolation may, in some cases, be less of a concern because this special population represents the norm and *all* the programs and activities are adapted, customized, planned, and executed around the needs of this population.

Whereas many students with CP who are educated in inclusive educational settings thrive, others can face difficult challenges of relative isolation that impacts their intellectual, social, emotional, and behavioral well-being, especially when these emotional issues are interwoven with severe motoric, health, and communication conditions. While younger, neurotypical students may be curious about a classmate's CP, they tend to be more accepting of differences. As students age, though, they can become more judgmental about a peer's physical or communication differences and may be less willing to believe that the "different" student has the potential to succeed or achieve.[250]

Students with CP have been observed to have the lowest levels of school participation in inclusion settings. This highlights the gap between the concept of inclusion and the practical, societal limitations of many schools to enable full participation of students with severe and complex physical disabilities.[251]

Potential School-Based Social-Emotional and Behavioral Realities

For the student with CP, the emergence of unhealthy emotions can go unrecognized and untreated if the barriers that arise from unconscious expectations to "fit in" are not anticipated, identified, and understood. If a student with CP perceives that they are expected to perform and keep pace with neurotypical peers, reduced motivation, withdrawal, and self-doubt can coexist with anxiety, depression, isolation, and feelings of being misunderstood. This struggle to feel oneself a meaningful part of the class can create attention problems, aggression, and frustration. This section identifies the range of social-emotional realities linked to behaviors and feelings that can emerge in all types of school settings for a student with CP:

- The student can be wounded by thoughtless comments by those who imagine that he or she can neither hear nor understand.
- The student resents being simply left to observe while others are being taught.
- The student may experience limited academic and social participation even when complex communication devices are used.
- The student finds the work too difficult, too confusing—or too easy.
- The student must rely on adult communication partners rather than on age-appropriate peers.
- The student participates in fewer skill-based and self-improvement activities.
- Social restrictions, rejection, and isolation can influence social maturity.
- Anger or degrees of depression may set in when students with CP

are not made intellectually aware of their conditions and are not encouraged to take ownership of the complexity of their conditions.

- Parental stress can exacerbate student stress and learning difficulties.
- Difficulties with self-regulation can compromise social interactions.
- Some students with CP may lack sufficient emotional and social stimulation.
- Poor social and emotional perception and comprehension can complicate social and emotional responses.
- The student may not be able to tell educators that he or she is looking for attention and from whom.
- Confusion or frustration may manifest themselves in disruptive and avoidance responses.
- The student is feeling wounded by not being seen or acknowledged.
- The student should be allowed to express the need for a break or a change of pace.

Certainly, students with CP can, despite their challenges, have positive outlooks and experience daily pleasure from having one or two good friends; from participating in satisfying art, music, drama, and sports activities; from achieving academic success; and from the dedication and support of faculty and caregivers. However, being overly self-focused and self-involved is not an uncommon reaction for some students with CP whose management has always been the intense focus of the adults who care for them. Extensive self-involvement may cause some of these students to lack the ability to understand the consequences of behaviors such as sharing and taking turns. Over-dependence on adult support can also precipitate an aversion to risk-taking, a lack of consideration for others, and the emergence of a demanding personality that makes it difficult to sustain relationships. These students tend to lag in social maturity.

These personal factors can cause students with CP to be victims of bullying and verbal and physical abuse. In 2006 Line Nadeau and Réjean

Tessier identified ten-year-old girls with CP as being at risk for rejection by nondisabled peers in inclusion settings because they didn't share behavioral similarities with neurotypical girls.[252] In this study, boys with CP faced slightly less rejection.[253]

Both psychologically and neurologically based difficulties with social connectivity may compromise the ability of students with CP to interact with others in both special and inclusive school settings. Brain-based disturbances can increase a student's difficulty in comprehending nonverbal communication and picking up on nonverbal clues. Disruptive behavior, a preoccupation with objects, and oppositional behavior may result from unaddressed frustrations in environments that fail to recognize and support the student's medical, physical, cognitive, and neurological needs.

Communicative inflexibility, demonstrated by an inability or unwillingness to vary from a conversational theme, and *perseveration,* the repetition of words and phrases, may characterize the spoken discourse of some students with CP, while neurological causes may explain why it is not uncommon for some of these students to exhibit poor emotional response to transitions.

Physical, medical, and management considerations can impact the quality of school socialization. Difficult-to-control drooling may discourage social interactions with neurotypical peers. The presence of chronic pain and discomfort may cause social withdrawal or limit the desire for socialization. Mood and emotional stability can be compromised not only by challenging social interactions but also by the effects of medication and chemical imbalance. Additionally, older students with CP may vigorously and emotionally resist having their private personal care needs met by adults of the opposite sex. Finally, higher rates of school absence due to illness or hospitalization can set students with CP apart from their neurotypical peers.

Some students with CP tend to feel more comfortable and less isolated when they are educated with others who share their experiences—where their experiences are the norm, not the exception. For these students, placement can shape self-awareness and self-concept. Intellectual awareness of the complexity of one's condition may produce anger and/or degrees of depression in settings where the student with CP has no peers who share his or her experiences.

Students with CP can experience problems with peers that lead to anxiety, stress, depression, and disruptive behaviors. These psychosocial consequences[254] may appear if the students feel that their presence precipitates negative or hostile emotional responses from peers. Some of these students may show signs of being self-conscious or embarrassed by their differences. At times they may prefer to play alone because classmates don't seek them out or because they realize that they can't keep up with peers. Often these students prefer the company of adults to that of peers, since adults tend to be more understanding and accommodating of differences. Insufficient attention may be paid to a student who is having trouble expressing emotions, because primary focus is being placed on the student's movement and health challenges.

In a more positive vein, sometimes the student with CP leads a school's disability awareness program. The student can explain and demonstrate their special equipment, and under appropriate supervision, others in the class may want to try using the devices. When this occurs, the experience can be very empowering for the student.

At other times, parents, school nurses, or physicians may speak with groups of students about disability issues. Professional groups that use puppets and dramatic presentations provide all students with a deeper, wider understanding of human differences. Particularly effective for students with and without CP is inviting, as speakers, adults with CP who have dealt with hurdles and have achieved successful, satisfying lives.

CP-Influenced Social-Emotional Responses in Some Profoundly Intellectually Disabled Students

As with other *primary* and *associated conditions* that characterize CP, the frequency, intensity, and duration of difficult behaviors varies with individual students. As there is a correlation between CP, epilepsy, lower cognitive abilities, and greater physical limitation, behavioral difficulties are more likely to be found in populations of students with severe or profound manifestations of CP.[255, 256] Often, but not always, severe behaviors are found in students who cannot verbally express themselves, who may be confused by their social or physical environments, or who struggle to maintain functional levels of stimulation and arousal.

Generally, the more significant forms of CP-associated emotional and behavioral challenges tend to appear in students who are educated in self-contained educational settings that serve a more significantly disabled population of medically and cognitively complex students. These students may be either under- or overstimuled and may find their physical environments uncomfortable in terms of temperature, light, and noise. Indeed, the challenging behaviors themselves may be an attempt to communicate discomfort, anxiety, or upset. Problematic behaviors can occur when a student seeks attention, is avoiding a situation, or has unmet needs. Students who exhibit challenging behaviors may also be signaling to caregivers situations of abuse, distress, anger, and frustration.[257] Students are highlighting the need for vastly improved staff awareness, training, and the use of alternate approaches.[258]

Neurological damage, difficult-to-control seizures, and significant learning disabilities can express themselves in such self-stimulating, self-injurious behaviors as hair pulling, skin scratching, head banging, sexualized behaviors, tantrums, rocking, hyperactivity, *perseverative* (repeated) speech and actions, and withdrawal from tactile contacts. It is also thought that foods containing caffeine or chemical additives may negatively impact behavior.

The uncontrollable need to eat nonedible items, screaming, biting, hitting, pinching, verbal abuse, and spitting are examples of extremely aggressive behavioral disruptions.[259] Behaviors that are directed not at people but at objects, such as the destruction of clothing and property, occur. These behaviors tend to be more characteristic of students with severe to profound CP who may also carry a diagnosis of *global developmental delay*.

Behavioral Interventions

Difficult social-emotional development, resulting in challenging behaviors that stem from existing health issues, can be identified by observation and comprehensive functional assessments. Ongoing discussions should be held with a student's family and staff to improve their mutual understanding of appropriate behavioral expectations for the student. Behaviors that occur at school may not always be seen in the home.

Assessments look for contributing factors during episodes of behavioral dysfunction, such as environmental contexts and emotional triggers. Often disturbing interpersonal responses and even treatment can exacerbate an unwanted behavior. Observations guide us toward identifying a host of corrective measures and interventions that help to eliminate or lower the intensity of the unwanted behaviors. Here are some suggested interventions:

- Change the activity or presentation.
- Give the student a break from a task or a demand.
- Gradually remove preferred objects or activities.
- Move in to provide reassuring one-on-one attention.
- Include the student with one or two partners, then gradually enlarge the group; this may diminish behaviors associated with the student's demanding individual attention.

Medications, many of them antidepressants, may lower the impact of difficult behaviors. *Applied behavioral analysis (ABA)* and teaching strategies may also help students with CP who exhibit autistic tendencies.

Unique Social and Emotional Challenges in the Middle and Upper Grades

As students with CP move into the middle and upper grades, particularly in inclusive school environments, adults are generally less involved in the formation of student friendships and social groups. Self-esteem and social participation research on students with CP during the middle and high school years reports infrequent opposite-sex contact and rare dating experiences for students in their teens. Girls with CP are reported to have fewer friends, feel socially isolated, and report more incidents of verbal and physical intimidation than are experienced by their neurotypical female peers.[260]

Far too many students who live with the conditions of CP are forced to simply observe life, not actively engage in it. Overprotective families, emotionally distant peers, confounded educators, and a disinterested wider public also unwittingly create barriers to achieving sound social-emotional growth.

Based on my extensive experience in the field as a special educator and from a careful reading of the literature on self-esteem, self-determination, and participation, I realize that some, but not all, students with CP may live with the effects of overtly or subtle stressors and barriers that result in unhappiness, isolation, and social rejections. For some individuals, these problems can be exacerbated when the student is the only one in their entire school community who lacks access to peers who truly share similar challenges.

Issues of Sexuality in Teens and Young Adults with CP

The topic of sexuality, sexual awareness, and sexual development in adolescents with CP is often met with anxiety and doubt by the adults in the young peoples' lives.

Some students with CP may exhibit early signs of puberty. Others experience puberty somewhat later than their neurotypical peers. For girls, when puberty is detected at an extremely early age, medication may be administered to suppress and delay the onset of menstruation.

Our acceptance of our sexuality is framed by familial and societal expectations. Unspoken societal insistence that sexuality is not appropriate for people with CP can confirm the widely held stereotype that disabled people are abnormal and even subhuman.[261] Harilyn Rousso carefully detailed the barriers to healthy sexual development that a student with CP may encounter.[262] Such a student may have limited opportunities to date and choose partners and may have scant opportunity to witness adults with CP in committed relationships.

Parental silence about sexuality may reveal either an inability to perceive the student with CP as a sexual being or may reflect rational fears of sexual abuse. Parents whose older children could have healthy sexual experiences fear that encouraging the expression of sexual desire could bring pain and disappointment to their sons or daughters with CP. These parents may also be reluctant to express any hope about their child's future.[263] In this atmosphere, the older student with CP may believe that they are expected to deny an essential part of what it means to be human by assuming an asexual identity and by despairing of ever having a meaningful, consensual sexual experience. If low self-concept is a component of a student's experience, then despair and depression may follow.

Sex Education Programs for Children and Adolescents with CP

Well-designed school programs expose students with CP to age-appropriate and intellectually appropriate information about their developing bodies. These programs should heighten a student's understanding of their sexual development and help them to believe in their right to be considered a sexual being. As they approach adulthood, these programs must also provide for these students the ability to help them make healthy and safe choices about sexual behavior.

In addition to the typical advice that would be provided a neurotypical teenager, teenagers with CP, as they age, need information about the unique challenges faced by individuals with atypical, physical functioning. They need to realize that they are not inherently asexual, a fact that may come as a surprise to parents. Students with CP need facts that help them to understand their feelings and emotions, the highs and lows of physical attractions, and the opportunity to express the pain they may feel if rejected.

However, students with CP, even young ones, are more vulnerable than their neurotypical peers and are therefore at a higher risk not only for sexual abuse but also for neglect and emotional abuse. Unfortunately, I am well familiar with the problem of sexual abuse of school-age females with CP and have appeared in court several times, supporting these students, as an expert witness for the prosecution. Although families acknowledge the need for sexual abuse screening, there is little consensus about how to do it, and many deny that their own daughter could ever be abused.[264] Members of the school-based support team should address issues of sexual abuse with students in an age-appropriate manner and offer themselves as safe, go-to individuals when students need help.

Across cultural settings, young people with both physical and intellectual disabilities are at higher risk for sexual abuse, and females are at higher risk than males.[265] Women with cerebral palsy, just as other patients with disabilities, may be more vulnerable to sexual abuse because of dependence on others for intimate care, increased exposure to a large number of caregivers and settings, inability to defend themselves and seek help or to report abuse, and lack of ability to understand sexual education and be aware of sexual contact.[266]

Therefore, these students must have access to self-protective strategies that include an awareness of appropriate and inappropriate touching. The occurrence of sexual abuse, especially among female students with CP, is a genuine concern. Perpetrators of this abuse, often members of the young woman's immediate or extended family, feel emboldened by several distorted assumptions: that the individual with CP has limited value, that the abuse would not be seen as a crime, that the person is dependent on the perpetrator's care and cannot or will not report the abuse, or if the student does report the abuse, they would not be believed.

Students with CP must also feel secure in the knowledge that they can go to informed, sympathetic school personnel or parents when their levels of discomfort lead them to realize that they are being abused and mistreated. Adults in their lives must be cognizant of the prevalence of sexual abuse incidents in populations of children and youth with physical disabilities and should be aware of subtle changes in behavior and affect that may signal the presence of sexual abuse.

Educators and administrators must also strengthen their awareness that students with CP may be at risk of bullying, since these students are often perceived by neurotypical peers as being physically, emotionally, and cognitively vulnerable. School personnel must take seriously any complaints of bullying and should make certain that the physical and emotional security of students with CP is protected.[267]

School-Based Interventions That Strengthen Social-Emotional Development

- Encourage the student with CP to express their emotions. Listen to and validate the student's feelings.
- Rather than allowing the student with CP just to simply sit and watch their classmates during unstructured periods in the day, take advantage of these periods to promote meaningful social engagement with reciprocity.
- Throughout the school day, work to increase the amount of time the student with CP interacts with an ever-wider circle of peers.
- Teachers who are well informed about the range of CP-related barriers and know each student's likes and dislikes (that relate to healthy social-emotional development) are in a strong position to support the student who experiences varying degrees of social maladjustment, loneliness, and isolation during their school years.
- Help the student to appreciate their strengths and opinions, and provide opportunities for classmates to appreciate those strengths.
- Help neurotypical students to move past stereotypes, to see that differences are a normal part of the human condition and that students with CP are valuable additions to a class who can accomplish meaningful goals and represent their own unique "normality."

- Realize that teachers at the elementary school, middle school, and high school levels all bear a responsibility to improve social adjustment and end social isolation for the student with CP. It is especially important for these educators to create interventions for that student that remove social barriers, with a goal of the student's participation in a wider, more diverse society.
- In both special and inclusive settings, create conversation circles during nonacademic periods.
- Include the student with CP in all academic activities that require group work and create ways for them to participate.
- When alternate methods need to be employed for instruction and completion of assignments and when alternative communication techniques are needed by the student with CP, the student must participate in class lessons to the greatest extent possible, thereby lessening feelings of isolation and separation.
- Participation by students with CP in class activities and nonacademic programs leads to greater independence, reduces negative peer interaction, shows others what these students are capable of, and ensures the development of well-adjusted adults.
- Self-esteem and social competence will increase when the student has access to the grade curriculum (with modifications as necessary).
- Reduce a student's dependence on a specific adult by ensuring that many staff members are familiar with the student.
- Require that the student with CP follow class rules.
- Understand the correlation between positioning-enhanced socialization and wider class participation.
- Encourage the student to demonstrate their understanding with any observable method possible in order to limit frustration and disengagement.
- Provide easy-to-understand procedures for students and adults for physical management activities.

- Use the facilitation of aides to explain group expectations and to improve a student's awareness of the needs, rights, and presence of others.
- Teach and constantly reinforce proper play skills and etiquette.
- Provide regularly scheduled counseling sessions with social workers, guidance counselors, and/or psychologists to address and target behaviors that highlight the presence of environmental stressors and/or neurological challenges to social-emotional development.
- Provide quality staff training in the causes and remediation of challenging behaviors, and ensure that the staff is made aware of how they speak about a student in the student's presence.
- Be aware of how to execute your legal obligation to report suspected abuse of the student with CP.

Motivation, Independence, and Self-Determination

Annette Majnemer and her colleagues stated that motivation in the face of challenge is dependent on past experiences, current abilities, environmental context, and the intrinsic desire to act and master difficult tasks.[268] A well-motivated student with CP will persistently solve problems or master skills that require both motoric and psychological effort.[269] Students with CP who are well-motivated experience fewer unwanted behaviors and derive feelings of pleasure, success, and accomplishment from their endeavors. Research has established a relationship between higher motivation and positive social behaviors.[270]

Strategies for Motivating Students with CP
- Don't miss a chance to create opportunities for independent action, no matter how small or minor.
- Never do for the student what they can learn to do for themself, and

when passivity and learned helplessness become an issue, constantly challenge, as much as is reasonable, the student's unproductive self-perception of inherent dependency.

- Safety is certainly important, but excessive adult help and overprotection at both school and home can physically, intellectually, and emotionally limit a student's potential.

- To diminish effects that signal the presence of self-involvement, self-pity, or entitlement, provide opportunities for the student with CP to demonstrate their ability to care about the needs and feelings of others.

- Through adaptation and accommodation, provide an ever-expanding number of real-life experiences for the student.

- With the consensus of the school team, make psychological counseling and/or regularly scheduled sessions with a social worker a supportive part of the student's education plan.

- The social worker, counselor, or psychologist can also work to enhance a student's sense of motivation by confronting issues of challenging family coping skills and stressful relationships with neurotypical siblings that can affect the student's motivation and feelings of empowerment.

- Allow students to compete with themselves without feeling defeated if they are unable to perform in the same manner and at the same rate as their neurotypical peers.

Self-Knowledge and Self-Esteem

Students with CP need to learn as much about their conditions as possible. Self-knowledge is fundamental to self-acceptance and emotional self-care, and these students need ongoing support in affirming the "normal" reality of their own bodies. Physical struggles with pain and other health dysfunctions can be unsettling and can damage a person's sense of self. Helping a student with CP achieve a sense of wholeness should be a goal of all who work with the student.

Students with CP are experts about their bodies. They know what works best for their own comfort and safety and should not feel pressured to meet society's interpretation of attractiveness or acceptability. We also need not assume that a student with a congenital disability perceives their physical differences as damaging and unacceptable.

If students with CP wish to explain their condition(s) to curious class-mates, they should be able to do so with pride in their accomplishments and a clear belief that being "different" is not to be equated with "unequal" or "less than." These students need to question the assumption that because of their CP, they should feel badly about themselves. Wanting to look and be like other students may be a strong motivator; however, the students should be strongly encouraged to question others' negative assumptions about them.

When possible, provide support or conversation groups, led by counselors or teachers, that enable students with CP to openly, freely, and honestly dis-cuss their thoughts with other students who share many of their experiences. These groups will afford these students a chance to express the pain and sadness they may occasionally feel at social rejection and help them to begin to establish the critical foundation for self-advocacy. As educators, we must engage in self-appraisal to be certain that we are not looking at a student's disability through the lens of our own fearful and negative perspectives. Their differences are challenges that need to be circumvented, not mourned.

Disability Awareness

School systems throughout much of the world, with the consent and guidance of parents and students, are developing a variety of innovative approaches to provide general information about individual differences to classmates, and in doing so, they are promoting the concept of *multiple norms*. All of the involved constituents benefit from these programs. Students with CP have an oppor-tunity to explain, if they wish, the nature of their challenges and subsequent coping strategies. The unasked questions of neurotypical students can lead to misinformation, discomfort, and rejection of the student with CP. Disability awareness activities help to replace fear and rejection with understanding, acceptance, admiration, empathy, and respect.

Families can feel more secure about the level of acceptance their child with CP receives in school when the student's conditions are appropriately and respectfully demystified. In situations where parents do not want a student's obvious difference discussed in school, there is a likelihood that faulty assumptions will further isolate the student with CP. Fortunately, many parents of students with CP realize the benefits of providing essential, age-appropriate information to neurotypical peers, who need an opportunity to ask questions about a classmate's CP. Parents, students with CP, and school personnel can decide on the appropriate terminology. By providing the school with information about the students and by anticipating questions, parents and students can help to shape what others need to know about the students. In designing disability awareness programs, schools should do the following:

- Provide some basic understanding of the student's physical, emotional, and cognitive limitations and strengths for staff members who do not come in direct contact with the student with CP.
- Reassure the parents of neurotypical students that the student with CP will not "upset" their children or draw too much classroom time from them.
- Let all parents know that the aide assigned to the student with CP can also help other students in the class.

Realizing that a student with CP may be at higher risk for bullying, teachers and classroom staff should heighten their awareness of this issue and do all that they can through observation and highly structured disability awareness and anti-bullying programs to eradicate this threat to the student's safety and overall well-being.

The following is a partial list of suggested behavioral interventions drawn from guidelines compiled by the disability awareness program Just Like You! published by Variety—the Children's Charity in Australia. The program initially grew out of an anti-bullying effort developed by Cerebral Palsy Alliance.[271]

- Use positive language when in the presence of individuals with disabilities.
- Find the positive features of differences.
- Imbue empathy in the presence of struggle.
- Inspire students with disabilities, much as you would students who are neurotypical.
- Find ways to celebrate and validate the often-unique realities of disability.
- Challenge preconceived attitudes about disabilities.
- Make disability presentations lively, interactive, and compelling.
- Create presentations that empower special-needs students.
- Provide intelligently presented information to imbue positive awareness and acceptance in inclusion environments.
- Integrate alternate modes of communication into daily classroom practice.
- Commit all students to treating one another with respect and understanding.
- Provide opportunities for students with CP to contribute to the welfare and happiness of others.

Use of Augmentative and Alternative Communication (AAC) to Enhance Socialization

Many types and levels of *augmentative and alternative communication (AAC)* devices have the potential to address and reduce the barrier of social and emotional isolation for students with CP who are dysarthric or nonverbal. Too often in schools, AAC devices are used primarily as academic tools, and their benefits as social communication tools are significantly underused and underrated.

Teaching the student with CP and their special or neurotypical classmates to undertake mutual communication using adaptive technology requires an ongoing concentrated effort. This effort must come not only from technology specialists and speech pathologists but also from school staff who continually enhance the social-emotional interactions among students. It also involves familiarizing neurotypical students with the operation of the communication devices. Having a student with CP sitting isolated while the rest of the class is chatting is simply unacceptable.

Socialization and Participation

Satisfying socialization and participation result from the creative input from multiple disciplines. School for students with CP should provide an emotionally satisfying experience. Certainly, these students need to be able to communicate with all the other students in the school environment. They also need to share activities even when this sharing requires innovative adaptations and modifications. The ability to share school spaces and activities speaks to the student's feeling of self-worth, acceptance, and belonging. The research of Nadeau and Tessier looked for a better understanding of personal factors, including interpretation of social situations, that interact with environmental factors that may cause social adjustment problems in children with CP.[272] "The discussion addresses the issue of age- and sex-related differences and provides avenues of intervention relating to personal and environmental factors that could facilitate or interfere with the social experience of children with CP in a mainstream environment."[273]

Sometimes this participation takes place in an inclusive school and community environment. Other times, participation will flower in an environment populated by those who share the student's unique, physical, medical, and cognitive characteristics. In all types of school settings, the use of social stories and narratives can be effective teaching tools in creating both internal satisfaction and empathy.

Peer Support

Peer support refers to the aid one students gives another. Here it describes assistance provided by a neurotypical student to a student with CP or a student with CP aiding a neurotypical student or a disabled peer. Particularly for the student with CP, offering help to others places them in a position of importance and value.

In inclusion settings, meaningful, nonsuperficial, supportive academic and/or social partnerships between students with CP and their neurotypical peers can greatly enhance the quality of each student's school experience. Mutually respectful bonding and friendships may occur when adults are able to facilitate the pairing of students who can support one another.

In special supportive school settings, peer relationships are critical in addressing the isolation that frequently accompanies significant, complex physical disability. It is in these special supportive educational settings that very complex and significantly disabled students are most likely to share functional educational activities, meaningful friendships, and recreational opportunities.

Mere physical presence is not enough. Inclusion settings, in addition to providing appropriate physical, medical, and academic modifications, need a strong commitment to understanding and addressing the unique behavioral and social-emotional competence challenges that a youngster with CP might exhibit. And, for this population of students, we need to help turn pity into admiration.

There exists a compelling need for educators and administrators in the upper grades in inclusive settings to acknowledge and identify these unique social-emotional challenges and plan collaboratively to effectively address them.

For older students with CP, the virtual world of the internet has afforded many the opportunity to create online groups of individuals who share lived experiences. When carefully and thoughtfully used, these virtual platforms can lessen isolation and build caring communities.

Aaron the artist: A student in Philadelphia uses a modified paintbrush.

CHAPTER 8
Assessment
Adine R. Usher

T his chapter addresses issues involved in choosing and administering both formal and informal academic assessment for students whose CP-related issues often make assessments challenging. These assessments may be administered by classroom teachers, educational psychologists, or neuropsychologists.

Assessing students with CP often involves considering competing goals. Do you compare students with their neurotypical peers, knowing that the student with CP may, because of the scope and reach of brain injury, fall short of the mark? Or do you assess the student in such a manner that allows hidden strengths, knowledge, and abilities to emerge? Rebecca Yin Foo and her colleagues made a compelling case for care and caution when assessing students with CP:[274]

> For children with minimal motor involvement, and both com-
> munication and visual impairments, there is a lack of appropriate
> standardized IQ [intelligence] assessments available; thus, other
> methods of evaluating a child's cognitive abilities must be used
> [(e.g., observations across environments). . . . Moreover,] the

cognitive abilities of children with more severe motor, communication, and/or visual impairments are likely to be underestimated
because the standardized procedures of such assessments are not
appropriate of the population as a whole. . . . [While] there are
standardized IQ assessments available that are potentially suitable
for children and young people with CP, at this time individual
assessments should be used and interpreted with caution.

It is important to examine cognitive functioning in CP because cognitive
deficits independently affect the performance of functional activities and
integration with community and school surroundings.[275] However, there has
been a paucity of studies on the relationship between physical and cognitive
functioning in children with CP, and only a few studies have demonstrated
significant relationships between physical and cognitive functioning.[276] Bridget
O'Connor and her colleagues found limited use of evidence-based assessments
for nongross motor functional issues.[277]

Research does suggest that physical functioning is positively related with
cognitive functioning in children with CP, since children who move more
actively showed higher scores in terms of physical and cognitive functioning
than did the children who showed fewer active movements.[278] For some students with CP, the brain injury that caused CP has likely influenced cognitive
difficulties when one considers the type of CP and the areas of the brain that
have sustained the greatest amount of damage. There is also a suggested correlation between the amount of voluntary movement possible and cognitive
performance.

Quadriparesis (quadriplegia) is the most severe form of cerebral palsy
and is often associated with moderate to severe intellectual challenges. It can
create widespread damage to the pathways of neurons in the motor cortex that
extend to and affect areas of the brain that determine cognition. Conversely,
degrees of hemiplegia and athetoid CP appear less likely to result in significant
cognitive dysfunction.

Although research on the correlation between cognition and diplegia, athetoid CP, and ataxic CP is not voluminous, years of careful classroom observation lead me to understand that in these populations of students, normal intellectual capacity accompanied by discrete elements of sensory-based learning disabilities is often the norm.

First, we will examine the administering of *standardized academic assessments*, which may require some or considerable modification in their delivery. Second, we discuss *neuropsychological assessments*, which have proven very effective in identifying strengths and challenges for students who sustained brain injury. And lastly, we will look at *alternate assessments* that are administered to students for whom the first testing category would yield less practical information; these assessments can be administered more informally over a period or in a structured delivery format that approximates mandated standard assessment.

Physical, occupational, and speech therapists, along with social workers, clinical psychologists, and counselors, all assess students with CP using a wide range of instruments in therapeutic settings, and the results of these assessments need to be shared with classroom teachers as they augment the crafting of effective instructional strategies. Also, the presence of a multidiscipline team lessens the chance that special considerations and modifications that might affect test performance will be missed.

The choice of educational testing instruments, the methods of assessment, and the interpretation of data should ideally be shared in collaboration with the student's in-school team. As with all types of assessments for students with CP, examiner experience and flexibility remain essential.

Standardized Assessments

Since no two students with CP present with identical strengths and challenges, we should exercise caution in making sweeping generalizations about the effectiveness of standardized assessment for this population of students. However, standardized cognitive and academic assessments generally rely on typical motor, speech, and sensory acuity and processing skills—all areas that may be significantly compromised in CP. For some students in this population, performance across testing domains may be difficult to fairly assess.

Students with CP who learn and process information within the range of average cognitive functioning, minus the presence of sensory processing-related learning disabilities, are usually able to successfully take formal standardized assessments when physical access, health concerns, sensory acuity issues, and communication difficulties are accommodated with appropriate modifications. Testing results under these circumstances retain their validity and reliability.

However, for those students with CP whose cognitive disabilities fall in the severe to profound range, standardized assessments, whether formal or informal, tell us what a student can't do but rarely yield results that reflect a student's abilities. For these students, cognitive limitations that stem from severe sensory acuity and processing disabilities render the results ineffective and less valid.

IQ is an important consideration in educating students with CP; however, there still exists insufficient psychometric information about these students.[279] Even now, when more appropriate tools are available, results must be read with the proviso that they, like the student's IQ assignment, can be misleading and have probably not fully captured a true picture of a student's cognitive abilities and future potential.[280]

There has been a misleading perception that most children diagnosed with CP function intellectually without learning challenges. This misperception continues to confound and confuse educational expectations, leaving teachers and parents (who may resist the reality of a student's educational complexity) unprepared for the complicated learning challenges that often accompany a diagnosis of CP.

Requiring students with highly complex CP to take standardized assessments that are not normed for students with their degree of complexity produces results that demonstrate what the students *can't do* and how *differently* they learn and process from their neurotypical peers. These assessments don't detail the cause of difficulties, nor do they recommend prescriptive interventions.

The effectiveness of standardized assessments for all students that are mandated by state and federal entities can be problematic in that they compromise the ability to gauge the potential of the student with CP or to reflect what the student has learned. The inappropriateness of these standardized assessments can also be a source of frustration for students, educators, and parents.

When there are no or few alternatives to the use of standardized assessments that have not been normed for populations with complex neuromotor disabilities, selected *subtests* (which will probably require modifications) may be extracted from the standardized instruments—subtests that afford the student a greater opportunity to demonstrate learning and strengths without completely voiding the reliability and validity of the instrument.

Before any manner of testing commences, examiners will need to understand, as much as possible, the student's total profile. This includes

- Familiarizing oneself with the student's medical history and researching unfamiliar terminology.
- Identifying fine and gross motor limitations that affect the way a student responds to instrument questions.
- Understanding the student's social-emotional coping skills, executive functioning skills, response to stress, and past and current academic achievement.
- Examining information gleaned from observations.
- Understanding social and family history.
- Understanding the need for and execution of adaptive functioning at home, in the school, and in the community.
- Identifying known sensory acuity, perceptual, and processing concerns.
- Determining how the student will communicate responses.

Challenges and Conditions That May Complicate Accurate Assessment

Certainly, there are performance variances between and among subsets of CP classifications; however, primary, secondary, and associated challenges that make learning so difficult for some students with CP are the same challenges that mask strengths and possibilities, making the assessment of progress and potential unreliable. The following is a list of conditions that can significantly limit the validity and reliability of results on standardized assessments for some students with CP, even when adaptations and modifications are in place:

- Limited physical movement, influenced by high and/or low muscle tone, which impedes access to the tools of assessment, including the immature production of writing products
- Poor bilateral motor speed
- Chronic health conditions, which can distract or debilitate
- Discomfort and pain, which distract from focusing
- Challenges to sensory acuity and perception, including somatosensory performance
- Visual motor problems, which affect higher cognitive abilities
- Limited movement, which disturbs perceptual exploration and consequently cognition
- Difficulty with memory, planning, and processing
- Fatigue, which slows work
- Waning initial eagerness as the student struggles to remain engaged, because of poorly regulated visual and auditory attention and distractibility
- Limited experience with the average, age-related activities of daily life that are reflected in test questions
- Compromised ability to indicate or articulate responses
- Uneven performance on subtests, which challenges the validity and reliability of the assessment

- Failure to meet academic proficiency standards
- Struggles with comprehending content area vocabulary
- Difficulties with semantic memory
- Inability to provide written responses
- Difficulty with both concrete and abstract problem solving
- Test anxiety
- Slow retrieval of visual and auditory comprehension
- Learning disabilities, which slow processing and performance
- Poor short-term (working) and long-term memory
- Difficulty with spoken fluency while responding verbally to questions (even when receptive language and verbal memory are stronger)
- Adequate comprehension of language but slow speaking, with mild to severe dysarthria, which can alter the intent of a response
- Difficulty with expressive and receptive language, verbal encoding, morphology, syntax, word retrieval, sequencing, and formulation[281]
- Engagement in spontaneous conversation that is inappropriate to the testing situation
- Mild or severely impaired paralinguistic features of gestures, intonation, and facial expression
- Perseveration
- Adequate capability to deal with simple challenges but struggles with higher-order thinking
- Weak organizational skills
- Below-average ability with simple and complex constructional skills
- Position below grade level in reading and math
- Challenges with response inhibition
- Possible depression and reduced motivation

When challenging conditions of CP appear either in isolation or in clusters, achieving a valid and reliable assessment can be difficult. In addition to the presence of these conditions, examiners need to be aware of barriers that are inherent both in the assessments themselves and in testing environments.

Importance of Preassessment Observation

Whether testing is formal or informal, ongoing observation of students with CP plays an essential role in pretesting preparation. The results of these observations not only help to inform the choice of testing accommodations and adaptations but also help us to anticipate student responses to the assessment itself as well as the testing environment. Even the most skilled examiner needs to observe the student with CP in several settings during the school day. This examiner must exercise thoughtful creativity that is enriched by prior observation if they hope to achieve a more accurate and valid reading of a student's cognitive potential and functional challenges.

Research supports the necessity of providing many students with CP a variety of testing adaptations and accommodations that are clearly written into their Individualized Educational Plans (IEPs).[282] Testing accommodations may be set by federal guidelines and are based on the collaborative consensus determined by a student's team members, who know the student well and who can carefully determine how to most effectively present test components. This collaboration sheds light on how the student with CP may approach assessment items and determines the ways in which a student is permitted to approach and respond to test questions.

Accommodations and Modifications

The effectiveness of accommodations and modifications must constantly be reevaluated, since the motoric, health, sensory, cognitive, and social-emotional conditions experienced by students with CP are not static but rather every-changing.[283] Accommodations and modifications must be carefully and thoughtfully chosen and well-engineered.

Barbara Wilson and Herman Davidovicz have articulated the professed goal of improving a student's ability to demonstrate skills without significantly altering the assessment's validity.[284] Even the most skilled tester must exercise thoughtful creativity to achieve a more accurate and valid reading of a student's cognitive potential.

These frequently used and recommended accommodations and adaptations are chosen to facilitate, optimize, and validate the successful administration of an assessment of a student with CP whose challenges negate the use of standard testing formats. The accommodations may be needed when administering *all* types of assessments and may often be identical to accommodations recommended for instruction. The following accommodations and modifications address an understanding of the student's physical, sensory, health, and cognitive profile:

- Assure that the student is comfortably positioned.
- Allow extended time to administer the assessment, either in one session or over a period of several days.
- Administer the assessment in locations that reduce visual and auditory distractions.
- Present instructions and assessment questions in a manner that ensures that the student can hear, see, and—when necessary—feel test items and materials.
- "Customize" response options. Offer as wide a range of alternative modes as necessary for the student when they respond to assessment questions, including low and high *assistive technology* supports.
- Present the assessment in digital formats that can be easily modified.
- When permitted, read questions aloud to the student, and when necessary, slow the pace of delivery and shorten reading passages.
- Allow adults to record a student's answers when the student is physically unable to do so.
- Allow the student to respond in any manner that is comprehended by the tester.
- Reproduce and modify testing materials by enlarging print and pictures, by increasing the space between written lines, and by decreasing the number of objects on a page, including written questions.

- Use all instructional implements and manipulatives that enable the student to demonstrate knowledge.
- Replicate visual icons for prior home use to establish comfort, consistency, and routine. This may influence a more positive reaction to the testing environment.
- Promote educator understanding of how individual students with CP function cognitively despite multiple barriers to learning.
- Heighten teacher understanding of the relationship between proper physical positioning and academic achievement, even for the mildly disabled student.
- When necessary, use special furniture, special seating configurations, seating pads, and weighted arms, hands, or vests. These devices help to relax and focus the student.
- Use the effective nonverbal responses of eye gaze, head pointing, eye blinking, and body movement.
- Be aware of the impact of medication on attention and stamina during testing.

The Neuropsychological Assessment

No one assessment can capture and address the full array of neurologically based variables that characterize many students with CP. There is a need for deeper understanding of the patterns of altered neurological functioning that are seen in the interactions within the brain and between the brain and the environment.

While the use of neuropsychological assessments is not deemed essential by all psychologists, many find that for some students with CP, a neuropsychological assessment can be a powerful tool that provides detailed, qualitative, not simply quantitative, results.[285] These assessments take into consideration the neuropathology of a student's CP diagnosis and can find associations with types of brain injury and motor-cognitive function. For example, understanding the effects of a thin corpus callosum may shed light on compromised perceptual reasoning. Many psychologists and educators feel that a neuropsychological assessment, in skilled hands, can provide a very accurate picture of a student's capabilities and challenges. These detailed assessments capture "the whole child" and take into consideration brain-based processing in physical, sensory, cognitive, and emotional domains. A neuropsychological exam can also provide insight into the changes that occur in student performance resulting from alterations in cognitive status, and these assessments recommend strategies that improve a student's adaptive functioning.

A well-executed, authentic neuropsychological assessment can greatly aid teachers, therapists, and families in identifying and understanding the ways in which CP affects students as learners. The assessment's descriptive and prescriptive results, once carefully studied, guide the integration of quantitative and qualitative information about the student and guide the teacher's interpretation of results in ways that shape effective instructional decisions and interventions.

Although further research on neuropsychological assessments will continue to widen and deepen the scope of their mission and impact, we know that these assessments

- Look at higher cortical activities that point to patterns of function and dysfunction.
- Consider the strong interconnection between movement, posture, attention, cognition, perception, learning, and communication.
- Identify typical and atypical cognitive patterns.
- Provide a specificity, a depth, and a wider scope to the assessment process.
- Add substantially to our understanding of the roots of a student's functional characteristics.
- Remind us that students with CP rarely have deficits in only one area, necessitating the need for varied instructional interventions.

- Provide a baseline for current cognitive and social-emotional functioning.
- Can guide future performance by identifying why and how instruction needs modifying.
- Increase their value as an assessment tool when the selection of subtests offers a clearer understanding of the student's motoric, cognitive, and social-emotional profile.

When the decision is made *not* to administer a neuropsychological assessment, educational assessments need to be administered by psychologists who are familiar with the manifestation of CP's varied presentations. These testers carefully select subtests from instruments designed both for students with neurological injury and from standardized educational assessments. Their choices should lead to achieving a clearer view of the strengths and needs of the student with CP. However, these assessments will probably need modifications and adaptations.

Informal Assessments

Informal assessments, usually administered by teachers or therapists, gather data in any subject area on students with CP and can be administered at any time. Informal assessments provide information on progress as well as learning challenges and barriers, and they open avenues to determining an individual student's subject mastery. The gathering of informal data that is paired with the results from more formal assessments becomes the foundation for adjusting curriculum, shaping instruction, and defining levels of progress.

Alternative Assessments Based on Modified Achievement Standards

There is a sizable population of students with CP who have very complex and extensive movement, medical, sensory, communication, and cognitive issues. The severity and extent of these conditions can render standardized assessments ineffective in describing a student's strengths and potential. To achieve educational accountability in these cases, great flexibility, substantial modifications, and alternative goals are needed.

Alternative assessments, sometimes referred to as formative assessments, may be informal and teacher-designed, or they can be created and approved by federal and state agencies. These assessments are designed or crafted to reflect the unique, individual student needs, both cognitive and affective. Alternative assessments do not compare student performance, and they yield qualitative information rather than quantitative data. They examine student progress over a long period and take into consideration various learning styles.[286] When it is appropriate, students can be encouraged and helped to participate in the planning and execution of these alternative assessments.

More formal alternative assessments are aligned with general educational standards; they parallel standard assessments in overall subject matter but not in academic goals or administration. These alternative assessments target more functional rather than academic goals. Achievement and proficiency, although based on grade level or alternative achievement standards, are defined differently for these students with CP, and achievement is demonstrated in different formats.

For the population of students with CP who take alternative assessments, standards of performance may be determined by some of the following methods:

- Portfolio creations (binders, photos, notes, self-described learning goals) that demonstrate student performance in tangible forms[287]
- Performance-based achievement

- A checklist of skills that the student with CP can perform
- Consistent uses of assistive technology to present questions, sustain attention, and promote responses[288]

How Effective Assessment Guides Instruction

Effective assessment is the foundation of effective teaching—whether standardized or alternative, formal or informal. It is allied with ongoing observation and with an informed understanding of a student's strengths, reactions to CP-related barriers, and the range of their performance on a variety of tasks at a given time and place. With or without early intervention, it is critical that the student's status and anticipated needs be assessed, addressed, and monitored in the following areas: physical, medical, therapeutic, communication, psychoeducational, social-emotional, and family coping status.

The results of appropriately administered, effective, and adapted assessments place the school's staff (through appropriate training), the student, and the family on the path toward the acquisition and use of newly acquired skills. Effective assessments provide tools for teachers that ease the strain of educational challenges and enhance the quality of the student's performance.

CHAPTER 9

Transitioning Students with Cerebral Palsy into Adult Life

Jeanette Glover and Adine R. Usher

Transitions are lifelong episodic passages that begin when students with CP are young. Each transition encompasses challenges that must be circumvented, hopes that may be completely or only partially realized, and planning that moves through unchartered waters. Careful, thoughtful, and creative planning is essential.

Students who live with the mildest to the most complex forms of CP are capable of much more than many people initially envision. Since there are still so many yet-to-be-discovered challenges and strengths in the school-age student with CP, it is well to assume that with a carefully chosen, well-thought-out collection of effective interventions, many students will be capable of living satisfying, meaningful, and contributory lives filled with self-determination and pride.

Determined parents, who know the student best, are usually the first to see potential in their child. However, as students age, many parents will have to face the reality that although many CP-related challenges can be accommodated, circumvented, improved, and strengthened, they can't currently

Nick with his siblings, Emilia and Luca, and his parents, Stefanie and Joe, in Venice, Italy, on a family trip.

be cured. Even without a cure, students with CP and their families need constant encouragement to stretch, expand, and actualize a student's hopes and potential.

The impact of specific, complex, CP-related conditions may change (both positively and negatively) as student's age, sometimes leaving educators and parents unsure of which paths to pursue and which interventions to prioritize. Rather than giving up or settling for minimum progress, school professionals and parents, confronted with this realization, may need to seek nontraditional and innovative instructional pathways that lead toward increasing independence and mastery.

Imbalance of School Focus

Often during the elementary school years, considerable time and energy is invested in trying to improve the student's physical and communication challenges. Understandably, from an instructional perspective, the predominant emphasis is on academic performance and socially appropriate development.

This academic focus may inadvertently deemphasize the concomitant acquisition of a wide range of critical functional skills for students with CP. Functional skills—including self-determination, self-knowledge, self-reflection, self-assessment, goal setting, problem solving, advocacy, and learning how to ask for and demand assistance and support—are crucial for the acquisition of an independent, meaningful life. These skills tend to be more easily and naturally acquired by neurotypical students.

The lack of a critical mass of students with CP in inclusive settings may leave school staff at a disadvantage in targeting and providing, from an early age, critical functional skills.

Intermediate and High School Focus

Upon high school graduation, students with CP will hopefully transition into higher-education settings or community-based work and residency programs that continue to support their strengths and desires. Although high school graduates with CP may desire and seek more independent living situations, either on their own or in supportive communities, many, due to their need for extensive physical support, personal preference, or limited appropriate options, will continue to live at home. Regardless of educational attainment, many transitioning students with CP will need degrees of support and encouragement for expressing their opinions and for making personal choices about critical aspects of their daily lives.

Formal Transition Planning

Formal transition planning is usually initiated when a student with CP reaches age fourteen, although parents and astute educators have, through observations of student performance, been developing a sense of the nature of the challenges and strengths the student brings into high school.

Early and carefully thought-out pretransition planning that becomes a part of a student's overall program, even in the early grades, broadens teacher and parental expectations for the student and helps to mitigate later transition difficulties. Indeed, many of us who have a more global view of CP can predict some of the future challenges and successes in the early grades.

As early as possible, guide students with CP to realistically think about their futures:

- Encourage the students to express their interests and passions.
- While continually working on skills that need strengthening, expose the students to activities in the community that may become a part of their adult lives.
- Give the students the widest possible range of options while helping

them to anticipate barriers they will undoubtedly meet that will need to be surmounted or circumvented.
- Embed educational goals into specific life skills, such as cooking, dressing, toileting, budgeting, and travel planning.
- Incorporate entrepreneurial endeavors, even in the earliest grades, that give young students with CP a sense of what skills a job requires.

Transition and postsecondary goals can be broken down into annual and short-term goals that are driven, in part, by results from assessments that identify a student's strengths, desires, and challenges. Educational and vocational assessments will inform the student as well as their parents about the student's state of preparedness. With available options, these assessments will also inform educators, job coaches, and transition specialists who prepare the student for their desired path.

Transition planning for students who live with the conditions of CP require the acquisition of knowledge and the implementation of well-thought-out strategies and skills that lead to the establishment of sound, achievable goals. Transition planning
- Considers the reality that many youths with CP have experienced limited involvement in community life.
- Assumes that students with CP need to learn to take on increasing degrees of personal responsibility.
- Encourages students with CP to value and strengthen decision-making skills.
- Helps foster independence, to the greatest extent possible, by fostering self-knowledge, self-acceptance, self-advocacy, self-determination, and self-help skills.
- Includes an in-depth grasp of legal supports and protections.
- Maximizes self-care by making certain that students with CP fully understand the ramifications of their own medical and health needs.
- Attempts to reduce the tendency to self-focus (to the exclusion of

being aware of the needs and feelings of others), even though the person with CP is dependent on others for help.

- Improves the ability of the student with CP to communicate thoughts, feelings, and desires by *whatever* methods are most effective.
- Strengthens competency in using needed assistive technology devices.

The Formal Transition Team: Its Membership and Responsibilities

The transition team meets at regularly scheduled intervals and convenes according to local educational directives. The team may be composed of the student, educators and therapists who know the student best, parents, and a community-based transition professional and/or a job case manager who works with schools and families to facilitate the student's transition to higher education, community education, work opportunities, supportive living environments, or day programs.

Through the strategy of transition planning, the core of this team is the student, who articulates their hopes, aspirations, and concerns. The student's abilities and skills are emphasized, with an understanding of the steps for transition that serve as a guide throughout the entire process. Encouraging students with CP to lead and participate in their own meetings builds self-awareness and accelerates self-monitoring and self-advocacy. Transition planning programs are usually offered as an integral part of the educational program but may be, on occasion, fee-based.

During the high school years, collaborative team decision making assures that the student with CP receives direct instruction on transition matters that

- Prepares the student for interviews and site visitations.
- Determines and evaluates the student's strengths, likes, skills, talents, and hopes, using assessments and prework opportunities in a variety of settings as well as in on-the-job work exposure.

- Introduces the student to the demands and expectations of the new challenges that will arise in the unfamiliar settings of the college campus, in work environments, and in the wider community.
- Strengthens those academic, functional, and social-emotional skills and attitudes that help to prepare the student for a satisfying, rewarding adult life.
- Teaches the student to understand and fully advocate for their need for individualized accommodations in educational, recreational, social, and work settings.[289]
- Prepares the student to integrate knowledge with experience, which then becomes generalized into postsecondary programs and activities.
- Helps the student to understand the parameters of legal emancipation.
- Provides financial and income information, including the management of savings.
- Helps the student to understand and negotiate federal and local income supports for their individual needs.
- Familiarizes the student with health-care systems, including the acquisition and payment sources for medical equipment.
- Helps the student to know how to manage mobility-related issues and individual transportation needs.
- Provides access to adapted driver education programs.

Transition Planning for Job Training and Employment

Preparing the student with CP for the world of work may involve experiences that are most effectively learned in community-based settings by

- Exposing the student to a variety of work situations.
- Teaching the student to apply for jobs that, with or without modifications, they may be able to perform.
- Realistically assessing the challenges of the world of work as reflected

in society's values—for example, staying on task, punctuality, and appropriate socialization.

- Meeting an employer's expectations.
- Accessing on-the-job information.
- Using the internet and community support to aid in the writing of a résumé and a job application.
- Being aware of the physical barriers in worksite spaces and developing the skill to articulate and demand the need for change and modification.
- Demonstrating the effective use of adaptive technology and augmentative and alternative communication, specialized for the workplace, to meet employer's expectations.

Building Social-Emotional Coping Skills

- Work with parents to help them enable and increase the independence of their teenagers with CP.
- Encourage students who out of necessity have been very dependent to engage in less familiar work and/or recreational activities.
- Assist students to effectively handle unanticipated challenges and crises in a civil manner.
- Use social-emotional learning modules to teach empathy, consideration, and social skills.
- Engage related service providers (RSPs) who are charged with enhancing age-appropriate work or college-related social communication.
- Develop and strengthen self-advocacy, organization, critical thinking, goal setting, communication, and decision making.[290]

Transitioning into (General) Higher-Education Programs

An ever-increasing number of colleges and universities are developing programs designed to improve their ability to work effectively with special-needs students and meet the myriad of unique needs that students with CP may have. Colleges expect students to know what they need prior to attending and can articulate these needs to professors, counselors, and others. In general, the college does not take direct responsibility for assisting students in the development of effective strategies for their success.

Statistics remind us that "students with disabilities don't complete college at the same rate as their typical peers."[291] Educators should be aware of the barriers that may be present in college programs so that high schools are better able to prepare students with CP to successfully complete higher-education programs.

Many college-bound students who have CP have unique needs that must be understood and addressed at *every* level of the college experience. Therapeutic attention to these needs, when addressed early in adolescence, has been associated with successful participation in postsecondary education by young adults with disabilities, including CP.[292] Transition programs for college-bound students with CP are most effective when they recognize that many of these students

- May have difficulty keeping pace with their nondisabled peers and may require assistance from a scribe and/or from adaptive technologies.[293]
- May need to be taught strategies (with or without adaptive technology) to help with note taking, test preparation, time management, written expression, reading, and tracking assignments.
- Have come from education environments where modifications and adaptations had been consistently implemented and, in many instances, need to be continued into higher education.
- Will attend schools where federal law does not require higher-educational institutions to replicate all the accommodations a student with CP received in high school.

- Must be prepared to negotiate the continued use of needed modifications and accommodations.
- Have not benefited from intense and extended collaboration and preparation between the sending high school and the receiving college.
- May benefit from college tours, which help students to visualize the college experiences and processes.
- Need to develop insight into both their areas of weaknesses and strengths, understanding how the weaknesses and strengths might affect them in the new academic environment.
- Need to know what specialized accommodations and services are available (some of which are free) and how and when to apply for them.
- When possible, need to hear from students with a range of CP conditions who have successfully navigated the college experience.
- Should, with their families, familiarize themselves with governmental resources that identify and explain the parameters of college programs for students with physical, health, and learning challenges.[294]
- Learn compensatory techniques to aid their survival in higher-education settings.
- Learn if, how, and to what extent the college is prepared to support assistive technology.
- Should anticipate the administration of a complete battery of cognitive and achievement tests near the completion of high school, tests whose results are most likely to further the college's understanding of each student's strengths and challenges.
- Should ascertain whether these assessments suggest further accommodations.
- Should investigate colleges that provide testing at a reduced cost for special-needs students.[295]
- Will want their high schools to create a detailed summary of performance (SOP), gathered by the transition team or the IEP team, and compile a historical overview of each student's needs and accommodations, including the efficacy of currently used accommodations.[296]

Transitioning into (Special) Higher-Education Programs

Students with CP who live with movement, health, and often communication challenges may also be dealing with complex and significant intellectual and social coping issues. Typically, they have had limited postsecondary opportunities and experiences. For this population, research registers poorer postschool outcomes when compared with neurotypical peers.[297]

Students with CP who have significant learning disabilities now have an increased opportunity to study in specially designed and modified programs at the college level. These programs, located in local colleges or universities, are designed for those who learn decidedly differently. Traditionally underserved students with CP who study in these specially designed programs have an increased opportunity to become productive citizens.[298]

Providing a purely academic program for a student with CP who is less likely to live or work independently because of intellectual challenges may not be as helpful as providing a modified, age-appropriate, academic program that is embedded into a functional daily-skills and social-support program.

Transitioning into Competitive Employment

In recent years, there has been a growing effort exerted on private and governmental agencies by schools that serve students with CP to prepare the students for employment and to help them find satisfying jobs and careers.

Despite federal legislation that addresses the employment needs of people with disabilities in many countries, employability has challenging facets for many in this population of young people. This low level of employability is dependent not so much on the young adult's ability to produce productive work but rather on the employer's overall attitude toward people with disabilities and their unwillingness to make the necessary physical accommodations for the young person's physical, health, and communication differences.[299]

Despite a noticeable improvement in societal attitudes and a concomitant move toward finding meaningful employment for this population, rates of employment for people with CP have seriously lagged. Students with CP who graduate from general education programs and who can do college-level work may have more difficulty in finishing college than their neurotypical peers and in finding employment after college if they are dealing with significant movement, health, and communication issues.

Flexibility in the ways that one can work and an awareness of evolving career opportunities are changing the face of employment expectations for those with CP who can work. Developing entrepreneurship and creating social enterprises along with the ability to work from home are just several of these innovations.

General and Important Transition Considerations for All Students with CP

From an early age, students with CP benefit greatly from learning about and being exposed to successful individuals with CP and other disabilities who have made a mark for themselves in the worlds of business, sports, music, and academics. This exposure to those who have distinguished themselves in the wider community not only offers students hope and engenders curiosity but also gives them an opportunity to think critically and independently about their own lives.

Students need to be clear in their understanding of required academic preparation for the postsecondary years. They need to be aware of the academic and social skills that will be expected of them. They should be discouraged from hiding their disabilities; rather, they should be able to articulate their questions, complaints, needs, and requests intelligently and forcefully. A successful transition program targets those requisite skills. Older students with CP must become prepared to take control over the monitoring of responsibilities and performance of those whom they will eventually hire to care for their daily personal care needs.

As students move from middle school to high school, they need instruction in identifying ways in which their CP may require them to seek special supports. Whether in higher education or on job sites, these young adults must learn to identify and understand the policies of state, federal, and non-governmental agencies that exist to support and fund their wider goals of independence and participation.

The student with CP needs to assume responsibility for and gain a thorough understanding of any educational and mobility device that they are dependent upon. This includes knowing when and why a device is not functioning properly, where repairs and temporary replacement devices can be found, and how these repairs, temporary replacements, or permanent replacements will be financed.

During the high school transition period, students with CP should strengthen their advocacy skills as they deal with accessibility issues that are certain to occur in areas outside of their schools and homes.

Supervised Community Employment

The population of transitioning students whose movement, health, social-communication, and intellectual challenges are significant requires formal vocational assessments and training, formal and informal observations, and a variety of possible job sites that train for service industry jobs, office jobs, and retail opportunities—all requiring extensive, ongoing support.[300]

As students with CP near the end of their secondary school years, traditional curriculum is embedded into a functional vocational core curriculum, and more school time is spent out in prospective work sites.

Community Day Programs

For transitioning individuals with CP who are unable to secure employment, local, state, and federally funded community day programs serve as gathering places—out of the home and during work hours—that provide therapy, medical services, companionship, meals, socialization, recreation, creative arts, and community trips. Day programs run by organizations such as United Cerebral Palsy are both privately and publicly funded. And, for the most significantly disabled high school graduates, these programs offer learning through sensory stimulation and exposure, which may include the use of therapeutic equipment that connects this population to persons, activities, and experiences outside of their own bodies. In such programs, activities of self-care and daily living continue to be worked on in order to awaken a degree of self-awareness and agency.

Using Technology to Enhance the Success of Transition into Adulthood

We know from research and practice that students with CP learn in a variety of ways, and the versatility of digital devices and software, simple and highly complex, can be critically important in connecting students to the wider community. It can be expected that by the time students with CP are entering a formal secondary school transition program, many have already used several forms of assisted, digital, and augmented technology tools that not only have enhanced their ability to perform academic and functional tasks but are equally important for communication.

The ever-changing, ever-growing range of low and high assistive technology tools offer many students with CP the chance to master more skills, complete ordinary academic and functional tasks, and communicate and interact successfully with nondisabled citizens in academic, recreational, and employment settings. Written and verbal communication, navigating the wider community, and accomplishing a range of personal care skills will all be instructional targets.

Ease of access to assistive technology for independence and engagement capabilities vary from student to student; therefore, an innovative willingness is required to assist the individual to discover and utilize methods of access that are specific to their physical capabilities (such as eye gaze, head switches, on-screen keyboard, etc.).

Learning to effectively navigate online communities and use social media, particularly those platforms that help to connect individuals who share the challenges of their conditions, is another powerful transitioning tool for the student with CP. Independence and self-determination will increase with the use of computers, small tablets (e.g., iPad, Surface Pro), and cell phones (e.g., Android, iPhone), all of which help to develop a student's confidence, lead to self-determination, and increase opportunities for both formal and incidental age-appropriate learning.

One also hopes, for students who require the assistance of augmentative and alternative communication (AAC) devices, that training on these devices, throughout elementary, middle, and high school years, not only has targeted academic learning and responses but also has strongly enhanced functional and social communication.

The mastery of AAC systems can decrease the isolation that is too often experienced by nonverbal and dysarthric students in the postsecondary period, isolation that can hinder or thwart independent, successful entry into higher education or the world of work. As the supports for students with CP are so specific and varied, there is a need for further research on the efficacy of apps on digital devices that meet the student's specific needs, particularly in the areas of physical and visual access in a higher-education or work environment.

For students with CP whose postsecondary years will most likely be spent in structured community settings and who may be less successful with written text, digital technology offers versatile possibilities for degrees of independence. For example, repeated presentation of pictures and words on the iPhone representing a shopping list teaches shopping skills and reinforces new, targeted vocabulary for older students.[301] Videos and recorded memos are also functional and effective communication tools that can connect some students to activities in the adult community.[302]

Many transitioning students who live with the conditions of CP need high-quality and lifelong medical, therapeutic, and recreational care that is provided in well-established publicly and privately funded organizations throughout the United States and in locations around the world. Not only do many of these centers actively seek to address these continuing needs by providing *physiatry* services (spasticity, gait, and pain management), but they offer a range of athletic, musical, dance, and performing arts opportunities.

Eubie, nineteen, with her brother, Romare, mother, Verna, and sister, Zaire, who also has CP.

CHAPTER 10
Family Voices

Adine R. Usher

Parental Responses to, and Experiences with, Disability That Need to Be Acknowledged and Understood

Love & Devastation
 Love & Fear
  Love & Anger
   Love & Embarrassment
   Love & Loneliness
    Love & Guilt & Blame
    Love & Frustration
    Love & Exhaustion
     Love & Depression
     Love & Disgust
      Love & Feelings of Loss
      Love & Resignation
       Love & Doubt & Denial
       Love & Confusion
Strength Hope Determination Gratitude Commitment Perseverance

Truly, every parent of a student with cerebral palsy could write their own book. Although similarities exist, no two families for whom CP is a constant presence journey on pathways of joys and challenges that are identical.

For the sake of clarification, the term *parents* will be used to define birth parents, relatives, caregivers, or other legal guardians who with willing and loving determination assume primary responsibility for the care, growth, and development of the student who lives with the conditions of CP.

It is critical to the well-being of students with CP and their parents that educators and other team members strive to grow in pedagogical knowledge, skills, and empathy.

For many years, to be supportive, I have walked in front of, behind, and beside families and their children with CP. Yet I have never walked in their shoes, so it is therefore incumbent upon me—and, indeed, upon all educators—to observe carefully and listen respectfully in order to discern what feelings, challenges, and information parents are and are not articulating. I am also keenly aware that parenting roles do not end until the parents draw their last breath. As educators, we must avoid hiding behind bureaucracy to separate ourselves from parental emotions and determination. Before we explain to families what we are going to do, we need to discover what they and their child need. As the late Verna Hart, mother extraordinaire, said, "Parents feel ill-equipped because society pays lip service to a system that is 'like a boat without paddles.'"

In the last half of this chapter, extensive interviews will record the experiences of seven parents who live with the reality of CP. Most parents' names have been altered for privacy, but their stories remain authentic.

Initial Parental Responses to a Diagnosis of Cerebral Palsy

From the moment a newborn or very young child is diagnosed with cerebral palsy, families may become overwhelmed and unsettled by feelings of grief, fear, trauma, shock, disbelief, frustration, anger, devastation, disappointment, depression, guilt, embarrassment, uncertainty, and loss—feelings that challenge a family's view of its self-worth.

Social status; financial restrictions; parental personalities; family support or its lack; cultural, religious, linguistic, and community pressures and practices; availability (or its lack) of medical support; endless medical procedures; medical terminology; the presence or lack of governmental support; and child-rearing practices may all influence a family's emotional health and management effectiveness.

The reaction of a stranger may be disconcerting, and families may be made to feel that the presence of a disability is a punishment. This confluence of issues can leave a family struggling for years.

Siblings may have difficulty accepting a sibling with CP, marriages can become strained, and generational attitudes about disability can devalue the student's inherent worth and strain the family structure.

Simply keeping the child with CP alive during the early months and years can become an all-consuming responsibility. These realities need to be acknowledged, understood, respected, and, as much as possible, accommodated.

Conversely, the arrival of a child with CP can be accompanied by a determination to fiercely love, accept, find joy in, fight for, and support the child born to them. These families realize that stress is an inevitable presence in their lives but can turn altered hopes into adapted possibilities and develop a resiliency that advances the welfare of the child and the family unit by finding a balance between their needs and the needs of their child. These are often fierce *warrior* parents, who can exhaust themselves trying to obtain the appropriate services that will improve the quality of their child's life. Intrafamily relationships are strengthened, and siblings in these families tend to embrace the sibling with CP, often becoming protective advocates.

The experiences of many parents of children with CP fall somewhere in between these scenarios.

Contributors to Parental Stress

All families caring for students with CP will experience some degree of stress, depending in part on the constitution of the family structure and the complexity of the student's physical, health, complex learning, and social-emotional status.[303] Family research on the effects of CP finds that there is higher parental stress felt by families with children with CP than is found in the general population.[304] Multiple experiences, described here, *may* contribute to parental and familial stress when caring for students with CP:

- Lack of sleep.
- Difficulty simply keeping a child with CP alive, properly hydrated, suctioned, fed, pain-free, breathing effectively, and relatively seizure-free, which can become an all-consuming, exhausting task.
- Reduced energy due to sadness and hopelessness.
- Unmet need for respite.
- Back strains from lifting a heavy student, a risk that increases as the student ages and becomes heavier.
- Reduction in the quality of parental self-care, leading to increased parental illness and problems with decision making.
- Marital instability, inconsistent or nonexistent partner support, and/or increased maternal stress. Research suggests that this instability can cause poorer maternal well-being, lower satisfaction with parenting, and the likelihood of mental health problems.[305]
- Anticipation of surgeries and postoperative home care.
- Burnout from providing care in dressing, feeding (oral or tube), and toileting and from providing for bodily cleanliness.
- Constant attention to swallowing problems that can lead to aspiration.
- A student's nonverbal status, especially when paired with significant physical limitations.
- Difficulty finding effective, qualified medical care.
- Difficulty affording necessary medical equipment and appliances.

- Difficulty finding or affording special transportation.
- Financial anxiety and insecurity over a lifetime of expenses, influenced by disability severity and family location.[306]
- Limits on the mother's earning power.
- Limits on parental recreation, self-care, and housekeeping.
- Abandonment by family members.
- Realization that interventions, both surgical and nonsurgical, may fail to produce hoped-for long-term benefits.
- The failure of staff to consider cultural, racial, religious, linguistic, and socioeconomic factors that influence the parent's attitudes and behaviors around disability.
- Feeling the need to take a constant combative stance in dealing with the school and the community.
- Difficulty finding appropriate schooling that accommodates a student's needs and improves his or her quality of life.[307]
- Difficulty finding caregivers outside of the family.
- Facing stigma and rejection from family, friends, and the community.
- Low racial or ethnic status in society.
- Facing social isolation.
- Exacerbating stress of minor daily problems.
- Vacillation between hopefulness and depression.
- Long-lasting feelings of parental shame.
- Negative effects on parental well-being, caused by a demanding, self-involved, and/or strong-willed student (from environmental and/ or neurological causes).[308]
- Realization that society may view the student as less valuable and productive.
- Concern about a student's social isolation and self-image at school.
- Comprehending vague and confusing information and instructions from health-care providers.
- Not having their voices heard at the child's school.

- Missing transitions related to life's typical milestones.
- Recurring bouts of grief and sadness at different stages of a student's development.
- Difficulty confronting realities related to a student's challenges.
- Demanding that a student "keep up" with neurotypical students when "different paths" are more effective. Students will generally reach the goals they need to achieve in their own, unique ways and in their own time.
- Feeling upset about a student's future, since CP has no real cure.
- Increased student stress brought on by the parental stress.
- Struggles to accept the scope and growing impact of a child's disability, including the presence of associated conditions.
- Defensive minimizing of the stress of caring for a child with CP.
- Feeling captive by all the of actions that the parents *believe* they should be taking.

Effective, Evidence-Based Practices and Attitudes That Help Reduce Parental Stress and Enhance Parental Satisfaction and Resilience

Although a child's CP may consume a parent's life, educational systems can play an important role in lessening stress and in improving the quality of parental life. Unfortunately, educators and educational structures that rely solely on administrative dictates and governmental policies fail to appreciate the sheer humanity of a family's situation. Understanding and addressing parental concerns bolsters parental emotional health. The following list of practices can begin to reduce parental stress, build parental resilience, and increase student well-being in all domains:

- Remind parents that *their* lives are important too.
- Strive to make the school the center for advocacy for students.
- Realize that parents can't "go it alone."

- Believe that schools and families learn from and rely on each other.
- Stress positivity and encourage parents to share what their student *can* do.
- Provide important information in a family's primary language.
- In inclusive settings, let parents know that you are learning about CP, and realize that the parent-school "dance" can be challenging.
- Know that parents may see more potential in a student than educators have been trained to see.
- Parents may be employing cognitive or behavioral strategies at home that the school can adopt.
- Because parental perceptions may be aspirational, parents may see more strengths and progress than the student is actually demonstrating.
- Appreciate the fact that school and home are not always on the same page.
- It may take a while for a family to understand the scope of the school's concerns. Conversely, educators can take a step back and allow parents to exercise the lead in sharing their considerable experience.
- Guide parents in understanding when there may be totally valid limits and parameters to a school's ability to provide, modify, adapt, and customize a service that the parents desire.
- Ascertain whether parents are emotionally ready to confront the full scope of the student's diagnosis.
- When fierce parental determination meets educator intransigence or defensiveness against a perceived challenge to the educator's role, adversarial relationships can cause friction that is time-consuming and that yields low parental satisfaction.
- Resist being judgmental, and instead work to make the school a comfortable, supportive, empathetic, safe, and accepting haven for parents who struggle daily.
- Encourage parents to ask questions, seek answers, and request clarifications.

- Inform yourself so that you can ground your interactions with parents through the lens of their cultural value system.
- It is of paramount importance that educators and parents grow in their ability to "read" each other emotionally.
- The frustration and anger that some parents bring to their relationships with school staff may result from the staff's own lack of understanding as well as from parental anxiety about the student's future.
- Empathize and offer the family respect.
- Help parents to recognize and find pride and motivation in what their child with CP *is* accomplishing.
- Listen to and learn from parents, and exercise humility as you encounter parental expertise. They understand a student's complexity best.
- Encourage parental involvement in networking and group collaboration, parent training, activism, and advocacy.[309] Parent support groups can and do move, shape, and influence local and governmental policies.
- Understand that throughout a student's school years, interactions with parents may have to be balanced between vacillations in student performance and parental expectations.
- Through transdisciplinary teamwork, help parents to appreciate the intersection of motoric, health, cognitive, and social-emotional issues.
- Encourage parents to openly share fears, concerns, critical health, and behavioral information that factor into the student's cognitive and social-emotional growth.
- Demonstrate your commitment to the belief that all students with CP, including the most profoundly disabled, can make improvement. We will never know how much can be accomplished until we employ all our innovative, creative strategies.
- Expand home-school communication with the daily use of e-messages, notebooks, phone calls, and journals, which allow educators and parents to lay out successes and concerns. These efforts encourage parents to articulate what is and is not working for them and the student.[310]

- Encourage parents and family members to hold high but realistic standards.
- Raise parental and familial expectations by gently pulling them into the educational process, even when there seems to be the willingness for the family to "leave it all to the school."
- Even as physical and health management responsibilities are undertaken at home, encourage parents to daily bring new sight, sound, and tactile experiences and stimulating communicative experiences into the student's life, no matter the student's academic level.
- Be aware that in both special and inclusive educational settings, the rate of performance and improvements in academic and social contexts will vary greatly among students with CP.
- Ensure that parents have access to adaptive and communication technology for their student as well as the knowledge and skill needed to operate the systems.
- Be aware that inclusion programs are less likely than special schools to offer parent support groups, thus increasing parental isolation.
- Children with CP are not born with instruction manuals in their hands, and teachers and team members should encourage parents to seek outside counseling when school-provided counseling is insufficient.
- Some parents are easily intimidated by authority figures in the educational and medical settings, so educators should help them understand that asking for help and insisting on responses is not a sign of weakness but rather an indication of strength.
- Ascertain the parents' level of comfort with their child's disability. Are the parents uncomfortable around others with CP? Have they expressed the desire that *their* student "not be around others who look like them"? Does a student's general lack of care and possible neglect, particularly in the middle school years, signal parental exhaustion, depression, or a feeling of having "given up"?
- Look out for less-than-healthy, overly dependent relationships between

parents and students, which can significantly impede a student's growth toward independence.

- Become allies of students with CP who are tired of "being fixed," who are no longer committed to "looking normal," and who are growing into becoming, not hiding, their authentic selves.
- Find ways to reduce parental overindulgence and overprotection.[311]
- Offer practical solutions and possibilities when parents seem to be avoiding difficult-to-accept realities.
- Exercise patience. Try not to correct what may appear to be illogical beliefs, and allow parents the right to be angry.
- Keep parents engaged and moving forward.
- Parents need a clear understanding of, and the freedom to express opinions about, what is being taught, how it is being taught, and why and how profound CP can challenge learning and instruction.
- Praise and encourage parental decision-making behavior.
- Be honest about the benefits and risks of trying new interventions and therapies that may or may not help the student with CP, but don't discourage parents from trying.
- Encourage parents to accept effective adaptive educational strategies that may apply only to their child with CP.
- Understand that parental attitudes and coping strategies are driven, in part, by the parents' belief systems, values, skills, hopes, and expectations for their child's future.

Having parents create a list of informational comments about their child with CP is extremely helpful for educators, related service providers (RSPs), and classroom support staff. This list, in addition to the Individualized Educational Plan (IEP), adds further, daily details to the contents of the student's "suitcase" and deepens educator knowledge. Here is how such a list can be headed: "This is what I would like you to know about our child and our family:"

- My child gets pleasure out of the following activities:
  _____

- My child appears most distressed when:
  _____

- My child communicates feelings in the following ways:
  _____

- The following strategies have worked best for my child in the past:
  _____

- The following activities bring discomfort and exhaustion to my child:
  _____

- These are my child's likes and dislikes:
  _____

- Here are some of the problems that my child and I have encountered in school, and here is how I think that those problems might be resolved:
  _____

- These are the goals and hopes I have for my child:
  _____

- These are some of the ways in which CP impacts my child and our family life at home and in the community:
  _____

- We are worried about lifelong care, quality of life, and degree of independence as our child becomes an adult.
- We are concerned about how the school is handling health-related absences.

Siblings

While research does not support significant difficulties between students with CP and their siblings,[312] problems do arise, and it is possible that siblings may feel stress if the parents are finding caring for a child with CP stressful.

While many siblings are supportive, protective, and empathetic and engage in heathy competition, others may send veiled or overt messages of embarrassment, resentfulness, and anger at the attention the sibling with CP requires. Occasionally, the nondisabled sibling may withdraw from family life. Parents should be aware that resentments exist and can use the support of school counselors and psychologists to address these challenges.

Global Perspectives: Strengths and Challenges

In 2006, the United Nations adopted the Convention on the Rights of Persons with Disabilities (CRPD), a human rights treaty, and many countries worldwide have signed on to the treaty as signatories and parties to the Convention. Unfortunately, not all these countries have been able to match their professed willingness to raise the general quality of life for people with physical disabilities, including CP, with their ability to actualize the Convention's goals.

There is great variability in the world concerning the value, care, and concern awarded students with CP and their families. The birth of a child with CP in a technological and socially advanced society may be met with medical and educational skill. However, the birth of a child with CP can pose significant challenges and adverse consequences for many who live in developing countries, and while parent-led efforts have begun to make substantive inroads in meeting the needs of children with CP, there is a critical need for governments to address those needs. The following are some of the extraordinary challenges that parents of children with CP frequently face in developing nations:

- The mother may face social stigma, isolation, and rejection, all based on cultural beliefs.
- The birth of a child with CP may keep a mother from earning a living.
- Parents in many countries find that there are few national conversations about CP, there is little information about the condition, and the media and governments fail to provide more than fragmented or limited medical, therapeutic, and educational support.
- Sometimes neurotypical students are pulled out of a classroom by their parents with the introduction of a student with CP.
- There may be a serious dearth of properly trained teachers.
- Parents of students with CP may have to rely on help from nongovernmental organizations (NGOs).
- Except for the mildest cases of CP, many school systems may insist on keeping students with CP in separate programs.
- Some highly selective educational systems relegate students with CP to the margins of the educational structures.
- In some countries, children with CP are cared for only by volunteers.
- A parent cooperative in Ghana trains parents of children with CP to make adaptive equipment out of paper and recycled materials.
- There is an international need for parents to receive psychological help to ward off depression.
- In some developing countries, mothers are creating their own CP centers to train unemployed mothers of children with CP to sustain the lives of their families.
- Parents are requesting that government provide day care centers for children with CP and are asking for properly trained teachers.
- Parents are wishing that many more children with CP had inclusive education or opportunities to interact with neurotypical peer children.

From a mother in Nigeria: "I have found joy in the purpose and love my child has given me."

Parent-Educator Alliances That Strengthen a Student's Social-Emotional Health

- Parent-educator alliances increase awareness of the potential pain of social isolation that is experienced by far too many students with CP (particularly in inclusion settings at the middle school and high school level).
- Older students are becoming more aware of the realities of their disabilities and need to view themselves as valuable social beings, not just as individuals who are in constant need of fixing.
- Parent-educator collaboration promotes inclusion of students with CP into the social life of the school and the wider community.
- Parents, educators, and counselors make students aware of the powerful myths and stereotypes that frequently surround disability and work to prevent negative attitudes from becoming internalized into each student's self-image.
- Parents play a critical role in helping students with CP to develop strategies for handling prejudices as they learn to navigate the non-disabled world—strategies that don't force them to disavow their disabilities but accept their differences as a realistic part of who they are. They need to know and feel that they are "all right" just as they are!
- Parents, teachers, and classroom staff should notice, and correct, instances when a student with CP becomes so attached and dependent on adults that they make little effort to sustain relationships with peers.
- A student may withdraw physically and socially, retreating to a place inside themselves when feeling anxious or stressed, and therefore may crave adult attention to the point of being manipulative.
- In helping a student to reach out independently, parents and educators should be aware that the nonjudgmental and patient interactions that students with CP find with adults will not necessarily be duplicated when students interact with neurotypical peers.

- Parents of students with CP bring a rich and vast array of cultural, linguistic, religious, racial, and socioeconomic experiences not only to the educational process but also to the place of disability in the family's life.
- As educators and team members, it is essential that we educate ourselves about these diverse experiences and ask questions to gain a deeper understanding, with the goal of bringing both educators and families to a place of greater cooperation and respect.

Parental Quotes That Can Elevate an Educator's Awareness

- "It took me two years to come to terms with my daughter's CP."
- "His CP tends to make my child sad."
- "My pain, as a mother, has made me more resolute."
- "There was a lot of crying in my family" (offered by one grandmother).
- "It takes so long to get the help you need."
- "Don't lose your aspirations for your child."
- "I am scared and cry a lot."
- "Always let your child with CP know how loved and valuable they are, despite the messages they may get from the wider society."
- "People don't think of my child as clever and bright just because she can't speak."
- "I give my child with CP every opportunity to make choices and decisions."
- "Insist that the school gives your child every opportunity to shine."
- "Stay in close constant contact with all the members of your child's school team."
- "I can't afford the kind of wheelchair I'd like my daughter to have. Many of them cost far too much."
- "My family really needs a special van for transporting our son, but

we will never be able to afford it."

- "My husband and I require a great deal of support to help us set realistic goals."
- "I believe that my daughter would enjoy spending more time around other kids with disabilities."
- "Look hard and create opportunities for enjoyment for your child and your family."
- "Work to release unrealistic goals, then work to set more realistic goals."
- "Allow yourself to grieve the birth you had expected, but move forward to find contentment in your new reality."
- "I can't stay angry forever because my child needs me at my best."
- "As I seek services and support for my son, I often find myself in places that are a lot less helpful."
- "Live your life as normally as you possibly can."
- "In trying to manage my son's needs for a lifetime, I needed to put on boxing gloves to deal with the school, doctors, and my wider community."
- "You really don't care if my child attends school if you use the excuse that it's too expensive to install automatic doors."
- "My son is just as valuable as any other student, and his future needs must be carefully considered."
- "Our son is a good student, and his CP should not determine the quality of the college he will be able to attend."
- "Don't excuse my son from part of the curriculum. Figure out a way to help him learn the material."
- "Accommodations do not give the student with CP an advantage over other students; they simply level the playing field."
- "Although my child has CP, don't give him an award for trying. Award him like any other student when he has achieved something."

- "Give me the truth. When there are problems at school, I want to know."
- "Please try my suggestions for working with my daughter. I am not trying to tell you how to teach; it's just that I may be able to make your job easier."

Here is an excerpt from an article written by a father, Chris Gabbard:[313]

My son, August, has a number of quirks that distinguish him from the typically developing ten-year-old. He lives with cerebral palsy, is a spastic quadriplegic, has cortical visual impairment (meaning he is legally blind), is completely nonverbal and cognitively disabled, has a microcephalic head, and must wear a diaper. Moreover, he is immobile—he can't crawl or scoot around or hold himself up or even sit in a chair without being strapped in it. If someone were to put him on the floor and leave him there, he would be in the same location hours later, give or take a foot.

Many such well-meaning people would like to put an end to August's suffering, but they do not stop to consider whether he actually is suffering. At times he is uncomfortable, yes, but the only real pain here seems to be the pain of those who cannot bear the thought that people like August exist. For many of those folks, someone with August's caliber of cognitive and physical disability raises the question of where humanity leaves off and animality begins. But that animal-human divide is spurious, a faulty either-or.

That is not to deny that August, along with my daughter and my wife, is the most amazing and wonderful thing that has ever happened to me, for he has allowed me an additional opportunity to profoundly love another human being.

Parents' Stories

Story Number 1

Ann Randall and her husband live in a suburban community in the northeastern part of the U.S. and have eleven-year-old twins who were born full term after an unremarkable pregnancy. At birth, their son was healthy; however, Jessica was born with the umbilical cord loosely sitting around her neck, and right after the birth, she had an APGAR score of 9 (out of 10) and was diagnosed with a condition called *single umbilical artery (SUA)*, in which the umbilical cord contained only a single artery rather than two arteries, affecting the blood supply between the mother and the developing fetus. The condition and the ensuing diagnosis of "cerebral palsy, spastic diplegia" was labeled idiopathic, indicating no known cause. Subsequent examination of hospital records by lawyers failed to reveal any further clarification.

Jessica is now in fifth grade, but she attended a preschool in the local public schools and has received physical therapy, occupational therapy, and speech therapy. She continued in inclusion classes; however, the parents realized in the middle of second grade that Jessica could not do addition and was falling behind her classmates. Her mother said, "I had to fight to persuade the school system to let Jessica repeat second grade. It was a beneficial decision."

In fourth grade, Jessica was pulled out for small-group instruction in math, reading, and comprehension, but her mother did not believe that the others in the group—who were either younger than Jessica or dyslexic—matched her unique needs, and after "fighting tooth and nail" with the school, she was able to secure the one-on-one support of a special ed teacher to help with math. "The school has been doing an okay job, and with this extra help, I've seen a great improvement in her math."

Jessica loves reading. She reads at a fifth-grade level, comprehends at a fourth-grade level, and is still receiving PT, OT, and speech services. Her mother says,

Jessica does not have visual-perception problems. She has insufficient conversion and wears glasses because one eye is having problems. She is at the bottom of the first percentile in math because she can't comprehend equations or word problems. I don't have a diagnosis for that. However, her writing is beautiful. She can write a story and a report. We are working on her script, which is a little simpler than probably the typical fifth grader. She also loves to read.

I do not feel that Jessica will be able to keep up in high school, because our high school is very competitive and highly rated. I hear that they have a good special-needs program, but I don't know too much about it. I'm trying to take one day at a time. Most of the special schools in our area focus on children with dyslexia, reading issues, or they serve students on the spectrum. There is nothing for children with physical disabilities. I think that school systems provide more money for students on the spectrum than they do for students like Jessica.

Jessica is extremely dysarthric, and it deeply affects her emotionally and socially. Group speech therapy did not work for her, because her speech is so difficult. I would be happy if she just stuttered, but she talks as if she is completely intoxicated. That's how it sounds.

Jessica also has drooling problems, but it's getting better. I got her ChapStick or lipstick and put a little mirror in her lunch box so she could see and get the food away from her mouth. It made her feel fancy to put on some lipstick, you know.

According to her mother, Jessica has chewing and swallowing problems.

She likes to eat soft foods and tells me that she is a vegetarian, although she loves meatballs too. She chokes a lot. Everybody in school—in the lunchroom, in the classroom, and at recess—is aware of the choking, and I requested and implemented the standard that everyone who worked around Jessica be CPR-trained. Jessica once "Heimliched" herself against a chair. I have done that procedure on her many times.

Ms. Randall describes her daughter as a little immature for her age but really a sweet girl.

Because of her speech problems, the kids sort of shy away from her. They don't understand her, so they just laugh or walk away. They have less patience to listen. I have great fears about her socialization as she gets older. I'm worried about her. This is the first year she hasn't had a playdate. I've tried to get to some other parents to find out what their daughters are doing for Halloween; however, no one has invited Jessica to join them in trick-or-treating.

Jessica is very close to her twin brother, who's very protective of her. She hasn't had a chance to really socialize with other students with CP. There is a boy with CP in the next town whom we see at therapeutic horseback riding, but there is really no connection.

Ms. Randall tried to explain the implications of low-incidence disabilities to the school, where there are not enough children to create a social group from which Jessica can choose a friend.

We are one of a kind, the first one to come through the school with mild CP, and they just don't know what to do or how to handle it. Yes, and there's not as much knowledge about how complex the conditions of CP can be. No two children with CP are alike, and of course, I'm a first-time parent, right? But my husband and I know her better than anyone else.

I do feel that our school is listening to us, but it has taken a long time. I had to fight tooth and nail to get our school system to pay for some of the neuropsychological assessment at New York University. I did not want an in-house assessment, and these assessments are quite expensive. I used a major medical center in our area, and when the results came in, the chips started coming into place. It was like, "Oh, okay, now I understand."

We do have an "It's Okay to Be Different" program, and when Jessica was in first grade, she went into each first-grade [class] to talk about CP. We showed a YouTube video that provided basic information on CP in its various degrees. Then she brought in some of her arm casts and other orthotics. When one student asked her how it felt to have CP, she answered, "It's hard. It's hard every day." At the end of the Q&A session, one little boy asked if they could have a playdate!

They had a talent show at school when Jessica was in second grade. She decided to go up on stage, even though she's completely tone-deaf, and her speech is so awful. In front of the whole second and third grade, she sang "Let It Go." The teachers told me that there wasn't a dry eye from any of the teachers, and all of the kids gave her a standing ovation.

I think that she feels valued, but I feel like things are changing, and it can be very upsetting. I worry that the other children and her peers are leaving her behind. I worry about how the social piece is affecting her. She does cry a lot when she hears that there is a party and no one has invited her. She thinks that she has a good friend, but I don't think that the girls are acting like good friends.

We got her a phone this summer. I know it's early, but we

just hoped that she could use it and be more social, but it just hasn't helped.

She doesn't get social studies until next year, but she does like science, and she is in a regular class as they study the weather and the moon. In this class, she has the support of a shared para, which helps.

I refuse to use adaptive technology. Doctors have asked me to have her talk through a keyboard—it would make it easier for people to understand her—but I said, "No, no." We're going to continue speech [therapy], and I have hope, and I'm not using a computer. It's not that bad. You can hear her. She just has to slow down and concentrate.

Her gait is still a little off, but she doesn't fall as much as she used to, but when we were in Disney last year, after the first day, we had to get a wheelchair because her legs were so tired from walking.

Did I mention that she has had serial casting, because as kids with CP grow, we know the bones grow and the muscles and ligaments follow, and the growing pain is the pain in the stretch. CP kids, you know, curl. They curl, and that's what happened. Her arm is bent at a ninety-degree angle. We have had seven weeks of seven casts.

She wasn't growing. We checked her growth hormones, and she wasn't producing growth hormones. We had her on growth hormones for a few years. She initially was predicted to be about four feet six, and now she's predicted to be five feet one.

When she speaks about her future, she says that she wants to be a veterinarian or a doctor so that she can help kids like her.

I had to get her a puppy because she doesn't have too many close friends.

Every time I talk to the school, they say, "Oh, she's doing great. She plays at recess . . . this and that. . . ." Unfortunately, I feel like it's more the parent's concern.

Maybe if I send an email over to Jessica's case manager, she will take an interest in the problem. Jessica was receiving one-on-one social support, but I changed it to a group social skills activity so that she could practice interacting with others.

I am definitely concerned about the social piece and wish that they just maybe had more coordinated recess with group activities as opposed to just letting them go off by themselves into little, small cliques where they think up games or the adults put out some balls in the grass and then go sit on the sidelines, talking to each other. This isn't effective—just watching the children. Or, all last spring, she was in the library playing Rat-a-Tat-Tat, a card game, with her aide. That's not helpful, and I should not have to tell them that.

Once, when Jessica was having a bad day, a bad moment, they put her in the safe place in the classroom, which was under her desk. Yeah, as a mom, it makes you sick to find that out. They put her under her desk in front of all those kids. . . . No, no, no, no! I told the school about this, and they changed the practice, but the teacher was a seasoned educator and should have been talked to at least.

At the beginning of the year, before school started, I spoke with her teacher about her choking, but it would be good for them to know more. I do communicate weekly by email with her one-on-one teacher, who keeps me posted on Jessica's progress, but as far as her classroom teacher goes—no, no, I have no contact with her whatsoever.

I think when teachers get a special-needs student in their classroom, or in the school, it should be part of the Child Study team's job to educate these teachers on what this condition is, what it entails, and how it can affect the student emotionally, cognitively, and physically. And, how to be prepared to deal with certain situations, like crying about friends. They certainly know enough about autistic kids and what to do, and they have a school in our neighboring town that has a therapy dog. Our high school has a therapy dog for special-needs kids. But I feel like unique kids, who have a unique situation . . . they should really be well versed on these situations. Well, I'm not going to go to a general internist if I need to have a tumor removed. I'd go to a specialist. And if you're going to deal with my daughter, you need to be a specialist in her world, not just a generalist.

When I asked Ms. Randall if she had more to share with me, she wanted to talk about several bullying episodes when Jessica was in third grade.

There were these two boys who would push her down at recess because she fell so easily, or they would kick dirt at her. One day, I arrived at school to pick her up, and she came over to me crying. When I asked what was wrong, she told me what had happened—again. I hadn't been made aware that it had happened five times before. I went right to the principal, who cried when she heard about it. She brought the boys and their parents in, and one parent said, "That's just an angry mother of a special-needs kid. She's just angry and wants to take it out on my child." The boys, however, were punished.

Several weeks later, when my children were playing in our yard, I stepped into the house for a moment, and my daughter came running in, crying. The same boys were hiding in the bushes, waiting for me to leave, and they pushed her off her bike and laughed.

I brought this to the school's attention, but nothing really happened. I should have called the police because it happened outside of school.

Jessica doesn't really see the school psychologist one-on-one. He is part of the team and shares with other team members what's going on. She sees her case manager for social skills group once a month. We need to find out what to do to improve her social skills.

Story Number 2

Ms. Anthony was interviewed in 2017, when her son was fifteen:

Our son, Danny, who was diagnosed with CP diplegia, began his schooling with early intervention and preschool in a public school that was, in theory, integrated with nonchallenged children, but it was pretty heavily special-needs with a couple of students in each class with some very committed teachers. I would say that kindergarten through third grade was probably the easiest in terms of getting him integrated inside of the classroom and probably when he had the most social interaction because kids are less judgmental, and the academics were not as challenging.

The challenge there was getting somebody to determine the nature of his slow learning and lack of ability, based on the way he was being taught. He lost a lot of time because of a lack of expertise and a lack of attention paid to his specific issues. Also, fourth, fifth, and sixth grades were very challenging because we were in a battle with the school system. We were not satisfied with his progress. We really felt on our own in terms of how to solve this problem. Are there any options, and how do we find out what they are? What's realistic and what's not realistic?

When Danny was twelve years old, we placed him in a private school that was partially funded by the public-school systems. We were so grateful to find this program, with the help of an educational consultant. We are suing the school system, and we have attorneys. If you are a high SES [social economic status] family, you can plug through all of that, but it is expensive, time-consuming, and stressful, so I feel that the last couple of years, we have been lucky in that we have found a good program.

This private program is a consortium of schools that offer specialty programs for children who have difficulty learning in the typical classroom. There are five other students in his classroom, and my son gets one-on-one instruction for the entire program. With his transition from elementary school and then after multiple years of real failure to progress in developing his reading and all his academic skills and simply being pushed from grade to grade, we thought it was time for a more focused intervention for him.

This represented both a failure of the public schools and a need for something more individualized. It was such an expensive way to educate a student. I understand why they can't provide those resources, but they were constantly pulling him out of the classroom, and the one-on-one instruction they were giving him was given by people who were not skilled enough. In moving to middle school, the program was going to be two-on-one or three-on-one student-to-teacher ratio. That was just not going to work for our son to learn.

Is this inclusion at any cost? Yes, and that's been the struggle for us, though Danny is absolutely not in the least restrictive environment, but we've made that choice. It came to us that we could produce a student who was integrated in the community and was illiterate, or we could produce a child who is achieving his academic potential in a much more restricted way. We had to do the work to get him integrated into the community as best as possible. His engagement in his education went up because it was something he could learn and respond to. The teachers were speaking a language he could understand. In fact, the first week of this new program, he did something a little bit against the rules, and the teachers were talking to him, and he was worried that they would not let him attend the school anymore because he was so excited to be in this program. He has stayed extremely motivated, and he has persevered, and we kept waiting for him to say that he missed his friends, but he was making friends, although not enough. There is small-group teaching, and each [student in the group] has his own issues. Danny has made progress in this program, although we are four years behind. However, he has good social interactions during school, but that doesn't extend to after school. So we've had to work, and that was really more than we could do to keep some friendships for him, which is hard.

One good thing about this program is that there is a consistency from year to year, and even the program director knows him deeply. His teachers teach each other and are willing to try this and that. They are learning from the experience of working with him. When Danny was in the inclusion program, every year we started over again because the teachers had no idea of how he learned, and then you're five months into the school year, and it's too late.

You asked if I have been given sufficient information about CP and its related conditions. In reflecting on this, my answer would be yes and no. On the one hand, when you have a youngster—a very young child with his condition—it's like everybody has an opinion about what you should be doing with the child, and none of them actually dovetail and integrate into what you want to do. And so, at one level, there is overload and too much information, and at another level, there is not the information you need to be an effective parent. In particular, around how to educate a child like this, if you are not highly motivated and able to search through a lot of ambiguity, it's terribly difficult.

Unfortunately, this special program does not have a high

school, and we are literally starting the neuropsychological process again and getting the gears churning to find a placement for next year. Danny's not coming back to a public high school. We've seen that it's a hard thing finding the right place, but we can plug away at it. Our state will just have to take the extra steps to further the process.

We still have our housekeeper, and now Danny has a couple of different, normal environments and a new half-sibling, since his dad remarried.

No one specifically explained the correlation between brain injury, motor challenges, and learning issues, but we had a very progressive neonatal neurologist who put the films up and said, "Here's the picture, and this is what can happen regarding motor and learning problems." We didn't know that, and it was terrible, because he was only two months old, but we had the information. For parents who don't have this transparency, it is much, much harder, and yes, most pediatricians have no idea.

I have to laugh when you asked me if school personnel helped or made our roles as parents more difficult. We understand that school personnel must adhere to legal mandates, but there is a slavery to the IEP [Individualized Educational Plan] and PPT [Planning and Placement Team] and a bureaucracy that just takes over and that does not address the actual education of the child. There is so much wasted time on things that have zero impact on the quality of your child's education, and everything gets bogged down.

I have empathy for the staff because they are following the rules and will be held accountable or even sued, but you feel that all your interactions are box-checking exercises rather than really trying to help the child.

Ninety percent of the teachers we worked with really wanted to do what was right and wanted to learn, but they were stuck within the constraints they were working in. Perhaps one teacher had a bad attitude toward Danny, but I felt that most of the teachers meant well.

Sometimes we felt that our opinions were respected and other times not. It very much depends on the tone of the administration at the time. There was a changing of cycles of attention and inattention, depending on where we were in that cycle. But I would say that staff were too quick to rely on their own judgment that Danny was a child who was not going to progress any faster. Was this a lack of education on their part or a part of sticking to budget constraints?

Doctors have done the same thing with a limited perspective when they give you a categorical answer to something that turns out not to be even close to the truth. They could be a lot more helpful, and you'd feel a lot more "heard" if they would say, "I actually don't know the answer." "What I've experienced is 'X,' but others may have experienced something different." "You might want to try something else."

How, you ask, am I managing all of this? I believe that the trick of managing your emotional and mental health in parenting a child with this challenge is living as much as you can in the moment because so much is unpredictable and invisible. We fool ourselves if we think that we can see the future for any child. So, on the one hand, you have to be mindful of the future because you want to make sure that you are putting in place whatever structure you can so that you can allow the child to achieve his potential just like any child, but on the other hand, know that our son is in competition with himself and creates his own path.

Has the special schooling sufficiently prepared him for a satisfying adulthood? I don't know—it's a little soon to tell.

I observe adults with CP doing all kinds of stuff at different levels, so it gives me a great deal of hope that Danny will find his way with direction and structure . . . but I don't know what that way is. But I feel that our society in general [has yet to create] a society where people with disabilities can have satisfying lives. So, it is a much bigger problem than CP. I don't know the answer.

I think, then, that the school system, though, is playing a very important role in that, but society has not caught up yet. When we were children, there was little mainstreaming, and it was not prevalent in many areas. Now, with the increasing prevalence of disabled students in our school systems, people are more familiar with and less frightened of children with disabilities, just like they are growing up with LGBTQ persons, but society has a long way to go.

I guess that I can say that if you've seen one child with CP, you've seen one child with CP [implying that there is great diversity in the population]. To teachers I would say, "Stop being afraid of the [perceived] fragility. Some certainly have fragile medical conditions, but many don't. It is really important to stop being afraid. . . . You are not going to hurt them. . . . Nothing bad is going to happen. . . . Try to resist your own personal fears of something going wrong and you not knowing what to do."

Resist making judgments about the child's abilities because unless you are a neuropsychologist, you can't make a judgment about a child's abilities. With Danny, after fifteen years of trying, [we realize] that he will not be a visual reader but primarily an auditory one. He can read, you know, and is coming along quite well, but he is never going to master complex material by reading something. But he can deeply understand. So, let's teach him that way rather than holding on to "this is the way we teach." If you don't know what to do, recommend someone who has the instincts to find out exactly how he learns. . . . Put it out there, so someone can pick up on that. That's better than making a judgment that he is not able, not capable, and always scores in the 5 percent in batteries of tests. Why do they do these tests?

What if someone decided in first grade that, okay, this child is not ever going to learn by reading. How much better it would be if there was acceptance that every piece of the curriculum, moving forward, could be learned differently.

Danny would be so much further along. So much time was spent with sight words and stressing fluency . . . moving from this stage to that stage . . . drilling the poor kid over and over on something that he just can't do. It's crazy, but it's the system. I think about the kids who don't have parents who will persistently advocate for them—who never become literate. What a waste of potential!

Understanding the whole child is so critical. At the beginning, when early intervention started, the OT would say, "Do this for twenty minutes a day," and the PT would say, "Do this every day for twenty minutes," and there was no time in the day to do the laundry—it was literally not possible. We were literally asked to do things that were impossible to do. You either don't do anything, or you randomly pick and choose because no one's taking care of the whole child, the whole family, the ecosystem, and deciding what's possible and what will matter.

We know more than we let on, and maybe we could move the dial. It would not hurt. We want to integrate technology into the student's program in ways that would benefit people impacted by CP, their caregivers, and teachers. School systems are not there yet.

Danny is primarily using Dragon for dictation, and depending on content, it is being dictated for him. Some textbooks will be read to him, and the tech is evolving enough so that Dragon understands him better than Siri, although he can use Siri on his phone and iPad. He still writes with a pencil and types sometimes because he wants to, and [he] still wants to read books sometimes and does not always want them read to him.

I don't think that his reading issues have affected his self-worth. Danny's a teenage boy, and I don't think that he is lacking in self-worth. The reading is challenging . . . he likes to be read to. He uses Audible books for Harry Potter and more sophisticated books, and [he] is multimodal, depending on where he is, in using several devices. If his speech isn't good enough for a device that speaks for him, it's not practical, so he doesn't want to do it. I don't blame him. You can understand him if both you and he will take the time.

Part of his education involves his being persistent at what he is good at. If I say, "I have no idea what you said," he tries again, and we get there—so then, his conversation works.

He's had several surgeries, including lengthening, so his spasticity is not worse, and he still gets around well with a walker, is learning to bathroom on his own, and is about 80 percent fairly independent in life activities with minimal assistance for putting on his shoes. Don't know when he will ever be able to do that.

It's really important that he maintain his physical abilities, and there is nothing worse than sitting all of the time. His current school is in an office building, and he can get around completely independently with his walker. He can get in and out of all the rooms and not be late to classes.

We haven't had a need for a wheelchair in an institutional setting, and he is not yet out in the world independently. I feel that Danny is going to know when the time is right, and he will tell us. He has a wheelchair that we push, and I told him that we can get a power chair. The school has been encouraging that, and Danny is becoming more assertive. In high school, he will be around more students who have multiple modalities of mobility, and this will encourage him to want to have a life.

Danny will absolutely want to go off on his own after twenty-one—no question in my mind—but now he is emotionally immature. . . . He's fifteen, but he is probably like a twelve-year-old.

We are challenging ourselves to ask if we really must do so much for him. Much of what we do is out of expediency. I mean, I don't want to wait twenty-five minutes for him to go to the bathroom.

I am at the stage where I must further adapt my home or move. I need to make it easier for us to get out of bed and get to the bathroom. I am trying to figure this out.

We've thought a lot about Danny's independent living in the future. I can see him living independently with someone who is there in the mornings and the evenings to help him with things he just can't do on his own . . . perhaps in a group setting where there is somebody on call. Danny can be by himself for hours, but if he falls off his walker, he is on the floor and can't figure out a way to get himself up.

He hasn't had a seizure in a while. He stays on his medicine, and he had an EEG three years ago. The brain patterns are still there, and we will probably have another EEG.

Story Number 3
Ms. Mercado and her husband spoke of their son, Robbie, who is a fifteen-year-old high school student.

Robbie began his education in his local public school; then, after surgery, [he] attended school as a day student, in a special education program that was embedded in a pediatric rehabilitation hospital. There he received eight years of special education and physical and occupational therapy. This is his second year in a special education program in his local public high school.

Robbie was diagnosed after birth with CP quadriplegia associated with PVL [periventricular leukomalacia]. Robbie had been using a walker but now ambulates fairly effectively without canes, thanks to the efforts of his adaptive physical education teacher. This teacher is an angel! He takes Robbie and other special-needs kids to games in different towns and engages them all year long. He's the only one who gives these students an environment that makes them feel that they are not alone.

Ups and downs with the medical community:

Our pediatrician was an awesome, good guy and made sure that Robbie was evaluated by a neurologist who gave us a lot of big words. After that, the therapy kicked in. But if you are not asking the right questions and not digging in further enough . . . I can't imagine [someone] who doesn't know English in this country and trying to raise a child who has a disability without any assistance from anyone who lives here. The complexity . . . it's like a thousand-piece puzzle.

I've had ups and downs with surgery. Robbie had one surgery that resulted in a bad infection in his leg, and another time, a scheduled surgery had to be delayed because the surgeon had gone to a seminar. However, at the same hospital, Robbie's gait analysis was fabulous, so you do get information, over time, from everybody.

Challenges and strengths:

Robbie's primary barriers to learning are fine motor issues that complicate his ability to functionally use writing and take notes. Delayed mental processing affects his rate of comprehension, and Robbie still tends to retreat into an imaginary world, a practice that is strongly discouraged at home. His mother says,

> I think that there are times when he does that to escape himself. . . . It's a coping mechanism for some things, and even though he is sixteen, he really has a lot of maturing to do. He still "zones out" and stares a lot. Once, when he was taking an exam with the IEP modification of a separate area for testing, I walked by and saw him through the glass—just sitting there, staring.
>
> Even now, I try to rush him, and he says, "Ma, you know it takes a little longer time." Why does he know this? I know that I am overprotective, and it's good to have casual conversations with his therapists.
>
> In first grade, in public school one day, as I pushed his wheel-chair through the hall, I questioned something a staff member had said, and she responded defensively, "Well, we've opened our arms to him." My mamma bear claws came out, and I reminded her that this was her job . . . this is what I pay her to do. I wish I could control my emotions more. I think that I could be a lot more powerful if I could control my emotions.
>
> Sometimes I believe that the special-ed/rehab school was make-believe land. The therapists tried to explain things to me, but I also thought that they coddled Robbie. I was willing to let Robbie be in photos, be in articles, do anything that would benefit people like him, but I was aware that staff was not particularly receptive when I pointed things out. I also sensed that some professionals who have the knowledge don't feel that you can understand that knowledge enough to interpret it for you.

The IEP-driven educational program:

With a few exceptions, our current local school district is a problem. Got to tell you, I don't understand the IEP process. It needs to be better explained. There doesn't seem to be a correlation between what's on the IEP and the school's expectations of Robbie. And no one seems to be coordinating all of the pieces.

When he reentered public school, he was first in a 15-1 co-teaching model and then a 12-1-1 model, but instruction moved so slowly in these settings. Now he is mainstreamed into the high school, but without communication, things are just crazy. I want to see results, and we don't want our son just graded on his personality.

Robbie called me from school once so upset because they scheduled two exams in one day, and he did not even finish the first one, and they did not give him the breaks and time extensions he required.

The IEP promises many modifications, but that information does not seem to be shared with all of his teachers, many of whom don't seem to understand what he needs. Also, he has not yet been assessed for the assistive technology device that would help with his note-taking. No reason has been giving for the delay ... no one cared or followed up.

Robbie complains about the speed at which the math teacher gives out information and his one-on-one has to take all of his notes. Once they had an IEP meeting without me and just invited Robbie. Our son needs information broken down for him, and I do want him to have a sense of ownership about himself, but once I kept him out of an IEP meeting because I didn't want him to hear negative things about himself.

Teachers should be required to know [specific information]

about the population and should ask about parent concerns. I would love to see educators more engaged and more knowledge-able. Perhaps they need to go to disability-specific courses. Even I need to take a yearly course because I have a disabled child, and it's required to maintain assistance through Medicaid. The courses were not always fruitful, because they applied to other disabilities. There is a program at a city hospital for parents and children with CP, and it's really nice that they get parents together.

Educators seem to fear his differences and are unaware that they have the "educational-speak" but not the disability-related information. Too many have no idea about how to accommodate Robbie's needs.

Robbie was supposed to participate in extracurricular activ-ities—it was on his IEP, but the music department knew nothing about it.

I don't need to have my son just walking out of high school with a piece of paper. He needs to be a participant in life. I don't want to set him up for failure because teachers can't deal with him.

In the coming years:

Jobs, that's where I am right now. I can't wait any longer. I don't want him to fear working at McDonalds or Walmart—don't want him to feel undervalued. He has this goal, and I don't want to discourage him, but there is always doubt in my mind that he won't achieve it because of this disability.

He wants to be a rapper, he wants to be a singer, so what I try to do is say, "That's great, but you know, why don't you try learning how to do the recordings, try to learn how to make beats?" He writes his own music, so we got him a machine where he can make sounds and create his own music. But we don't know how to teach him, and I know that society limits kids with CP. At some point I have to say, "Listen, you've got to get a job." I don't want him to just sign up at Social Security and get money. I want him to be able to say that he has his own money.

Story Number 4

Early educational experiences:

Rick's mom describes him as a surviving twin from a premature birth who lives with CP spastic diplegia.

At six months of age, Rick's schooling began with Early Intervention in the home-based 0-3 program, and at age three he began nursery school at a private children's center, where he did phenomenally. He left that program walking with a walker and talking. People thought at that point that Rick would be ready for inclusion in public school. However, teachers in a public-school program that was our first choice, which has an ICT [integrated co-teaching] class, felt that he was too young to start kindergarten. Since we did not want to send him back for another year of preschool, we decided to try the ICT class in our local, zoned public school, which promised to offer collaborative team teaching.

That school was a disaster. Going from a class of seven to a pre-K class of twenty was a huge jump, but we were very hopeful. The school did not have much experience with kids with physical disabilities. The building had four stories, the elevator was out of service much of the time, and PT was on the fourth floor.

I remember the OT calling me at some point during the middle of the school year suggesting that maybe Rick had oppositional defiant disorder because he was hard to work with. Let's just say, I just couldn't wait to get out of that school because, I mean, he is the opposite of having a defiant disorder.

Teachers did not know how to adapt materials for Rick, and the special ed teacher had just graduated. Now, that can go either way. She could have been full of new ideas and enthusiasm, but she was just stuck. We knew that the kindergarten year was going to be a practice run, since Rick would be going to our first choice the next year. Rick's old preschool teacher came two weeks after school started, to adapt his homework and work with him on it.

Elementary school experiences:

We reapplied and got him in [repeat kindergarten] in our first school of choice. Initially, the school was amazing, and people were kind. Rick had two wonderful, experienced veteran teachers. The school had a lot of experience with kids with physical disabilities. Elevators worked all the time, and they had wonderful therapists. They were able to get him a laptop and some different technologies, and he flourished.

But the class was a mix of things. The class was bigger, and he began on a slow, downhill trajectory as the program became more academic and harder.

We had a neuropsychological assessment done (as much as they work for a six-year-old) and realized that although he had average intelligence, we knew that there were learning and focusing issues, and his experiences would be more than physical.

The teacher suggested that we might want to look into another smaller class, with more support, and I just sort of blew that off, saying, "Oh no, he's fine where he is.... We love it."

We had another neuropsychological assessment done, but we didn't think that it was very thorough. Although it took place over three or four sessions, I don't think that they got enough information. First grade was getting more difficult for Rick to keep up with. The class size was getting bigger, and Rick just slowly started to check out—he was completely lost. It was really hard.

During first grade, Rick had a teacher who had lied and said that she had a lot of experience, and [it turned out, she] had not worked where she said she had worked. Her references had not been checked. On the first day of school, I introduced myself and asked for time to talk to her and discuss different accommodations. She looked like a deer in the headlights—was overwhelmed and had no idea. Then, at Back-to-School Night, it was apparent that she still did not know what she was doing, and I left there crying.

Finally, his former kindergarten teacher came to replace that teacher, and that was great, but [even] she could only do so much. It was also a great disruption for him, and during that time, things switched pretty drastically to a Common Core focus on reading and writing—which are very hard for him.

Slowly, he just sort of shut off and turned inward. He had such a hard time in school, and it was hard to watch this really sweet, outgoing, bubbly, curious kid just become depressed, anxious, and overwhelmed. As the year wore on, it was obvious that he needed a lot more.

In March, we asked for another IEP meeting and could not get one until the last day of school. This was very traumatizing because I went into the meeting thinking that we were going to get more support, and they completely blindsided me. They said, "We can't meet your child's needs, and we are referring him to a different setting." No one—not the teacher, not the psychologist—had told me that this was in the works. I was beside myself. I had no idea of what to do. This was the end of June, and I had no idea where to look.

A pleasant person was assigned to us by the CBST

[central-based support team] to help us find a state-approved, nonpublic school, but there were not very many choices. We looked at a number of options, but they were not for him. One program had a PT room the size of a closet. It had an exercise ball, and that was about it.

We liked some of the public schools because they had resources and relationships that private schools didn't have, like the Roadrunner Club and adaptive physical education. Other programs were too far away. Some were in buildings with no elevators and kept children in wheelchairs on the first floor. In others, students were doing stuff he had done in pre-K.

There was a long waiting list for one area school that is known for its success with students with complex physical and medical challenges. Since we couldn't get in there, we called his old preschool to ask for suggestions. They told us of a new school [within their organization], with an individualized curriculum and very small classes, and because of our [positive] experiences in the nursery school at that site, we had high hopes.

Rick started there in second grade and stayed through the end of fifth grade. The first teacher, who had absolutely no experience in special ed, was terrible, and it was a disaster. Everyone complained, and we got a new teacher for the next two years. The first year, [however,] was not a total loss. He gained confidence and was happy.

Rick has highs and lows and manages to fall into the low-average intelligence category. He started with a reading tutor because nobody at his school quite knew how to approach the dyslexia that affected everything he learned. And it wasn't just hiring a reading tutor, because there were a whole bunch of other things that needed to be addressed.

The neuropsychological assessment pointed to some

visual-perceptual problems, which explained the trouble he was having. His fine motor control is not good, and even though it has gotten better, he still struggles with paper and pencil, which he finds hard. The school shied away from computers and adaptive technology, and I have been asking for its use. He came to the program with a laptop, but nobody ever uses it.

During the first year in kindergarten, I was listened to, but now I don't think that I am heard so much. It didn't seem as if the teachers followed the information I shared with them about who Rick was, nor did they follow through with the information from the neuropsychological assessment.

I don't think that the school helped him to meet his potential. Long time ago, I thought that he could go to college. In the past couple of years, that expectation has fallen because he is not progressing, not getting to where he is supposed to be. We just want him to be happy.

In this school, he had no opportunity to make any social connections, since almost all of the kids were on the spectrum. The kids in his class were so different and impossible to teach. Everyone was on a different level, and many had behaviors that the teachers spent most of their time managing. Teachers didn't have time to teach, and the assistants were not educated. There were so many distractions, and it was hard for Rick to focus and learn.

We got him on meds, and his anxiety and depression were well under control, and since 2016, we had been trying to find a focus medicine for him that worked because everything that we had tried had not worked, or the stimulants had made him very aggressive and belligerent. I think he had the worst reaction to Zoloft, and it was really scary. I wasn't sure if I needed to call 9-1-1. He was just so agitated, he was throwing like these little metal Thomas trains, and it was really scary, so we switched psychiatrists, and then there was this push to stabilize his mood, his anxiety, and we got that under control in third and fourth grades.

Rick's language skills and vocabulary are great. He is a strong auditory learner, but in the classroom, they rely on visual skills. His latest neuropsychological assessment offered good suggestions on using more concrete approaches to math, along with the use of ongoing assessments. The report also found that he has a real strength for learning, but focusing is a major issue. The program director sort of danced around all of this and says that everything is individualized, but it is not. They tell me what they do, but they don't tell me how they do it. For instance, he came home with core words from Boardmaker. Every year it's the same words: "Hi and Me." With six students in the class and four assistants, they are not individualizing. All the kids are doing the same thing. They go on the same field trips all the time, every year.

Middle school experiences:

At this point at the end of fifth grade, we got a placement letter from the Department of Education for a special middle school program. [That was for] an 8-1-1 program, and I thought, "Oh my God, these people understand a learning disability. They understand dyslexia. They understand that he needs technology." I mean I was just blown away because I wasn't expecting that at all. He started sixth grade there, and his first year was great, and his teacher was amazing. He learned by leaps and bounds, and for seventh grade, I really wanted him to stay with that teacher, but he couldn't, and so we got a new teacher who just didn't really have the training. So, he's in eighth grade now, and it's been kind of a struggle.

In talking about goals, the teacher is saying he needs to be able to read a paragraph and write something about it, but these goals basically center around his dyslexia struggles. It's really hard for him to read a paragraph. He's come very far, and if you read to him, he comprehends at an eighth-grade level. Reading is always going to be a struggle for him, and it is weird because I wasn't ready to [be] here.

In math, he's on a third-grade level. He's interested in it, but it's hard for him. He can tell time on a digital clock. I don't know whether I should keep pushing or step back.

Functional skills and attitudes:

He did lose some skills during the pandemic, but he gained so much in independence. At the beginning of the pandemic, I was the schedule keeper, getting him on the meetings and the Zoom calls. Then, over the course of the summer and fall, he took charge of it, and he managed it 100 percent by himself. He knows his schedule and gets on his meetings and manages his schedule. That is a potential work skill, and it is amazing and marvelous. His transformation has been great.

He does miss being in the classroom with the other kids, but again, these kids are on the spectrum, and Rick has expressed many times that their behaviors can be very distracting [like rocking]. He says that he would rather be back in an ICT class. Rick has an innate drive to learn, is curious, and expresses his frustration when some things seem too easy.

Not since he was very young has he been in a class with other kids with CP. That's both a strength and a weakness. He loves talking about his disability and explaining to people what CP is. He advocates for himself, and he has done CP presentations in the middle school.

When my youngest was in kindergarten, Rick went to school and did a presentation (with my help) that used photos, slide-shows of him doing adapted activities. And [he] brought his AFOs [ankle foot orthoses] to show the students.

When he was younger, he felt uncomfortable around kids in wheelchairs, and I could not understand that he might not want to identify with those children. However, in seventh grade, he attended a sleepaway camp for physically disabled kids, and he didn't seem uncomfortable at all. He is comfortable in his skin, but I think it would be helpful for him to be around kids with physical disabilities because it doesn't have to feel like he's the only one all the time.

He complained in sixth and seventh grades that he didn't understand why he couldn't go out to recess, why he had to be watched all the time [like the other kids who needed that], and why he was being babied. Rick loves sports and has been involved in special-needs sports programs, but the kids in his class don't have any physical disabilities, so it's just different.

Last year I met with the team frequently, and the teacher was accessible. It was a difficult year, with the neuropsychological assessment and two surgeries. This year's teacher keeps everyone at arm's length and doesn't see this as a joint learning experience. Teachers can get defensive, and some don't want you to know what they don't know. Finding expertise with a low-incidence population is hard.

Before upcoming surgery, his anxiety got in the way of his focus medication and made him so drowsy that it was hard for him to get through the day, and by the end of the day, he fell apart. Although he went up three reading levels with the meds, the benefits did not outweigh the fact that he was a mess, so we took him off the meds.

For him, surgery always come with anxiety. A rhizotomy, the six-week in-hospital stay, and being dependent in a wheelchair frustrated him. He worried about the pain, and not even the Child Life specialist was able to allay his fears.

He had been seeing a psychologist since kindergarten when he was showing a lot of aggression. Although the play therapist was less experienced with CP, the play therapy helped him a lot with hospitalization and emergencies. However, the long, two-year commute of taking him to the psychologist was too much. We found a therapist close to home [whom] he sees weekly, and that's been great. I needed some help and am in therapy.

Rick's reading is affected by distractibility in the environment. When we read to him, he starts looking around and just guesses at what the words are. His neurologist decided to go to a stimulant med, but that caused Rick terrible panic attacks, and because he was paralyzed with fear, she took him off that medicine and decided that we should see a psychiatrist. Some psychiatrists don't take insurance and don't know much about CP!

Rick is very aware of his physical and learning differences. He does not really talk about it, but I have always explained his muscle issues and his birth at twenty-five weeks.

When he was little, he could not walk but would crawl around. I took him everywhere because we wanted him to feel that [he] could do anything and be a part of the world. He does feel like a part of the world and is okay with it. We are using augmentative communication at home. The iPad has good programs, and he enjoys using the help of voice searching. A local speech specialist is helping us, and this gives us much hope.

He'll be attending a new high school in September, and we've hired a reading tutor for him who uses the computer and who has worked with CP kids. We also found an amazing psychologist at a major medical school who is doing play therapy and concrete things, like breathing and meditation. He has seen her three times, and although he is still on Zoloft, with a lot of tweaks, his anxiety and dysregulation have been reduced.

Planning for high school:

We've been looking at special high school programs and found ones that focus on ADHD, dyslexia, learning disabilities, and social issues, but they don't understand CP and the physical part. We are looking at an inclusion program with [an] 8-1-1 pupil-teacher ratio. They offer a lot of academic support with adapted homework for students like Rick, who are on an alternate assessment track.

There's another thing. He has an iPad with some dictation software and Co:Writer, but it's limited, and I'm trying to get him a laptop with more technology, but nobody knows what to put on it; they're not familiar with what he needs. His current speech teacher is great, and she is looking to find programs like Writing Revelation that will help him write and organize his thoughts. Another problem: Dictation software is for people who have perfect diction, which he does not have, so there is a lot of revising and fixing; he needs something else.

Transition hopes:

I don't know if Rick can go to college, but he really, really wants to have that experience. Also, he loves to talk about going into a helping profession and helping other people. He actually talked about becoming a police officer, and I just nodded. There may be something in that profession that he could do. I try to be very supportive of what he wants to do—because why not?

They do a lot of transition programs in his current school,

but there are no kids with CP.

There are still some physical things he struggles with, like drying his back after he showers, and cutting is hard, but he's getting better, and over the course of the pandemic, he's learned to wash himself independently. The hardest thing for me is to step away from expecting him to do things the way everyone else is doing them, and a big problem for the public schools is that they don't have any wiggle room. There is only one way.

Story Number 5

Ms. Langley is a nurse who has two sons, one of whom has spastic diplegia CP. She and her husband are divorced, but they share concerns and decision making about Ryan. She says,

> Ryan is nineteen now, and we started Early Intervention services at home before his first birthday. At nineteen months, he wound up in a children's rehab center. We kept him in this center-based program that had all of the therapies, including preschool speech and medical services, and then by age five, we transitioned him over to the local school district for kindergarten. He attended public school until his sophomore year in high school, and since then, he has been in private school out of state. After completing high school, he has been attending a transition program affiliated with the private school and housed in a neighboring community college.

Elementary school experiences:

> Ryan was always a likable and happy kid, so that was his strength. We were in a good school district, and he was safe. However, there were challenges, even going back to kindergarten. I remember

his kindergarten teacher saying, "I think he is going to be a motivational speaker." But then she had him for first grade, and by first grade, she was frustrated. By second grade, we got a great teacher, we thought. I liked the second-grade teacher and thought that Ryan had a good relationship with him, but he turned on me. He became so angry, so angry, because Ryan was not fully capable in the bathroom. He didn't want to hear about it, because Ryan needed a little bit of assistance. "What do you want me to do, wipe his ass?"

There was one boy with severe CP in his class who was in a wheelchair and couldn't move and who had an aide assigned to him. The school made her a shared aide. Maybe the teacher was angry that I didn't push for a second aide. But I told them that if Ryan has toileting issues, he will need help and will be mortified and devastated [without it], but they did not want to hear that.

Since this placement failed, we moved Ryan to a second elementary school in the district. His new teacher was a much nicer, much kinder female teacher who wasn't as angry. As she was a newbie, she could roll with it. I worked in the district, and the teacher felt that I should have gotten more support and advocated better for my son to have an aide. This was definitely one of the downsides of having my child go to school in the district I worked in.

For third grade we went to another school in our district and found that our district will say yes to anything. His teachers for third, fourth, and fifth grades truly cared about Ryan, but I sensed that there was a growing anger from the district. He was in a self-contained class, and there was some integration before he went to middle school. The school psychologist was a little bit blunt. She said, "You know, he is not going to do much. He's a nice kid, but he does not have much cognitive ability."

Socially, things were easier at the elementary level. He got invited to parties, and he participated in the playground.

Middle school experiences:

In middle school, he was in a Life Skills class that was very, very low-functioning, and we made it through because our middle school is divided into four houses. Ryan was allowed to go between the four houses, and they gave him extra music. They did not focus on his academics, anyway; they put together a dummy program for him, and that made him happy during the school day.

I had been told that in our district, they sent students who didn't have autism out of the district. But again, I wasn't ready to transfer him out. My kid was happy, was getting something, but I felt that because he was a sweet kid, they put him in the corner while the behavioral kids got all of the attention. It was just easy.

Physical versus cognitive:

Physicians give you the medical pieces of CP, but they don't know the other pieces. Most medical people see Ryan as really low, and they don't see the beautiful things that he can do. I was low in my expectations for the first six years of his life. I was a nervous wreck, waiting for the next shoe to drop. Even though I am a medical person, the school staff was afraid to discuss his complex challenges with me. One special education director said, "He's not really educable." All of his evaluations were below the first percentile.

He had one OT in the third, fourth, and fifth grades who was trying so hard to get through, but everyone else just skirted around his challenges, threw up their hands, and did what they just had to do. A specialist in CP hit the nail on the head by telling me that Ryan's visual motor skills were probably his most disabling condition, but the school would not talk with me about what would be best. They thought he was so low that he would never do anything. They wanted to keep him happy and smiling. Once I got an email that said, "Ryan is smiling, he is happy."

Public high school:

I recall that before [Ryan started] our local high school, the staff wanted to see if he could walk through the building. They were anticipating his needing a wheelchair and an aide to push him around. Ryan walked, with his braces, through the whole building with no fatigue, and they said, "You know, I don't think he needs an aide." He really showed them that day!

Ryan was great at music. He had such an affinity for singing, and they gave him extra music, and everyone wanted him in their chorus. That was a happy year, and he had social connections. He was involved in our church as an altar boy, and we were doing Saturday morning Alternative League. We had enough going on, had nice workers in the house, so we made it through.

The district realized that we wanted out because academically Ryan was making poor progress, but the district made it clear that they were not "kicking him out." Ryan was rejected by several other districts and then accepted by only one.

However, for this new school, our district was offering Ryan a class in the basement with a bunch of behavioral kids again. So stigmatizing! The teacher in the new class was a lovely human being, but academically, things were not working, and Ryan was becoming more unhappy as a teenager. That is when we brought

in an educator who was a specialist in CP, and the district made
the decision to send him to an out-of-state private school.

Private high school and community college:

The out-of-state private school offered a very busy program,
and later the school program complemented his activities at the
community college. This school, his third high school placement,
has shown what he can do.

Ryan completed his last three years in the private, residential, out-of-state high school and is starting his second year in a
special program at a community college that is allied with the
private school. At the community college, he did an exploratory
rotation, where he got to check out different vocational areas.
Last year he concentrated on hospitality, and this year he will be
working on communication, literacy, consumer math, social skills,
current and office skills. He's busy all day long. We also had to
fit in personal training and massage. At the school-community
college program, he also gets travel training, health and wellness,
banking, and planning and organization at the business center.
During Ryan's last year in the program, he did internships in PT
technology, office work, maintenance, and food services.

The intersection of medical and emotional concerns:

When Ryan's neurologist saw him last, she said that his eyes
were working better together, but although he seemed a bit more
coordinated, his gait was off a little. We may need to do more
Botox while holding off on more medications and any additional
EEGs. She also felt that his short-term memory issues were affected by attention problems, and she increased that medication

a bit. Initially, he perseverated, and although he never complains, everything hurts.

Ryan has a lot of anxiety. I think it is because he can remember stuff that he cares about—that he is interested in and can remember so well. If he is listening to one of our conversations, he can recall everything. His functional ability day to day is all over the place. If he is not committed or focused, there is the attention and forgetting piece that is larger. It's anxiety.

His therapist at the private school said that the few CP kids she has seen have a tendency to get very dark. I did not see that in Ryan in his initial year, but I see it now, and I know that that is part of being a teenager, but he tends to go very dark and stay there. You have got to pull him out with humor. Everything becomes black and white, and when he gets dark, it's like all bad. Everything is bad and that's been really challenging with him emotionally.

When he entered his second local high school program, Ryan said, "If I want to meet girls, I have to get into the hall." Richard Lavoie, author of *It's So Much Work to Be Your Friend*, talks about the "hidden curriculum." Ryan's hidden curriculum is so much more important to him than the standard curriculum. No one was addressing my son's emotional and personal needs that make him feel so isolated in that basement of the second public high school. They were not really looking at him and trying to figure out what he really needed. They thought if they made him a little bit happier with the other stuff, he would come back and focus.

Recently, Ryan said that he didn't want to stay at his private school for the summer program. I don't think it's about his academics, it's about girlfriends and social situations. The staff at the private school told me that Ryan was fixated on girls, and although he gets along with everybody and has friends, he hasn't connected with anybody. Ryan did eventually get a girlfriend, but when they broke up shortly after they got back to school, he posted on a media platform that he was single, and all of his relatives had to come to his rescue.

Ryan's biggest stumbling block right now is his anxiety about his performance and his future. Recently he worried about a large bunion on his left foot and feared that he would have to have surgery sooner than later, and that would have been awful. We try to keep him supple and buy him sneakers that he can change daily, that lace up all the way and keep support around his ankles.

He came home one day and could not walk [because the bunion was so enflamed], and I thought, "Oh my God, he is overdue for Botox that loosens up those muscles." I've asked the private school's health-care center to check in with him every two weeks because if he complains, then something is really wrong.

I am very worried about his orthopedic issues right now. He will have to be non-weight-bearing for a couple of months, and I don't know what we will do. He would have to come home, and I would have to fully put him in respite care.

His degree of spasticity has remained the same, but I can't get him in for procedures as much as I would like. We are probably two months behind in scheduling appointments, but we wanted him to go to the summer program, and he has too many activities and mitigating factors.

Financing Ryan's education and life:

Ryan is going to be expensive and will rely on a lot of public funding forever because he needs a lot. Our state has supported his out-of-state education, and we have spent a lot out of pocket for services and activities not covered by insurance or by our state. With the help of a broker, it is taking us a lot of anxiety and work to put it all together.

The immediate future:

We are looking at further college programs, group homes or independent living situations, and supportive job opportunities. I would like for him to stay near his out-of-state school/college location and take advantage of job training opportunities that, in collaboration with his private school, are opening up. I have heard that a new group home is going up locally, and Ryan is on the short list.

There are an increasing number of college and community college programs for young adults with complex medical, so-cial-emotional, and learning issues that are opening up locally and nationwide. Some are funded by Medicaid.

I would prefer that Ryan not return to our home but rather stay in his out-of-state school placement with his friends. At home, he regresses, and his forgetfulness increases. Also, because I work, I can't set up the kind of structure he needs.

When Ryan returned from the out-of-state college program, he enrolled in another special, local college program, but after a year, that program was sidelined by the pandemic, and he is still waiting for a similar program to be up and running.

Before the local college program shut down, Ryan had extensive, successful orthopedic surgery, which allowed him to climb three flights of stairs to his dorm room. Now that he is back home, I'll just have to find a group home and programs for him that include adult schooling and enrichment activities, because right now, he is in a sort of a slump about everything. Although I've asked him to focus on finding a passion, and he says he liked his hospitality rotation, he's not committed to anything right now.

Teachers and administrators:

With the exception of the angry second-grade teacher, most of the time I have had really good relationships with teachers and administrators, and for the majority of the time, our discourse has been honest.

Ms. Langley realizes that teachers can have problems too.

I feel that too many times, teachers are closemouthed because they feel that they are going to get in trouble with their supervisors for telling the truth as they see it. I get the pressure that teachers are under, what with all the different levels in the class. I was very impressed when one of Ryan's teachers described a situation in her class that was not optimal for Ryan, and even her supervisor seemed to respect her comments.

A lot of well-meaning educators do not understand the neurology of CP [and how the neurology affects their cognitive and social-emotional development]. Administrators and teachers want to give students the best opportunities, but they just don't understand what I'm trying to do. The staff doesn't understand that kids may be getting a lesson even if they can't tell you that they are getting it.

One of the stumbling blocks is the lack of teacher education in the use of technology.

In his first high school they were great with him in music, but when he attended his second high school, they said that since their music program was very competitive, he could not participate. Then, because he just felt bad about himself and was upset, he did not want to participate in the chorus or plays at the private school. It made me so sad because music was such a strength for him.

Story Number 6

I interviewed Ms. Velasquez, mother of Samuel, who lives with athetoid CP, is dependent in all areas of daily living, is G-tube-fed, is functionally nonverbal, and has limited motor skills that affect the use of his hands. However, he can maneuver his power wheelchair with a joystick, and he uses an augmentative and alternative communication (AAC) system.

My son graduated two years ago from a special high school, and although he had the opportunity to go to a vocational program, he chose a community college.

His education began in a UCP [United Cerebral Palsy] program, then moved to the special school for elementary, middle school, and high school. When he took his community college entry exam, he placed into the remedial courses, so he had a bit of work to do before he started regular courses.

He started off with math and reading, then realized that it was a heavy workload. His elementary, middle school, and high school experiences in the special school were perfect because the school was equipped for students like him. That school was very team-oriented, and that helped me and Samuel to make transitions. In his community college setting, Samuel has to maneuver on his own.

There is very little support built into the community college. They give him a scribe to take notes, write for him, or help with test-taking. There is no adaptive equipment in the college. His transition into a mainstream college has been daunting for him, for us, and even for the advisor at the college.

The college has ramps, but there is a shortage of scribes. He needs a letter of accommodation from each instructor, allowing the instructor to share notes, but that has not really happened. Without these letters, the instructors cannot make accommodations. This frustrates the instructors too. It's a paradox. They want to help, they understand, but they are not going to lower their expectations or their standards.

At first, they didn't even give him a scribe. We had to fight for that. He cannot highlight. He needs to be able to point out different questions, different answers. He needs to be able to say, "This is how fast I'm reading." But he cannot dictate that to someone. He cannot do that physically himself. Samuel has never had a para, and when he had an incident at the college where he got stuck on a ramp, he had to call his father to come and get him.

When he finally got a scribe, she spoke to him like he was a baby and took on the role of a mother or a grandmother. She forgot that she was working with an adult with CP who is cognitively intact, whose maturity level is up to par in many ways, and that she was there to assist, not comfort!

I hired a student to help with his homework—a tutor—and she works with him about four hours a week, but there is still no social structure for him to engage in.

We have to almost kind of manipulate Samuel's body and feed him at times that will not result in his needing to use the bathroom at college, because there is no one there to help him. The person who is his scribe only does that. It is not her job to help him with his coat, to unbuckle his belt, or to take things out of his book bag. They don't see the human part. I tell them, "Ask him if he needs help": "Do you need anything?" and make sure that he's fine. One semester, he had an accident, and in calling us, he couldn't say it out loud, because he was using his speakers. Now he has an earpiece.

Today his father is taking him to college because he has an exam, but his father can't go in the room and assist him. But the people with him in the room don't know how to use his aug com system [augmentative and alternative communication system]. I just want enough accommodations so that he can succeed. I don't want to set him up to fail. After the first semester, we were all frustrated, and we withdrew him and lost over two thousand dollars in tuition. His workload was heavy, and he had a lot of concerns.

This is the challenge. I think the nonverbal piece is what they are not used to. Samuel uses a wheelchair, cannot work on his own at all, and needs assistance for everything. My son's receptive language has always been his greatest strength. He can absorb and learn like a sponge. I think that he is worrying about other things that may impact his learning ability because there are so many aspects of him that are impaired.

One day I asked Samuel, "If you were able to ask God for one ability out of the ones you are missing, what would it be?" I thought it would be sports, but he replied, "Talk, communicate." Language impacts him socially and academically, and it impacts his understanding of adult relationships. His communication limitations were difficult for him in high school when it came to dating, and he started getting in trouble because of it. Fundamentally, Samuel is not a disrespectful kid, but unless someone understands his communication device, he cannot clearly present his point of view and adequately advocate for himself. So even in his amazing special school, everyone, not just the speech therapist, who dealt with Samuel needed to know how to work with his device. Even I, as a parent, must improve my understanding of his communication device as Samuel learns to communicate in whole sentences, not just one word. In the teacher's defense, the teachers need a lot of training, and it takes a lot of time to program the device.

Samuel's father and I have felt disoriented since we left the special school. My ex-husband said, "The special school was amazing, but it created a false sense of reality when kids graduated—like you're not in Kansas anymore—and it's so disheartening to see my son struggle, 'cause he really struggles." Maybe after high school, the receiving school has to have a stronger transition partnership with the special school—to make things easier for the kids. The advisor at the community college now realizes that the more challenges [that are] in an individual's disability, the more difficult it is for the college.

The transition program in the special school needs to be focused on the reality of going to college classes, meeting with instructors, and communicating using email. In that transition program, my son needed a bit more structure that included strengthening his academic weaknesses.

I suggested the idea of a bridge between the sending school and the receiving school, and the college advisor not only found the idea amazing but offered, in her spare time, to spearhead such an effort and write something up that described what this program should look like.

In his first year of college, Samuel said, "I can't socialize, I don't know how to socialize, and I don't know where to socialize." I feel terrible that he just goes to school, does homework, and comes back. And I'm like, "What about a basketball game?" "Do you want to go?" "Do you want to hang out with your peers?" I'm trying to figure out how we can get him more socially engaged at the college, and I can't do it, because I don't know how to do it there. There is no bridge that makes faculty more empathetic about special-needs populations. In a way, we all have to be empathetic advocates because it is hard for Samuel to communicate his thoughts and feelings.

He also said, "I don't understand my scribe; she is overwhelming me." Now, this is the person who's supposed to be helping him. As a scribe, she was trying too much. You can't feed him the answers. You have to be careful. . . . It goes back to academic integrity. If you got it wrong, you got it wrong. She hasn't been trained. Everyone who comes into Samuel's life needs to be highly trained.

It is hard for people at the community college to understand that you have an augmentative communication system, but you're cognitively intact. There also has to be a transition orientation of some sort, where special-needs kids and mainstream kids get to know each other. I think that in small community colleges, some special-needs students are really on their own.

Whenever his father and I try to strategize and coordinate Samuel's needs, he says, "I'll be okay" to make us feel that he's really okay.

He did find an ally in the college librarian, who told him that he could come to the library anytime he needed something. When he is out in the community, there is a store in the mall where he has found a safe place. He moves around with his iPhone strapped to his leg, in his power chair, and his communication system. If any of those things give up, we have an issue. Once his phone was acting up, but Samuel wasn't able to get that message to his father, who had to drive all the way to the college to discover what was happening.

We've asked for extra support, but they [the college] just don't have it. We tried to get Samuel into a sports program, just keeping score, but that expressive language is such a big challenge.

I tried to hire an aide to just sit outside of the classroom, but I couldn't get anybody. I have done it, his father has done it, and there was one lovely scribe who was willing to take him to the bathroom, but he's a young man—so, no.

When his father runs late in picking him up, Samuel is really outside by himself. Folks don't communicate with Samuel, because when they see all the equipment and stuff, they're probably thinking he's not understanding and wonder how to approach him. So we have told Samuel, "That's why you have your communication system. Use it. Ask others, 'How are you doing?' You communicate with everyone else."

His socialization is really poor. I think it's poor because people are afraid of how he presents. And to be honest and fair, even before I had a child with special needs, if I was to see someone drooling excessively, I probably wouldn't approach the person. We tell Samuel that he has to try to control the drooling because it can be a social turnoff, but that takes a lot of concentration. And when he's stressed and concentrating with academics, he's going to drool more. So, do we want him to focus on not drooling, or do we want him to focus on actually learning?

He really won't use his communication system a lot, because he thinks it's silly or stupid or whatever. We tell him that nowadays, everyone has digital devices, and it's actually cool to have an iPad. We are looking for another aug-com device that resembles an iPad and is smaller, thinner, and cooler. His current aug-com device is bulky and sits in front of him and blocks his peripheral vision.

Once, his father had to go to the community college just to open the sliding doors that did not accommodate a wheelchair, just so Samuel could take an exam. The advisor knew about this, but she is overwhelmed.

The first time we removed Samuel from the college program, he felt really bad. He's like, "Oh no. I don't want to be a dropout." We explained that we withdrew him so he would have the opportunity to go back and start fresh. This is what happened, but now he is taking one course at a time, and so far, so good, but it has taken a lot out of his father and me.

Finally, we constantly tell Samuel that he has to write his advisor, tell her what he needs right now. "Then you have to cc us because there are privacy laws, and they are not going to call us. You are on your own, baby. I don't care what you are telling your advisor, but you have to share with us if you want us to help you."

Story Number 7

Ms. Maldonado, a general-ed teacher and a nurse, is Marco's adopted mother. She believes that educator expectations are often more limiting than the disability itself.

Expectations are set too low, and students are not seen as completely different from one another, and the one-size-fits-all approach with CP doesn't work. Rather than say they can't, we need to let them try.

The fear of the unknown makes people defensive and afraid to try things. Often when we don't know how to do things, we don't want to do things.

In general ed, too, if you're uncomfortable, not just with CP but with a race or religion, we are not as kindhearted as we should be.

Marco was not forecasted to do much of anything. I was encouraged to put him in a nursing home in infancy and pretty much give up. It was a big deal when he was in the side lyer as an infant and actually reached for something. They said if he sat up by two, he might walk. Now he walks, runs, and jumps.

Despite initial low expectations, he reads pretty well, thanks to a lot of teachers who have taught him everything they could.

One former teacher used the principles of guided reading and elementary literacy education, like I would use in a regular classroom, and Marco benefited.

His OT worked on books with him and did research projects. He's benefited greatly from music and art education. His time spent at a school in a rehab hospital was tremendous. They taught him manners, how to pick up after himself, and how to say please and thank you. He had to do things the right way. He wasn't given a pass on behavior because of lack of ability. He's developed positively, both socially and educationally. A lot of his conversation is good because teachers taught him like he was a normally abled kid. So, they got that right. We have been very blessed over the years that we've had a lot of people who have been very open about providing education and experiences. The integration of the therapies, PT, OT, and speech, into the classroom was also really well done at both schools. He was able to scaffold his knowledge into different areas, and they identified and used his interests for instruction.

Marco's skills are scattered. That makes it really hard for people because if there is a failure to function in one area, educators tend to extend that failure to all areas. That is a mistake because deficits in one area don't necessarily extend to all areas of functioning.

I am finding this year, for the first time, I'm frustrated. I'm happy that this is the first year I am having this problem. I think educators totally missed math with him. He hasn't had the math instruction he should have had. Perhaps time is limited, and perhaps some teachers are not as comfortable mathematically as they are with literacy.

A recent Task Performance Report noted that Marco was having difficulty in the store organizing shoes by the whole sizes and the half sizes. He has never had any instruction on fractions. I don't think that he knows what "whole" and "half" mean. When there is a deficit in performance in the child in special ed, there is a deficit in the child, but in general ed, there's a deficit in the teacher. Why is it almost June and this is the first I am hearing that he doesn't know fractions? I could have been teaching him fractions. And I could have taken him to the store, try on a pair of shoes that are a half size too small and a half size too big, and he would have understood. I don't know that that's been attended to, even though it's been cited as a difficulty for him. Giving him a chart [is not enough].

Schools also fail by putting program needs before the student needs. This year they make the student fit into the blocks of time and space, and it doesn't matter that Marco's needs are different and can't be accommodated with the staff and program they have. So, what should drive what? In my opinion, his needs should drive the program. But in their opinion, the opposite.

Unfortunately, some educators have a real can't-do attitude: "We can't do this" or "We don't do that" instead of trying to figure out what *can* be done. For example, one of his teachers said that Marco should be able to self-advocate. He's a compliant don't-rock-the-boat kind of guy, but when he's made an effort to self-advocate, they've shut him down completely.

There was a girl he liked in his class, and he did not want to move to a new class and be away from her. Although we had been telling him that he could see her, since this was her last year there, once he changed classes. Faculty said, "No, you can't go and see her." Now graduation is approaching, he is really upset, and he wanted me to get in touch with her father and see if there was some way that they could meet up after graduation.

One day they sent him to the office and told him that if he

did the errands, maybe he'd be able to see her. He walked around the block of classrooms, hoping to see her, and he got caught and in trouble. He was crushed.

Then Marco was planning to see her at the school dance in the evening, where I would be able to meet the father and ask for their phone number. The school then rescheduled the dance during the day, denying parents the right to attend.

They have done no sex education with the kids, and I've asked about that too. They have not even addressed that, and I suppose it is my responsibility as much as theirs. I've always had the attitude that whatever he asks, I'll answer, and he hasn't. The school only wants them to be friends. They don't accept the attitude that he may want a girlfriend. They said that they were not going to encourage this friendship, because it did not have any future. I put my thoughts in writing because I did not think that was the school's decision. Must people with CP be asexual in school?

I went through my litany of complaints, including telling the teacher that she was culturally tone-deaf in trying to exclude parents. We [Latino parents] hang together, and it's not the role of the classroom educator to change our culture. I don't understand "The children have to separate." They are going to separate soon enough. You don't need to tell us that we can't come to the dance. I have been coming all these years, and dances always have parent chaperones.

The PLOP was a little tone-deaf too. It said that Marco was a mouth breather. He has a mouth that has been structurally unable to close. He has had his tonsils and his adenoids out; he breaths just fine. Now, with the braces, he is starting to have lip closure.

I provided the assessments that they requested, but they would not give Marco the kind of speech therapy for his stuttering and feeding issues that I requested for his different needs—needs that I believe can't be met with the collaborative speech intervention. It's almost an insult to my intelligence. They told me every speech therapist has the same training, but no, we have different skills that we develop through the years.

For months, I've asked for referrals to other schools, programs, and homeschooling, but I've gotten nothing. I asked whether Marco could get services if I did homeschooling; I got nothing.

I worked for months to make Marco eligible for paratransit, and now the school is telling me that he can't take paratransit, because I have to be at school every morning to sign him in. Well, he takes the school bus, and nobody has to sign him in.

I put it in writing that I want him to be able to use paratransit to get to school after I have taken him to the speech therapist. They say that it is a liability issue. If so, it's my liability.

The teacher insisted that I get permission from the district to have him use paratransit, even though I wanted to try it out first. When I called the district, they told me I could get him to school any way I wanted to. There is a real learning curve on this transit business, and I wanted to get the times just right, and it took a while for me to figure out how to do it, and I had to be sure that he could handle it okay. For a while, he was taking paratransit from home to speech and from speech to school, and I was driving behind the whole time. We did this twice a week for a couple of months. So I know that he can do this.

He was using paratransit one day and had to travel a distance. I'm with the OT, waiting for him, and she said, "Where is he?" Just then he called from the bus, telling me why he was late and where the bus took him first. "Everything is fine," he said. "We're coming to you now. I just didn't want you to worry."

Marco will be eighteen; he can do this. He can go into Disney World on his own and find his way home to the hotel and use the transportation in Disney without a problem. If he rides with me somewhere we've gone before, he goes, "No, you've got to turn ..."

Then there's the matter of the pureed diet. I've resuscitated and cleared airwaves, and I'd rather Heimlich a chunk than puree that can't be cleared. If he can't swallow, then he needs a nurse traveling with him at every feeding with suctioning.

It's not logical, and I told them that a modified barium swallow trumps a five-minute observation by a speech pathologist who has never met him before and who recommended the MBSS [Modified Barium Swallow Study]. The MBSS revealed that he could have a soft chop because he needs to learn to chew. As long as he has puree, he is never going to learn that. It's just illogical. I wrote it all down because I'm tired of talking, and there's no record of what I say.

I didn't attend the last IEP meeting, because even though I'm entitled, I'm not getting to review the IEP draft. What we talk about and what comes in writing are not the same, and I'm done with talking and meetings. They denied me that and proceeded to schedule the meeting. I submitted a fifty-page PowerPoint for the last meeting, and they are not thrilled with me. I can't sign off on something I only saw five minutes before the meeting.

When I did not appear at the meeting, they went to my son and made him sign something saying I couldn't come to the meeting so they could not have it. I wrote a note right away to the principal, saying "What is this?" She replied, "No, at a certain age, the students have to participate." "I asked for his participation months ago, and you said no. So why does he have to sign if there is no meeting?"

Up until now, I have had a good rapport with the school. I told them that I wanted him out of the class. He wants out of the class, has talked about self-harm, and says that he wants to punch the teacher in the face. He is internalizing the chastisement that other students are getting. He's feeling bad for the other kids. Why is he feeling that way?

I want him in the mechanics class. They said that he may not be able to get a job, and I said, "I don't care. There are too many stairs for him to get to the mechanics shop, so he'll have to use the back door." They replied that nobody does that and the walkway isn't always shoveled. Can't, can't, can't, can't! If I get an IEP, and after I've told them what I want, then we'll see. I can't protect him from ever having an accidental injury. Taking him around the back for the shop class is a reasonable accommodation.

They said that he had some small progress with the stuttering, and I thought, "Are you kidding?" At first there was a lot of stuttering, then he went mute, and now there is real improvement. The outside speech therapist and the one in school have yet to communicate, and I understand that there have been missed calls. It's unconscionable that they have not spoken; I want there to be integration of services. They should not each be spinning in their own orbits.

Marco's grown sister briefly joined the conversation and noted a disconnect between teacher perceptions and Marco's progress and challenges:

There is nothing in his IEP about his gait, although his walking has become more difficult. He leans on me or puts his hand on me when we're walking down the street. He's walking much slower than he used to. I don't know why. I don't know if he needs more therapy.

Ms. Maldonado added,

The school did acknowledge that he was slower than he should be, but they did not give a reason for his increasing spasticity.

They also said that he uses one hand, not two, to tie his shoes. His fingers are very rigid.

They have also not acknowledged the significant improvement in his speech. He is also not as verbal with them, because I think he is intimidated by them. He's afraid to do something wrong. He thinks his teacher is mean, says people get in trouble, and he's afraid to buck her and say anything.

Marco wanted them to change the key of the song that they use at graduation. He said that he found the low key annoying. He's been asking them to do this for six months. They said we're going to bring him to the committee to make that request. Why does it take so much? I can guarantee you that 80 percent of the people who come to a musical would not notice the pitch, but he is very musical. There is so much out of his control; his friends are leaving. Can't we just give him this? This is so little, and I don't think anyone will know the difference anyway.

It appears that for functions or activities, they deliberately try to keep the parents and families out. Marco performed on a talent show, and he wanted us to come. They said that it was not necessary, but we came.

Marco says that come September, he's not going back there. Don't know where he will be, because our home district has not provided referrals.

I am getting guardianship now. Am getting all the assessments done now. I'm looking at an institute for individuals with degrees of developmental disabilities that is not far from us. I also could register him in the special program in our local high school, then let him drop out.

This year we had a specific teacher problem, not a program problem. Never had this before. It's okay if he doesn't work, because he has my Social Security for the rest of his life and he can earn only so much a year. A little part-time job would be fine; then he can go to a social program. He has received no academic instruction this year—also no music and no art. The kids go out to work five days a week. Marco doesn't need to be putting shoes in boxes five days a week.

I told the school that I would like him in a different class. He enjoyed writing and reading books last year. He needs some of these academic activities that he finds so pleasurable.

I'm not happy, because I don't know where we are going. We have no referrals to other places, and the school will not talk to me. I am stuck. Looks like we are getting close to impartial time. It's particularly challenging as they age. The psychologist is the most understanding, and the OT and PT are good too. At least Marco is being heard. It's terrible if you don't have a choice. Marco brought his crush flowers for Christmas, and I will send my phone number to the girl's father, and the four of us can get together.

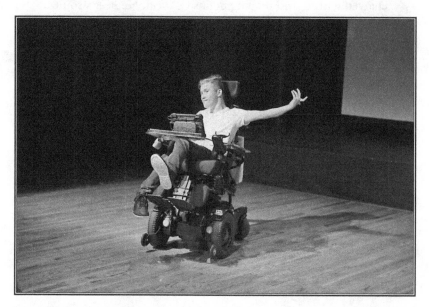

Tom in his off-off-Broadway show in 2017.

CHAPTER 11

Student Voices

Adine R. Usher

In this chapter, thirteen students speak for themselves as they reflect on and answer the question, "What would you like your teachers to know about your school experience?" Each of these students live with a unique presentation of CP, and even though they all share aspects of the same umbrella diagnosis, each student has different gifts, strengths, challenges, and experiences. Some have been educated entirely in either special or general education settings. Others have had both experiences. Listen to their powerful and profoundly individual perspectives.

Mateo

Mateo, fourteen, has received all of his education in special settings for students with significant disability. Although he has to contend with significant learning challenges, he has a warm, caring, and generous personality, makes friends easily, has a great social memory, can be amazingly perceptive, and enjoys the warmth and security of a loving family.

With a diagnosis of spastic diplegia, Mateo, who is ambulatory, has significant gastrointestinal issues and has had several surgeries to correct jaw malformations that have affected his ability to eat and speak. He appears to have outgrown earlier seizures and is no longer on seizure medication.

Mateo reports that he has had both good and bad school experiences. He said,

> I was very upset and frightened in my last school because I felt that my teacher was not being kind to my classmates. I like my new high school placement much more because my shop teacher respects my curiosity and determination and is willing to spend extra time with me to teach me about taking care of cars and changing tires.

Stephanie

Stephanie, whose K–12 education was always in general education settings, lives with spastic quadriplegia, uses a wheelchair most of the time, but walks daily with assistance to keep her muscles from becoming too tight. She bemoans how low people's expectations go when they see someone in a wheelchair.

An excellent student, Stephanie applauded her general education teachers who learned to approach her instruction differently in order to accommodate her visual and working-memory issues. In recalling her high school years, she applauded those teachers who "assumed that if I was in their class, I could do the work." These teachers "treated me like any other student."

> I relied on these teachers' curiosity, creativity, and willingness to understand why I worked the way I did, and I valued their efforts to help me work more efficiently. I also let it be known that my disability is not the central focus of my life. I don't feel

the need to be a spokesperson for people in wheelchairs, nor do I want every school project to be disability-related. Teachers who understood that improved my school experience.

My high school had a requirement that students take courses in the arts. I went to see my guidance counselor to discuss how I could experience an art class that did not involve studying and writing a paper on art history (yet another paper!). My guidance counselor thought about it and went to one of the art teachers—a person who was creative and who was receptive to trying something unusual. The art teacher found a way to include me in her art class, doing the art projects, using techniques that were adapted to my physical skills. It was one of the greatest classes that I took in high school, and I still have some of the art I produced hanging on my walls. I never thought that I could create art like that! I will always be grateful to both teachers for making that happen. I was grateful for teachers who could "think outside of the box" and who cared about what I wanted.

My adaptive PE teacher and physical therapist also thought out of the box and weren't afraid to get me out of my wheelchair. They understood how important it was for me to keep my body strong and in shape. It also contributed to my self-esteem and my sense of self-efficiency.

Adaptive PE can take many forms. I was lucky to have an APE instructor throughout high school who did not structure her class in traditional ways, with everyone basically doing the same thing. Instead, she designed a program for each of us individually, which allowed us not only to use our bodies but to increase our strength and physical skills. Looking back, I realize how much extra work this meant she had to do, and I will always be grateful to her and to my physical therapist. My physical therapist also went more than the extra mile: She not only treated me like an individual, she cared about why I wanted to do things and about finding ways for me to do more things, even outside of her sessions with me. She scheduled our sessions around my school day, instead of pulling me out of my classes to suit her schedule. She trained my aide to walk with me at lunchtime, using my walker. She even came to the homecoming dance as my "aide" for the evening, so I could get up out of my wheelchair and be part of the crowd.

School did not always work out well. *I'm a student first and someone with a disability second*, but some teachers couldn't see it that way. In my freshman year, I had an honors-level literature class that I was very excited about. But the first day, the teacher suggested to me that I might be "more comfortable" in "another kind of class"—meaning, an integrated class where there would be a special ed teacher in the room. She didn't even know me yet; she knew nothing about the type of work I had done up to that point, what kind of student I was, or anything else—except that I was in her class in a wheelchair with an aide. The notion that only a special ed teacher can teach someone with a disability is ridiculous; and as I mentioned before, many of my general ed teachers were amazing, creative, and never flinched at my disability. But there were enough like the literature teacher to make me think that schools should give general education teachers both better training and/or better information about the students assigned to their classes.

Aides are not mutually interchangeable when you have a complex physical disability. In my high school, when my regular aide was out, I spent the day with whoever took the substitute opportunity when they called around that morning. The idea was, the nurse could help me with toileting, so the sub didn't need any training. But there is so much more that my aide had to know so I could access what was being done in class that day:

how to position my laptop and slant board so I could see the materials and process them; how to scribe (printing, not cursive; regular straight lines; big enough for me to see); where I needed to sit in class; how to assist me without getting between me and the teacher or me and the other students. I can't even describe how stressful it was when the person with me didn't know any of these things. It took years, but my high school finally set things up in my senior year so that there was another aide in the building who worked with me regularly whenever my main aide was out.

If someone is supposed to take notes for a person with a disability, it should be someone capable of taking notes. I went through high school in general education classes, mainly honors level, and some advanced placement level. Yet, at the start of my senior year, a competent aide who had been with me for three years was let go "for union reasons"—i.e., because the district negotiated a contract with their aides, assuming that they are all interchangeable and where the only measurement of their performance was how long they had been in the job. She was replaced with a very nice person who had no idea how to take notes in the AP level classes that I was taking. When she very honestly told her supervisor that this was the case, she was told to "just copy whatever the teacher writes on the board and don't worry about it." Not only did this reflect underlying low expectations for someone with a disability like mine—which was hurtful and depressing for me—it also made my work ten times harder because I had to get through my classes without notes.

Letting physical barriers go unaddressed makes a physically handicapped student feel not only like they have to fight just to be part of the school, but also like nobody really cares. Not one entry door to my high school building was automatic. I could not open any of them on my own. The parking lot had handicapped spots. But to get from the handicapped spot into the building, you had to cross a section of sidewalk with a gap in the concrete that was wide enough and deep enough that a wheelchair would get its wheel stuck in the gap. I could not get from the car into the building alone. The ADA had been in force for decades. Independence? Seriously?????

Curtis

Listening to ten-year-old Curtis was revealing. He lives in an inner-city neighborhood in a major U.S. city. He is in a fifth-grade general education class but goes to resource room for reading and math. He complained that he has had to deal with teasing and bullying about his physical challenges both inside and outside of school.

Diagnosed with CP, right hemiplegia, Curtis says, "Everything just takes me a little longer, and a lot of times, I feel really tired." Curtis uses crutches and walks slowly with an unsteady gait.

> I don't like it when people just stare at me, and sometimes, I just stare back. People forget that I have feelings. I hate it that some people treat me like I'm a baby. I think that if I could walk better, people would not stare at me so much.
>
> I am pretty independent and try to do what the teacher asks me to do, but sometimes she talks so fast, and I can't understand what she is saying, and it is hard to keep up. My hand hurts when I write, and I write really slow and can't always read what I have written. My eyes don't work for me so good, and I can't read everything that the teacher puts up on the board. I wear glasses, but they don't work so good either. Sometimes the teacher makes the homework a little easier for me, but also, sometimes it is

real hard—especially the math—I really don't like math 'cause it confuses me. I like resource room better because the class is small—only two boys and a girl—and the teacher helps me a lot and gives me more time to finish my work. I am a real good storyteller, and the resource room teacher writes my stories down, and I feel proud we read them in the resource room class.

Gym is hard because I try, but I can't move fast like the other kids, and they just kind of ignore me. Last year, there was a special-ed gym teacher at my school, and he gave me fun things to do, but he left and nobody has come to take his place.

Some of the girls in my class are friendly and help me do things that are hard, and sometimes they sit with me at lunch and help me open my juice and stuff, but the boys in the class don't want to be my friend—even the boys who live in my apartment building. Some of them call me a "retard," and that makes me feel mad and sad.

I would like art better if the art teacher didn't make me do what the other kids are doing. When I work just with finger paint, I can make some pretty cool pictures.

I love music, and at home, I dance a lot with my brother, but at school, the kids laugh at me when I try to dance to the music in music class. The teacher tells them to stop, but when she is not looking, they still laugh at me.

My mom and my brothers are really good to me and tell me that I can do anything I want, but I don't believe them. Except for my family, I feel lonely, and sometimes I don't feel too good about myself—but I still try really hard to do what people ask me to do.

Candance

Candance is fourteen and started her schooling in a small general education private school. Her gross and fine motor challenges stem from spastic quadriplegia. She uses a wheelchair, communicates well, is a hard worker, and has a friendly smile and a very positive attitude. In addition to her gross motor limitation, she has had to contend with problems with hand-eye coordination, and she has significant learning difficulties that appear related to visual-processing issues. In her private school setting, Candance required the assistance of a one-on-one aide in school.

In kindergarten and first grade, Candance tried to make friends but had difficulty getting their attention and keeping up with her classmates physically and academically. She remembers "enjoying table activities because I could talk with the other kids." In grades two through six, she spent a lot of time with her aide.

> The teacher would teach the whole class, then give instructions to my aide, then the aide would teach me. A special-ed teacher would come to help me a couple of times a week, but I had difficulty keeping up with the rest of the class.
>
> When I was in fifth grade, I figured out that some of my classmates were a little afraid of my CP, so I talked to them about what CP was and how it sometimes changed my life. We talked about how anyone would feel if they had no friends and felt alone. The other students in the class talked about their own experiences and agreed that they would be unhappy if that happened to them. My aide helped me to write a report on CP that I thought was pretty good, and everyone in the class got a copy of my report.
>
> By the time I got to sixth grade, things were getting hard. The schoolwork really confused me, I just didn't have any real friends in my class, and I never got invited over to anyone's

house after school. I guess some regular kids don't feel cool if they have a disabled friend. I asked my parents if I could go to a school with kids like me. At first, they didn't like that idea, but then they said yes.

Now, in my new school, I am really happy, and I don't feel sorry for myself. The entire building is barrier-free, and getting around is super easy. Everyone here has some kind of physical disability, and we just kind of understand each other, and I have lots of friends to talk to. I still have trouble with reading and math, but I don't need a one-on-one aide, because all of my teachers know how to help me do a little better with my work. I think that my parents are surprised to see what I can do in this new school. My PT thinks that I could use a power chair, and that gets me super excited because now I will be able to move about faster and more easily on my own.

Randy

Randy, who is nonverbal, lives with significant spastic quadriplegia. He just graduated from a public suburban junior high school and was the only student with CP in the school at the time. He received physical therapy, occupational therapy, speech therapy, resource room, adaptive physical education, and the services of a one-on-one aide.

He receives a lot of emotional and physical support from his parents; however, they are finding his care more challenging as he gets older and heavier. At school, Randy's demeanor is generally friendly, calm, and well-regulated; however, when frustration sets in, he can be difficult to deal with as he yells, cries, and thrashes about.

Except for his related services, Randy attended all inclusion classes with an aide in full attendance. The speech teacher was responsible for building his communication skills on his augmentative and alternative communication system and created a weekly conversation group that included Randy and two general ed students. He responded that he "enjoyed his group and looked forward to these sessions." As he was pushed through the halls from class to class, many students waved and said "Hi," but it was impossible for Randy to sustain conversations with peers outside of the conversation group.

Randy was totally dependent in all activities of daily living, had to be fed, and took a long time to eat. Therefore, lunchtime did not provide much opportunity for socialization.

Randy's attention was well focused in his academic classes, and with his aide taking notes for him, classroom teachers tried to include him in lessons by eliciting yes and no answers. His science teacher tried to adapt lessons and experiments to his interests and abilities and encouraged him, with his aide's help, to research and present a report on a marine biology topic using his AAC system. He smiled and responded "Yes, I think so" when I asked him if his classmates were impressed by the work he had done.

Art class was a challenge because of Randy's gross and fine motor limitations. Initially, the art teacher was unsure of how to modify art lessons assigned to the classroom. By collaborating with the PT, the art teacher was able to lightly restrain the movement of the upper part of Randy's right arm (with his permission and cooperation) by loosely tying it to the upper frame of his wheelchair. This allowed him greater control of his wrist and hand, thereby enabling him to participate to some extent in the art activity. His intense concentration on the task demonstrated a degree of satisfaction with the project.

Lauren

Lauren, a high school freshman in a general education class, is a very quiet, extremely shy, hardworking student who speaks freely only with adults with whom she feels comfortable. She says, "I feel shy and don't like it when people judge me." Her diagnosis of CP hemiplegia challenges her ability to write, walk, or swallow with ease. Lauren appears exceptionally dependent on the aide who accompanies her throughout the school day.

> I don't think the other students like me, because they just talk to each other and kind of pretend I am not there, so I pretend that they are not there either. I really don't know what the other students think of me—I guess that they must think that I am weird because I can't walk the way they do. I like most of my teachers because they help me when I have trouble writing and will give me extra time to finish my work. I particularly like my resource room teacher because she spends a lot of time helping me to understand my math homework. I feel good about myself when I leave her classroom. I talk to my aide because she keeps me safe and listens to me. I feel a little afraid when she is not with me, and I feel comfortable when she is helping me. I don't know if I can take care of myself in school.
>
> I don't know if my teachers know that lots of time, I feel lonely. My teachers try to understand my learning problems, and they let me write all of my reports using my Dragon system, but I don't think that they are aware that no one really likes me. I am pretty good at simple math, but word problems and geometry give me a lot of trouble.

Ronald

Seventh-grader Ronald says,

> I like school and have several good friends in my general ed classes, even though I think that there are some kids who don't

want to be around me because I am different. I go to the therapy rooms for PT and OT, where they help me to get stronger. The rest of my time is spent in general education classes.

I am not as smart as the other kids, but the teachers try to help me. Reading and understanding what I read takes a lot of time, and I can get really confused, and the classroom aide spends extra time with me. I don't like to do things different from my friends, but sometimes I have to. Homework takes me a long time, and my mom can't help me too much. I am pretty good at art, and I really like music class.

I try to keep up with my friends during recess and during gym. I can do some of the things that everyone else can do, and lunch is my favorite subject.

With his diagnosis of CP spastic diplegia, Ronald, who uses Canadian crutches, admits,

I get tired easily, and I don't sleep a lot at night. Now that I am in middle school, there is a lot more walking, and I've got to figure out a way not to be late to my classes because I have a lot of classes all over the school. I think that if I could improve my walking, it would change the way people look at me. I feel kind of clumsy, you know, and I am afraid that I'm not perfect.

When I asked about speaking out in class, he offered this:

I like asking questions. I don't mind asking questions in class. I guess that I just try to make the best of whatever I can do, but I wish that people outside of my family would include me in more fun stuff. There is a sports program for kids like me in my town, but my mom has to work a lot, and she can't get me there.

Ronald added, "I also worry about my parents' divorce and wonder if it was my fault."

Gina

Gina is currently a seventh-grader in a special education school in a midwestern American city, although she began her schooling in general education and was pleased for a while to attend her local public school. Gina is an intelligent, articulate, intense, and self-aware student. She is aware of her learning difficulties, which manifest themselves with reading, writing, and math challenges.

> I have difficulty writing because my hands start to cramp up, and I struggle with reading because the words seem to show up in funny ways on the page. But I am very determined, and I keep on trying, and I'm good at math when I use my calculator.

Gina lives with spastic CP diplegia. She walks occasionally with a walker but uses her wheelchair during most of the school day.

> I think that I am doing more than my family expected me to do, and I really try to help myself. I am looking forward to doing more for myself as I get older because I think a lot of people don't have high expectations for me. A lot of therapists helped me to move better, but sometimes I felt that I was really broken, and I wished that people could focus on the things I *could* do. It would have helped if teachers in my old school could have talked about CP in school. I think that more of my classmates would have been more understanding.
>
> The one thing about my old school is that I didn't really have friends, and some of the girls were kind of mean. Sometimes I

felt kind of shy, and I didn't like being judged by people, but I guess that just happens. There was one girl who really didn't like me and told the other girls not to talk with me. My aide just told me to ignore her.

This is my first year in my new school, and I really like it. I asked my parents if I could move to this school because the old school was making me sad, and the kids here are like me and many of them use wheelchairs too. I have lots and lots of friends and feel comfortable just being myself. I even have a boyfriend. I don't need an aide, and all of the teachers help me a lot with my schoolwork. I don't feel stupid when I have to ask the same question several times.

My hands are getting stiffer, and so I have a special computer with a cool keyboard that is easier to use, and now I am writing some of my own poetry.

There are a lot of people here who are interested in getting to know the "real me." Everything . . . art, music, gym, and special drama performances are just a lot of fun. Everyone here is trying to help me, not fix me. I've decided to stop worrying about what other people think of me.

Now I am starting to think about what I am going to do after high school and what I plan to do after I attend college.

Jamal

Jamal is a fifth-grader in a public-school inclusion class in a small American town. He has attended this school since he was a preschooler and says that he is "really happy with the way my family, therapist, and teachers take care of me." Jamal, who has CP quadriplegia, is nonambulatory, wears a back brace to aid his posture, has limited control of his hands and fingers, experiences difficulty keeping his head up, and has speech that, at times, is difficult to understand.

> I like being around my classmates, but I spend most of my time with my aide and wish that I had more friends at school. My teacher talks to my aide about my lessons, but she [the teacher] doesn't talk to me too much.
>
> My aide writes for me because my writing is slow and not so good, but I am getting an iPad that can maybe help a little bit. It takes me a long time to finish my work. . . . I have too much work. I don't always understand the words and math problems that are on the board. Maybe I can do more for myself when my iPad arrives.
>
> There is a special gym teacher who comes to work with me two times a week, and he gives me activities that are fun and I can do. When the other kids in my class go to gym, I work with my aide on reading and stuff. I really love basketball, and my mom and dad take me to watch basketball games in my town. I don't get to visit with the other kids too much—even at lunchtime—because my aide has to help me eat. It's hard for me to speak up because my voice will not get loud, and people have a hard time hearing me, so they just ignore me. Sometimes I feel embarrassed about my speech when people can't understand me at first.
>
> I like art too because things are not so confusing, and I don't get upset, but drawing is difficult for my hands, and my aide has to help me. My pictures don't look like the other kids' pictures, but I like them anyway.
>
> In school, sometimes people just stare at me. When they do that, I just stare back. Sometimes I hate myself and feel sad and hate school. But there is one girl who is really nice to me and,

when she can, comes and sits by my desk and shows me books from the library shelf. I don't think that she is afraid that she is going to "catch CP," and she doesn't talk to me like I am a baby.

My dad and my PT are trying to get me a power chair. When I learn how to steer that, I can go places by myself, and no one has to push me. I try not to feel sorry for myself. I know that I have challenges, but I enjoy what I can.

I have already had eight surgeries, and sometimes I have pain in my legs and in my back, but I still try to do as much as I can. I get worried a lot when I go to see the doctors because I'm afraid of more surgery.

Marcus

Marcus is a third-grade student in an inclusion class in an inner-city school and says that he really likes school.

I play with my friends in the classroom but can't run as fast as the other boys in the schoolyard. Some kids wait for me, but some don't. I can play baseball, but I am slow running around the bases. On the climbing ladder, I am pretty strong. In class, I am a good reader, and I'm really good at math, and I'm really good at games that we play in the class. Science is my favorite subject, and I bring insects and bugs from the garden across the street from my apartment to show my class.

Marcus lives with CP hemiplegia and says that by the end of the school day,

I really get tired, and my school has too many steps. My mom has asked the school to build more ramps on the outside of the school building, but they haven't done that yet. I hope that they

really do build some ramps because I really get tired. Then my
teacher tells me not to fall asleep in class.

Marcus uses the services of a PT and an OT. He is supposed to receive
counseling, but there is currently no counselor available for him.

> I really don't need too much help in school 'cause I'm strong
> and I can figure things out. My right hand works better than
> my left hand, but my new computer/word processor and iPad
> makes writing easy and fun. My art teacher has art activities that
> are fun for me to do, and my artwork looks just as good as the
> other kids' in my class.
>
> My hearing is not too good—that's why I wear two hearing
> aids. In class, I miss some things that the teacher says when she
> doesn't speak louder. I have to ask my friends what she said.
>
> When kids in my school ask me what's wrong with me, I tell
> them I have CP, and many of them want to try out my crutches.
> One of my teachers says that maybe I could talk to everyone in
> my class so that they can learn more about CP.
>
> Sometimes I think about my disability, and sometimes I
> forget it. When I get tired, I wish I could use a wheelchair, just
> for a little while, but my parents don't want me to do that. They
> want me to walk.

Jennifer

Communication for eighteen-year-old Jennifer is difficult because she is
nonverbal, significantly intellectually delayed, and lives with severe spastic CP
quadriplegia. Even though she is dependent in all activities of daily living, given
the extent of her multiple challenges, she often appears happy and engaged
in her special-school setting, where all of the adults around her are attuned
to her need for, and responses to, sensory stimulation.

When she is feeling well, Jennifer cooperates with her teachers and caregivers. She turns her head in response to her name. Watching and listening to cartoons that are accompanied by music elicits excitement and prolonged smiles. She registers pleasure, vocalizes, and smiles when food is brought near her and when her wheelchair is pushed rapidly in response to music. Jennifer responds positively to gentle touch, a soothing voice, and soft brushing against her arm. And when settled, she will reach out to touch the arm of the adult trying to interact with her. She will also reach out to touch someone nearby, adult or student, to get their attention.

Rocking and sucking on her hand appear to be self-soothing responses to boredom and a lack of attention. Jennifer's reactions are decidedly negative when she is unhappy, unsettled, unwell, or uncomfortable. In those circumstances, she cries and pinches others, or she exhibits a self-injury pattern by biting her hand and arm.

For Jennifer, this is her norm, and within the parameters of her abilities, she is quite predictable and capable of communicating what she thinks, feels, and needs.

Della

Tenth-grader Della says, "I try to like school, but it is not always easy." She is a member of a special education class in a large general education public high school.

> There is only one other girl in my class. . . . I'm not like the other kids in the class, and I really am not friendly with anyone in my class.

Della lives with CP diplegia. She walks with an uneven gait, mounts stairs slowly, has spasticity in her hands and fingers, and deals with significant visual-perception difficulties that make navigating the school, writing, and reading quite challenging.

Sometimes I have pain in my legs and back—the pain is worse this year—and it is hard to concentrate and remember what the teachers are saying. Walking from class to class can also be tiring, but I don't think that too many students know that about me.

I think about my religion a lot and hope that maybe a miracle will make the CP go away—but I don't know.

My teacher gives me a lot of attention each day, but things are boring because we do the same thing every day. My OT is helping me to write and use a computer, but in the computer lab, there is no one to help me, so I just try to copy what other students are doing on their screens. I don't see the PT as much as I used to, but he helps me to get stronger on the stairs and gives me stretching exercises in the therapy room.

The part of school that I like is when I visit with a group of students in the regular school once a week. These kids make me laugh, help me, make me feel special, and wait for me when I have trouble explaining what I mean. A couple of times this year, I was allowed to go off-campus with this group, and we went to a bagel shop at lunchtime and just hung out. My aide went too, but she stayed out of sight.

I wish that I was more independent and didn't need an aide to walk around the school with me because I still get lost a lot. That makes me feel like a baby. I get a little bit embarrassed that I can't be like the other kids in the school. My mom and my older sister are great, but at home, they can't be around a lot. So even at home, I have to have a sitter, and I get tired of watching TV so much.

I worry about what I will do when I graduate from high

school. I know that I have a lot of problems, but I also think that I am smart, but nobody sees that.

Dominick

Fourteen-year-old Dominick was an enthusiastic interviewee. He is entering high school and was anxious to talk about his life. Dominick, who has spastic diplegia with expressive speech challenges, says, "I was born a twenty-five-week-old preemie, an amazing kid and amazing guy who has been blessed by God. I had a twin, but my twin didn't make it." Dominick required a good deal of redirection in our conversation, but he said that he was excited about being interviewed for a book because he has wanted to write a book.

> I love school, but sometimes I am bored, like, with science. We are learning about the weather, but I already learned about the weather. My grandmother was a teacher, and I like reading and am very good at math, but sometimes division is difficult. If I had a choice, I'd like to dissect a frog. I have a dog. Her name is Ziggy, she's a mutt from Russia, and I've had her for six months. My mom walks her—I haven't done that.
>
> I have been to about five or six special ed schools, and I think that high school [a special class in a general ed school] is going to be the best. I had a real good teacher in sixth grade—she was just very experienced. She made me feel like we had picked the right school, the right district. She made me feel smart and was very patient because sometimes it takes me a long time to learn things. I also had a very good preschool teacher, but I've not seen her in about nine years.
>
> I have two friends. They are not from school . . . I just know them. I had not seen one of them since the holidays, but I just

went on a picnic with them in the park.

I love sports. I think after the pandemic I'll try baseball. I played baseball for about four years, then I took a break. It was adaptive baseball. I also did soccer, I did basketball . . . I did every kind of sport. On TV, I watch football. After the pandemic, I think I'll play on one of those traveling baseball teams.

After I get out of high school, I want to go to college and study Catholic catechism, Italian, and Spanish. My grandpa speaks Italian, and my great-grandpa used to own, like, a bodega. He was born in Italy, but I have not been to Italy. My great-grandmother, my great-aunt Jane, my great-uncle Mike, and my great-grandma Esposito spoke Italian.

I did go to church, but during the pandemic, my mom has been looking out for me.

When I asked about CP, Dominick had a lot to say:

It's like the way I put it. . . . I might have a different fingerprint than my mom or my sister or my dad. Everyone has a different fingerprint. Even my dog has a different paw print. Sometimes CP can make life difficult. When I get to go swimming, the wetness makes my bones tight.

When asked if he had tried a heated pool, he responded,

I never have been to a Jacuzzi, but I heard that they are nice. Didn't know about the heated pool.

If we go to an amusement park like Coney Island on the boardwalk, there is a roller coaster on the other side. . . . I can't walk from point A to point B. I get tired. I only use a wheelchair for, like, amusement parks. Sometimes it is hard to do sports because all of your muscles are working at the same time—like running the bases on the baseball diamond.

I would like teachers to know that every case of CP is different. People with CP might make strange noises or move their bodies as just a way of expressing themselves. It might take us a while . . . please don't rush us.

And there is something that really bothers me. This is for the bullies: Please, please, please, I beg you, don't bully us because of the way we walk. We might walk differently, we might have a tilt, we might move our bodies in a different way, but this actually makes me so mad, please don't mock us on the way we walk, because it might be posted on Facebook, and your mom or your grandpa is going to see it, and your mom is going to be so pissed at you because you mocked a child. I never get bullied, and my school counselor taught me to "be a buddy, not a bully." If I saw a bully, I would step in and say, "That's not cool, dude," because that's what my parents taught me to do . . . help.

If I have anything else to tell you, I can use Speech to Text on my iPad.

CHAPTER 12
Complementary and Alternative Interventions for Cerebral Palsy

Adine R. Usher

Complementary interventions for students who live with the conditions of CP describe practices with are employed *in addition to* traditional medical, therapeutic, and educational interventions. Some examples of complementary interventions for students with CP are

- Yoga
- Healing touch
- Aquatic therapy
- Music therapy
- Art therapy
- Hippotherapy
- Massage

These interventions are usually delivered outside of the school setting and outside of school hours.

Alternative interventions are nontraditional practices that *may replace* the more traditional interventions when families feel that they are not deriving the desired outcomes from traditional and complementary interventions. The choice to use alternative interventions may occur when families fear that not all is possibly being done to reduce the impact of CP's challenging conditions. Families may believe that alternative interventions offer a greater chance for more dramatic corrections and, perhaps, a cure. Alternative interventions may also provide families with a sense of greater control and even increase a sense of bargaining with a higher power in the face of grief. Cultural and religious beliefs may further fuel a rejection of traditional and complementary interventions. The following alternative interventions are used to either replace or supplement accepted practices and are not accepted clinical practice:[314]

- The Adeli suit was first designed in Russia for cosmonauts to counter the effects of weightlessness in space. Designed in Poland, the Penguin suit, modeled after the Adeli suit, is a therapeutic device designed to improve independent movement for children with CP and other neuromuscular disabilities. It is composed of antigravitational bands and springs that hopefully can normalize the functioning of joints, ligaments, and muscles controlled by the central nervous system (CNS).[315]

- Conductive education (CE) is a philosophy and educational approach to habilitation that was designed by Dr. András Pető in Hungary. CE guides students, many with CP, in group settings, to be aware of and adjust their bodies to their environments through active engagement with highly motivating, interrelated physical and cognitive tasks.[316]

- Stem cell therapy is currently being explored as a safe and effective treatment for CP.

- Modified constraint-induced therapy, in which the less affected upper limb is constrained and the more effective opposite limb receives intensive therapy. This well-studied therapy has yielded mixed results, with some studies showing improvement over a short period.[317]

- Craniosacral therapy is a widely discredited alternative therapy in which light touch is applied to a child's skull. Medical research has to date found insufficient evidence to support any specific therapeutic effect of craniosacral therapy for improvement in motor function, although caregivers have reported some positive global effects.[318]

- Hyperbaric oxygen therapy involves inhalation of 100-percent oxygen for a period of treatments. Many parents have hoped to see an improvement in motor function for children with CP after hyperbaric oxygen therapy; however, there is currently little scientific support for its beneficial use.[319]

- Fish oil may be a healthy food supplement, but there is currently no research that supports the taking of fish oil to reduce the effects of CP.

- Amino acid therapy: There is currently no reliable scientific research on the efficacy of amino acid therapy for CP.

- Acupuncture: National Institutes of Health (NIH) research at the University of Arizona shows some improvement in the reduction of muscle tone in children with CP, but feelings are mixed in the medical community. Acupuncture might reduce chronic pain and spasticity.

- Cannabis, specifically cannabidiol (CBD) oil, is currently being researched as an answer to reducing the pain incurred in some individuals with CP.

Traditional care, if evidence-based, poses a lower risk than do some alternative interventions. Despite great enthusiasm for alternative interventions, they are difficult to validate and are not subject to peer review. Providers may have difficulty supporting their claims, and their practices may, at times, counter medical advice. Although most alternative therapies for CP pose no physical harm, their investment in time, travel, and cost can cause significant strain and eventual disappointment for many families.

Parents can be strongly influenced by alternative and therapeutic information from online sites and from personal stories shared by other families, information that can exert greater influence than medical statistics.[320] This information can appear promising, convincing, and yet often confusing—offering hope that goes beyond traditional prognosis and may even be contrary to traditional recommendations.

In defense of alternative interventions, those that employ stretching and patterning exercises to lessen the discomfort of contracture can foster self-awareness of body functioning, increase relaxation, and spur the desire to work toward self-initiated movement. Evidenced-based interventions and strategies change over time. Alternative interventions may become mainstream, and current practice may be altered or discarded.

Teachers should know that there will always be a need for multifaceted approaches that employ, whenever possible, the concurrent use of traditional, complementary, and alternative techniques. If parents of students with CP are to make informed, objective choices, they need the full nonjudgmental support, guidance, understanding, patience, and respect of the transdisciplinary team.

The occurrence of age-related transition may cause home-school conflicts with service providers over the type and duration of interventions. During the early school years, parents exert considerable influence in decision making and often believe that "more is better."

Therapists are often faced with upset parents when a decision is made to reduce therapy hours and replace traditional therapy with other movement activities that could meet similar therapeutic goals.

As students with CP age, decisions are increasingly made by the students themselves. They assert their own opinions and preferences, and they balance medical and therapeutic demands with educational, personal, and vocational realities. Age-related challenges reflect the need for all team members to re-examine the value of complementary or alternative therapies, expenditure of energy, risk-taking, self-reliance, and emerging independence.[321]

CHAPTER 13
Cerebral Palsy Research, Organizational Support, Publications, and Resources

Adine R. Usher

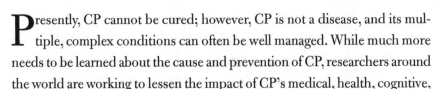

Presently, CP cannot be cured; however, CP is not a disease, and its multiple, complex conditions can often be well managed. While much more needs to be learned about the cause and prevention of CP, researchers around the world are working to lessen the impact of CP's medical, health, cognitive, communication, and social-emotional impairments.

Prevention, improved management, and hoped-for cures are more typically the goals of the medical community. For educators and therapists, functionality in cognitive, communicative, movement, and social-emotional areas is the major focus. Dr. Peter Rosenbaum believes that those who interact with students with CP require an understanding of the importance of the F-words of the International Classification of Functioning, Disability and Health (ICF)—function, family, fitness, fun, friends, and a future—which lead to satisfying employment while also having a functional understanding of the medical conditions that underlie the conditions of CP. [322] More research is needed that examines the complex integration and interrelation of the medical, therapeutic, cognitive, communication, and social-emotional aspects of CP.

U.S. Organizations Supporting CP Research

The following is a partial list of organizations based in the United States that support cerebral palsy research and provide and disseminate research findings worldwide to governmental, nongovernmental, and community-based agencies:

- The **American Academy for Cerebral Palsy and Developmental Medicine (AACPDM)**, aacpdm.org, is an academy more than 1,100 health professionals dedicated to providing multidisciplinary scientific education and promoting excellence in research and services for the benefit of people at risk for cerebral palsy and other childhood-onset disabilities.
- The **Center for Parent Information & Resources (CPIR)**, parentcenterhub.org, is the central "hub" of information and products created for the network of parent centers serving families of children with disabilities.
- The **Centers for Disease Control and Prevention (CDC)**, cdc.gov, monitors a range of birth defects, including CP; runs clinical trials on CP; and coordinates communication among many organizations concerned with the welfare of individuals with disabilities.
- The **Cerebral Palsy Foundation (CPF)**, yourcpf.org, a nonprofit, raises funds for research and education for causes, cures, and care for individuals with CP and other developmental disabilities.
- The **Cerebral Palsy Research Network (CPRN)**, cprn.org, coordinates the research of many centers, studies research goals and gaps, supports important clinical research on CP, and in many cases provides client services.
- **Easterseals**, easterseals.com, is community-based and is dedicated to increasing the independence of disabled persons.
- The **Eunice Kennedy Shriver National Institute of Child Health and Human Development (NICHD)**, nih.gov, is a major organization that is currently conducting intense research on CP.

- **Family Voices,** familyvoices.org, is a national family-led organization of families and friends of children and youth with special health-care needs and disabilities.

- The **Intellectual and Developmental Disabilities Research Center (IDDRC),** health.ucdavis.edu, is composed of twenty-seven nationwide centers that each support research into discrete causes of intellectual disabilities. The IDDRC evaluates the effectiveness of interventions and receives funding from the NICHD and the NIH.

- The **Kennedy Krieger Institute,** kennedykrieger.org, is internationally recognized for improving the lives of tens of thousands of children, adolescents, and adults with neurological, rehabilitative, and developmental needs through inpatient and day hospital programs, outpatient clinics, home and community services, education, and research.

- The **March of Dimes,** marchofdimes.org, is a nonprofit that works to prevent birth defects and premature births.

- The **National Center on Birth Defects and Developmental Disabilities (NCBDDD),** cdc.gov, works under the CDC and focuses on health risk factors for the developmentally disabled.

- The **National Institute of Neurological Disorders and Stroke (NINDS),** ninds.nih.gov, researches traumatic and genetic defects, including treatment options for cerebral palsy. It also studies the reduction of spasticity, drugs that reduce spasticity, and their method of delivery.

- The **National Institutes of Health (NIH),** nih.gov, is the largest source of funding for medical research worldwide. NIH, known as one of the world's largest research centers, conducts research on disorders of the brain and nervous system.

- **Sibling Support Project,** siblingsupport.org, is a national program dedicated to the lifelong and ever-changing concerns of millions of brothers and sisters of people with special developmental, health, and mental health needs.

- United Cerebral Palsy (UCP), ucp.org, is an international network of independent nonprofit organizations that offer direct care and advocacy for individuals with developmental disabilities.

International Organizations Supporting CP Research

The following are international organizations that conduct and disseminate research information on CP:

- The **Australasian Academy of Cerebral Palsy and Developmental Medicine (AusACPDM)**, ausacpdm.org.au, provides multidisciplinary scientific education for health professionals and promotes excellence in research and best-practice clinical care for children and adults with cerebral palsy and developmental conditions.
- The **British Academy of Childhood Disability (BACD)**, bacdis.org.uk, is the primary organization in the U.K. to provide support to professionals working in the field of pediatric disability.
- The **British Paediatric Neurology Association (BPNA)**, bpna.org.uk, a registered British charity, is the professional organization for doctors who specialize in the care of children with neurological disorders.
- The **Cerebral Palsy Alliance Research Foundation and Institute**, cerebralpalsy.org.au, funds Australian and international research to find a prevention and cure for cerebral palsy.
- The **International Cerebral Palsy Society**, cpint.org, is an organization for families and professionals that operates in forty-two countries that don't have formalized cerebral palsy organizations.
- The **Mexican Academy for Cerebral Palsy and Neurodevelopmental Disorders (Academia Mexicana para la Parálisis Cerebral y Trastoronos del Neurodesarrollo, AMEXPCTND)**, amexpctnd.org, is made up of health professionals dedicated to providing multidisciplinary scientific education and promoting excellence in research and services

for the benefit of people with developmental deficiencies as well as malformations associated with said deficiencies.

- **Surveillance of Cerebral Palsy in Europe (SCPE)**, eu-rd-platform.jrc. ec.europa.eu, represents a collaborative network of fourteen centers in eight countries in Europe. It has developed a central database of children with cerebral palsy. SCPE monitors trends, disseminates information, and provides a collaborative framework.
- The **World Health Organization International Classification of Functioning, Disability and Health (ICF)**, who.int, guides clinical thinking, practice, and research in the field of cerebral palsy.[323]

Other Support Organizations

Among their many functions, the following organizations try to predict the size of the CP population, detail the needs of individuals with CP, and make recommendations that guide improvements in health-care outcomes, education, and full membership in society worldwide.

- The **Health Resources and Services Administration (HRSA)**, usa. gov, seeks to improve access to health care for people who are uninsured, isolated, or medically vulnerable.
- **Leadership Education in Neurodevelopmental and Related Disabilities (LEND)**, aucd.org, disseminates skills and knowledge and promotes the integration of services in thirty-two centers nationwide.
- The **United Nations World Health Organization (WHO)**, un.org, is responsible for providing leadership on global health matters, shaping the health research agenda, setting norms and standards, articulating evidence-based policy options, providing technical support to countries, and monitoring and assessing health trends.
- **University Centers for Excellence in Developmental Disabilities (UCEDD)**, aucd.org, envisions nationwide centers that help

individuals with developmental disabilities and their families to participate in their communities more fully and productively. The Association of University Centers on Disabilities (AUCD), the U.S. Department of Education, and the Centers for Disease Control and Prevention (CDC) are a few of the organization that fund UCEDD.

- The **U.S. Department of Health & Human Services (HHS)**, hhs. gov, is the leading national agency dedicated to protecting the health of all Americans, while providing essential human services. HHS maintains several divisions that focus on prevention and wellness; public health and safety; education and training; social services, providers, and facilities; and emergency preparedness and response.

Efforts of Current Research Projects

Here is a list of what some current cerebral palsy research projects seek to do:
- Investigate the possible relationship between lowering body temperature and decreasing brain injury.
- Look at risk factors in the prenatal, perinatal, and postnatal periods that can lead to the conditions of CP.
- Examine factors that disrupt neuron connectivity in brain development.
- Discover abnormalities in brain formation and brain development that may have genetic roots.
- Further understand the role played by chemicals in disrupting the development of newborn infants' fragile brains.
- Look at the correlation between white matter damage in the brain's ventricles (spaces) and movement disorders in CP.
- Study the use of controlled, medical cooling of the body (systemic hypothermia) to protect the pre- or full-term infant who has suffered from a lack of oxygen.
- Research the reduction of CP-related neurological damage by improving oxygen-monitoring systems.

- Research ways of improving the production of myelin (the protective white matter that shields the axon of a neuron).
- Develop anti-inflammatory medicine that reduces white matter inflammation, which leads to white matter damage.
- Improve techniques for pain management.
- Develop biomedical technology that provides students with CP with greater motor control.
- Investigate the aerobic endurance benefits of treadmill training.
- Understand how adding low-intensity vibration treatment to existing locally injected Botox decreases spasticity and improves bone structure.
- Improve gross motor and gait function using robotic therapy and low-level and electrical stimulation to muscles (functional electrical stimulation [FES]).
- Study the physical and emotional benefits of massage for students with CP.
- Use constraint-induced therapy that seeks to strengthen the weaker limb by forcing it to perform after restraining the stronger limb.
- Investigate the use of eye gaze combined with brain and computer interfaces (*text-to-speech [TTS]* or *thought-to-speech technology*) to improve receptive and expressive language for those with CP who are nonverbal or who have significant articulation difficulties.
- Reduce the incidence of prematurity through epigenetics, the study of inherited changes in genes.
- Use deep brain stimulation (DBS) combined with genomic findings that may lead to success in controlling dystonia.
- Investigate the root cause of the chronic or occasional pain experienced by 80 percent of people with CP that affects movement and sleep.
- Study the effects that sleep disorders in CP have on cognition, seizures, and quality of life.
- Investigate possible correlations between parental age at conception and the increased use of reproductive technology.[324]

- Reduce the incidence of prematurity (a significant cause of CP) by administering doses of magnesium sulfate to mothers just before birth.
- Conduct stem cell research that takes stem cells from the skin, the placenta, the umbilical cord, amniotic fluid, and bone marrow. It is thought that these stem cells will be able to regenerate and repair damaged neurons that cause CP.
- Conduct hematology research that studies ways to address the lowered oxygen levels in a baby's system after birth, a situation that can kill or injure neurons.
- Explore ways of improving eye-tracking technology.
- Become more proactive about long-term health maintenance through observation and screening.
- Study ways of eliminating jaundice in infants.
- Explore the possible connections between brain abnormalities and genetics.
- Investigate chemicals that can injure neurons and find ways of blocking this effect.
- Use stem cells to limit the occurrence of CP.
- Study how the care of preterm infants affects the prevalence of CP.[325]
- Investigate whether stem cells might have a regenerative effect on CNS disorders.[326]
- Study the possible correlation between hypoglycemia and the risk for infant brain damage during delivery.
- Study bone density problems that lead to fractures in severe cases of CP and possible use of vitamin, growth hormone, and bisphosphonate treatments.[327]

Professional Journals Covering CP-Related Topics

Here are some professional journals that cover topics related to cerebral palsy:

- *American Journal of Diseases of Children*
- *Current Opinion in Neurology*
- *Developmental Medicine & Child Neurology*
- *Indian Journal of Cerebral Palsy*
- *International Journal of Neurorehabilitation*
- *International Journal of Vascular Medicine and Surgery*
- *Journal of the American Medical Association (JAMA)*
- *Journal of Child Neurology*
- *Pediatrics* (official peer-reviewed flagship journal of the American Academy of Pediatrics)

Other Resources

The following list includes online resources, books, businesses, and magazines that address the needs of students with cerebral palsy. Educators can also direct parents to these resources.

- Adaptive Design Association, adaptivedesign.org.
- American Printing House for the Blind, aph.org.
- Anderson, M. E. 2000. *Taking Cerebral Palsy to School* (Bohemia, NY: Jayjo Books), goodreads.com.
- Baniel, A. 2012. *Kids Beyond Limits: The Anat Baniel Method for Awakening the Brain and Transforming the Life of Your Child with Special Needs* (New York: Penguin, TarcherPerigee), penguinrandomhouse.com.
- Betancourt, J. 2001. *He's My Pony!* (New York: Scholastic), goodreads.com.
- Boardmaker, goboardmaker.com.

- Bugaj, C., K. Janowski, M. Marotta, and B. Poss. 2021. *Inclusive Learning 365: Edtech Strategies for Every Day of the Year* (Portland, OR: International Society for Technology in Education), amazon.com.
- Card, C. F. 2006. *Ceana Has CP* (Lansing, MI: Royal Blue Books), amazon.com.
- Center for Parent Information & Resources, parentcenterhub.org.
- *Cerebral Palsy Experience Journal* (Boston Children's Hospital), experiencejournal.com.
- Cerebral Palsy Guide. N.d. "Cerebral Palsy Help for Parents and Caregivers," cerebralpalsyguide.com.
- *Cerebral Palsy Magazine* (Cerebral Palsy Source), cerebralpalsysource.com.
- Cerebralpalsy.org.uk. "We Support People Who Are Affected by Cerebral Palsy," cerebralpalsy.org.uk.
- Cerebral Palsy Worksheets & Teaching Resources (Teachers Pay Teachers), teacherspayteachers.com.
- Draper, S. M. 2012. *Out of My Mind* (New York: Athenium Books for Young Readers), goodreads.com.
- Emmert, M. 1989. *I'm the Big Sister Now* (Park Ridge, IL: Albert Whitman), goodreads.com.
- Enabling Devices. N.d. "Sensory Rooms (Commercial and Customized Adaptive Devices for Students with CP)," enablingdevices.com.
- *Exceptional Parent*, ep-magazine.com.
- Friedlander, B. S. 2016. *Assistive Technology: What Every Educator Needs to Know*, 2nd ed. (Katonah, NY: National Professional Resources, Dude Publishing), amazon.com.
- Geralis, E. 1998. *Children with Cerebral Palsy: A Parents' Guide*, 2nd ed. (Bethesda, MD: Woodbine House), amazon.com.
- Hassan, A. 2020. "Social Attitudes Towards Individuals with a Disability," Cerebral Palsy Midlands, cpmids.org.uk.
- Kennedy Krieger Institute and its *Potential Magazine*, kennedykrieger.org.

- Marshak, L. E., and F. P. Prezant. 2007. *Married with Special-Needs Children: A Couple's Guide to Keeping Connected* (Bethesda, MD: Woodbine House), amazon.com.
- Martin, S. 2006. *Teaching Motor Skills to Children with Cerebral Palsy and Similar Movement Disorders: A Guide for Parents and Professionals* (Bethesda, MD: Woodbine House), amazon.com.
- Meyer. D.J. 1995. *Uncommon Fathers: Reflections on Raising a Child with a Disability* (Bethesda, MD: Woodbine House), amazon.com.
- Miller, F., and S. J Bachrach. 2006. *Cerebral Palsy: A Complete Guide for Caregiving* (Baltimore: Johns Hopkins University Press), amazon.com.
- My Cerebral Palsy Child. N.d. "Cerebral Palsy Resources," mycerebralpalsychild.org.
- *Parenting Special Needs Magazine*, parentingspecialneeds.org.
- Patel, R. 2013. "Synthetic Voices, as Unique as Fingerprints." TED Talks (December), ted.com.
- Philip, A. 2016. *This Kid Can Fly: It's About Ability (NOT Disability)* (New York: HarperCollins, Balzer + Bray), amazon.com.
- Quality Indicators for Assistive Technology Services. N.d. "Guiding the Provision of Quality AT Services." qiat.org.
- Waldman, B., R. Rader, and S. P. Perlman. 2020. "A More Positive View of Children with Disabilities." *Exceptional Parent Magazine* 50, no. 3 (March): 15–16, epmagazine.com.
- *Web*MD. N.d. "How to Care for a Child with Cerebral Palsy," webmd.com.

Acknowledgments

This book was a long time in coming. Life's challenges slowed the writing process, but my constant proximity to amazing students with CP has strengthened, educated, and inspired me. The spectacularly wonderful parents of these students have kept me focused and on track. These extraordinary parents and guardians—some with great resources, others with limited or no resources—fiercely love their sons and daughters and spend their entire lives moving unimaginable barriers that stand in the way of maximizing the quality of life and potential for these truly valuable young people.

Relevance is important, so I've been careful not to promote specific tools or assistive devices that may in a short time become outdated. Instead, I believe that recognizing and comprehending CP-related conditions or needs should dictate the use of both established and current effective interventions.

I am so grateful for the late Verna Hart, an extraordinary mother of three special-needs students (two with CP), who epitomized the skill and fierce dedication of parents who stop at nothing to improve the quality of life for their sons and daughters. She literally gave her life for this cause.

I feel immense gratitude for the encouragement of my beloved family members, dear friends, and supportive colleagues.

As I wrote chapter 1, I received valuable guidance from Randolph S.

Marshall, MD, MS, Elisabeth K. Harris Professor of Neurology, Columbia University Irving Medical Center, New York.

My gratitude also goes to Sarah Winter, MD, neurodevelopmental-behavioral pediatrician at the Intermountain Primary Children's Hospital at the University of Utah in Salt Lake City for her recommendations in chapters 2 and 3.

I am exceptionally grateful for the skilled practitioners who have contributed to chapters in the book (see "Contributor Biographies"). Their collective expertise and dedication to students with CP has added immeasurably not only to the book's contents but also to the wider field of special education.

Glossary

AAC: *See* augmentative and alternative communication (AAC).

ABA: *See* applied behavioral analysis (ABA).

absent seizure: *Formerly called* petit mal seizure. The mildest form of epileptic seizure, defined by a short, momentary loss of attention, which approximates drifting off momentarily.

activities of daily living (ADLs): Basic, daily self-care tasks.

adaptive technology: Items that are specifically designed for persons with disabilities.

ADHD: *See* attention-deficit hyperactivity disorder (ADHD).

aerobic endurance: Any exercise that provides sufficient oxygen to sustain energy.

alternating tone: Muscle tone that is sometimes too high and other times too low. This condition characterizes athetoid CP.

alternative assessment: A modified, adapted assessment that adheres to the general principles of standardized assessments.

alternative intervention: A plan of action that is different from the usual or the established intervention.

ambient sound: A distracting sound or noise in a person's environment.

amblyopia: "Lazy eye," reduced vision when one eye moves from side to side.

amniotic fluid: The protective nutrient and chemical-filled fluid that cushions the growing fetus.

amygdala: The small almond-shaped group of neurons located in the temporal lobes that process memory, emotions, and especially fear. The amygdala is found in both brain hemispheres.

anterior: Pertaining to the front of the brain or the frontal sections of the brain.

Apgar score: A 1–10 rating scale that looks for abnormalities in newborns. A score between 7 and 10 represents a normal, nonproblematic range.

apoptosis: Programmed cell death.

applied behavioral analysis (ABA): A form of behavioral therapy that targets learning, communication, and socialization primarily for students on the autistic spectrum.

articulation: The ability to produce distinct, clear speech.

asexual: Having neither sexual feelings nor the desire to engage in sexual activity.

aspiration: The inhaling or breathing in unwanted objects or substances into one's airway.

assistive technology (AT): The use of rehabilitative devices for individuals with disabilities that enable them to function and learn.

associated health conditions: The scope of health conditions experienced by individuals with cerebral palsy in addition to the orthopedic conditions of movement disorders.

associative vision areas: Areas of the brain, outside of the occipital lobes, that are also involved in processing vision.

astigmatism: A condition when light incorrectly focuses on the retina of the eye because of a refractive error, causing blurred vision.

AT: *See* assistive technology (AT).

ataxic cerebral palsy: A form of cerebral palsy controlled in the cerebellum that affects muscle control and balance.

athetoid cerebral palsy: A subtype of dyskinetic cerebral palsy. It is characterized by fluctuating muscle tone that arises from damage to the neurons of the basal ganglia.

attention-deficit hyperactivity disorder (ADHD): A disorder characterized by impulsivity, inattention, and hyperactivity that compromises functioning and development.

auditory acuity: The sharpness and clarity with which one hears.

auditory cognition: A series of brain processes that help us to make sense of the sounds we hear.

auditory discrimination: The ability of the brain to make sense of and organize sounds so that language can be developed.

auditory perception: The ability to make sense and meaning out of what one hears.

augmentative and alternative communication (AAC): A variety of strategies and tools used to help individuals communicate who are unable to produce typical speech.

autism spectrum disorders: The range in severity of the conditions that constitute a diagnosis of autism.

autonomic nervous system: A part of the nervous system that innervates smooth and cardiac muscle and glandular tissues and governs involuntary actions (such as secretion and peristalsis).

axon: The part of a nerve cell (neuron) that helps in transferring messages from one neuron to the next.

baclofen: A drug that reduces muscle pain, spasms, and stiffness.

basal ganglia: A cluster of neurons that lie below the cerebral cortex. Part of their function is to control voluntary movement.

behavioral optometrist: *See* developmental optometrist.

bilateral integration: The coordination of visual and motor systems, including tracking and scanning with the added ability to use both hands when crossing the midline.

biological: Pertaining to living material.

bisphosphonate: A drug that slows the loss of bone density.

bone marrow: Spongy tissue inside of a bone that makes red blood cells.

Botox: A drug that is used to reduce muscle tightness.

botulinum toxin: A toxic neuroprotein used medically to relax muscle spasms.

brain hemispheres: The two, equally divided front-to-back divisions of the human brain.

brain shunt: A piece of narrow tubing that is surgically implanted in the brain and runs from a brain ventricle to the stomach. This procedure prevents a dangerous buildup of cerebral spinal fluid that has been blocked from normal circulation in the brain.

brain stem: A part of the brain that sits at its base and connects motor nerves to the spinal cord.

breakthrough seizure: An unexpected seizure that occurs in a person who has had previously well-controlled seizures.

breech birth: A birth in which the baby presents feetfirst rather than headfirst.

cardiac problems: Difficulties surrounding the health of the heart.

cardiorespiratory function: The cooperative functioning between the heart and the lungs to exchange oxygen and carbon dioxide in the blood.

casting or **splinting:** External supports that protect damaged bone and soft tissue.

catheter: *See* urinary catheter.

CAT scan: *See* computed tomography (CT) scan.

central nervous system (CNS): The brain and the spinal cord.

cerebellum: A section of the brain that lies at the base of the skull in both hemispheres and that, among many functions, enables one to control one's sense of balance.

cerebral cortex: The gray folded, neuron-rich outer layer of the brain.

cerebral spinal fluid (CSF): A clear fluid that protects the brain and spinal cord.

chest percussions: Pressure or clapping on the chest or the back to loosen mucus in the airways to improve breathing.

chorea: Uncontrollable, involuntary movement of the arms and legs. Chorea is often found in individuals with athetoid (dyskinetic) CP.

cleft lip: An opening or split of the lips.

cleft palate: An opening or split of the roof of the mouth.

CNS: *See* central nervous system (CNS).

cochlear implant: An electrical device that when surgically placed in the ear stimulates the auditory nerves and improves hearing.

cognitive visual dysfunction (CVD): Brain-based injuries that simultaneously disrupt cognitive and visual functions.

communicative inflexibility: The inability to pair vocalization with intentional, interactive speech processes.

compensatory conditions: Behaviors or skills that make up for or overcome a physical loss or weakness.

complementary interventions: Responses and interventions that are complementary to recommended treatments and procedures.

computed tomography (CT) scan: A noninvasive imaging technique that provides detailed internal images of the body.

conception: The moment at which an egg and a sperm meet to form a new human being.

conductive hearing loss: The condition that occurs when sound is blocked from moving from the outer ear to the inner ear.

congenital: Pertaining to a condition that a person is born with.

constraint-induced therapy: A therapy for persons with neuromuscular disabilities, which constrains the stronger arm to induce improved movement in the weaker arm.

contractures: Loss of joint motion because of changes to muscles, ligaments, and tendons that lose their elasticity.

contralateral: Pertaining to neurons on one side of the brain that control activity on the opposite side of the brain.

co-occurring: Happening at the same time.

corpus callosum: A bundle of neurons that are positioned between the brain's left and right hemispheres and that help to connect and coordinate functions between the two hemispheres.

cortical visual impairment (CVI): A condition that results from damage in the brain's visual cortex.

CSF: *See* cerebral spinal fluid (CSF).

CT scan: *See* computed tomography (CT) scan.

CVD: *See* cognitive visual dysfunction (CVD).

deep brain stimulation (DBS): A surgical device, like a pacemaker, that is implanted in the brain and that sends out electrical impulses to reduce some uncontrollable movements.

dendrites: Branches that extend from the cell body of a neuron to receive electrical and chemical messages from a previous neuron.

developmental optometrist: *Also called* behavioral optometrist. An optometrist who cares for the totality of a child's vision.

diagnostician: One who observes, reports observations, and makes recommendations for improvement.

diaphragm: A thin muscle that sits at the bottom of the chest, which helps a person to breathe in and out.

differentiated instruction: Teaching students in the same class, using the same topics, but instructing in different ways based on each student's strengths and challenges.

Dilantin: An antiseizure medicine.

disseminated intravascular coagulation: When blood clots form in the body, thereby blocking small blood vessels. A person can experience chest pain, shortness of breath, leg pain, speaking difficulties, and challenges in moving body parts.

domain: A specific, discrete area of learning or instruction.

drooling: *Also called* sialorrhea. The inability to control the flow of saliva in the mouth because of difficult-to-control fine motor muscles of the face, mouth, and lips.

dysarthric: Pertaining to significant difficulty in producing articulate speech due to fine muscle dysfunction in the mouth, face, lips, and neck.

Dysem: A thin, flexible rubberlike mat that helps individuals with fine motor challenges to stabilize handwork, including writing.

dyskinetic: Pertaining to involuntary movement characterized by repetitive twisting.

dyskinetic cerebral palsy: The second of three primary forms of CP, characterized by involuntary movements. Athetoid, dystonia, and chorea are subtypes of dyskinetic CP.

dysphagia: Difficulty swallowing.

dyspraxia: *Also called* developmental dyspraxia. A childhood disorder of coordination with the ineffective planning of movements.

dystonia: An abnormality of movement and muscle tone, marked by abnormal posture, that is found in both spastic and dyskinetic forms of CP.

encephalitis: An inflammation of the brain that is usually caused by a viral infection.

encoding: Relating new information to that which has already been learned.

epigenetics: A study of the way behavior and environment can affect the way one's genes work.

esophagus: The pipe that runs from the throat to the stomach and through which food passes.

esotropia: The turning in of one or both eyes.

etiology: The medical history or trajectory of a disease or a condition.

executive functioning: Functions that are both cognitive and emotional, spanning problem solving, memory, and self-regulation. Executive functioning is thought to be controlled in the frontal and prefrontal lobes of the brain.

exotropia: When one or both eyes turn out uncontrollably due to weak eye muscles.

expressive language: Being able to speak or make one's wishes and thoughts understood by alternative means.

extrapyramidal: Pertaining to paths of motor neurons that lie outside of the motor cortex–spinal cord pathway.

eye-gaze technology: Digital technology that enables the user to control digital functions on a screen with eye gaze and eye movements.

failure-to-thrive: The condition exhibited by an undernourished or under-developed child.

FES: *See* functional electrical stimulation (FES).

fetal toxins: Environmental toxins that adversely affect the development of the fetus.

fine motor dysfunction: A condition resulting from damage to neurons that control small movements in the toes, fingers, lips, mouth, and face. Independent movement in these body parts can be significantly challenging.

fixate: To concentrate with a steady visual focus. This focus may, at times, become excessive.

Floortime: An educational strategy for significantly neurologically injured children where the adult enters the child's world until an emotional connection is established. Then the adult attempts to engage the child in venturing out of their own isolated world.

FM system: An electronic classroom system that magnifies the teacher's voice for students with hearing deficits.

fMRI: *See* functional magnetic resonance imaging (fMRI).

focal seizure: *Also called* partial seizure. A seizure of short duration that affects only one part of the brain. If the focal seizure is *simple*, the person usually remains conscious. A *complex* focal seizure often starts in the temporal lobes and may involve loss of consciousness and involuntary movement of arms and legs.

frontal lobes: Sections of the brain that, along with the prefrontal lobes, are behind the forehead and control, among other behaviors, reasoning, thought, and self-regulation.

functional electrical stimulation (FES): A technique that delivers low-level electric stimulation to improve function in areas of the body that have sustained neuromuscular injury.

functional magnetic resonance imaging (fMRI): An imaging technique that maps and shows images of brain areas to better explain brain functioning.

gastroenterologist: A physician who trains as an internist and who specializes in the digestive system.

gastroesophageal reflux disease (GERD): When stomach acids back up from the stomach into the mouth.

gastrointestinal disorders: Disorders that describe the abnormal movement of food and liquids through the body from the mouth to the rectum.

gastrostomy tube (G-tube): A feeding tube that is surgically inserted through the abdomen and into the stomach for those who can't take food by mouth.

genetic factors: Factors that either are hereditary or are caused by gene mutation and that can influence the existence of a medical condition.

GERD: *See* gastroesophageal reflux disease (GERD).

gestational age: The age of a pregnancy, beginning at the mother's last menstrual period.

glial cells: Cells that support and protect neurons. In the central nervous system, glial cells are astrocytes, microglia, ependyma, and oligodendrocytes. In the peripheral nervous system, glial cells are Schwann cells and satellite cells.

global developmental delay: A medical term used to describe a child who is severely to profoundly delayed in both physical and intellectual development. In these instances, injury is thought to be widespread throughout the brain.

GMFCS-E&R: *See* Gross Motor Function Classification System Expanded and Revised (GMFCS-E&R).

grand mal seizure: *See* tonic-clonic seizure.

graphomotor impairments: Difficulties with the muscular movement required for writing.

gross motor dysfunction: A condition that describes difficulties encountered in walking, sitting, and using mobility devices. In cerebral palsy, gross motor issues usually concern the large muscle groups that control the arms, legs, body core, and neck.

Gross Motor Function Classification System Expanded and Revised (GMFCS-E&R): A universal standard for determining the five levels of physical functioning for children with cerebral palsy with level I being the least severe and level V being the most severe. This classification system was developed by the World Health Organization and the Surveillance of Cerebral Palsy in Europe.

G-tube: *See* gastrostomy tube (G-tube).

high-frequency wave vests: Vests that are used as therapy for airway clearing by individuals with neuromuscular disabilities.

high tone: A condition where there is too much tension in the muscle.

hip dislocation: *See* subluxation.

hip osteotomy: A surgical procedure that reshapes and realigns hip bones.

hippocampus: Important structures in both brain hemispheres that strengthen the movement of memories from short term to long term. These structures help to create new memories.

hippotherapy: Horseback riding therapy for children with neuromuscular challenges.

hydrocephalus: A condition caused by a potentially dangerous buildup of cerebrospinal fluid in the ventricles (cavities) of the brain.

hyper-: A prefix indicating an excess of (or too much of) something.

hyperactivity: A state of being persistently overactive and excitable.

hyperopia: Farsightedness, a condition where objects seen close up become blurry.

hypersensitivity: Exaggerated sensitivity to touch or to reactions in the body's immune system.

hyperthermia: Abnormally high body temperature.

hypertropia: When an eye turns upward and is out of alignment with the other eye.

hypo-: A prefix indicating less than normal or too little of something.

hypoglycemia: Low levels of sugar (glucose) in the blood, a condition that can lead to disturbances in physical orientation, seizures, loss of consciousness, or death.

hypothalamus: An area of the brain lying below the frontal lobes that controls the autonomic nervous system, including the pituitary gland, body temperature, hunger, thirst, emotion, and sleep.

hypotonia: *See* low tone.

hypoxia: A condition that occurs when tissues in the body are deprived of sufficient oxygen. Cerebral palsy can occur when tissues in the developing brain are deprived of oxygen.

idiopathic: Describing a condition that has no known cause.

IEP: *See* Individualized Educational Plan (IEP).

inclusion: In an educational context, the practice of including students with disabilities in the general education classroom.

incontinent: The inability to control one's flow of urine or bowel movements.

Individualized Educational Plan (IEP): A written document that serves as a collaboratively created educational plan for a student who is eligible to receive special education services.

inhaler: A portable device that delivers medicine, usually through the mouth. An inhaler is designed to open airways.

inhibition: The blocking or restraining of a process. The term can refer to a chemical process in a neuron or to an executive function governed by the frontal lobes.

inhibition of return (IOR): The slowed visual process of attending to an object that had previously been seen or attended to.

intestinal malformations: A condition found in some severe cases of CP, where the bowels may be twisted, leading to intestinal obstructions, reduced blood flow, and possible death of tissue.

intracranial bleeding: Bleeding that occurs within the skull.

intrathecal space: The fluid-filled area located between the innermost layer of covering of the spinal cord and the middle layer of covering.

IOR: *See* inhibition of return (IOR).

ischemic stroke: When arteries in the brain narrow and become blocked, restricting blood flow in the brain.

jaundice: A condition commonly found in newborns and that shows up with a yellow cast to the eyes and skin. Jaundice can be a risk factor for CP if the body is unable to remove bilirubin, a substance found in red blood cells of the newborn with jaundice.

kinesthetic: Pertaining to one's awareness of the positions and movement of parts of one's body through the sensory receptors in his or her joints and muscles.

kyphosis: A malformation of the spinal cord that forces the upper back into an exaggeratedly rounded position.

lability: Difficulty regulating moods and behavior.

laterality: The side of the brain that controls specific activities.

lethargy: Extreme, unusual drowsiness.

limbic system: Both neuroanatomical and conceptual, the system involving several structures in the brain that are thought to be important in forming behavior and emotion.

lobes: Clearly defined subsections of the brain that appear in pairs. One lobe is found in each brain hemisphere.

low-incidence: Pertaining to less common disabilities that occur in smaller numbers in the population.

low tone: *Also called* hypotonia. A condition characterized by loose, floppy, weak muscles.

magnesium sulfate: A chemical compound used against seizures as an anticonvulsant.

magnetic resonance imaging (MRI): A medical imaging technique that creates detailed images of body tissues and organs.

malformation: A part of the body that has developed incorrectly.

malocclusions: Problems with tooth decay, gum disease, and misaligned teeth, frequently found in children with cerebral palsy.

meconium aspiration: When newborn babies breathe in amniotic fluid before, during, or right after birth, and this fluid contains the baby's stool. Meconium aspiration is a risk factor for CP.

meningitis: A swelling of the membranes (tissues) that surround the brain and the spinal cord, caused by either viruses or bacterial infections.

metabolic: Having to do with the chemical reactions and processes in the cells of the body.

microcephaly: An abnormally small skull, resulting from a poorly developing brain.

mirror neurons: Neurons that cause an individual to duplicate or repeat the actions and emotions of others as he or she observes these actions and emotions.

mixed cerebral palsy: A diagnosis that includes, in equal part, two of the three primary categories of cerebral palsy.

morphology: The investigation of the shape, form, or structure of living beings.

motility: Rapid changes in movement.

motor cortex: The strip of motor neurons that run across the top of the brain in both hemispheres and that control movement.

motor planning: The ability to organize, plan, and execute movements.

MRI: *See* magnetic resonance imaging (MRI).

multiple norms: Multiple standards for ways of being or performing.

muscle contractures: A loss of elasticity and a shortening of muscles and tendons that sometimes is accompanied by poor joint formation.

muscle tone: A muscle's resistance, while resting, to passive stretching.

musculature: How muscles are arranged in body parts.

myelination: The growth of a fat-rich covering (sheath) over the axon of a neuron.

myopia: Because of faults in the eye's retina, the condition where clear vision is possible at near distances but not at far distances.

myotomy: A minimally invasive surgical procedure that makes a cut in the lower part of the esophagus, stopping spasms and thus making it easier for food and liquids to pass into the stomach.

myringotomy: A surgical procedure in which infected fluids are drawn out of the inner ear through a small hole made in the eardrum.

nasogastric tube (NG tube): A thin tube inserted into the nose and leading to the stomach that delivers food and liquids to an individual who, because of neuromuscular conditions, can't take food or liquid by mouth.

nebulizer: An electric (battery-operated) device that turns liquid asthma medicine into a fine mist, which is then inhaled into the lungs. The medicine is delivered either by mouthpiece or face mask.

neural pathways: Connections of neurons throughout the nervous system in the body.

neurectomy: A surgical procedure that removes part or all of a nerve.

neurodevelopmental: Pertaining to the brain's development of pathways of neurons that control movement, learning, and emotion.

neurogenic bladder dysfunction: A bladder dysfunction caused by neurological injury.

neuroimaging: Imaging of the structures of the brain.

neurological: Pertaining to conditions that stem from injuries to neurons in the nervous system.

neuromotor disorder: A disorder that affects gross and fine motor movement, posture, and muscle tone.

neuromuscular: Pertaining to the behavior of muscles as they are controlled by neurons.

neuron: A nerve cell.

neuropsychological assessment: An assessment that looks at the physical and cognitive aspects of learning through the lens of brain function and yields both descriptive and prescriptive information.

neuropsychologist: A specialist whose focus is the impact of neurology on behavior, learning, and emotion.

neuroscience: The science that studies brain cells and the nervous system.

neurotypical: Pertaining to neurological responses expected from one who has not experienced neurological damage.

NG tube: *See* nasogastric tube (NG tube).

normed: A standard against which other behaviors and outcomes are judged.

nuclei: A cluster of neurons that communicate and perform a similar function.

nystagmus: Jerking, rapid, rhythmic up-and-down, side-to-side, or circular movement of both eyes.

occipital lobes: Sections in the upper back part of the brain, in both hemispheres, that primarily control the processing of vision.

ocular convergence: The condition of eyes moving inward until they can visually create an image of one singular object.

oculomotor dysfunction: Difficulty with the ability to fix one's eyes on an object or to move evenly in a desired direction.

olfactory nerves: Nerves that connect the brain to the nose and make smelling possible.

ophthalmologist: A medical specialist for the eyes and vision.

optometrist: A technical vision specialist who performs eye exams and provides prescriptions for eyeglasses.

oral-motor control: Muscular control of the cheeks, jaw, tongue, and lips in eating, speaking, drinking, and forming emotion-related facial expressions.

orthographic coding: The process of keeping written words in memory long enough to study the word and move it into long-term memory, using the help of meaning and pronunciation.

orthopedist: A physician/surgeon who specializes in correcting disabling conditions of the bones and muscles.

orthotic devices: Implements such as braces, casts, and other devices used by orthopedists to correct bone and muscle deformities.

otitis media with effusion: Fluid in the inner ear that does not involve infection.

paralinguistic features of nonverbal communication: Communicating with nonverbal signals. gestures, facial expressions, or body language.

parietal lobes: Parts of the brain found in the upper rear of the brain that interpret and integrate sensory information throughout much of the body.

partial seizure: *See* focal seizure.

pathological: In a medical context, pertaining to the cause of a medical condition.

pedagogical: Having to do with the philosophy and methodology of teaching.

perceptual: Pertaining to the ability to comprehend, be aware of, and interpret the meaning of sight, hearing, touch, smell, and the position of the body in space.

periodontal disease: A disease of gums in the mouth.

peripheral nervous system (PNS): Nerves that are outside of the brain and spinal cord.

periventricular leukomalacia (PVL): A type of brain injury that is often found in premature infants. PVL appears when holes develop in the brain's fluid-filled ventricles (spaces in the brain). The resulting damage to the white matter of the brain's neurons can affect motor development.

perseveration: Brain-based difficult-to-control repetition of familiar words and phrases.

petit mal seizure: *See* absent seizure.

phenomenological: Pertaining to an investigative method of inquiry that involves intense observation and perception of individuals, environments, and behaviors.

phonological memory: Storing and recalling the sounds of speech in working or short-term memory.

physiatry: A branch of medicine that focuses on rehabilitation and physio-logical management.

placenta: During pregnancy, an organ attached to the wall of the uterus and connected to the baby by the umbilical cord, which transfers nutrients, reg-ulates temperature, removes waste, and protects the fetus against infection. The placenta is expelled after birth.

PNS: *See* peripheral nervous system (PNS).

posterior: Pertaining to the back or end parts of the brain.

prefrontal lobes: The most forward parts of the brain, which sit in both hemispheres just behind the forehead.

prematurity: The birth of a newborn before the end of a nine-month gestation period in the womb.

premotor cortex: The strip of neurons at the top of the brain, behind the frontal cortex and before the motor cortex. Its neurons signal the initiation of movements.

prenatal: Pertaining to the period before birth.

presynaptic vesicle: The area at the end of a neuron that contains chemicals ready to be sent through the synapse (the space between neurons) over to the dendrites of the next neuron.

primary conditions of cerebral palsy: Basic gross and fine motor movement, balance, posture, and coordination are adversely affected by neurological injury.

processing disorders: The inability to make sense of sensory information.

proprioception: Knowing and feeling where one's body is in space.

proteinuria: Having an excess of proteins in the urine.

psychometric: Pertaining to the construction and measurement of assessment tools.

psychosocial: Pertaining to social and psychological forces that affect mental health.

pull-out: An educational practice that removes students with disabilities from the classroom so that they might receive instruction or therapy in another location.

pulmonary aspiration or asphyxiation: When food, drink, or secretions enter the pulmonary tract and pose a danger to breathing.

pureed diet: A diet consisting of easily ingested food that has a soft, pudding-like texture.

push-in: An educational practice where therapeutic services are delivered in the classroom.

PVL: *See* periventricular leukomalacia (PVL).

pyramidal cerebral palsy: Cerebral palsy that occurs as result of damage to neurons in the central nervous system.

receptive language: The comprehension of language that is heard.

reflux: The backup of stomach juices, acids, or food into the mouth.

refractive errors: When light coming into the eye is poorly focused on the retina because of the shape of the eye, causing either nearsightedness or farsightedness.

regeneration: The regrowth of old or injured tissue.

related services: Services received in a school setting in addition to traditional educational instruction.

resource room: A small classroom led by a special education teacher for special education students who require remediation of materials presented in the general education classroom.

respiratory dysfunction: Breathing difficulties that stem from various conditions.

Rh incompatibility: A condition that develops during pregnancy when the baby's blood type is positive and the mother's blood type is negative. Jaundice may increase with this incompatibility, and if untreated, the condition can lead to CP.

robotic therapy: The use of robots in therapy, often to aid an individual in walking or improved hand function.

saccadic movement: Smooth, rapid eye movement from one object to another.

scaffolding: Support provided a student during the learning process that addresses individual needs and leads the student toward the achievement of a goal.

Schwann cells: Cells that help to form the myelin covering of a neuron's axon.

scoliosis: A sideways curve of the spine.

scribe: A person who writes for an individual who has difficulty with fine motor coordination.

SDR: *See* selective dorsal rhizotomy (SDR).

secondary conditions of cerebral palsy: Functional disorders caused by the primary movement disabilities of cerebral palsy.

seizure disorder: An unexpected electrical brain disturbance that may result from conditions outside of the brain and that can lead to changes in movement, degree of consciousness, feelings, or behavior.

selective dorsal rhizotomy (SDR): A surgical procedure performed on children with CP that locates and cuts selective motor neurons in the spine in order to reduce spasticity.

sensorimotor: Pertaining to the coordinated use of the senses and movement.

sensorineural: Pertaining to when sense perception is controlled by neurons.

sialorrhea: Another name for drooling.

single photon emission computed tomography (SPECT): A nuclear scanning procedure that aids in exploring and analyzing the body's internal organs.

single umbilical artery (SUA): An umbilical abnormality in which the fetus has only one umbilical artery instead of two. In 25 percent of cases, this condition may signal other abnormalities.

skeletal anomalies: Improper development of the body's bones.

sleep apnea: When pauses in breathing occur during sleep, reducing the steady flow of oxygen to the lungs and heart.

somatosensory cortex: A part of the brain that lies directly behind the motor cortex and directly in front of the parietal lobes. It receives and processes sensory data from every part of the body.

spastic cerebral palsy: The most common form of CP, characterized by tight, stiff, jerky (high-tone) muscles and exaggerated reflexes.

spastic diplegia: A type of spastic cerebral palsy that primarily affects the legs.

spastic hemiplegia: A type of spastic cerebral palsy that affects one side of the body.

spastic quadriplegia: A type of spastic cerebral palsy that affects both arms, both legs, the head and neck, and the body's central core.

spatial problems: When students lack the perception or awareness of the correct position of objects (including their own bodies) in a space.

SPECT: *See* single photon emission computed tomography (SPECT).

splinting or **casting:** External supports that protect damaged bone and soft tissue.

standardized academic assessment: An assessments that is normed for students who perform within the average IQ range.

stem cells: The cells from which all other cells in the body originate.

strabismus: The condition wherein the eyes don't align with each other and may appear "crossed."

structural anomalies: Atypical and unusual forms or structures of body parts.

subluxation: *Also called* hip dislocation. A condition for children with CP who have not walked by the age of five. Subluxation is often painful, as tight muscles force the leg bone out of the hip socket.

suctioning: Regarding cerebral palsy, the removing or sucking out of material in the respiratory passages that the child is unable to cough up.

synapse: The space between the end of one neuron and the beginning of another neuron. Electrochemical messages that determine the neuron's function are passed from one neuron to the next over the synaptic space or cleft.

"syndrome" of cerebral palsy: A way to define CP as a group of complex, interrelated conditions.

systemic: Relating to a system, such as affecting the body generally. *Also*, describing a method of doing things.

systemic hypothermia: When the body temperature falls below 95 degrees.

tactile: Having to do with the sensation of touch.

task analysis: Breaking a learning or teaching process into small units and then identifying and analyzing the reasons for breakdowns in the process.

temporal lobe epilepsy: A series of seizures that originate in the temporal lobes of the brain.

temporal lobes: Lobes in each brain hemisphere that help process auditory stimulation, language, visual memories, emotions, and pain.

tenotomy: A surgical procedure used to lengthen a muscle that has become short or contracted.

text-to-speech (TTS) technology: Technology that turns text into recognizable speech. *See also* thought-to-speech technology.

thalamus: A pair of egg-shaped organs in the brain that act as a relay station, sending nerve messages to the cerebral cortex in the outer layer of the brain from other areas of the brain.

therapeutic: Pertaining to a treatment designed to improve the body's functions.

thought-to-speech technology: Technology that turns thoughts into recognizable speech. *See also* text-to-speech (TTS) technology.

tonic-clonic seizure: *Formerly called* grand mal seizure. A seizure that is severe in nature, that causes violent muscle contractions and a total lack of bodily control, and that often is accompanied by a loss of consciousness.

tooth enamel: The smooth white outer covering of a tooth.

transdisciplinary collaboration: Cooperation among educators, parents, and therapists to collectively create and administer strategies that advance the progress of a student with a disability.

transparency: The state of being clearly and easily seen and understood by the observer.

TTS technology: *See* text-to-speech (TTS) technology.

tympanic membrane: The eardrum.

umbilical cord: The cord that connects the fetus (unborn child) to the placenta.

universal architectural design: A construction strategy that ensures total environmental access without regard to physical ability.

urinary catheter: A plastic tube that is inserted into the bladder to help expel urine when urination can't be performed naturally.

ventricles: Four spaces in the top, center, and lower parts of the brain that help the continuous circulation of cerebral spinal fluid throughout the brain and the spinal cord.

ventriculoperitoneal shunt: A shunt (tube) placed in the brain to remove excess cerebrospinal fluid that then drains into the abdominal cavity.

vestibular system: The link between the brain and the inner ear that helps to maintain balance.

visual acuity: The clarity with which one sees objects in the environment.

visual closure: The ability to visualize an entire picture when only part of the picture is presented.

visual convergence: The situation where eyes move inward simultaneously to fixate and focus on an object.

visual field: All that can be seen when the eyes are focused on a single object.

visual laterality: The unconscious awareness of areas to both the left and right of the visual focus.

visual perception: The ability to correctly interpret and comprehend that which is seen.

visual sequential memory: The ability to remember the proper order of letters, words, and narratives that have been seen.

visuo-constructive: The combining of fine motor skills with visual perceptive abilities.

visuospatial: Pertaining to the ability to accurately see and perceive the size of distances between objects.

vocalizations: Nonverbal sounds that have meaning and are meant to convey communication.

white matter: In a neurological context, the myelin protective covering on the axon of a nerve cell (neuron).

white matter damage: Damage sustained by the protective myelin covering on the axon that can lead to a diagnosis of cerebral palsy.

working memory: Memory of short duration, which requires repetition if a concept is to move into long-term memory.

zone of proximal development: A concept promoted by Lev Vygotsky, a Russian psychologist who described student learning where support (*scaffolding*) is provided as needed until the student can proceed on his or her own.

Scaffolding's initial intense adult support is gradually removed as the student begins to master a task. Depending on the activity, their student's progress may require adaptations that may need to remain in place for a considerable period.

Endnotes

1. Centers for Disease Control and Prevention. 2015. "Data and Statistics for Cerebral Palsy." Accessed July 7, 2015.

2. Dormans, J. P., and L. Pellegrino, eds. 1998. *Caring for Children with Cerebral Palsy: A Team Approach* (Baltimore: Paul H. Brookes), p. 5.

3. Dormans and Pellegrino, p. 5.

4. Dormans and Pellegrino, p. 4.

5. Esben, P. 2003. "From Around the World." In *"New CP": Hold to the Light* (Copenhagen: Danish Society for Cerebral Palsy), p. 8.

6. Cerebral Palsy Alliance Research Foundation. 2018. "Cerebral Palsy Facts." Accessed December 10, 2021.

7. Vincer, M. J., A. C. Allen, K. S. Joseph, D. A. Stinson, H. Scott, and E. Wood. 2006. "Increasing Prevalence of Cerebral Palsy Among Very Preterm Infants: A Population-Based Study." *Pediatrics* 118, no. 6 (December): e1621–e1626.

8. Abdel-Hamid, H. Z., A. T. F. Bazzano, A. Kao, B. Ratanawongsa, and A. S. Zeldin. 2015. "Cerebral Palsy." *Medscape* (December 23), updated August 22, 2018. Accessed July 10, 2016.

9. Esben, "From Around the World," p. 8.

10. Willis, J. 2012, July 27. "A Neurologist Makes the Case for Teaching Teachers About the Brain." Edutopia (George Lucas Educational Foundation).

11. Sylwester, R. 2005. *How to Explain a Brain: An Educator's Handbook of Brain Terms and Cognitive Processes* (Thousand Oaks, CA: Corwin Press), pp. xv, xvi.

12. Sylwester, pp. 124–125.

13. Wolfe, P. 2001. *Brain Matters: Translating Research into Classroom Practice* (Alexandria, VA: Association for Supervision and Curriculum Development), p. 37.

14. Dolan, V., J. Krainin, and R. Senelick. 2020. "Parietal Lobe: Function, Location and Structure." Spinalcord.com.

15. Sylwester, *How to Explain a Brain*, p. 107.

16. Seladi-Schulman, J. 2020. "What to Know About Your Brain's Frontal Lobe." Healthline.com.

17. Çikili Uytun, M. 2018. "Development Period of Prefrontal Cortex." In *Prefrontal Cortex*, edited by A. Starcevic, chapter 1 (London: IntechOpen).

18. Saikat, R. N.d. "What Is the Difference Between the Prefrontal Cortex and Frontal Lobe?" *Socratic Q&A*. Accessed May 4, 2017.

19. Straub, K., and J. Obrzut. 2009. "Effects of Cerebral Palsy on Neuropsychological Function." *Journal of Developmental and Physical Disabilities* 21, no. 2 (April): 153–167.

20. Jin, S. C., S. A. Lewis, S. Bakhtiari, X. Zeng, M. C. Sierant, S. Shetty, S. M. Nordlie, A. Elie, et al. 2020. "Mutations Disrupting Neuritogenesis Genes Confer Risk for Cerebral Palsy." *Nature Genetics* 52, no. 10: 1046–1056.

21. E. G. Fowler, T. H. A. Kolobe, D. L. Damiano, D. E. Thorpe, D. W. Morgan, J. E. Brunstrom, W. J. Coster, R. C. Henderson, K. H. Pitetti, J. H. Rimmer, J. Rose, and R. D. Stevenson. 2007. "Promotion of Physical Fitness and Prevention of Secondary Conditions for Children with Cerebral Palsy: Section on Pediatrics Research Summit Proceedings." *Physical Therapy & Rehabilitation Journal* 87, no. 11 (November): 1495–1510.

22. Neupsy Key. N.d. "Management of Clinical Problems of Children with Cerebral Palsy." Neupsy Key: Fastest Neupsy Insight Engine. Accessed August 13, 2021.

23. Saavedra, S., A. Joshi, M. Woollacott, and P. van Donkelaar. 2009. "Eye Hand Coordination in Children with Cerebral Palsy." *Experimental Brain Research* 192: 155–165.

24. Fennell, E. B., and T. N. Dikel. 2001. "Cognitive and Neuropsychological Functioning in Children with Cerebral Palsy." *Journal of Child Neurology* 16, no. 3 (March): 58–63.

25. Pape, K. N.d. "Muscle Imbalance Hurts Growing Bodies." *Karen Pape, MD* (blog). Accessed November 2020.

26. Dormans and Pellegrino, *Caring for Children with Cerebral Palsy*, p. 11.

27. National Institute of Neurological Disorders and Stroke (NINDS). 2020, March. "Cerebral Palsy: Hope Through Research (What Are the Different Forms?)." National Institutes of Health.

28. NINDS, "Cerebral Palsy: Hope Through Research."

29. Centers for Disease Control and Prevention, "Data and Statistics for Cerebral Palsy."

30. Dormans and Pellegrino, p. 84.

31. Dormans and Pellegrino.

32. Gosling, A. S. 2017. "Recent Advances in the Neuroimaging and Neuropsychology of Cerebral Palsy." *Applied Neuropsychology: Child* 6, no. 1 (January–March): 55–63.

33. Gosling, 60.

34. Fennell and Dikel, "Cognitive and Neuropsychological Functioning in Children with Cerebral Palsy."

35. Geralis, E., ed. 1998. *Children with Cerebral Palsy: A Parents' Guide*, 2nd ed. (Bethesda, MD: Woodbine House), p. 79.

36. Geralis, *Children with Cerebral Palsy*.

37. Santos, M. V., V. M. Carneiro, P. Oliveira. C. Caldas, and H. R. Machado. 2021. "Surgical Results of Selective Dorsal Rhizotomy for the Treatment of Spastic Cerebral Palsy." *Journal of Pediatric Neurosciences* 16, no. 1 (January–March): 24–29.

38. Santos et al., "Surgical Results of Selective Dorsal Rhizotomy for the Treatment of Spastic Cerebral Palsy."

39. Cerebral Palsy Group. N.d. "Cerebral Palsy Surgery Options." Accessed May 8, 2020.

40. Cerebral Palsy Guide. 2021. "Medications for Cerebral Palsy." Accessed December 13, 2021.

41. Molenaers, G., A. Van Campenhout, K. Fagard, J. De Cat, and K. Desloovere. 2010. "The Use of Botulinum Toxin A in Children with Cerebral Palsy, with a Focus on the Lower Limb." *Journal of Children's Orthopaedics* 4, no. 3 (June): 183–195.

42. Seattle Children's Research Division. N.d. "Baclofen Pump, Condition, Cerebral Palsy." Accessed May 9, 2020.

43. Quinn, B. L., E. Seibold, and L. Hayman. 2015. "Pain Assessment in Children with Special Needs: A Review of the Literature." *Exceptional Children* 82, no. 1: 44–57.

44. Association of Child Life Professionals. 2021. "The Case for Child Life: The Need for Child Life Services."

45. Heller, K. W., P. E. Forney, P. A. Alberto, S. J. Best, and M. N. Schwartzman. 2009. *Understanding Physical, Health, and Multiple Disabilities*, 2nd ed. (London: Pearson).

46. Heller et al., p. 101.

47. Datchuk, S. 2015. "Teaching Handwriting to Elementary Students with Learning Disabilities: A Problem-Solving Approach." *TEACHING Exceptional Children* 48, no. 1 (September–October): 20.

48. Datchuk, 21.

49. Esben, "From Around the World," p. 23.

50. Hermann, B., and M. Seidenberg. 2007. "Epilepsy and Cognition." *Epilepsy Currents* 7, no. 1 (January): 1–6.

51. Knežević-Pogančev, M. 2010. "Cerebral Palsy and Epilepsy." *Medicinski Pregled* 63, no. 7–8 (August): 527–530.

52. Hermann and Seidenberg, "Epilepsy and Cognition."

53. "Temporal Lobe Seizure: Symptoms and Causes." N.d. Mayo Clinic. Accessed December 13, 2021.

54. Hermann and Seidenberg, "Epilepsy and Cognition."

55. Van Rijckevorsel, K. 2006. "Cognitive Problems Related to Epilepsy Syndromes, Especially Malignant Epilepsies." *Seizure* 15, no. 4 (June): 227–234.

56. Ramstad, K., R. Jahnsen, O. H. Skjeldal, and T. H. Diseth. 2011. "Characteristics of Recurrent Musculoskeletal Pain in Children with Cerebral Palsy Aged 8 to 18 Years." *Developmental Medicine & Child Neurology* 53, no. 11 (November): 1013.

57. Ramstad et al., 1013–1018.

58. Alriksson-Schmidt, A., and G. Hägglund. 2016. "Pain in Children and Adolescents with Cerebral Palsy: A Population-Based Registry Study." *Acta Paediatrica* 105, no. 6 (June): 665–670.

59. Ramstad et al., "Characteristics of Recurrent Musculoskeletal Pain in Children with Cerebral Palsy."

60. Ramstad et al., 1018.

61. Rodriguez-Raecke, R., A. Niemeier, K. Ihle, W. Ruether, and A. May. 2013. "Structural Brain Changes in Chronic Pain Reflect Probably Neither Damage Nor Atrophy." *PLOS ONE* 8, no, 2: e54475.

62. Children's Hospital Colorado, Chronic Pain Clinic. N.d. "Chronic Pain in Children." Accessed May 29, 2020.

63. Chaleat-Valayer, E., F. Roumenoff, R. Bard-Pondarre, C. Ganne, S. Verdun, A. Lucet, and J-C. Bernard. 2019. "Pain Coping Strategies in Children with Cerebral Palsy." *Developmental Medicine & Child Neurology* 61, 11 (November): 1329–1335.

64. Quinn et al., "Pain Assessment in Children with Special Needs: A Review of the Literature."

65. Schulze, S., ed. N.d. "Cerebral Palsy and Sleep Issues." Cerebral Palsy Guidance. Accessed December 13, 2021.

66. FlintRehab: Tools to Spark Recovery. N.d. "Cerebral Palsy and Sleep Problems: Causes, Risks, and Treatment." *Neurological Recovery* (blog). Accessed July 30, 2019.

67. Ghorbanpour, Z., S. A. Hosseini, N. Akbarfahimi, and M. Rahgozar. 2019. "Correlation between Sleep Disorders and Function in Children with Spastic Cerebral Palsy." *Iranian Journal of Child Neurology* 13, no. 3 (Summer): 35–44.

68. Schulze, "Cerebral Palsy and Sleep Issues."

69. Ghorbanpour et al., "Correlation between Sleep Disorders and Function in Children with Spastic Cerebral Palsy."

70. FlintRehab: Tools to Spark Recovery, "Cerebral Palsy and Sleep Problems: Causes, Risks, and Treatment."

71. FlintRehab: Tools to Spark Recovery.

72. Newman, C J., M. O'Regan, and O. Hensey. 2006. "Sleep Disorders in Children with Cerebral Palsy." *Developmental Medicine & Child Neurology* 48, no. 7 (August): 564–568.

73. Newman et al., 565.

74. Adiga, D., A. Gupta, M. Khanna, A. B. Taly, and K. Thennarasu. 2014. "Sleep Disorders in Children with Cerebral Palsy and Its Correlation with Sleep Disturbance in Primary Caregivers and Other Associated Factors." *Annals of Indian Academy of Neurology* 17, no. 4 (October–December): 473–476.

75. Dutt, R., M. Roduta-Roberts, and C. A. Brown. 2015. "Sleep and Children with Cerebral Palsy: A Review of Current Evidence and Environmental Non-Pharmacological Interventions." *Children* 2, no. 1: 78–88.

76. Newman et al., "Sleep Disorders in Children with Cerebral Palsy," 564–568.

77. Blasco, P. 2012. "Prevalence and Predictors of Drooling." *Developmental Medicine & Child Neurology* 54, no. 11 (November): 970.

78. Reid, S. M., J. McCutcheon, D. S. Reddihough, and H. Johnson. 2012. "Prevalence and Predictors of Drooling in 7-to-14-Year-Old Children with Cerebral Palsy: A Population Study." *Developmental Medicine & Child Neurology* 54, no. 11 (November): 1032–1036.

79. Arvedson, J. C. 2013. "Feeding Children with Cerebral Palsy and Swallowing Difficulties." *European Journal of Clinical Nutrition* 67, suppl. 2 (December): S9–12.

80. Van Roon, D., and B. Steenbergen. 2006. "The Use of Ergonomic Spoons by People with Cerebral Palsy: Effects on Food Spilling and Movement Kinematics." *Developmental Medicine & Child Neurology* 48, no. 11 (November): 888–891.

81. Arvedson, "Feeding Children with Cerebral Palsy and Swallowing Difficulties."

82. Del Giudice, E., A. Staiano, G. Capano, A. Romano, L. Florimonte, E. Miele, C. Ciarla, A. Campanozzi, and A. F. Crisanti. 1999. "Gastrointestinal Manifestations in Children with Cerebral Palsy." *Brain & Development* 21, no. 5 (July): 307–311.

83. Del Giudice et al.

84. Vernon-Roberts, A., J. Wells, H. Grant, N. Alder, B. Vadamalayan, M. Eltumi, and P. B. Sullivan. 2010. "Gastrostomy Feeding in Cerebral Palsy: Enough and No More." *Developmental Medicine & Child Neurology* 52, no. 12 (December): 1099–1105.

85. Goldfarb, R. A., A. Pisansky, J. Fleck, P. Hoverstein, K. J. Cotter, J. Katorski, D. Lieberman, and S. P. Elliott. 2016. "Neurogenic Lower Urinary Tract Dysfunction in Adults with Cerebral Palsy: Outcomes Following a Conservative Management Approach." *Journal of Urology* 195, no. 4 part 1 (April): 1009–1013.

86. Vargus-Adams, J. N. 2012. "An Urgency About Bladder Dysfunction in Cerebral Palsy." *Developmental Medicine & Child Neurology* 54, no. 10 (October): 877–878.

87. Children's Health Queensland Hospital and Health Service. N.d. "Children's Health Fact Sheets: Management of Constipation in Children with Cerebral Palsy." Queensland Government. Accessed December 14, 2021.

88. Vargus-Adams, "An Urgency About Bladder Dysfunction in Cerebral Palsy."

89. Children's Health Queensland Hospital and Health Service, "Children's Health Fact Sheets: Management of Constipation in Children with Cerebral Palsy."

90. Seddon, P. C., and Y. Khan. 2003. "Respiratory Problems in Children with Neurological Impairment." *Archives of Disease in Childhood* 88, no. 1 (January): 75–78.

91. Prashant. 2017, May 15. "Respiratory Problems in the Child with Cerebral Palsy." Health in Physio. Accessed December 14, 2021.

92. Seddon and Khan, "Respiratory Problems in Children with Neurological Impairment."

93. Dormans and Pellegrino, *Caring for Children with Cerebral Palsy*, p. 81.

94. Ayo-Ogunseye, O., and T. Hamzat. 2016. "Respiratory Function and Motor Performance in Children with Cerebral Palsy." *European Respiratory Journal* 48, suppl. 60: PA1380.

95. Shin, H-K., E-J. Byeon, and S. H. Kim. 2015. "Effects of Seat Surface Inclination on Respiration and Speech Production in Children with Spastic Cerebral Palsy." *Journal of Physiological Anthropology* 34, no. 1: 17.

96. Erasmus, C. E., K. van Hulst, L. J. C. Rotteveel, P. H. Jongerius, F. J. A. van den Hoogen, N. Roeleveld, and J. J. Rotteveel. 2009. "Drooling in Cerebral Palsy: Hypersalivation or Dysfunctional Oral Motor Control?" *Developmental Medicine & Child Neurology* 51, no. 6 (June): 454–459.

97. Geralis, *Children with Cerebral Palsy: A Parents' Guide*, p. 82.

98. Glader, L., C. Delsing, A. Hughes, J. Parr, L. Pennington, D. Reddihough, K. van Hulst, and J. van der Burg. 2018, June 4. "Sialorrhea: Bottom-Line 'Evidence-Informed' Recommendations for Children/Youth with Cerebral Palsy Who Have Sialorrhea." American Academy for Cerebral Palsy and Developmental Medicine (AACPDM) Care Pathways. Accessed December 14, 2021.

99. Rodwell, K., P. Edwards, R. S. Ware, and R. Boyd. 2012. "Salivary Gland Botulinum Toxin Injections for Drooling in Children with Cerebral Palsy

and Neurodevelopmental Disability: A Systematic Review." *Developmental Medicine & Child Neurology* 54, no. 11 (November): 977–987.

100. Walshe, M., M. Smith, and L. Pennington. 2012. "Interventions for Drooling in Children with Cerebral Palsy." *Cochrane Database of Systematic Reviews*, issue 11 (November 14): CD008624.pub3.

101. Alliance for Oral Health Across Borders. N.d. Accessed December 14, 2021.

102. Project Accessible Oral Health (PAOH). 2018, November 1. "Viscardi's 1st 'Take a Dental Health Day.'" Accessed December 14, 2021.

103. Geralis, *Children with Cerebral Palsy: A Parents' Guide.*

104. Geralis.

105. Stadskleiv, K. 2020. "Cognitive Functioning in Children with Cerebral Palsy." *Developmental Medicine & Child Neurology* 62, no. 3 (March): 283–289.

106. CanChild. N.d. "Research in Practice: F-Words in Childhood Disability" (Hamilton, ON: McMaster University). Accessed December 15, 2021.

107. Stadskleiv, "Cognitive Functioning in Children with Cerebral Palsy," 283.

108. Lindmeier, C. 2018, June 18. "WHO Releases New International Classification of Diseases (ICD 11)." World Health Organization. Accessed December 15, 2021.

109. Cheyne, J. A., and D. Tarulli. 2005. "Dialogue, Difference and Voice in the Zone of Proximal Development." In *An Introduction to Vygotsky*, edited by H. Daniels (London: Routledge), p. 122.

110. Greenspan, S. I., S. Wieder, and R. Simons. 1998. *The Child with Special Needs: Encouraging Intellectual and Emotional Growth* (Reading, MA: Perseus).

111. United Nations Department of Economic and Social Affairs, Disability. 2006. "Convention on the Rights of Persons with Disabilities (CRPD)." Accessed December 15, 2021.

112. Rosenbaum, P., and D. Stewart. 2004. "The World Health Organization International Classification of Functioning, Disability and Health: A Model

to Guide Clinical Thinking, Practice and Research in the Field of Cerebral Palsy." *Seminars in Pediatric Neurology* 11, no. 1 (March): 5–10.

113. Center for Parent Information and Resources. 2017, August. "Supporting the Parent Centers Who Serve Families of Children with Disabilities." Accessed December 15, 2021.

114. Wolf, P. S., and T. E. Hall. 2003. "Making Inclusion a Reality for Students with Severe Disabilities." *TEACHING Exceptional Children* 35, no. 4: 57.

115. Gonzalez-Monge, S., B. Boudia, S. Marignier, C. Gardie, and A. Rochel. 2010. "Multiple-Cognitive Deficits/Dysfunctions and Cerebral Palsy: Different Diseases or a Continuum." *Neurological Approaches to Children* (December): 960–965.

116. Stadskleiv, "Cognitive Functioning in Children with Cerebral Palsy," 284–285.

117. Huang, X., X. Du, H. Song, Q. Zhang, J. Jia, T. Xiao, and J. W. 2015. "Cognitive Impairments Associated with Corpus Callosum Infarction: A Ten Cases Study." *International Journal of Clinical and Experimental Medicine* 8, no. 11: 21991–21998. PMCID: PMCA4724017, PMID: 26885171. Accessed April 21, 2020.

118. White, D. A., and S. E. Christ. 2005. "Executive Control of Learning and Memory in Children with Bilateral Spastic Cerebral Palsy." *Journal of the International Neuropsychological Society* 11, no. 7 (November): 920–924.

119. FlintRehab: Tools to Spark Recovery. 2019, June 6. "Effective Ways to Manage a Learning Disability in Children with Cerebral Palsy." *Neurological Recovery* (blog). Accessed April 22, 2020.

120. Schatz, J., S. Craft, D. White, T. S. Park, and G. S. Figiel. 2001. "Inhibition of Return in Children with Perinatal Brain Injury." *Journal of the International Neuropsychological Society* 7, no. 3 (March): 275–284.

121. Wolfe, *Brain Matters*, pp. 74–129.

122. Wolfe, p. 56.

123. Wolfe, pp. 71–73.

124. FlintRehab: Tools to Spark Recovery. "Effective Ways to Manage a Learning Disability in Children with Cerebral Palsy."

125. Bouck, E., and R. Satsangi. 2014. "Evidence-Base of a Functional Curriculum for Secondary Students with Mild Intellectual Disability: A Historical Perspective." *Education and Training in Autism and Developmental Disabilities* 49, no. 3 (September): 478–486.

126. Leko, M. M. 2015. "To Adapt of Not to Adapt: Navigating an Implementation Conundrum." *TEACHING Exceptional Children* 48, no. 2 (November–December): 80–85.

127. Dormans and Pellegrino, *Caring for Children with Cerebral Palsy*, p. 11.

128. Wolfe, *Brain Matters*, p. 37.

129. Fazzi, E., S. Bova, A. Giovenzana, S. Signorini, C. Uggetti, and P. Bianchi. 2009. "Cognitive Visual Dysfunctions in Preterm Children with Periventricular Leukomalacia." *Developmental Medicine & Child Neurology* 51, no. 12 (December): 974–981.

130. Bourne J. A. 2010. "Unravelling the Development of the Visual Cortex: Implications for Plasticity and Repair." *Journal of Anatomy* 217, no. 4 (October): 449–468.

131. Hagen, S. 2012. "The Mind's Eye." *Rochester Review* 74, no. 4 (March–April). Accessed December 17, 2021.

132. Hirvonen, M., R. Ojala, P. Korhonen, P. Haataja, K. Eriksson, M. Gissler, T. Luukkaala, and O. Tammela. 2018. "Visual and Hearing Impairments After Preterm Birth." *Pediatrics* 142, no. 2 (August): e20173888.

133. Fazzi, E., S. G. Signorini, R. La Piana, C. Bertone, W. Misefari, J. Galli, U. Balottin, and P. E. Bianchi. 2012. "Neuro-Ophthalmological Disorders in Cerebral Palsy: Ophthalmological, Oculomotor, and Visual Aspects." *Developmental Medicine & Child Neurology* 54, no. 8 (August): 730–736.

134. Mercuri, E., G. Baranello, D. M. M. Romeo, L. Cesarini, and D. Ricci. 2007. "The Development of Vision." *Early Human Development* 83, no. 12 (December): 795–800.

135. Guzzetta, A. 2014. "Visual Disorders in Children with Cerebral Palsy: Is the Picture Still 'Blurred'?" *Developmental Medicine & Child Neurology* 56, no. 2 (February): 103–104.

136. Fazzi, Signorini, et al., "Neuro-Ophthalmological Disorders in Cerebral Palsy: Ophthalmological, Oculomotor, and Visual Aspects," 732.

137. Philip, S. S., A. Guzzetta, O. Chorna, G. Gole, and R. N. Boyd. 2020. "Relationship Between Brain Structure and Cerebral Visual Impairment in Children with Cerebral Palsy: A Systematic Review." *Research in Developmental Disabilities* 99 (January): 103580.

138. Baranello, G., S. Signorini, F. Tinelli, A. Guzzetta, E. Pagliano, A. Rossi, M. Foscan, I. Tramacere, D. M. M. Romeo, and D. Ricci. 2020. "Visual Function Classification System for Children with Cerebral Palsy: Development and Validation." *Developmental Medicine & Child Neurology* 62, no. 1 (January): 104–110.

139. Fahn, S., J. Jankovic, and M. Hallett. 2011. "Chorea, Ballism, and Athetosis." In *Principles and Practice of Movement Disorders*, 2nd ed. (Amsterdam: Elsevier), p. 347.

140. National Eye Institute. 2014, July 14 (updated). "Cerebral Visual Impairment (CVI)." Accessed December 17, 2021.

141. Saavedra, S., M. Woollacott, and P. van Donkelaar. 2010. "Head Stability During Quiet Sitting in Children with Cerebral Palsy: Effect of Vision and Trunk Support." *Experimental Brain Research* 201 (September): 13–23.

142. Ryalls, B. O., R. Harbourne, L. Kelly-Vance, J. Wickstrom, N. Stergiou, and A. Kyvelidou. 2016. "A Perceptual Motor Intervention Improves Play Behavior in Children with Moderate to Severe Cerebral Palsy." *Frontiers in Psychology* 7 (May): 643.

143. Geralis, *Children with Cerebral Palsy: A Parents' Guide*, p. 71.

144. Dutton, G. N., J. Calvert, D. Cockburn, H. Ibrahim, and C. Macintyre-Beon. 2012. "Visual Disorders in Children with Cerebral Palsy: The Implications for Rehabilitation Programs and School Work." *Eastern Journal of Medicine* 17, no. 4: 178–187. Accessed December 17, 2021.

145. Straub and Obrzut, "Effects of Cerebral Palsy on Neuropsychological Function," 153.

146. Gonzalez-Monge, S., B. Boudia, A. Ritz, F. Abbas-Chorfa, M. Rabilloud, J. Iwaz, and C. Berard. 2009. "A 7-Year Longitudinal Follow-Up of Intellectual Development in Children with Congenital Hemiplegia." *Developmental Medicine & Child Neurology* 51, no. 12 (December): 959–967.

147. Gonzalez-Monge et al., 966.

148. Fazzi, Signorini, et al., "Neuro-Ophthalmological Disorders in Cerebral Palsy: Ophthalmological, Oculomotor, and Visual Aspects."

149. Fazzi, Bova, et al., "Cognitive Visual Dysfunctions in Preterm Children with Periventricular Leukomalacia."

150. Berthoz, A., and M. Zaoui. 2015. "New Paradigms and Tests for Evaluating and Mediating Visuospatial Deficits in Children." *Developmental Medicine & Child Neurology* 57, suppl. 2 (April): 15–20.

151. Geralis, *Children with Cerebral Palsy: A Parents' Guide*, p. 70.

152. Good, W. V. 2012. "Cerebral Palsy: The Central Nervous System Informs the Visual System." *Developmental Medicine & Child Neurology* 54, no. 8 (August): 678.

153. "Adaptive vs. Assistive Technology." *Dakota Center for Independent Living* (blog). Accessed April 26, 2022.

154. Morales-Angulo, C., N. Azuara Blanco, J. Gallo Terán, A. González Aledo, and J. Rama Quintela. 2006. "Sensorineural Hearing Loss in Cerebral Palsy Patients." *Acta Otorrinolaringologica Española* 57, no. 7 (August–September): 300–302.

155. Morales-Angulo et al., 302.

156. National Institute of Neurological Disorders and Stroke (NINDS). 2020, March. "Cerebral Palsy: Hope Through Research (What Is Cerebral Palsy? What Other Conditions Are Associated with Cerebral Palsy)." National Institutes of Health. Accessed December 17, 2021.

157. Hidecker, M. J. C., N. Paneth, P. L. Rosenbaum, R. D. Kent, J. Lillie, J. B. Eulenberg, K. Chester, B. Johnson, L. Michalsen, M. Evatt, and K. Taylor.

2011. "Developing and Validating the Communication Function Classification System for Individuals with Cerebral Palsy." *Developmental Medicine & Child Neurology* 53, no. 8 (August): 704–710.

158. Dormans, J. P., and L. Pellegrino, eds. 1998. *Caring for Children with Cerebral Palsy: A Team Approach* (Baltimore: Paul H. Brookes), p. 21.

159. Reid, S. M., M. B. Modak, R. G. Berkowitz, and D. S. Reddihough. 2011. "A Population-Based Study and Systematic Review of Hearing Loss in Children with Cerebral Palsy." *Developmental Medicine & Child Neurology* 53, no. 11 (November): 1038–1045.

160. Eyvazzadeh, A. 2020, March 10. "What Is Sensorineural Hearing Loss?" Healthline.com. Accessed December 17, 2021.

161. Weir, F. W., J. L. Hatch, T. R. McRackan, S. A. Wallace, and T. A. Meyer. 2018. "Hearing Loss in Pediatric Patients with Cerebral Palsy." *Otology & Neurotology* 39, no. 1 (January): 59–64.

162. Johns Hopkins Medicine, Health Conditions and Diseases. N.d. "Ear Infection (Otitis Media)." Accessed July 26, 2020.

163. Dorman, C. 1987. "Verbal, Perceptual and Intellectual Factors Associated with Reading Achievement in Adolescents with Cerebral Palsy." *Perceptual and Motor Skills* 64, no. 2: 671–678.

164. Johns Hopkins Medicine, Health Library. N.d. "Ear Tube Surgery." Accessed December 19, 2021.

165. Schmidler, C., ed. 2018, April. "Myringotomy." Healthpages.org. Accessed December 17, 2021.

166. Reid et al., "A Population-Based Study and Systematic Review of Hearing Loss in Children with Cerebral Palsy."

167. Reid et al., 1044.

168. Gandevia, S., and U. Proske. 2016. "Proprioception: The Sense Within." *The Scientist*, August 31.

169. Duque-Parra, J. E. 2004. "Perspective on the Vestibular Cortex Throughout History." *The Anatomical Record* 280B, no. 1 (September): 15–19.

170. Kranowitz, C. S. 2005. *The Out-of-Sync Child: Recognizing and Coping with Sensory Processing Disorder* (New York: Skylight Press, TarcherPerigee), p. 321.

171. Mirpur, D., and I. Sultana. 2018, March 9. "Sensory Integration Difficulties in Children with Cerebral Palsy," *Daily Sun.*

172. An, S-J L. 2015. "The Effects of Vestibular Stimulation on a Child with Hypotonic Cerebral Palsy." *Journal of Physical Therapy Science* 27, no. 4: 1279–1282.

173. Williams, N. 2015, September 18. "Dyspraxia and Cerebral Palsy: The Similarities and Differences." *Natalie Williams* (blog). Accessed June 12, 2017.

174. *Psychology Today.* N.d. "Dyspraxia." Accessed June 30, 2020.

175. Chambers, H., M. Tourne, D. Hrubec, A. Sarafian, L. Vogtle, N. Truba, and J. Chambers. 2019, January 1. "Navigating the Journey." AACPDM eCourses, American Academy for Cerebral Palsy and Developmental Medicine.

176. Heller et al., *Understanding Physical, Health, and Multiple Disabilities*, p. 85.

177. Heller et al.

178. Heller et al., p. 86.

179. Sigudardottir, S., and T. Vik. 2011. "Speech, Expressive Language, and Verbal Cognition of Preschool Children with Cerebral Palsy in Iceland." *Developmental Medicine & Child Neurology* 53, no. 1 (January): 74–80.

180. Sigudardottir and Vik, 77.

181. Sigudardottir and Vik.

182. Exploring Your Mind. 2020, June 11 (updated). "Causes and Symptoms of Dysarthria." Accessed December 20, 2021.

183. Straub and Obrzut, "Effects of Cerebral Palsy on Neuropsychological Function," 153.

184. Pennington, L., N. Miller, S. Robson, and N. Steen. 2010. "Intensive Speech and Language Therapy for Older Children with Cerebral Palsy: A Systems Approach." *Developmental Medicine & Child Neurology* 52, no. 4 (April): 337–344.

185. Mouse4All. N.d. "Mouse4All Switch." Accessed June 28, 2019.

186. Birth Injury Help Center. 2020. "Cerebral Palsy Hearing, Speech & Vision Problems." Accessed December 21, 2021.

187. Straub and Obrzut, "Effects of Cerebral Palsy on Neuropsychological Function," 153.

188. Vimont, C. 2017, July 26. "Vision Training Not Proven to Make Vision Sharper." American Academy of Ophthalmology: EyeSmart. Accessed February 19, 2020.

189. Coats, D. K. 2002. "What Does Independent Research Show About the Effectiveness of Vision Therapy for Children?" American Optometric Association. Documentation on the Clinical Research & Scientific Support Underlying Vision Therapy. Accessed February 19, 2020.

190. Kress, N. E. 2015. "Vision Therapy in the Cerebral Palsy Population: Utilizing Vision Therapy Techniques to Remediate Motor and Sensory Deficits of the Visual System." *Optometry & Visual Performance* 3, no. 5 (November): 265–271.

191. Mitchell, L. E., J. Ziviani, and R. N. Boyd. 2015. "Characteristics Associated with Physical Activity Among Independently Ambulant Children and Adolescents with Unilateral Cerebral Palsy." *Developmental Medicine & Child Neurology* 57, no. 2 (February): 167–174.

192. Mitchell et al., 173.

193. Imms, C. 2008. "Review of the Children's Assessment of Participation and Enjoyment and the Preferences for Activity for Children." *Physical & Occupational Therapy in Pediatrics* 28, no. 4: 389–404.

194. Imms, 402.

195. Ryan, J. M., E. E. Cassidy, S. G. Noorduyn, and N. E. O'Connell. 2017. "Exercise Interventions for Cerebral Palsy." *Cochrane Database of Systematic Reviews*, issue 6 (June 11): CD011660.

196. Johnson, C. C. 2009. "The Benefits of Physical Activity for Youth with Developmental Disabilities: A Systematic Review." *American Journal of Health Promotions* 23, no. 3 (January–February): 157–167.

197. Lauruschkus, K., I. Hallström, L. Westbom, Å.Tornberg, and E. Nord-mark. 2017. "Participation in Physical Activities for Children with Cerebral Palsy: Feasibility and Effectiveness of Physical Activity on Prescription." *Archives of Physiotherapy* 7 (November 28): 13.

198. Palisano, R. J. 2012. "Physical Activity of Children with Cerebral Palsy: What Are the Considerations?" *Developmental Medicine & Child Neurology* 54, no. 5 (May): 390–391. This commentary is on the following original article: Van Wely, L., J. G. Becher, A. C. J. Balemans, and A. J. Dallmeijer. 2012. "Ambulatory Activity of Children with Cerebral Palsy: Which Characteristics Are Important?" *Developmental Medicine & Child Neurology* 54, no. 5 (May): 436–442.

199. Estelle I. The CP Diary, N.d. "Warming Up & Cooling Down." *The CP Diary* (blog). Accessed February 25, 2020.

200. Piškur, B., A. J. H. M. Beurskens, M. J. Jongmans, M. Ketelaar, and R. J. E. M. Smeets. 2015. "Enabling Participation of Children with a Physical Disability: Parents' Role." *Developmental Medicine & Child Neurology* 57, no. s4 [Special Issue: "Abstracts of the European Academy of Childhood Disability 27th Annual Meeting," May 27–30, Copenhagen, Denmark]: 20–21.

201. Tunjungsari, E., C. J. Chrysolite, and K. Jackson. N.d. "Barriers and Facilitators to Physical Activity in Individuals with Cerebral Palsy." *Physiopedia*. Accessed December 7, 2020.

202. "VSA (Kennedy Center)." 2020, November (updated). Wikipedia. Accessed December 23, 2021.

203. Agar, A, and A. Patro. 2013. "Music Therapy and Children with Cerebral Palsy." *Physiopedia*. Accessed February 27, 2020.

204. Agar and Patro.

205. Agar and Patro.

206. Agar and Patro.

207. Oshman, T. 2015, November 25. "The Magic of Music Therapy for Cerebral Palsy Patients." The Oshman Firm News Center. Accessed March 1, 2020.

208. Agar and Patro, "Music Therapy and Children with Cerebral Palsy."

209. Jäncke, L. "Music, Memory and Emotion." 2008. *Journal of Biology* 7: 21.

210. Husain G., W. F. Thompson, and E. G. Schellenberg, E. G. 2002. "Effects of Musical Tempo and Mode on Arousal, Mood, and Spatial Abilities." *Music Perception* 20, no. 2: 151–171.

211. Marrades-Caballero, E., C. S. Santonja-Medina, J. M. Sanz-Mengibar, and F. Santonja-Medina. 2018. "Neurologic Music Therapy in Upper-Limb Rehabilitation in Children with Severe Bilateral Cerebral Palsy: A Randomized Controlled Trial." *European Journal of Physical Rehabilitation Medicine* 54, no. 6 (December): 866–872.

212. Oshman, "The Magic of Music Therapy for Cerebral Palsy Patients."

213. Guy, J., and A. Neve. 2005. "Music Therapy & Cerebral Palsy Fact Sheet." The Music Therapy Center of California. Accessed December 24, 2021.

214. Marrades-Caballero et al., "Neurologic Music Therapy in Upper-Limb Rehabilitation in Children with Severe Bilateral Cerebral Palsy: A Randomized Controlled Trial."

215. Van Criekinge, T., K. D'Août, K. J. O'Brien, and E. Coutinho. 2019. "Effect of Music Listening on Hypertonia in Neurologically Impaired Patients: Systematic Review." *PeerJ: Brain, Cognition and Mental Health*: e8228. Accessed December 4, 2020.

216. Nicosia, D. N.d. "Johns Hopkins Study Finds Music Increases Dopamine Release." *Recovery Unplugged*. Accessed January 4, 2019.

217. "Music Therapy." N.d. My Child at CerebralPalsy.org. Accessed December 5, 2020.

218. Guy and Neve, "Music Therapy & Cerebral Palsy Fact Sheet."

219. Jäncke, "Music, Memory and Emotion."

220. "Music Therapy," My Child at CerebralPalsy.org.

221. Oshman, "The Magic of Music Therapy for Cerebral Palsy Patients."

222. Guy and Neve, "Music Therapy & Cerebral Palsy Fact Sheet."

223. Oshman, "The Magic of Music Therapy for Cerebral Palsy Patients."

224. Jäncke, "Music, Memory and Emotion."

225. Husain et al., "Effects of Musical Tempo and Mode on Arousal, Mood, and Spatial Abilities."

226. Giangreco, M. F., S. Yuan, B. McKenzie, P. Cameron, and J. Fialka. 2005. "Be Careful What You Wish For: Five Reasons to Be Concerned About the Assignment of *Individual* Paraprofessionals." *TEACHING Exceptional Children* 37, no. 5 (May): 28–34.

227. Carter, E. W., C. K. Moss, J. Asmus, E. Fesperman, M. Cooney, M. E. Brock, G. Lyons, H. B. Huber, and L. B. Vincent. 2015. "Promoting Inclusion, Social Connections, and Learning Through Peer Support Arrangements." *TEACHING Exceptional Children* 48, no. 1 (September): 9–18.

228. Giangreco, M. F. 2003. "Working with Paraprofessionals." *Educational Leadership* 61, no. 2 (October): 50–53.

229. "Toilet Training Children with Special Needs." N.d. American Academy of Pediatrics. Accessed December 4, 2020.

230. FlintRehab: Tools to Spark Recovery. 2020, February 7. "Cerebral Palsy and Incontinence: What's the Link?" *Neurological Recovery* (blog). Accessed December 24, 2021.

231. Children's Hemiplegia and Stroke Association (CHASA). 2022. "Dressing." Accessed March 7, 2022.

232. "Nine First Steps to Student-Directed IEPs." 2015, June 9. *Brookes* (blog). Accessed December 24, 2021.

233. Thoma, C. A., and P. Wehman, P. 2010. *Getting the Most out of IEPs: An Educator's Guide to the Student-Directed Approach* (Baltimore: Paul H. Brookes).

234. Hamblet, E. C. 2014. "Nine Strategies to Improve College Transition Planning for Students with Disabilities." *TEACHING Exceptional Children* 46, no. 3 (January–February): 53–59.

235. Winfree, L. "Multidisciplinary Teams in Special Education: Members, Roles & Functions," chapter 12, lesson 2. Study.com. Accessed December 5, 2020.

236. "Importance of Collaboration in Special Education." 2016, February 9 (updated on June 19, 2018). Arkansas State University. Accessed December 24, 2021.

237. Weber, P., P. Bolli, N. Heimgartner, P. N., Pierina Merlo, T. Zehnder, and C. Kätterer. 2015. "Behavioral and Emotional Problems in Children and Adults with Cerebral Palsy." *European Journal of Paediatric Neurology* 20, no. 2 (December): 270–274.

238. Shields, N., A. Murdoch, A. Y. Loy, K. J. Dodd, and N. F. Taylor. 2006. "A Systematic Review of the Self-Concept of Children with Cerebral Palsy Compared with Children Without Disability." *Developmental Medicine & Child Neurology* 48, no. 2 (February): 151–157.

239. Vignes, C., E. Godeau, M. Sentenac, N. Coley, F. Navarro, H. Grandjean, and C. Arnaud. 2009. "Determinants of Students' Attitudes Towards Peers with Disabilities." *Developmental Medicine & Child Neurology* 51, no. 6 (June): 473–479.

240. Majnemer A., M. Shevell, M. Law, C. Poulin, and P. Rosenbaum. 2010. "Level of Motivation in Mastering Challenging Tasks in Children with Cerebral Palsy." *Developmental Medicine & Child Neurology* 52, no. 12 (December): 1120–1126.

241. Colver, A. 2010. "Why Are Children with Cerebral Palsy More Likely to Have Emotional and Behavioural Difficulties?" *Developmental Medicine & Child Neurology* 52, no, 11 (November): 986.

242. Sigurdardottir, S., M. S. Indredavik, A. Eiriksdottir, K. Einarsdottir, H. Gudmundsson, and T. Vik. 2010. "Behavioural and Emotional Symptoms of Preschool Children with Cerebral Palsy: A Population-Based Study." *Developmental Medicine & Child Neurology* 52, no. 11 (November): 1056–1061.

243. Colver, "Why Are Children with Cerebral Palsy More Likely to Have Emotional and Behavioural Difficulties?"

244. Lavoie, R. 2005. *It's So Much Work to Be Your Friend: Helping the Child with Learning Disabilities Find Social Success* (New York: Simon & Schuster, Touchstone). pp. 73–111.

245. Sprayberry, T. L. 2014. "Disability Doesn't Need Your Pity." *The Huffington Post,* June 17. Accessed April 27, 2022.

246. Guyard, A., J. Fauconnier, M.-A. Mermet, and C. Cans. 2011. "Impact on Parents of Cerebral Palsy in Children: A Literature Review." *Archives of Pediatrics* (official organ of the French Society of Pediatrics) 18, no. 2 (February): 204–214.

247. Sigurdardottir et al., "Behavioural and Emotional Symptoms of Preschool Children with Cerebral Palsy: A Population-Based Study."

248. Shields et al., "A Systematic Review of the Self-Concept of Children with Cerebral Palsy Compared with Children Without Disability."

249. Usher, A. R. 1996. "Effects of Program Placement on the Self-Concept of Students with Orthopedic Disabilities." EdD dissertation, Teachers College, Columbia University. pp. 104–130.

250. Martins, I. C. 2015. "This Is My Best Friend Anna: Asking Peers of Children with Cerebral Palsy." *Developmental Medicine & Child Neurology* 57, no. 4 (May): 18.

251. Schenker, R., W. Coster, and S. Parush. 2005. "Participation and Activity Performance of Students with Cerebral Palsy Within the School Environment." *Journal of Disability and Rehabilitation* 27, no. 10 (May): 539–552.

252. Nadeau, L., and R. Tessier. 2006. "Social Adjustment of Children with Cerebral Palsy in Mainstream Classes: Peer Perception." *Developmental Medicine & Child Neurology* 48, no. 5 (May): 331–336.

253. Nadeau and Tessier, 335.

254. Yude, C., R. Goodman, and H. McConachie. 1998. "Problems of Children with Hemiplegia in Mainstream Primary Schools." *Journal of Child Psychology and Psychiatry* 39, no. 4 (May): 533–541.

255. Carlsson, M., I. Olsson, G. Hagberg, and E. Beckung. 2008. "Behaviour in Children with Cerebral Palsy with and Without Epilepsy." *Developmental Medicine & Child Neurology* 50, no. 10 (October): 784–789.

256. Cerebral Palsy Alliance Research Foundation. 2018. "How Does Cerebral Palsy Affect People?" Accessed December 24, 2021.

257. Cerebral Palsy Alliance Research Foundation, "How Does Cerebral Palsy Affect People?"

258. Cerebral Palsy Alliance Research Foundation.

259. Nadeau and Tessier, "Social Adjustment of Children with Cerebral Palsy in Mainstream Classes: Peer Perception," 331–336.

260. Rousso, H. 1984. "Fostering Healthy Self-Esteem, Part One: What Parents and Professionals Can Do." *Exceptional Parent* 14, no. 8 (December): 9–10.

261. Rousso, "Fostering Healthy Self-Esteem, Part One: What Parents and Professionals Can Do," 9.

262. Rousso, 10.

263. Majnemer et al., "Level of Motivation in Mastering Challenging Tasks in Children with Cerebral Palsy," 1123.

264. Gray, S. H., M. Wylie, S. Christensen, A. Khan, D. Williams, and L. Glader. 2021. "Puberty and Menarche in Young Females with Cerebral Palsy and Intellectual Disability: A Qualitative Study of Caregivers' Experiences." *Developmental Medicine & Child Neurology* 63, no. 2 (February): 190–195.

265. Lin, L.-P., C.-F. Yen, F.-Y. Kuo, J.-L. Wu, and J.-D. Lin. 2009. "Sexual Assault of People with Disabilities: Results of a 2002–2007 National Report in Taiwan." *Research in Developmental Disabilities* 30, no. 5 (September–October): 969–975.

266. Fasen, M., S. Elamsenthil, J. Thompson, B. Saldivar, L. Edwards, L. Fouad, and R. Jacob. 2020. "Gynecological Care and Contraception Considerations in Women with Cerebral Palsy." *Journal of Childhood & Developmental Disorders* 6, no. 5 (April): 4.

267. Cerebral Palsy Guidance. "Children with Cerebral Palsy at Greater Risk of Bullying." *National Safe Place Network, Cerebral Palsy Guidance and Networking and News* (blog). Accessed April 27, 2022.

268. Majnemer et al., "Level of Motivation in Mastering Challenging Tasks in Children with Cerebral Palsy," 1122.

269. Majnemer et al., 1120.

270. Variety—the Children's Charity: Just Like You! 2015. "A Free Disability Awareness Program." Accessed December 24, 2021.

271. Nadeau and Tessier, "Social Adjustment of Children with Cerebral Palsy in Mainstream Classes: Peer Perception."

272. Nadeau and Tessier, 335.

273. Nadeau and Tessier, 331.

274. Yin Foo, R., M. Guppy, and L. M. Johnston. 2013. "Intelligence Assessments for Children with Cerebral Palsy: A Systematic Review." *Developmental Medicine & Child Neurology* 55, no. 10 (October): 916–918.

275. Song, C-S. 2013. "Relationships Between Physical and Cognitive Functioning and Activities of Daily Living in Children with Cerebral Palsy." *Journal of Physical Therapy Science* 25, no. 5 (May): 619–622.

276. Song.

277. O'Connor, B., C. Kerr, N. Shields, and C. Imms. 2016. "A Systematic Review of Evidence-Based Assessment Practices by Allied Health Practitioners for Children with Cerebral Palsy." *Developmental Medicine & Child Neurology* 58, no. 4 (April): 332–347.

278. Song, "Relationships Between Physical and Cognitive Functioning and Activities of Daily Living in Children with Cerebral Palsy."

279. Yin Foo, Guppy, and Johnston. "Intelligence Assessments for Children with Cerebral Palsy: A Systematic Review," 916–918.

280. Esben, "From Around the World," p. 11.

281. Wilson, B. C., and H. M. Davidovicz. 1987. "Neuropsychological Assessment of the Child with Cerebral Palsy." *Seminars in Speech and Language* 8, no. 1 (February): 1–18.

282. Jamgochian, E. M., and L. Ketterlin-Geller. 2015. "The 2% Transition: Supporting Access to State Assessments for Students with Disabilities." *TEACHING Exceptional Children* 48, no. 1 (September–October): 28–35.

283. Jamgochian and Ketterlin-Geller, 30.

284. Wilson and Davidovicz, "Neuropsychological Assessment of the Child with Cerebral Palsy," 7–8.

285. Wilson and Davidovicz, 8.

286. Richter, J. "Assessment: Definition & Examples, Alternative Assessments, What Is Alternative Assessment?, Characteristics." Accessed September 30, 2020. Study.com.

287. Richter.

288. Richter.

289. Think College. 2019. "Think College Learn." Institute for Community Inclusion at the University of Massachusetts, Boston. Accessed December 28, 2021.

290. 1st Cerebral Palsy of New Jersey. N.d. "We Are a Pioneer in Providing Educational and Therapeutic Services for a Variety of Students with Special Needs." Accessed December 28, 2021.

291. Hamblet, "Nine Strategies to Improve College Transition Planning for Students with Disabilities," 53.

292. Vogtle, L. K. 2013. "Employment Outcomes for Adults with Cerebral Palsy: An Issue That Needs to Be Addressed." *Developmental Medicine & Child Neurology* 55, no. 11 (November): 973.

293. Hamblet, "Nine Strategies to Improve College Transition Planning for Students with Disabilities."

294. Office for Civil Rights. 2002. "Students with Disabilities Preparing for Postsecondary Education: Know Your Rights and Responsibilities. U.S. Department of Education. Accessed December 28, 2021.

295. Hamblet, "Nine Strategies to Improve College Transition Planning for Students with Disabilities."

296. Hamblet, 58.

297. Sanford, C., L. Newman, M. Wagner, R. Cameto, A-M. Knokey, and D. Shaver. 2011. "The Post-High School Outcomes of Young Adults with Disabilities up to Six Years after High School: Key Findings from the National Longitudinal Transition Study-2 (NLTS2)." U.S. Department of Education, Institute of Education Sciences, National Center for Special Education Research, SRI International: NCSER 2011-3004, pp. 1–3. Accessed December 28, 2021.

298. Think College. "Think College Learn."

299. Centers for Disease Control and Prevention, Disability and Health Promotion. 2019, September 9. "Common Barriers to Participation Experienced by People with Disabilities." U.S. Department of Health & Human Services. Accessed December 28, 2021.

300. Vogtle, "Employment Outcomes for Adults with Cerebral Palsy: An Issue That Needs to Be Addressed."

301. Douglas, K. H., K. M. Ayres, and J. Langone. 2015. "Comparing Self-Management Strategies Delivered via an iPhone to Promote Grocery Shopping and Literacy." *Education and Training in Autism and Developmental Disabilities* 50, no. 4 (December): 446–465.

302. Douglas et al., 450.

303. Lalvani, P., and L. Polvere. 2013. "Historical Perspectives on Studying Families of Children with Disabilities: A Case for Critical Research." *Disability Studies Quarterly* 33, no. 3.

304. Wang, H-Y., and Y-J. Jong. 2004. "Parental Stress and Related Factors in Parents of Children with Cerebral Palsy." *Kaohsiung Journal of Medical Sciences* 20, no.7 (July): 334–340.

305. Fritz, H., and C. Sewell-Roberts. 2020. "Family Stress Associated with Cerebral Palsy." *Cerebral Palsy*, edited by F. Miller, S. Bachrach, N. Lennon, and M. E. O'Neil (New York: Springer), pp. 515–545.

306. Marshak, L. E., and F. P. Prezant. 2007. *Married with Special-Needs Children* (Bethesda, MD: Woodbine House). Pp. 115–132.

307. Wharton, R. 2020, September 16. "Cerebral Palsy Government Assistance, Cerebral Palsy Guidance. Accessed December 29, 2021.

308. Sipal, R. F., C. Schuengel, J. M. Voorman, M. Van Eck, and J. G. Becher. 2010. "Course of Behaviour Problems of Children with Cerebral Palsy: The Role of Parental Stress and Support." *Child: Care, Health and Development* 36, no. 1 (January): 74–84.

309. Resource Directory. N.d. "United We Stand of New York." Cerebral Palsy Family Network. Accessed December 29, 2021.

310. "Cerebral Palsy: Parents Talk (Video)." N.d. Nemours Children's Health, Kidshealth.org. Accessed December 29, 2021.

311. Ho, S. M. Y., B. K. K. Fung, A. S. M. Fung, S. P. Chow, W. Y. Ip, S. F. Y. Lee, E. Y. P. Leung, and K. W. Y. Ha. 2008. "Overprotection and the Psychological States of Cerebral Palsy Patients and Their Caretakers in Hong Kong: A Preliminary Report." *Hong Kong Medical Journal* 14, no. 4 (August): 286–291. PMID: 18685161.

312. Cerebral Palsy Alliance Research Foundation. 2018, November. "The Amazing Role Siblings Play in Disability." Accessed December 29, 2021.

313. Gabbard, C. A. 2010. "A Life Beyond Reason." *The Chronicle of Higher Education*, November 7. Accessed April 27, 2022. There are several iterations of this article. Sometimes the son is referred to as "my son." Other times, the son is referred to by his given name, August. These articles are now part of a book entitled *A Life Beyond Reason: A Father's Memoir* (Boston: Beacon Press, 2020).

314. Mayo Clinic. N.d. "Cerebral Palsy: Diagnosis and Treatment." Mayo Clinic, Patient Care & Health Information: Diseases & Conditions. Accessed December 29, 2021.

315. Mehl-Madrona, L. N.d. "Treatment for Cerebral Palsy: The Adeli Suit." Forum on Alternative and Innovative Therapies for Children with Developmental Delays, Brain Injury and Related Neurometabolic Conditions and Disorders. Accessed December 29, 2021.

316. Conductive Education Center of San Francisco. 2012, February 23. "The Benefits of Conductive Education for Children with CP." Accessed December 29, 2021.

317. Wallen, M., J. Ziviani, O. Naylor, R. Evans, I. Novak, and R. D. Herbert. 2011. "Modified Constraint-Induced Therapy for Children with Hemiplegic Cerebral Palsy: A Randomized Trial." *Developmental Medicine & Child Neurology* 53, no. 12 (December): 1091–1099.

318. Ernst, E. 2012. "Craniosacral Therapy: A Systematic Review of the Clinical Evidence." *Database of Abstracts of Reviews of Effects (DARE): Quality-Assessed Reviews* [Internet] (York, UK: Centre for Reviews and Dissemination).

319. Bell, E., T. Wallace, I. Chouinard, M. Shevell, and E. Racine. 2011. "Responding to Requests of Families for Unproven Interventions in Neurodevelopmental Disorders: Hyperbaric Oxygen 'Treatment' and Stem Cell 'Therapy' in Cerebral Palsy." *Developmental Disabilities Research Reviews* 17, no. 1: 19–26.

320. Cerebral Palsy Guide. N.d. "Alternative Therapy." Accessed December 30, 2021.

321. American Academy of Cerebral Palsy and Developmental Medicine. 2018. "AACPDM eCourse: Navigating the Journey." Accessed December 31, 2021.

322. Rosenbaum, P., and J. W. Gorter. 2011. "The 'F'-words in Childhood Disability: I Swear This Is How We Should Think!" *Child: Care, Health and Development* 38, no. 4 (July): 457–463.

323. Rosenbaum, P., and D. Stewart. 2004. "The World Health Organization International Classification of Functioning, Disability, and Health: A Model to Guide Clinical Thinking, Practice and Research in the Field of Cerebral Palsy." *Seminars in Pediatric Neurology* 11, no. 1 (March): 5–10.

324. Vincer, M. J., A. C. Allen, K. S. Joseph, D. A. Stinson, H. Scott, and E. Wood. 2006. "Increasing Prevalence of Cerebral Palsy Among Very Preterm Infants: A Population-Based Study." *Pediatrics* 118, no. 6 (December): e1621–e1626.

325. Clark, S. L., and G. D. V. Hankins. 2003. "Temporal and Demographic Trends in Cerebral Palsy—Fact and Fiction." *American Journal of Obstetrics and Gynecology* 188, no. 3 (March): 628–633.

326. Ruff, C. A., S. D. Faulkner, and M. G. Fehlings. 2013. "The Potential for Stem Cell Therapies to Have an Impact on Cerebral Palsy: Opportunities and Limitations." *Developmental Medicine & Child Neurology* 55, no. 8 (August): 689–697.

327. Houlihan, C. M., and R. D. Stevenson. 2009. "Bone Density in Cerebral Palsy." *Physical Medicine and Rehabilitation Clinics of North America* 20, no. 3 (August): 493–508.

Contributor Biographies

Lead Author

Adine R. Usher, EdD, is a special educator who has taught, lectured, consulted, and advocated for students with orthopedic and neuromuscular disabilities for nearly six decades. Cerebral Palsy has been her focus. She has served as a classroom teacher, a staff developer, and a health coordinator who facilitated the activities of teachers, related service professionals (RSPs), and support staff, serving physically disabled students in the New York City public school system.

Dr. Usher was a member of the Special Education Graduate School faculty at Bank Street College of Education in New York City, and since 2003, she has worked with families and school systems as a consultant and advocate for students with physical disabilities in New Jersey, Connecticut, and New York State. She serves as a behavioral specialist for the four children's programs run by United Cerebral Palsy of New York City (now ADAPT) and continues to provide professional development locally, nationally, and internationally at the National Centre for Disabled Persons in San Fernando, Trinidad and Tobago.

Dr. Usher has written articles for professional journals on the education ʌts with cerebral palsy; has received awards from Very Special Arts

(VSA), the Council for Exceptional Children (CEC), and the Child Life Association of New York; and is a member of the Council for Exceptional Children, Project Accessible Oral Health, and the American Academy of Cerebral Palsy and Developmental Medicine (AACPDM).

Dr. Usher received her degrees from Oberlin College and Teachers College, Columbia University.

Book Contributors

Daniel Cuddy, BA, has been the adaptive physical education teacher at the Cotting School, Lexington, Massachusetts, since 1988. Cotting is a private day school for students, ages three to twenty-two, with varying degrees of moderate to severe learning and physical disabilities, communication deficits, health and medical impairments, and post-traumatic injuries. Mr. Cuddy received his degree from Westfield State College.

Beverly Ellman, director, MS, holds New York State Permanent certification in school administrator and supervisor and is the supervisor/administrator for ADAPT Bronx Children's Program (formerly United Cerebral Palsy of New York City). Educated at Hunter College in New York City, Ms. Ellman is affiliated with the Bronx Developmental Disabilities Council and Advocates for Children of New York.

Eiko Fan, MFA, is a wood sculptor who came to the United States from Japan in 1970. She received degrees from the Professional Academy of Fine Arts and the University of Pennsylvania. In her multimedia performance called Live Wood Sculpture, Ms. Fan makes costume-like sculptures to bring sculpture to live performances with dancers and musicians. She has taught sculpture classes to visually impaired students at the Philadelphia Museum of Art and has created artists out of students with cerebral palsy at the HMS School for

Children with Cerebral Palsy in Philadelphia since the 1980s. Ms. Fan says, "I feel that inventing and empowering my students is also my art."

Ronald Friedman, PhD, has been the coordinator of psychological services at the Henry Viscardi School in Albertson, New York, since 1972. During his career, Dr. Friedman has served in psychological supervisory positions at Brooklyn College, St. John's University, and Hofstra University. He was a panel psychologist for New York State Department of Education's Vocational and Educational Services for Individuals with Disabilities, is chairperson of the Town of Mamaroneck Committee on the Disabled, and has volunteered his services with the Muscular Dystrophy Association of Westchester, the Multiple Sclerosis Society of Westchester, and the New York Diabetes Association. Dr. Friedman earned degrees from Lehman College, the New School for Social Research, and Hofstra University.

Diane L. Gallagher, PhD, retired in 2019 as the president of the HMS School for Children with Cerebral Palsy in Philadelphia. HMS is a highly specialized private school dedicated to meeting the diverse needs of children, teens, and young adults with significant disabilities from cerebral palsy or other neurological disabilities. Dr. Gallagher's extensive experience spans studies in human development, early childhood special education, and teaching and administration for both neurotypical students and those with disabilities. She received her formal training at Pennsylvania State University and Temple University.

Jeanette Glover, BS, MS, is the clinical support services and admissions coordinator at the Henry Viscardi School. She is responsible for the delivery of the related services, which includes overseeing the transition program for graduating students.

An occupational therapist, Ms. Glover has provided direct care to children and adults in both hospital and educational settings. She began her career working in acute care at both Harlem Hospital and New York Hospital. Later, she became the independent living specialist at the Human Resources School in Albertson, New York, where she worked directly with students with physical disabilities in all areas of daily life, including personal care and community activities. Ms. Glover was the occupational therapy supervisor at Western Suffolk Board of Cooperative Educational Services (BOCES) and has been an assistant adjunct professor for Hofstra University's occupational therapy program. Ms. Glover received her degrees from Columbia University and Adelphi University.

Amanda Buonora Jung, MA, has spent her twenty-six-year career as a pediatric physical therapist, working with infants, children, and young adults with medically fragile physical disabilities. She has extensive exposure to adaptive seating; wheelchair training (power and manual); adaptive equipment, technology, and orthotics; and prosthetics. She is coordinator for the Orthotic/Prosthetic Clinic at the Henry Viscardi School. She is also a clinical instructor for multiple universities in the metropolitan New York City area. At the Euromed Rehabilitation Center in Mielno, Poland, she became familiar with the Adeli suit and its use for children with cerebral palsy. Ms. Jung has guest-lectured at Queens College and Teachers College at Columbia University. She worked collaboratively with Dr. Carol Goossens on the "Enhancing Circle Time: Going Holistic" workshop and has spoken in Sigüenza, Spain, at the International Conference for Osteogenesis Imperfecta.

Patrice McCarthy Kuntzler, MS, is an experienced special educator and administrator with over forty-five years of experience in the field. Ms. Kuntzler received her degrees from Bloomsburg University and Hofstra University and a professional diploma in school administration from Stony Brook University. After teaching a variety of grade levels at the Henry Viscardi School, a school for children with physical disabilities and medical frailties, she became the school's executive director.

Ms. Kuntzler was the founder and the chair of the National Consortium of Specialized STEM Schools, which connects schools that serve children with severe physical disabilities. She is past president of the Division for Physical, Health and Multiple Disabilities of the Council for Exceptional Children and is an adjunct instructor and member of the Special Education Advisory Board at Molloy College in Hempstead, New York.

Charles McClinton, PhD, is a retired health education and health association professional and graphic artist. During his working career, Dr. McClinton, who now lives in Tampa, Florida, worked for the American Medical Association, Rush Medical College, the Arthritis Foundation National Office, Morehouse School of Medicine, North Carolina Central University, and Massachusetts Institute of Technology. He earned his degrees at South Carolina State College, Medical College of Virginia, and Kent State University. Reviving an earlier serious interest in art, Dr. McClinton is currently venturing into drawing, using graphite pencils to create and re-create illustrations.

Catherine McGrath, MS, ATP, has served as an occupational therapist for over twenty-five years at the Henry Viscardi School, where she serves students who are medically fragile and physically disabled. She holds degrees from Ulster University in Northern Ireland and Misericordia University in Pennsylvania. She is a certified assistive technology professional.

Judy Portelli is a board-certified family nurse practitioner, certified for critical care. Ms. Portelli works at the Henry Viscardi School and has extensive experience in adult and pediatric nursing, particularly with those living with developmental disabilities.

Hadassah P. Rubin, LCSW, MSW, has served as a social worker at the Brooklyn Children's Program run by ADAPT Community Network (formerly United Cerebral Palsy of New York City) since 1992 and in that position has acted as a liaison with the Department of Education's Committee on Special Education. She is also currently serving clients at the Young Adult Institute (YAI) in Brooklyn, New York. Over the past thirty-one years, Mr. Rubin has provided counseling services for the Adult Day Treatment Program for United Cerebral Palsy of New York City, Brooklyn Program. She provided socially appropriate behavior and grief and loss programs for the Beacon Group in Brooklyn. Additionally, she offered therapeutic and home counseling services at Yeled v'Yalda in Brooklyn. Ms. Rubin received her degrees from Brooklyn College and Hunter College.

Liz Viducich, PsyD, MA, is a school psychologist certified in New York and New Jersey. She has worked as an elementary school psychologist for twenty years in Darien, Connecticut. Ms. Viducich provides mental health, learning, and behavioral support to students in both general and special education programs. She also develops prereferral intervention strategies, conducts psychoeducational evaluations, provides group and individual counseling and social skills training, conducts staff training, and develops behavioral intervention plans. The students she works with have ADHD, anxiety disorders, depression, mood disorders, Down syndrome, autism, and cerebral palsy. She received her degrees from Manhattan College, College of Mount Saint Vincent, and Fordham University.

Index

Numbers in italics refer to pages with photos or illustrations.

architecture
  bathroom design and, 234–235
  universal architectural design
  principles in, 2, 29–30
articulation challenges
  brain and computer interfaces in,
  421
  educational consequences of,
  144
  expressive language with, 66,
  111, 168
  music and, 216
  low-technology systems for, 175
  speech therapy for, 174
art teachers and therapists, 153,
  223, 224–225, 226, 391, 405
art therapy, 222–226, 411. *See also*
  visual arts
  benefits of, 222–223
  example of one teacher's approach to, 224–225
  parent's story about, 380, 387
  profound disabilities and, 104
  student's story about, 391, 395,
  398, 400, 402, 403, 405
asexual identity, 275, 382
aspiration, 64
assessment, 287–300
  accommodations and modifications in, 294–296

adaptations to tests used in,
  196–197
alternative, 289, 299–300
behavioral interventions with,
  273
challenges and conditions com-
  plicating, 292–293
effective teaching using foundation of, 300
of health status by school nurses,
  188–189
importance of observation before
  starting, 294
informal, 298
neuropsychological, 289,
  296–298
by psychologists, 194, 195–197
range of staff administering, 287
sharing information from with
  teachers, 289
standardized, 289–291
subtests used in, 196–197, 291,
  292, 298
by support team members, 153
transition planning using, 305
understanding a student's total
  profile before starting, 291
using care and caution in performing, 287–288
assistants, 228–236

gastroenterologists, 60

gastroesophageal reflux disease
(GERD), 60

gastrointestinal disorders, 59–61
causes and description of, 59–60
failure-to-thrive issues in, 61
medications for, 25
sleep difficulties and, 55, 56
tubes and feeding procedures
used in, 60–61

gastrostomy tube (G-tube), 60

genetic factors, 10, 417, 420, 422

GERD (gastroesophageal reflux
disease), 60

German measles, 9

gestational age, 122

Giangreco, Michael, 233

glial cells, 3

global developmental delays, 93,
272

Glover, Jeanette, 301–316

GMFCS-E&R, 23

go-around-the-circle method of
instruction, 105–106

Gonzalez-Monge, Sibylle, 91

government guidelines. *See* federal
guidelines; state guidelines

grand mal seizures (tonic-clonic
seizures), 47, 48

graphomotor impairments, 130

graphomotor skills, 16–17, 39. *See*

also handwriting

Greenspan, Stanley, 82

gross motor functions
motor planning for, 39
music and rhythm for strengthening, 218, 220
physical therapist's focus on,
156–157, 161
teacher's observation of, 109

gross motor impairments
adaptive physical education
(APE) for, 206, 210, 212
assessment and, 291
assistive technology for, 167, 177
description of, 16
dressing and undressing and,
235
impact of, 30
robotic therapy and electrical
stimulation for, 421
speech production and, 170
student's story about, 396

Gross Motor Function Classification
System Expanded and Revised
(GMFCS-E&R), 23

group size
go-around-the-circle method of
instruction, 105–106
whole-group versus small-group
instruction in, 98–99

G-tube (gastrostomy tube), 60

hydrocephalus, 8, 24, 190
hyperactivity, xvii, 55, 272
hyperbaric oxygen therapy, 413
hyperopia, 124
hypersensitivity, 149
hyperthermia, 190
hypertropia, 125
hypoglycemia, 422
hyposensitivity, 149
hypothalamus, 7, *13*
hypotonia. *See* low muscle tone
hypoxia, 9

ICF framework, 73, 87, 415, 419
idiopathic brain injury, 8
IEP. *See* Individualized Educational
    Plan (IEP)
"I hear" games, 147
imaging, 22. *See also specific types of
    imaging*
inclusion programs, 88–90
    assistants' role in, 229
    classmates' learning about a
    student's CP in, 200–201
    co-teaching in, 228
    critical functional skills acquired
    in, 303
    one-on-one support for students
    in, 229
    peer support in, 285
    profound learning, medical, and

movement disabilities and, 103
psychologist's assessment for,
    195
resource room services for,
    227–228
school participation levels in,
    268
social-emotional concerns of
    students in, 198, 267, 270, 273,
    284, 285
social workers in, 204
teachers in, 226–227
teachers' support for parents in,
    323, 325
voluntary buddy system in, 202
incontinence, 61–63
    causes and description of, 61–62,
    63
    nurse's role in managing,
    192–193
    teacher's role in managing, 62,
    63
Individualized Educational Plan
    (IEP)
    adaptive physical education in,
    206–207
    description of, 108, 245
    items included in, 115, 176, 181,
    206, 294, 310, 326
    parents' stories about, 344, 351,
    352–353, 356, 384, 385

wheelchair transfers and, *33*
proteinuria, 9
psychologists, 194–203
  adaptations to tests used by,
  196–197
  assessment information shared
  with teachers by, 289
  communication with parents by,
  197
  counseling by, 197–198, 279
  example of work of, 194–195
  helping students gain greater
  control and independence as
  they age, 199–200
  issues considered by, 195–196
  neuropsychological assessment
  and, 296, 297
  parents' support by, 202–203
  primary roles of, 194
  social-emotional concerns and,
  198–203
  social skills group training by,
  201–202
  students' dealing with stress and,
  198–199
psychometric information, 290
psychosocial support. *See* counselors; psychologists; social
  workers
PTs. *See* physical therapists
"pull-out" delivery model, 155–156
pulmonary aspiration or

asphyxiation, 57, 58, 64, 191
pureed diet, 62, 384
"push-in" delivery model, 155–156
PVL (periventricular leukomalacia),
  7, 9, 129, 350
pyramidal cerebral palsy, 18

quadriplegia. *See* spastic
  quadriplegia

reading, *14*
  instructional strategies for,
  135–137, 138–139
  parents' stories on, 342, 346,
  348, 356, 357, 360, 361, 362,
  380
  students' stories on, 334, 392,
  400, 401, 403, 408
  visual memory and, 133
reading materials, *14*
reading programs, 138, 139
reading records, 86
receptive language, 168
  computer interfaces for, 421
  mild to moderate communication
  challenges with, 168–169
  parent's story about child's use
  of, 375
  teacher's observation of use of,
  111–112
receptive language challenges
  assessment issues from, 293

speech assistive and AAC
technology responsibilities of,
180–181
staff collaboration and, 241
staff training responsibilities of,
240–241
transdisciplinary teams and, 238
school nurses, 187–193
choking episodes and, 190
educational roles of, 193
feeding procedure and, 27, 53,
60, 187, 190, 191–192
health status assessment by,
188–189
intrathecal baclofen pump malfunctions and, 190
medication administration by,
188
pain and discomfort management
and, 52, 53, 188
parents' support by, 193
respiratory difficulties and, 64,
191
responsibilities of, 187–188
routine medical procedures performed by, 26–27
seizures and, 189–190
shunt malfunctions and, 190–191
teacher's need to know specific
conditions that require calling,
26

toileting support and, 62, 193,
392
transportation needs and, 114
urinary and bowel incontinence
and, 62, 192–193
schools
disability awareness programs in,
200–201, 271, 281–283
effective instructional strategies
in, 99–102
government support for, 87
inclusion programs in, 88–90
Life Skills programs, 102, 366
placement options in, 88
postsurgical reentry planning in,
28
special, dedicated schools, 90
team teaching in, 88, 102
transportation responsibilities in,
114–115
whole-group versus small-group
instruction in, 98–99
school systems
assistive technology needs and,
164, 176, 181
disability awareness programs
and, 281
parents' stories about, 335, 337,
341, 346
training responsibilities of,
230–233

speech
impact of communicative inflexibility and perseveration on, 270
production problems in. *See* dysarthria
symbolic and nonsymbolic, 167
speech and language pathologist (SLP), 147, 190
speech issues. *See* communication issues
speech pathologists. *See* speech therapists
speech production problems. *See* dysarthria
speech therapists (speech pathologists), 167–185
AAC technology for social communication and, 284
assessment information shared with teachers by, 289
causes and description of language disorders and, 168
classroom supports for expressive and receptive language challenges and, 174–175
communication challenges with intellectual disability and, 171–172
feeding procedures and, 184–185
low-tech communication devices

and strategies used by, 175
mild to moderate communication challenges and, 168–169
multilevel systems of assistive and AAC technology used by, 175–183
receptive language disorders and, 172–174
school's responsibilities and, 180–181
significant communication challenges with average cognitive ability and, 170–171
speech-hearing connection and, 183–184
speech-to-text systems, 41, 182–183
splinting or casting, 24, 36, 338
sports. *See* adaptive physical education (APE); athletic programs
Sprayberry, Trisha Lynn, 264
staff. *See* occupational therapists; physical therapists; school nurses; support team; teachers; *and specific staff members*
standardized academic assessment
accommodations and modifications in, 295–296
conditions affecting, 299
description of, 289–291
effective teaching using foundation of, 300

subtests from, 298

using care and caution in performing, 287–288

standers, 28, 31, 32, 33, 36, 161, 252

state guidelines

leadership's responsibilities for, 238, 241

legal parameters and requirements of delivery of services under, 238

standardized assessments under, 291

training of staff on, 241

stem cells, research using, 422

stem cell therapy, 412

storage, of adaptive equipment, 36–37

strabismus, 125, 134

Straub, Kathryn, 173

structural anomalies, 57

students with CP

stories by, about their experiences with the reality of CP, 389–410

stories by parents about their children's experiences as, 317–387

as support team members, 237–238

as transition team member, 306

stuttering, 66, 216

dysarthric speech with, 171

parents' stories about, 335, 382, 385

subluxation (hip dislocation), 22, 189

subtests, 196–197, 291, 292, 298

suctioning, 64–65

"suitcase" description of personal experience of living with CP, xxi

summary of performance (SOP), 310

superintendents, 238. *See also* school leadership

supervised community employment, 313

Supine Stander, 252

support services

"pull-out" versus "push-in" delivery model for, 155–156

scribes and, 41, 232, 309, 373, 374, 377, 378, 393

support team, 153–159. *See also individual team members*

assessment of a student's status and needs performed by, 153

collaboration by, 153, 245

communication and information sharing among, 244

description of work of, 153

frequency of meetings of, 243

IEP and, 244–245

impact of overdependence on support from, 269

members of, 153, 243–244

optimizing the effectiveness of, 243–246

outside medical personnel and specialists' consultations with, 154–155

parents as members of, 236–237

parents' list of informational comments for, 326

"pull-out" versus "push-in" delivery model and, 155–156

related service providers and, 155

sexual abuse education by, 276

skills and practices used by, 245–246

students as members of, 237–238

teachers and, 239–240

surgical interventions

range of, 23–25

scheduling of, 28

school reentry planning after, 28

staff knowledge of and responses to, 26–28

therapies needed after, 28

swallowing difficulties. *See* dysphagia

Sylwester, Robert, 2, 6

synapse, 4, *10*

"syndrome" of cerebral palsy, 45

systemic hypothermia, 420

systemic infection, 67, 68

table activities, student's enjoyment of, *396*

tables

adaptive design of, 34–35, 232, *249*

educational equipment used with, 35

example of, *249*

mounting of adaptive equipment on, 220

seating decisions and height of, 31, *33*

tablets. *See also* computers

writing technology on, 41, 164–165

tactile challenges, 148–149

causes and description of, 149

impact on students of, 148

instructional responses to issues in, 150–151

task analysis, 101, 104, 107, 155

taste

CP-related challenges to, 149–150

sensory brain processing in, 120

teachers

CPSIA information can be obtained
at www.ICGtesting.com
Printed in the USA
JSHW031023090323
38672JS00001B/1